MODELS FOR WRITERS

SHORT ESSAYS FOR COMPOSITION

Sixth Edition

Editors

Alfred Rosa
Paul Eschholz
University of Vermont

ST. MARTIN'S PRESS
NEW YORK

Sponsoring editor: Donna Erickson
Director of development: Carla Kay Samodulski
Development editor: Meg Spilleth
Managing editor: Patricia Mansfield Phelan
Project editor: Deirdre Hare
Production supervisor: Kurt Nelson
Art director: Lucy Krikorian
Text design: Patricia McFadden
Cover design: Lucy Krikorian
Cover art: Molly Heron

Library of Congress Catalog Card Number: 97-65207

Manufactured in the United States of America.
3 2 1 0 9 8
f e d c

For information, write:
St. Martin's Press, Inc.
175 Fifth Avenue
New York, NY 10010

ISBN: 0-312-15310-4

Acknowledgments

Acknowledgments and copyrights are found at the back of the book on pages 547–551, which constitute an extension of the copyright page. It is a violation of the law to reproduce these selections by any means whatsoever without the written permission of the copyright holder.

PREFACE

Over the course of the previous five editions, *Models for Writers* has provided students and instructors with lively, readable essays that model rhetorical elements, principles, and patterns. While models are extremely helpful to students as they learn to write college-level essays, we believe students also need plenty of writing activities to help them stitch the various rhetorical elements together into coherent, forceful essays of their own. *Models for Writers* combines the best collection available of examples for student writers, with the most useful and abundant support to help them master the writing skills needed for their college classes.

Favorite Features of *Models for Writers*

- **Lively Examples.** Most of the selections in *Models for Writers* are comparable in length (two to three pages) to the essays students will write themselves, and each clearly illustrates a basic rhetorical element, principle, or pattern. Just as important, the essays deal with subjects that we know from our own teaching experience will spark the interest of most college students. Drawn from a wide range of sources, the essays represent a variety of popular contemporary prose styles.
- **Abundant Study Materials.** To help students link reading to their writing, every essay is accompanied by ample study materials:

  Questions for Study and Discussion focus on the content, the author's purpose, and the particular strategy used to achieve that purpose, with at least one question in each series focusing on a writing concern other than the one highlighted in the chapter to remind students that good writing is never one-dimensional.

  Vocabulary sections identify several words from each reading that students will find worth adding to their vocabularies, with exercises asking students to define each word as it is used in the context of the selection and then to use the word in a new sentence of their own.

Classroom Activities provide brief exercises enabling students to work in the classroom (often in groups) on rhetorical elements, techniques, or patterns. These activities range from developing thesis statements to using strong action verbs and building argumentative evidence.

Suggested Writing Assignments provide two writing assignments for each essay, one encouraging the use of the reading selection as a direct model, and the second asking students to respond to the content of the reading.

- **Rhetorical Organization.** Each of the nineteen chapters in *Models for Writers* is devoted to a particular element or pattern important to college writing. Chapters 1 through 7 focus on the concepts of thesis, unity, organization, beginnings and endings, paragraphs, transitions, and effective sentences. Chapter 8 illustrates the importance of controlling diction and tone, and Chapter 9, the uses of figurative language. Chapters 10 through 18 explore the types of writing most often required of college students: illustration, narration, description, process analysis, definition, division and classification, comparison and contrast, cause and effect, and argument. Finally, Chapter 19, "Combining Rhetorical Strategies," is new to this edition and includes four essays that highlight how writers combine multiple strategies in support of a thesis.
- **Flexible Arrangement.** Each chapter is self-contained so that instructors may easily follow their own teaching sequences, omitting or emphasizing certain chapters according to the needs of their students. Whatever sequence is followed, thematic comparisons among the selections can be made by referring to the alternate Thematic Table of Contents at the beginning of the book.
- **Useful Introduction.** The book opens with an introduction that shows students how the text can be used to improve their writing. Included in the introduction are three student essays demonstrating the three major types of writing students need to master—a personal narrative (new to this edition and on the topic of sports), an expository essay, and an argumentative essay.
- **Concise and Helpful Chapter Introductions.** Users have been generous in their praise for the memorable chapter introductions, which explain the various rhetorical elements and prin-

ciples. In each one, students will find illuminating examples of the feature or principle being studied.

- **A Glossary of Useful Terms.** Whenever possible in the questions or writing assignments throughout the book, we refer students to this helpful list, which covers all rhetorical and literary terms, and we encourage them to connect the terms with concrete examples.
- **Instructor's Resource Manual.** The editors have used all of the material in *Models for Writers* and offer insights into the rhetorical features of each essay as well as advice on how best to use the materials in class. Suggested answers for study questions, vocabulary, and classroom activities are included.

Highlights of the Sixth Edition of *Models for Writers*

- **For Your Journal** activities precede each reading and prompt students to explore their own ideas and experiences regarding the issues presented in the reading.
- **Classroom Activities** provide instructors with numerous creative strategies to help students apply concepts modeled in the readings to their own writing as they work either on their own or with other students.
- **Chapter 19, "Combining Rhetorical Strategies,"** includes four essays in which the writers have used more than one rhetorical pattern. These essays show how good writers use effective combinations of rhetorical development to fulfill their purposes.
- **Essays on topics of current interest** are available, with selections on stereotyping, education, urban violence, and technology, and a special thematic focus on sports that includes five essays.
- **New readings,** comprising almost half of the sixth edition, were chosen with an eye toward critical thinking and writing as well as for their brevity, clarity, and suitability for student writers. Among the exciting new pieces included in this edition are essays by popular writers such as Sandra Cisneros, Pat Mora, Anne Lamott, and Gary Soto.
- **A more comprehensive introduction to argument** opens Chapter 18, with increased coverage of types of appeals and a series of steps to follow when writing an argument.

- **A new workbook for developmental and ESL students** is provided, with activities and exercises that will help developmental and advanced ESL students get the most out of the readings and instruction in *Models for Writers.*

Acknowledgments

In response to the many enthusiastic users of this book, we have kept the solid foundation of previous editions of *Models for Writers* while adding fresh readings and writing topics to stimulate today's student writers.

We are indebted to many people for their criticism and advice as we prepared this sixth edition of *Models for Writers.* We are especially grateful to Joan Angelis, Woodbury University; Andrea Berta, University of Texas, El Paso; Stephanie Bertoni, Butte College; Dee Bielecki, North Greenville College; Colin E. Bourn, Fitchburg State College; George P. Castellitto, Felician College; Linda Lee Cooper, Front Range Community College; Joan Fry, Glendale College; Richard Hascal, Contra Costa College; Judy Hathcock, Amarillo College; Susan Martell Huebner, Milwaukee Area Technical College; Devonee McDonald, Kirkwood Community College; Michele Miller, Fullerton College; Margaret A. Morrison, Mount Ida College; Barbara Peterson, Isothermal Community College; June Roque, Milwaukee Area Technical College; Karen A. Russikoff, California Polytechnic University; Ronni Soffian, Florida International University; and Barbara P. Thompson, Columbus State Community College.

It has been our good fortune to have the editorial guidance of Meg Spilleth, Donna Erickson, Carla Samodulski, and Deirdre Hare of St. Martin's Press as we worked on this new edition. Thanks to our colleagues Phoebe Bryan, Wright Dannebarger, Sue Dinitz, Dick Sweterlitsch, and Alex Vardamis who have shared with us their experiences using *Models for Writers* in the classroom. Thanks also go to Brian Kent, Mark Wanner, and Susan Wanner for their cheerful and prompt editorial assistance with both the text and the Instructor's Resource Manual. Our greatest debt is, as always, to our writing students, for all that they have taught us over the years.

Alfred Rosa
Paul Eschholz

CONTENTS

THEMATIC CONTENTS

Family and Friends

People and Personalities

Social Behavior

Men and Women

The Minority Experience

Science and Technology

Controversies

Work

Language and Thought

Enduring Issues

Popular Culture

Education

Sports

Health and Medicine

INTRODUCTION

Models for Writers is designed to help you learn to write by providing you with a collection of model essays, essays that are examples of good writing. We know that one of the best ways to learn to write and to improve our writing is to read. By reading we can begin to see how other writers have communicated their experiences, ideas, thoughts, and feelings. We can study how they have used the various elements of the essay—words, sentences, paragraphs, organizational patterns, transitions, examples, evidence, and so forth—and thus learn how we might effectively do the same. When we see, for example, how a writer like James Lincoln Collier develops an essay from a strong thesis statement, we can better appreciate the importance of having a clear thesis statement in our writing. When we see the way Lisa Brown uses transitions to link key phrases and important ideas so that readers can recognize clearly how the parts of her essay are meant to fit together, we have a better idea of how to achieve such clarity in our own writing.

But we do not learn only by observing, by reading. We also learn by doing, by writing, and in the best of all situations we engage in these two activities in conjunction with one another. *Models for Writers* encourages you, therefore, to write your essays, to practice what you are learning, as you are actually reading and analyzing the model essays in the text.

The kind of composition that you will be asked to write for your college writing instructor is most often referred to as an essay—a relatively short piece of nonfiction in which a writer attempts to develop one or more closely related points or ideas. An effective essay has a clear purpose, often provides useful information, has an effect on the reader's thoughts and feelings, and is usually a pleasure to read.

All well-written essays also share a number of structural and stylistic features that are illustrated by the various essays in *Models for Writers*. One good way to learn what these features are and how you can incorporate them into your own writing is to look at each of them in isolation. For this reason we have divided *Models for Writers* first into three major sections and, within these sections, into nineteen chapters, each with its own particular focus and emphasis.

"The Elements of the Essay," the first section, includes chapters on the following subjects: thesis, unity, organization, beginnings and endings, paragraphs, transitions, and effective sentences. All these elements are essential to a well-written essay, but the concepts of thesis, unity, and organization underlie all the others and so come first in our sequence.

Briefly, "Thesis" shows how authors put forth or state the main ideas of their essays and how they use such statements to develop and control content; "Unity," how authors achieve a sense of wholeness in their essays; and "Organization," some important patterns that authors use to organize their thinking and writing. "Beginnings and Endings" offers advice and models of ways to begin and conclude essays, while "Paragraphs" concentrates on the importance of well-developed paragraphs and what is necessary to achieve them. "Transitions" concerns the various devices that writers use to move from one idea or section of an essay to the next. Finally, "Effective Sentences" focuses on techniques to make sentences powerful and create stylistic variety.

"The Language of the Essay," the second major section of the text, includes a chapter on diction and tone and one on figurative language. "Diction and Tone" shows how carefully writers choose words either to convey exact meanings or to be purposefully suggestive. In addition, this chapter shows how the words a writer uses can create a particular tone or relationship between the writer and the reader—one of irony, for example, or humor or great seriousness. "Figurative Language" concentrates on the usefulness of the special devices of language—such as simile, metaphor, and personification—that add richness and depth to one's writing.

The final section of *Models for Writers,* "Types of Essays," includes chapters on the various types of writing most often required of college writing students: "Illustration" (how to use examples to illustrate a point or idea); "Narration" (how to tell a story or give an account of an event); "Description" (how to present a verbal picture); "Process Analysis" (how to explain how something is done or happens); "Definition" (how to explain what something is); "Division and Classification" (how to divide a subject into its parts and place items into appropriate categories); "Comparison and Contrast" (how to demonstrate likenesses and differences); "Cause and Effect" (how to explain the causes of an event or the effects of an action); "Argument" (how to use reason and logic to persuade someone to your way of thinking); and finally, "Combining Rhetorical Strategies" (how to utilize a combination of rhetorical patterns). These types of writing are referred to as *rhetorical patterns.*

Studying the rhetorical patterns and practicing using them is very important in any effort to broaden one's writing skills. In *Models for Writers* we look at each pattern separately, one at a time; we believe this is the simplest and most effective way to introduce them. However, this does not mean that a well-written essay is necessarily one that chooses a single pattern and sticks to it exclusively and rigidly. Confining oneself to comparison and contrast throughout an entire essay, for instance, might prove impractical and may yield a strained, unnatural piece of writing. In fact, it is often best to use a single pattern to organize your essay, and then to use the other patterns as your material dictates. When you read the student essays that follow, notice how, for example, Trena Isley's essay is basically a narrative, but also includes comparison and contrast. Jon Clancy's essay is an argumentative one that makes its point with strong illustrations and vivid narrative examples. As you read the model essays in this text, you will find that in the service of the dominant pattern a good many of them utilize a combination of other patterns.

Combining rhetorical patterns is probably not something you want to plan or even think about when you first tackle a writing assignment. Rather, such combinations will develop naturally as you organize, draft, and revise your materials. As the essays in "Combining Rhetorical Strategies" demonstrate, the combination of patterns also enhances the interest and impact of the writing.

All of the chapters are organized in the same way. Each opens with an explanation of the element or principle under consideration. These introductions are intended to be brief, clear, and practical. Here you will also usually find one or more short examples of the feature or principle being studied. Following the introduction, we present three or four model essays (Chapter 18, with nine essays, is an exception), each with a brief introduction of its own providing information about the author and directing your attention to the way the essay demonstrates the featured writing technique. Every essay is followed by study materials in four parts: *Questions for Study and Discussion, Vocabulary, Classroom Activity,* and *Suggested Writing Assignments.*

Models for Writers, then, provides information, instruction, and practice in writing essays. By reading carefully and thoughtfully and by applying what you learn, you can begin to have more and more control over your own writing. Trena Isley, Courtney Smith, and Jon Clancy, three of our own writing students at the University of Vermont, found this to be true, and their work is a good example of what can be achieved by studying models.

Three Model Student Essays

After reading several personal narratives—Helen Keller's "The Most Important Day" and Dick Gregory's "Shame" in particular—and discussing in general significant changes in life that are signaled by memorable events, Trena Isley decided to write a narrative of her own. Trena focused on the day that she told her father she no longer wished to participate in sports. Recalling that event led her to reconsider her childhood experiences of running track. Trena welcomed the opportunity to write about this difficult period in her life. As she tried to make her dilemma clear to her classmates, she found that she clarified it for herself. She came to a deeper understanding of her own fears and feelings about striking out on her own and ultimately to a better appreciation of her difficult relationship with her father. What follows is the final draft of Trena's essay.

On the Sidelines

Trena Isley

Point of View: first person

It was a Monday afternoon and I was finally home from track practice. The coach had just told me that I had a negative attitude and should contemplate why I was on the team. My father greeted me in the living room.

"Hi honey. How was practice?"

"Not good, Dad. Listen, I don't want to do this anymore. I hate the track team."

"What do you mean <u>hate</u>?"

"This constant pressure is making me crazy."

"How so?"

"It's just not fun anymore."

"Well, I'll have to talk to Coach—"

"No! You're supposed to be my father, not my coach."

"I am your father, but I'm sure . . ."

"Just let me do what I want. You've had your turn!"

He just let out a sigh and left the room. Later he told me that I was wasting my "God-given abilities." The funny part was that none of my father's anger hit me at first. All I knew was that I was free.

OPENING: critical dialogue between writer and her father highlights conflict

My troubles began the summer I was five years old. It was late June and the sticky weather had already settled over Vermont. My father was yanking my hair into a ponytail in preparation for the first day of the summer track and field season.

FLASHBACK: writer returns to beginning of her story and sets context

As our truck pulled into the upper parking lot I could look down on the scene below. The other kids resembled ants against the massive black track, all of them parading around with no obvious purpose. I stepped out of the truck, never taking my eyes off the colony beneath me, and fell. As I stood there, both knees skinned and bleeding, the last thing I wanted to do was join the other kids. My father quickly hushed my sobs and escorted me down into the throng of children. Around the track we ran, each step stinging my knees as the water in my eyes continued to rise. Through blurred vision I could see my father on the sidelines, holding his stopwatch in one hand and wearing a grin from ear to ear.

Echo of Title

Organization: chronological sequence of events

For most of my childhood I was content to let my father make me a track star. As my collection of blue ribbons grew, I was perfect in my father's eyes. By the time I was ten, college coaches were joking with me about scholarships. So I continued to run. It was fun in the beginning, and Dad always had nice things to say about me. I can remember him talking to my grandmother over the holidays: "Trena's got a real shot at winning the 200 meters at the state meet this year, but she's got to train hard."

I began to alter my opinion of competition as I entered my teenage years. At this point I wasn't having fun anymore. My father took me to the gym for "training" sessions four days a week before school. I knew my friends weren't getting up at 5:00 a.m., so I didn't understand why I had to. At thirteen years old all I wanted was to be considered normal. I wanted to fit in with the other kids and do regular teenage stuff.

My father didn't understand my waning interest in track. He still looked forward to my competitions and practice every morning. When my alarm would go off, I would not get out of bed right away, often claiming that I didn't feel well or pretending to oversleep. I began not winning all or even most of my races. My father pushed me to work harder. He would talk incessantly about other competitors and how often they practiced. He never stopped trying to coax me into practicing by buying me breakfast or taking me out to lunch. He tried endlessly but I just didn't care about track. I resented him more and more with each attempt. I needed to do something that I was truly interested in. And I needed to do it alone.

"Hey Dad, what do you think about me trying out for the school play this term? I was told I have a good shot at a part."

DIALOGUE: shows instead of tells

"I don't think you'd have time. Track practice is every day isn't it? I've been talking with the coach and he says the team is looking strong this year. He tells me the state meet should be tough, though. Do you need new spikes?"

"No, Dad. The ones I have are fine, but I just thought . . ."

"Great, 'cause you'll need good spikes when you run on some of those dirt tracks."

So that was that. It got so bad that my father didn't hear me unless "track" was in the sentence. I was starving for my own identity. The mold "Trena the track star" that my father had created for me was crumbling rapidly. Sadly, he wasn't noticing; however, I knew I wanted to quit the track team, but I was afraid that if I gave up sports there would be nothing left for me to be good at. The worst thing someone could be in my family was average.

Return to Opening Scene

When I finally did it—told my father the pressure was making me crazy and that I was quitting—I felt three times lighter. I came to find out, though, that this freedom did have its price. I got to sleep late, but Dad didn't ask me how my day was anymore. He didn't ask me much of anything except when I'd be home at night and whom I was going out with. He wasn't my coach anymore—he was my warden. Every night I was grilled for details. He needed to know everyone I was with and what we were doing. When I'd tell him, he never seemed to believe me. My dreams of living on a farm and building my own house were laughed at. In the same conversation my younger sister could tell my parents that she was hoping to work for the United Nations, and she would be applauded. The shift had been made. I gained my personal and creative independence but lost a parent.

Organization: time reference

It has been five years since I retired from athletics and slipped out of my father's graces. Presently my father and I do speak, but it's all on the surface. I now realize that I didn't need the extra morning practices to be good at something. This transition was normal and healthy. It happened quickly, so quickly that I left my father holding the remains of our relationship. The problem was that neither of us bothered to reinvent one for our future as adults. It's not hard for me to understand why we still have a hard time relating to each other. We really don't know each other very well.

Ending: reflections on meaning of relationship

Eventually we'll be able to talk about my quitting track as just that, a small incident that marked the turn of a page in both our lives. We both have unresolved feelings that are standing in the way of our friendship. I need to stop blaming him for my blemished self-image and he needs to realize that I can succeed without his coaching. In the end we both have to forgive each other.

For an assignment following one of the readings in the chapter on unity, Courtney Smith was inspired by a television commercial to choose an unusual topic: cockroaches. In order to develop a thesis about these creatures, Courtney did some preliminary reading in the library, spoke to her biology professor (who had some interesting exhibits to show her), and surveyed the roach-control products available at her local supermarket. In sorting through the information she gathered, she was particularly surprised by the ability of cockroaches to survive under almost any circumstances. This ability seemed to her to provide a suitably narrow focus for a short, unified essay, so she began to analyze the various reasons for the insects' resiliency. By first making lists of the points she wanted to include in her essay, Courtney discovered that she could cluster the reasons into three groups. She was then able to formulate the following thesis: "Cockroaches are remarkably resilient creatures for three basic reasons." This thesis, in turn, helped Courtney to map her organization; she decided that her essay would have three major paragraphs to discuss each of the basic reasons cockroaches are so durable and that she would also need an introductory paragraph and a concluding paragraph. This five-paragraph pattern provided the basis for her first draft.

What follows is the final draft of Courtney's essay, which incorporates a number of changes she made based on a critical evaluation of her first draft.

Cockroaches

Courtney Smith

BEGINNING: captures readers' attention

Have you ever tried to get rid of cockroaches? Those stupid little bugs refuse to go. You can chase them, starve them, spray them, and even try to squash them. But no matter what you do, they always come back. I have heard they are the only creatures that can survive a nuclear explosion. What do cockroaches have that enables them to be such extremely resilient insects? The answer is simple.

THESIS

Cockroaches have survived in even the most hostile environments because they possess several unique physical features, an amazing reproductive process, and an immune system that has frustrated even the best efforts of exterminators to get rid of them.

FIRST POINT: "physical features"

DESCRIPTION

Cockroaches are thin, torpedo-shaped insects. Their body shape allows them to squeeze into small cracks or holes in walls and ceilings or dart into drains, thus avoiding all dangers. Their outer shell is extremely hard, making them almost impossible to crush. Cockroaches have sticky pads on their claws that enable them to climb walls or crawl upside down on ceilings. They also have two little tails called "cerci" to alert them to danger. These cerci are covered with tiny hairs that, like antennae, are sensitive to things as small as a speck of dust or as seemingly innocent as a puff of air. Finally, if cockroaches can't find food, they can sustain themselves for up to a month without food, as long as they have water. Combined with their other physical features, this ability to go for long periods without food has made the cockroach almost invincible.

TOPIC SENTENCE: PARAGRAPH UNITY

SECOND POINT: "reproductive process"

Cockroaches give credence to the old adage that there is safety in numbers. They reproduce at a truly amazing rate. About two months after a mating, a new generation of cockroaches is born. One cockroach can produce about two dozen offspring

ILLUSTRATION: hypothetical example

each time it mates. To get some idea of their reproductive power, imagine that you start with three pairs of cockroaches that mate. Approximately three weeks after mating, the females lay their eggs, which hatch some forty-five days later. If we assume two dozen eggs from each female, the first generation would number seventy-two offspring. These roaches would continue to multiply geometrically so that by year's end the colony's population would total more than 10,000 cockroaches. Stopping this process is almost impossible because, even if we were successful in annihilating the adult population, it is more than likely that a new generation would already be on the way.

THIRD POINT: "immune system"

Finally, cockroaches have frustrated scientists with their ability to immunize themselves against drugs, poison, and bomb gases. The cockroaches then pass this new immunity on to the next generation quicker than a new poison can be made. Although scientists have studied the cockroach for a long time, they have not discovered the biological mechanism that enables them to develop immunity quickly. It is only natural, therefore, that many scientists have been at work on a "birth control" solution for cockroaches. By rendering at least some portion of the adult population sterile, scientists hope to gain a measure of control over the pesky creatures.

ENDING: prediction for the future

Today there are 3,500 different species of cockroaches. They have survived on this planet since the Carboniferous Era some 350 million years ago. Whether or not scientists are successful in their

> latest efforts to rid us of cockroaches is yet to be determined. Odds are that they won't succeed. Given the cockroach's amazing record of survivability, it is not likely to turn up on the world's list of endangered species.

Jon Clancy's paper grew out of his reading the essays in Chapter 18. His assignment was to write an argument and, like Trena and Courtney, he was free to choose his own topic. He knew from past experience that in order to write a good essay he would have to write on a topic he cared about. He also knew that he should allow himself a reasonable amount of time to find such a topic and gather his ideas. After studying Russian for four years and French for six, Jon had begun to wonder why he wasn't learning the languages as quickly and as well as other people. Then, after meeting a Soviet couple and their eight-year-old daughter, he understood. The girl, after only a few months in the United States, spoke English with only a slight accent while her mother was not progressing nearly as quickly. Never before did he realize how the difference in age affected the attainment of fluency. This gave Jon the idea to write an essay on the need to teach languages at an early age rather than only at the secondary and post-secondary levels, an approach that would have helped him, as well as many others, he thought.

Jon began by brainstorming about the topic. He made lists of all the ideas, facts, issues, arguments, opposing arguments, and refutations that came to mind as a result of his own reflections on the topic, as well as ideas he had gathered from several educators he interviewed about the teaching of foreign languages. Once he was confident that he had amassed enough information to begin writing, he made a rough outline of an organizational pattern he felt would work well for him. Keeping this pattern in mind, Jon wrote a first draft of his essay, then went back and examined it carefully, assessing how it could be improved.

Jon was writing this particular essay in the second half of the semester, after he had read a number of essays and had learned the importance of such matters as good paragraphing, unity, and transitions. In rereading his first draft, he realized that his organizational pattern could be clearer if he did not mix the reasons why Americans need to learn foreign languages with his suggestion for how we should actually go about teaching and learning them. He also found places where phrases and even whole sentences could be added to make his meaning clearer. He repositioned some sentences, added some key transitions, and changed a number of words to create a more forceful effect.

The final draft of Jon's paper illustrates that he has learned how the parts of a well-written essay fit together, and how to make revisions that emulate some of the qualities of the model essays he has read and studied. The following is the final draft of Jon's essay.

Where Is Le Bathroom?

Jon Clancy

An American in Paris. To the French, this is a most hideous thought. Thousands of travelers from Boston to Boise head for the City of Lights each year, and very few know enough French to ask for directions to the nearest Metro stop, police station, or bathroom. Americans think that knowing the language of a foreign country is not necessary. The basic, arrogant assumption is, "Not to worry! The whole world knows English."

BEGINNING: a problem is announced

The typical traveler is in for a rude awakening when it is 3 a.m. on a remote European road and suddenly the engine overheats. The last gas station is 10 kilometers back, and there's not one English-speaking Austrian to be found. Quickly now! Refer to that dime-store phrase book and attempt to say, "My car is broken." Too bad. What actually came out was, "My! Look at all the hedgehogs!" We Americans just do not have a strong knowledge of

ILLUSTRATION: hypothetical example

THESIS

languages, and something should be done to change this.

RHETORICAL QUESTION

But why should we begin emphasizing foreign language study? Actually, the benefits are great. For

ORGANIZATION: first argument

example, the knowledge of a second language helps in learning others. Strong similarities exist within linguistic groups, such as the Romance and Slavic families. Of course it's not possible for Americans to know every language, but once someone understands the concepts of verb conjugation, noun cases, and noun gender, a foreign tongue will seem less intimidating.

ORGANIZATION: second argument

We deal with many foreign speakers right here in the United States. For instance, those areas of the United States that are near French-speaking parts of Canada, such as New England, and those near Mexico are often visited by our foreign neighbors. However, many Americans who often deal with them do not know the most basic French or Spanish phrases. People will argue that those traveling in the United States should know English. Fine. But when we travel to Quebec, what do we speak? That's right . . . "Garkon, I'd like un Coca-Cola, seel voos plate."

ORGANIZATION: third argument

Also, most urban areas in the United States, especially those in the southern states, are home to Mexican, Cuban, and other Latin American immigrants. These people have made Spanish our second language, yet most people do not bother to learn it at all. Wouldn't it be beneficial if these Hispanics and Americans who work and live with each other took the time to learn each other's native tongue, thus taking a big step in bettering the understanding between these two different but inevitably inseparable cultures? Latin Americans are making the more sincere effort in this case, and as usual, the arrogant, lazy Americans cannot be bothered broadening their horizons beyond "America's Funniest Home Videos" and "Wheel of Fortune."

ORGANIZATION: fourth argument
QUOTATION: supporting opinion

Linguistically, politically, and economically, the world is growing closer each year. According to former Senator Paul Simon of Illinois, "Cultural isolation is a luxury the United States can no longer afford" (qtd. in Seligmann 37). Places like China and the Soviet Union do not seem quite as far away as they used to, and international business is on the rise. With the advent of international companies and a global economy, we need to enhance inter-nation communication. How can we expect to understand these new neighbors and business partners without knowing their language? Each culture has its own, distinct vocabulary that reflects its way of life. For example, the Russian word "blat," which is the highly developed system of favors between merchant and consumer, does not have a direct English translation, but it has significant economic, social, and political ramifications in Russia. One surely cannot appreciate the importance and beauty of foreign cultures by reading such classics as Arabic at a Glance and Just Enough Serbo-Croat.

EVIDENCE: example used as illustration

RHETORICAL QUESTION

But exactly how should we go about making the United States more aware of the world and the languages it speaks? Because a person's cognitive learning skills are at their peak at an early age, the first grade would be an excellent place to begin foreign language instruction. At birth, according to noted brain surgeon Wilder Penfield, there is a large area of the brain, known as the uncommitted cortex, that is not used. This part of the brain becomes a perfect tool for learning a second language in the early years—especially before the age of 12 (389).

SOLUTION TO PROBLEM

EVIDENCE: paraphrase of scientific authority

Some would argue that the most efficient way of solving the language problem would be to work on the existing programs at the junior high and high school levels. However, these programs have been in effect for many years, and the results have been anything but promising. A high school student will study a language for two, three, or even four years and afterwards will not have attained fluency.

ORGANIZATION: opposing argument

REFUTATION OF OPPOSING ARGUMENT

It should come as no surprise that students in the teenage years do not excel in the area of language study. On the other hand, younger children are still learning English in the first grade, so the teaching of a second tongue would not be a hindrance, but rather a complement. The children surely will not protest this addition, for if it is incorporated as part of their learning from day one they will always associate French, Spanish, or even Russian with math and English, as part of the school day. Also, there is a good chance that children would consider learning a foreign language to be fun.

Children all over the world begin to study English as a second language at a very early age and, despite its complexity, do amazingly well. For example, I just met the eight-year-old daughter of a Soviet family now living in the United States who participated in an intensive English instruction program. After only a few months, she learned the language so well that she was able to enter the fourth grade, speaking English with only a slight accent. On the other hand, her mother is taking much longer; she still has a strong accent and often stumbles over vocabulary. Young children have a clear advantage in learning languages.

EVIDENCE: personal experience

Young children have little difficulty switching between two languages. Many schools, such as those in Montreal and in Gates County, North Carolina, have instituted bilingual school days. The morning lessons are taught in French and the afternoon lessons in English. The direct method, when a parent speaks to a child in a second language from day one, is the best way to create proficient speakers.

EVIDENCE: examples of effective programs

In order for Americans to better understand the world, we must be able to expand and grow with the world. The best way is through a second language. The present system of beginning instruction in junior high school does not create effective speakers and listeners. At this stage, the ability to learn a second language is severely diminished. However, starting in the primary years of a child's education, as has already been shown, will create a group of adept, bilingual people who will have no problems communicating in and learning

ENDING: argument summarized

ENDING: concluding sentence echoes title

from other cultures. Let's not raise another generation of ignorant Americans who can't communicate with their foreign neighbors and are forced to walk the streets of Europe in agony because they can't find le bathroom.

WORKS CITED

Penfield, Wilder. "Conditioning the Uncommitted Cortex for Language Learning." Brain 88.4 (1965): 387–398.

Seligmann, Jean. "Speaking in Tongues." Newsweek Fall/Winter Special Edition, 1990: 36–37.

1

THESIS

The *thesis* of an essay is its main idea, the point it is trying to make. The thesis is often expressed in a one- or two-sentence statement, although sometimes it is implied or suggested rather than stated directly. The thesis statement determines the content of the essay: everything that the writer says must be logically related to the thesis statement.

Because everything you say in your composition must be logically related to your thesis statement, the thesis statement controls and directs the choices you make about the content of your essay. That does not mean your thesis statement is a straitjacket. As your essay develops, you may want to modify your thesis statement. This urge is not only acceptable, it is normal. You can develop a working thesis by determining a question that you are trying to answer in your paper. A one- or two-sentence answer to this question often produces a tentative thesis statement. For example, one of our students wanted to answer the following question in her essay:

> Do men and women have different conversational speaking styles?

Her preliminary answer to this question was:

> Men and women appear to have different objectives when they converse.

After writing two drafts, she modified her thesis to better fit the examples she had gathered:

> Very often, conversations between men and women become situations in which the man gives a mini-lecture and the woman unwittingly turns into a captive audience.

Usually the thesis is presented early in an essay, sometimes in the first sentence. Here are some thesis statements that begin essays:

> One of the most potent elements in body language is eye behavior.
>
> Flora Davis

> Americans can be divided into three groups—smokers, non-smokers, and that expanding pack of us who have quit.
>
> Franklin E. Zimring

> Over the past ten to fifteen years it has become apparent that eating disorders have reached epidemic proportions among adolescents.
>
> Helen A. Guthrie

> Clutter is the disease of American writing. We are a society strangling in unnecessary words, circular construction, pompous frills, and meaningless jargon.
>
> William Zinsser

Each of these sentences does what a good thesis statement should do—it identifies the topic and makes an assertion about it.

Often writers prepare readers for a thesis statement with one or several sentences that establish a context. Notice, in the following example, how the author eases the reader into his thesis about television instead of presenting it abruptly in the first sentence:

> With the advent of television, for the first time in history, all aspects of animal and human life and death, of societal and individual behavior have been condensed on the average to a 19-inch diagonal screen and a 30-minute time slot. Television, a unique medium, claiming to be neither a reality nor art, has become reality for many of us, particularly for our children who are growing up in front of it.
>
> Jerzy Kosinski

On occasion a writer may even purposely delay the presentation of a thesis until the middle or end of an essay. If the thesis is controversial or needs extended discussion and illustration, the writer might present it later to make it easier for the reader to understand and accept it. Appearing near or at the end of an essay, a thesis also gains prominence.

Some kinds of writing do not need thesis statements. These include descriptions, narratives, and personal writing such as letters and diaries. But any essay that seeks to explain or prove a point has a thesis that is usually set forth in a thesis statement.

The Most Important Day

Helen Keller

Helen Keller (1880–1968) was afflicted by a disease that left her blind and deaf at the age of eighteen months. With the aid of her teacher, Anne Sullivan, she was able to overcome her severe handicaps, to graduate from Radcliffe College, and to lead a productive and challenging adult life. In the following selection from her autobiography, The Story of My Life *(1902), Keller tells of the day she first met Anne Sullivan, a day she regarded as the most important in her life. As you read, note that Keller states her thesis in the first paragraph and that the remaining paragraphs maintain unity by emphasizing the importance of the day her teacher arrived, even though they deal with the days and weeks following.*

For Your Journal

Imagine what your life would be like without the use of your eyes and your ears. What would your other senses be able to tell you? Try to imagine how you would communicate with others.

The most important day I remember in all my life is the one on which my teacher, Anne Mansfield Sullivan, came to me. I am filled with wonder when I consider the immeasurable contrast between the two lives which it connects. It was the third of March, 1887, three months before I was seven years old. 1

On the afternoon of that eventful day, I stood on the porch, dumb, expectant. I guessed vaguely from my mother's signs and from the hurrying to and fro in the house that something unusual was about to happen, so I went to the door and waited on the steps. The afternoon sun penetrated the mass of honeysuckle that covered the porch and fell on my upturned face. My fingers 2 lingered almost unconsciously on the familiar leaves and blossoms which had just come forth to greet the sweet southern spring. I did not know what the future held of marvel or surprise for me. Anger and bitterness had preyed upon me continually for weeks and a deep languor had succeeded this passionate struggle.

Have you ever been at sea in a dense fog, when it seemed as if 3 a tangible white darkness shut you in, and the great ship, tense and anxious, groped her way toward the shore with plummet and sounding-line, and you waited with beating heart for something to happen? I was like that ship before my education began, only I was without compass or sounding-line, and had no way of knowing how near the harbor was. "Light! give me light!" was the wordless cry of my soul, and the light of love shone on me in that very hour.

I felt approaching footsteps. I stretched out my hand as I sup- 4 posed to my mother. Someone took it, and I was caught up and held close in the arms of her who had come to reveal all things to me, and, more than all things else, to love me.

The morning after my teacher came she led me into her room 5 and gave me a doll. The little blind children at the Perkins Institution had sent it and Laura Bridgman had dressed it; but I did not know this until afterward. When I had played with it a little while, Miss Sullivan slowly spelled into my hand the word "d-o-l-l." I was at once interested in this finger play and tried to imitate it. When I finally succeeded in making the letters correctly I was flushed with childish pleasure and pride. Running downstairs to my mother I held up my hand and made the letters for doll. I did not know that I was spelling a word or even that words existed; I was simply making my fingers go in monkeylike imitation. In the days that followed I learned to spell in this uncomprehending way a great many words, among them *pin, hat, cup* and a few verbs like *sit, stand* and *walk.* But my teacher had been with me several weeks before I understood that everything has a name.

One day, while I was playing with my new doll, Miss Sullivan 6 put my big rag doll into my lap also, spelled "d-o-l-l" and tried to make me understand that "d-o-l-l" applied to both. Earlier in the day we had had a tussle over the words "m-u-g" and "w-a-t-e-r." Miss Sullivan had tried to impress it upon me that "m-u-g" is *mug* and that "w-a-t-e-r" is *water,* but I persisted in confounding the two. In despair she had dropped the subject for the time, only to renew it at the first opportunity. I became impatient at her repeated attempts and, seizing the new doll, I dashed it upon the floor. I was keenly delighted when I felt the fragments of the broken doll at my feet. Neither sorrow nor regret followed my passionate outburst. I had not loved the doll. In the still, dark world in which I lived there was no strong sentiment or tenderness. I felt my teacher sweep the fragments to one side of the hearth, and I had a sense of satisfaction that the cause of my discomfort was removed. She brought me my hat, and I knew I was going out into the warm sunshine. This thought, if a wordless sensation may be called a thought, made me hop and skip with pleasure.

We walked down the path to the well-house, attracted by the 7
fragrance of the honeysuckle with which it was covered. Someone was drawing water and my teacher placed my hand under the spout. As the cool stream gushed over one hand she spelled into the other the word *water,* first slowly, then rapidly. I stood still, my whole attention fixed upon the motions of her fingers. Suddenly I felt a misty consciousness as of something forgotten—a thrill of returning thought; and somehow the mystery of language was revealed to me. I knew then that "w-a-t-e-r" meant the wonderful cool something that was flowing over my hand. The living word awakened my soul, gave it light, hope, joy, set it free! There were barriers still, it is true, but barriers that could in time be swept away.

I left the well-house eager to learn. Everything had a name, and 8
each name gave birth to a new thought. As we returned to the house every object which I touched seemed to quiver with life. That was because I saw everything with the strange, new sight that had come to me. On entering the door I remembered the doll I had broken. I felt my way to the hearth and picked up the pieces. I tried vainly to put them together. Then my eyes filled with tears; for I realized what I had done, and for the first time I felt repentance and sorrow.

I learned a great many new words that day. I do not remember 9
what they all were; but I do know that *mother, father, sister, teacher* were among them—words that were to make the world blossom for me, "like Aaron's rod, with flowers." It would have been difficult to find a happier child than I was as I lay in my crib at the close of that eventful day and lived over the joys it had brought me, and for the first time longed for a new day to come.

Questions for Study and Discussion

1. What is Helen Keller's thesis in this essay? What question do you think Keller is trying to answer? How does this question help focus her subject? Does her thesis answer her question?
2. What is Helen Keller's purpose in this essay? (Glossary: *Purpose*)
3. What was Helen Keller's state of mind before Anne Sullivan arrived to help her? To what does she compare herself? (Glossary: *Analogy*) How effective is this comparison? Explain.
4. Why was the realization that everything has a name important to Helen Keller?
5. How was the "mystery of language" (7) revealed to Helen Keller? What were the consequences of this new understanding of the nature of language for her?
6. Helen Keller narrates the events of the day Anne Sullivan arrived (2–4), the morning after she arrived (5), and one day several weeks after her arrival (6–9). Describe what happens on each day, and explain how these separate incidents support her thesis.

Vocabulary

Refer to your dictionary to define the following words as they are used in this selection. Then use each word in a sentence of your own.

dumb (2)	plummet (3)
preyed (2)	tussle (6)
languor (2)	vainly (8)
passionate (2)	

Classroom Activity on Thesis

One effective way of focusing on your subject is to brainstorm a list of specific questions about it at the start. This strategy has a number of advantages. Each question narrows the general subject area, suggesting a more manageable essay. Also, simply phrasing your topic as a question gives you a starting point; your work has focus and direction from the outset. Finally, a one- or two-sentence answer to your question often provides you with a preliminary thesis statement.

To test this strategy, develop a list of five questions about the subject of "recycling paper waste on campus." To get you started, here is one possible question: Should students be required to recycle paper waste?

1. ______________________________
2. ______________________________
3. ______________________________
4. ______________________________
5. ______________________________

Suggested Writing Assignments

1. Think about an important day in your own life. Using the thesis statement "The most important day of my life was ______," write an essay in which you show the significance of that day by recounting and explaining the events that took place.
2. For many people around the world, the life of Helen Keller is a symbol of what an individual can achieve despite seemingly insurmountable disabilities. Her achievements have also inspired many who have no disabilities, leading them to believe that they can accomplish more than they ever thought possible. Consider the role of disabled people in our society, develop an appropriate thesis, and write an essay on the topic.

ANXIETY: CHALLENGE BY ANOTHER NAME

James Lincoln Collier

James Lincoln Collier is a freelance writer with more than six hundred articles to his credit. He was born in New York in 1928 and graduated from Hamilton College in 1950. Among his published books are many works of fiction, including novels for young adults. His nonfiction writing has often focused on American music, particularly jazz. Collier has produced biographies of Louis Armstrong, Duke Ellington, and Benny Goodman, but his best-known book is The Making of Jazz: A Comprehensive History *(1978), still regarded as the best general history of the subject. In 1993, he added* Jazz: The American Theme Song *to his list of publications. As you read the following essay, pay particular attention to where Collier places his thesis. Note also how his thesis statement identifies the topic (anxiety) and makes an assertion about it (that it can have a positive impact on our lives).*

FOR YOUR JOURNAL

Many people tend to associate anxiety with stress and to think of it as a negative thing. Are there good kinds of anxiety, too? Provide an example of anxiety that has been beneficial to you or to someone you know.

Between my sophomore and junior years at college, a chance came up for me to spend the summer vacation working on a ranch in Argentina. My roommate's father was in the cattle business, and he wanted Ted to see something of it. Ted said he would go if he could take a friend, and he chose me. 1

The idea of spending two months on the fabled Argentine Pampas was exciting. Then I began having second thoughts. I had never been very far from New England, and I had been homesick my first few weeks at college. What would it be like in a strange country? What about the language? And besides, I had promised to teach my younger brother to sail that summer. The more I thought about it, the more the prospect daunted me. I began waking up nights in a sweat. 2

In the end I turned down the proposition. As soon as Ted asked somebody else to go, I began kicking myself. A couple of weeks later I went home to my old summer job, unpacking cartons at the local supermarket, feeling very low. I had turned down something I wanted to do because I was scared, and had ended up feeling depressed. I stayed that way for a long time. And it didn't help when I went back to college in the fall to discover that Ted and his friend had had a terrific time. 3

In the long run that unhappy summer taught me a valuable lesson out of which I developed a rule for myself: *do what makes you anxious; don't do what makes you depressed.* 4

I am not, of course, talking about severe states of anxiety or depression, which require medical attention. What I mean is that kind of anxiety we call stage fright, butterflies in the stomach, a case of nerves—the feelings we have at a job interview, when we're giving a big party, when we have to make an important presentation at the office. And the kind of depression I am referring to is that downhearted feeling of the blues, when we don't seem to be interested in anything, when we can't get going and seem to have no energy. 5

I was confronted by this sort of situation toward the end of my senior year. As graduation approached, I began to think about taking a crack at making my living as a writer. But one of my professors was urging me to apply to graduate school and aim at a teaching career. 6

I wavered. The idea of trying to live by writing was scary—a lot more scary than spending a summer on the Pampas, I thought. Back and forth I went, making my decision, unmaking it. Suddenly, I realized that every time I gave up the idea of writing, that sinking feeling went through me; it gave me the blues. 7

The thought of graduate school wasn't what depressed me. It was giving up on what deep in my gut I really wanted to do. Right 8 then I learned another lesson. To avoid that kind of depression meant, inevitably, having to endure a certain amount of worry and concern.

The great Danish philosopher Søren Kierkegaard believed that anxiety always arises when we confront the possibility of our own development. It seems to be a rule of life that you can't advance without getting that old, familiar, jittery feeling. 9

Even as children we discover this when we try to expand ourselves by, say, learning to ride a bike or going out for the school play. Later in life we get butterflies when we think about having that first child, or uprooting the family from the old hometown to find a better opportunity halfway across the country. Any time, it seems, that we set out aggressively to get something we want, we meet up with anxiety. And it's going to be our traveling companion, at least part of the way, into any new venture. 10

When I first began writing magazine articles, I was frequently required to interview big names—people like Richard Burton, Joan Rivers, sex authority William Masters, baseball-great Dizzy Dean. Before each interview I would get butterflies and my hands would shake. 11

At the time, I was doing some writing about music. And one person I particularly admired was the great composer Duke Ellington. Onstage and on television, he seemed the very model of the confident, sophisticated man of the world. Then I learned that Ellington still got stage fright. If the highly honored Duke Ellington, who had appeared on the bandstand some 10,000 times over 30 years, had anxiety attacks, who was I to think I could avoid them? 12

I went on doing those frightening interviews, and one day, as I was getting onto a plane for Washington to interview columnist Joseph Alsop, I suddenly realized to my astonishment that I was looking forward to the meeting. What had happened to those butterflies? 13

Well, in truth, they were still there, but there were fewer of them. I had benefited, I discovered, from a process psychologists call "extinction." If you put an individual in an anxiety-provoking situation often enough, he will eventually learn that there isn't anything to be worried about. 14

Which brings us to a corollary to my basic rule: *you'll never eliminate anxiety by avoiding the things that caused it.* I remember how my son Jeff was when I first began to teach him to swim 15 at the lake cottage where we spent our summer vacations. He resisted, and when I got him into the water he sank and sputtered and wanted to quit. But I was insistent. And by summer's end he was splashing around like a puppy. He had "extinguished" his anxiety the only way he could—by confronting it.

The problem, of course, is that it is one thing to urge somebody else to take on those anxiety-producing challenges; it is quite another to get ourselves to do it. 16

Some years ago I was offered a writing assignment that would require three months of travel through Europe. I had been abroad a couple of times on the usual "If it's Tuesday this must be Belgium" trips, but I hardly could claim to know my way around the continent. Moreover, my knowledge of foreign languages was limited to a little college French. 17

I hesitated. How would I, unable to speak the language, totally unfamiliar with local geography or transportation systems, set up interviews and do research? It seemed impossible, and with considerable regret I sat down to write a letter begging off. Halfway through, a thought—which I subsequently made into another corollary to my basic rule—ran through my mind: *you can't learn if you don't try.* So I accepted the assignment. 18

There were some bad moments. But by the time I had finished the trip I was an experienced traveler. And ever since, I have never hesitated to head for even the most exotic of places, without guides or even advanced bookings, confident that somehow I will manage. 19

The point is that the new, the different, is almost by definition scary. But each time you try something, you learn, and as the learning piles up, the world opens to you. 20

I've made parachute jumps, learned to ski at 40, flown up the Rhine in a balloon. And I know I'm going to go on doing such things. It's not because I'm braver or more daring than others. I'm not. But I don't let the butterflies stop me from doing what I want. Accept anxiety as another name for challenge and you can accomplish wonders. 21

Questions for Study and Discussion

1. What is Collier's thesis in this essay? Based on your own experiences, do you think that Collier's thesis is a valid one? Explain.

2. What is the process known to psychologists as "extinction"?
3. What caused Collier to come up with his basic rule for himself: *"Do what makes you anxious; don't do what makes you depressed"* (4)? (Glossary: *Cause and Effect*) How did he develop the two corollaries to his basic rule?
4. What do you think Collier's purpose was in writing this essay? (Glossary: *Purpose*) Explain.
5. Identify the figure of speech that Collier uses toward the end of paragraph 10. (Glossary: *Figures of Speech*)
6. Explain how paragraphs 17–19 function within the context of Collier's essay. (Glossary: *Illustration*)

Vocabulary

Refer to your dictionary to define the following words as they are used in this selection. Then use each word in a sentence of your own.

daunted (2)	butterflies (5)
proposition (3)	crack (6)
anxiety (5)	venture (10)
depression (5)	corollary (15)

Classroom Activity on Thesis

A good thesis statement identifies the topic and makes an assertion about it. Evaluate each of the following sentences as a thesis statement, and explain why each one either works or doesn't work as one.

1. Americans are suffering from overwork.
2. Life is indeed precious, and I believe the death penalty helps to affirm this fact.
3. Birthday parties are loads of fun.
4. New York is a city of sounds: muted sounds and shrill sounds; shattering sounds and soothing sounds; urgent sounds and aimless sounds.

5. Everyone is talking about the level of violence in American society.
6. Neighborhoods are often assigned human characteristics, one of which is a life cycle: they have a birth, a youth, a middle age, and an old age.

Suggested Writing Assignments

1. Building on your own experiences and the reading you have done, write an essay in which you use as your thesis either Collier's basic rule or one of his corollaries to that basic rule.
2. Write an essay in which you use any of the following as your thesis:

   Good manners are a thing of the past.
   We need rituals in our lives.
   To tell a joke well is an art.
   We are a drug-dependent society.
   Losing weight is a breeze.

Why "Model Minority" Doesn't Fit

Diane Yen-Mei Wong

Diane Yen-Mei Wong writes about Asian American issues in a column that appears in the Hawaii Herald. *She currently lives in Oakland, California. In the following selection, which appeared in* USA Weekend *in January 1994, she discusses the dangers of stereotypes and how personal experience has forced her to re-evaluate her own ethnic community. Wong begins her essay with an extended example in which she explains the circumstances of the murder of her best friend's mother. This example sets the context for her somewhat surprising thesis about images of Asian American communities.*

For Your Journal

What images do you have of Asian American communities? On what experiences do you base your impressions? Do you think that the images you have are shared by your community at large?

I stopped by a peaceful lake on one of Seattle's rare sunny days to watch a wonderfully multiracial, multiethnic parade of people walk, jog, bicycle and skate along the bike path. For them, life looked good and the whole weekend lay ahead. The irony did not escape me. 1

Just a few hours before, I had been inside a windowless courtroom listening to a judge render a final sentence of 70 years in prison to a Vietnamese-American man, Dung Hoang Le, barely out of his teens. He had fatally stabbed my best friend's mother, Mayme Lui, a petite septuagenarian Chinese-American widow. He had mutilated her body to wrench off a jade bracelet, then at- 2 tempted to extort money from her family as he led them to believe she was still alive.

He needed money fast. He had just wrecked his cousin's car and discovered his girlfriend was pregnant. Without a job or marketable skills, he was at a critical juncture. Rather than earn money through hard work, he chose crime. This decision changed our lives forever. 3

I used to see my friend's mother whenever I was visiting in town; we laughed and talked and ate. Now I try to comfort the family as they negotiate their lives around her absence. I am haunted by frequent nightmares of the terror and pain she must have felt. But this man's act also has compelled me to rethink how I view my own community of Asian Americans. 4

For more than two decades, I have argued that the diverse Asian-American community cannot be stereotyped. One of the most troubling and persistent images is that we are a "model minority," people who have succeeded when other people of color have not. We are held up as proof that racial discrimination either does not exist or, if it does, is not much of a handicap. I have argued that this stereotype negates the existence of the large segments of our ethnic communities that live in poverty, have little or no education, and work in sweatshops for less than the minimum wage or in family-owned businesses for no wages. 5

Violence in the Asian-American community, like violence in many other communities, is growing at such an alarming rate that several cities, including Seattle, have assigned special units to investigate crimes committed by Asian-American gangs. City officials in Seattle say that from 1988 to 1993, for example, the number of Asian-Pacific Islander youths involved in gangs increased eightfold. 6

Despite this reality, too many Asian Americans and others cling to the mythical model-minority image. They want to believe that crime, especially violent crime, happens in other communities, not in one that spawns valedictorians and scientists and espouses respect for authority and close family ties. 7

The model-minority mantra, however, no matter how frequently repeated, cannot protect us against the intensifying violence perpetrated by our own. 8

I have heard "experts" say that some immigrants and refugees may commit crimes because of cultural unfamiliarity or a lack of 9 sophistication about the American way of life. Some say there is a heightened sense of detachment adopted by refugees dulled by the horror of seeing so many deaths in war.

Even if true, these arguments do not explain why many other people facing similar circumstances do not extort, kidnap and murder. Surely killing someone for money is not an acceptable act in any country. 10

And it may get worse. As the interaction among the different Asian-American ethnic groups grows, crimes increasingly will cross ethnic lines. 11

A Chinese-American wedding reception becomes the target of non-Chinese-American criminals whose eyes see not the ethnicity of the newlyweds but only the jade and gold jewelry worn just for the special occasion. Is it any wonder that some wedding parties now include security guards? 12

At the sentencing, I happened to sit next to a small, elderly well-to-do and prominent Chinese American. I found myself wondering how much of her interest in the outcome was related to how unsafe she felt now that her ethnicity no longer could protect her. 13

Asian Americans have been considered different from other minorities. We are supposed to be harmless and somehow exotic, the least offensive minority group to have around if one must have any around at all. Tragically, it may be the rising crime rate within our own "model-minority" community that finally proves, once and for all, that we are more like everyone else than some of us ever thought. 14

Questions for Study and Discussion

1. Reread paragraphs 1–3. Why does Wong use them to begin her essay? (Glossary: *Beginnings and Endings*) In what way do they help unify the essay?
2. What is Wong's thesis? (Glossary: *Thesis*) Where is it stated? What does Wong gain by stating her thesis where she does?
3. Who is Wong's audience? (Glossary: *Audience*) Explain your answer.

4. Why does Wong think that the "model minority" stereotype of the Asian American community is harmful? Identify how she illustrates her argument. (Glossary: *Illustration*)
5. Why does Wong think violence in the Asian American community might get worse? Do you agree with her assessment? Why or why not?
6. What purpose does paragraph 13 serve? How does it help Wong unify her essay?

Vocabulary

Refer to your dictionary to define the following words as they are used in this selection. Then use each word in a sentence of your own.

render (2)	valedictorians (7)
septuagenarian (2)	espouses (7)
extort (2)	mantra (8)

Classroom Activity on Thesis

Based on your reading of Wong's essay, write at least one thesis statement for each of the following questions:

1. How has the "model minority" label hurt Asian Americans?
2. Why did the "model minority" stereotype come into being?
3. What do Asian Americans have to learn about themselves with respect to stereotyping?

Suggested Writing Assignments

1. Explore how a personal experience changed your thinking about a particular subject. It can be about any subject you choose—how you view your peers or another group of people, an issue in current events, political beliefs, etc. Write a unified essay in which you incorporate your revised opinion

or belief into the thesis statement. Make sure that each paragraph contributes to your exploration of how and why your thinking has changed.

2. Write a unified essay using the following sentence as a thesis: "Ethnic stereotypes, whether positive or negative, are harmful."

2

UNITY

A well-written essay should be unified; that is, everything in it should be related to its thesis, or main idea. The first requirement for unity is that the thesis itself be clear, either through a direct statement, called the *thesis statement,* or by implication. The second requirement is that there be no digressions, no discussion or information that is not shown to be logically related to the thesis. A unified essay stays within the limits of its thesis.

Here, for example, is a short essay called "Over-Generalizing" about the dangers of making generalizations. As you read, notice how carefully author Stuart Chase sticks to his point.

> One swallow does not make a summer, nor can two or three cases often support a dependable generalization. Yet all of us, including the most polished eggheads, are constantly falling into this mental peopletrap. It is the commonest, probably the most seductive, and potentially the most dangerous, of all the fallacies. 1
>
> You drive through a town and see a drunken man on the sidewalk. A few blocks further on you see another. You turn to your companion: "Nothing but drunks in this town!" Soon you are out in the country, bowling along at fifty. A car passes you as if you were parked. On a curve a second whizzes by. Your companion turns to you: "All the drivers in this state are crazy!" Two thumping generalizations, each built on two cases. If we stop to think, we usually recognize the exaggeration and the unfairness of such generalizations. Trouble comes when we do not stop to think—or when we build them on a prejudice. 2
>
> This kind of reasoning has been around for a long time. Aristotle was aware of its dangers and called it "reasoning by example," meaning too few examples. What it boils down to is failing to count your swallows before announcing that summer is here. Driving from my home to New Haven the other day, a distance of about forty miles, I caught myself saying: "Every time I look around I see a new ranch-type 3

house going up." So on the return trip I counted them; there were exactly five under construction. And how many times had I "looked around"? I suppose I had glanced to right and left—as one must at side roads and so forth in driving—several hundred times.

In this fallacy we do not make the error of neglecting facts altogether and rushing immediately to the level of opinion. We start at the fact level properly enough, but *we do not stay there.* A case of two and up we go to a rousing oversimplification about drunks, speeders, ranch-style houses—or, more seriously, about foreigners, Negroes, labor leaders, teen-agers. 4

Why do we over-generalize so often and sometimes so disastrously? One reason is that the human mind is a generalizing machine. We would not be people without this power. The old academic crack: "All generalizations are false, including this one," is only a play on words. We *must* generalize to communicate and to live. But we should beware of beating the gun; of not waiting until enough facts are in to say something useful. Meanwhile it is a plain waste of time to listen to arguments based on a few handpicked examples. 5

Everything in the essay relates to Chase's thesis statement, which is included in the essay's first sentence: ". . . nor can two or three cases often support a dependable generalization." Paragraphs 2 and 3 document the thesis with examples; paragraph 4 explains how over-generalizing occurs; paragraph 5 analyzes why people over-generalize; and, for a conclusion, Chase restates his thesis in different words. An essay may be longer, more complex, and more wide-ranging than this one, but to be effective it must also avoid digressions and remain close to the author's main idea.

One way to check that your essay is indeed unified is to underline your thesis and then to explain to yourself how each paragraph in your essay is related to the thesis. If you find a paragraph that does not appear to be logically connected, you can revise it so that the relationship is clear.

My Name

Sandra Cisneros

Sandra Cisneros was born in Chicago in 1954. After attending the Iowa Writers' Workshop in the late 1970s, she moved to the Southwest and now lives in San Antonio, Texas. Cisneros has had numerous occupations within the fields of education and the arts and has been a visiting writer at various universities. Although she has written two well-received books of poetry, My Wicked, Wicked Ways *(1987) and* Loose Woman *(1994), she is better known for the autobiographical fiction of* The House on Mango Street *(1984)—from which the following selection was taken—and for* Woman Hollering Creek and Other Stories *(1991). In 1995 she was awarded a grant from the prestigious MacArthur Foundation and is currently at work on a novel. As you read "My Name," pay particular attention to how tightly Cisneros unifies her paragraphs by intertwining the meanings of her name (originally Esperanza) and her feelings about the great-grandmother with whom she shares that name.*

For Your Journal

Are you happy with your name? Why do you think your parents chose the name they did for you? Does the name have a special meaning for them? What does your name mean to you?

In English my name means hope. In Spanish it means too many letters. It means sadness, it means waiting. It is like the number nine. A muddy color. It is the Mexican records my father plays on Sunday mornings when he is shaving, songs like sobbing. 1

It was my great-grandmother's name and now it is mine. She 2
was a horse woman too, born like me in the Chinese year of the horse—which is supposed to be bad luck if you're born female—but I think this is a Chinese lie because the Chinese, like the Mexicans, don't like their women strong.

My great-grandmother. I would've liked to have known her, a 3
wild horse of a woman, so wild she wouldn't marry until my great-grandfather threw a sack over her head and carried her off. Just like that, as if she were a fancy chandelier. That's the way he did it.

And the story goes she never forgave him. She looked out the 4
window all her life, the way so many women sit their sadness on an elbow. I wonder if she made the best with what she got or was she sorry because she couldn't be all the things she wanted to be. Esperanza. I have inherited her name, but I don't want to inherit her place by the window.

At school they say my name funny as if the syllables were 5
made out of tin and hurt the roof of your mouth. But in Spanish my name is made out of a softer something like silver, not quite as thick as my sister's name Magdalena which is uglier than mine. Magdalena who at least can come home and become Nenny. But I am always Esperanza.

I would like to baptize myself under a new name, a name more 6
like the real me, the one nobody sees. Esperanza as Lisandra or Maritza or Zeze the X. Yes. Something like Zeze the X will do.

Questions for Study and Discussion

1. What is Cisneros's thesis? (Glossary: *Thesis*) Where does she state it? How does each paragraph relate to her thesis to produce a unified essay?
2. In what way do you think a name can be like the number nine? Like a muddy color? What is your impression of the author's name, based on these similes? (Glossary: *Figures of Speech*)
3. What is Cisneros's purpose in writing the essay? (Glossary: *Purpose*) Explain your answer.
4. Identify all of the metaphors and similes used by Cisneros in paragraphs 3–5. Discuss the importance of each to her purpose. (Glossary: *Figures of Speech*)

5. What is Cisneros's tone in the essay? (Glossary: *Tone*) How does she establish the tone? What does it tell the reader about how she feels about her name?
6. Why does Cisneros wait until the end of paragraph 4 to reveal her given name?
7. Why do you think Cisneros chose "Zeze the X" as a name that better represents her inner self?

Vocabulary

Refer to your dictionary to define the following words as they are used in this selection. Then use each word in a sentence of your own.

chandelier (3)   baptize (6)

Classroom Activity on Unity

Follow Cisneros's example in the first paragraph of her essay, and associate your name with familiar things. What is the literal meaning of your name? What color would you associate with it? What else would you associate with it? If you were to write a short essay, how might you organize these details so as to achieve maximum unity?

Suggested Writing Assignments

1. If you could choose a different name for yourself, what would it be? Write an essay that reveals your choice of a new name and explains why you like it or why it might be particularly appropriate for you. Make sure the essay is unified and that every paragraph directly supports your name choice.
2. Choose a grandparent or other relative at least two generations older than you about whom you know an interesting story. What impact has the relative, or the stories about him or her, had on your life? Write a unified narrative essay about the relative and what is interesting about him or her.

A Chance to Pursue My Dreams

Cynthia Inda

Cynthia Inda was born in Santa Barbara, California. During her sophomore year in high school, after achieving little academic success in public schools, she transferred to Brighton Academy in Grants Pass, Oregon, where she fared much better. She then spent two years at Santa Barbara City College before going on to Harvard University, where she is now studying government. As you read the description of her academic background in the following essay, take note of how the first five paragraphs establish a supporting context for the thesis presented in paragraph 6. In the remaining paragraphs, she maintains a strong sense of unity by pursuing her main point about the importance of leadership in producing "not only good students, but good people."

For Your Journal

Think about your high-school experience. How would you characterize the atmosphere in your school? Did you find this atmosphere conducive to learning? What could have been done to improve the atmosphere?

By the end of my freshman year at a public high school in Santa Barbara, California, I had had enough. 1

Enough of the lewd comments and harassment I encountered daily. Enough of watching students come to class stoned or drunk. And enough of the racial tension that culminated for me when I was physically threatened by a gang of Hispanic girls because I had white friends. 2

To make matters worse, no one at the school seemed to care about any of this. Administrators didn't protect students from harassment in the hallways. Teachers didn't reprimand the students who disrupted class. Few showed concern if a student flunked all 3 of his courses. I went for weeks without attending class, but no teacher ever said a word and my parents never found out.

I came very close to dropping out, which would not have sur- 4
prised my teachers. I am the youngest of seven children, born to immigrant parents from rural Mexico. My father has a third-grade education, and my mother never attended school. They never learned to speak English. My older brothers did not attend college; my older sisters became pregnant at an early age and dropped out of high school.

If I had stayed in my public school, I would surely have lost 5
all interest in education. But I was lucky to have parents who scrimped and saved to send me, beginning in my sophomore year, to a private school that emphasized competence and character. It was a turning point: I rediscovered my ardor for learning. I graduated with honors and I was admitted this fall as a transfer student to Harvard University.

What was it about Brighton Academy, a small private school 6
in Grants Pass, Oregon, that helped turn me around? In a word: leadership. The faculty and administration were interested in producing not only good students, but good people. I was once again free to focus on academics because I was no longer wasting my energy living in fear of school.

At my private school, adults weren't afraid to exercise author- 7
ity in a sensitive yet firm manner, and for this they earned the students' respect. Teachers wouldn't tolerate tardiness, inappropriate dress, or disruption. When a student was caught with drugs, not only was he punished and his parents informed, but the administration addressed the entire student body about it.

Our teachers emphasized discipline and character. They taught 8
us not to capitulate to peer pressure, reminding us that it takes strength and individuality to stand for what one believes. School officials regularly rewarded good conduct, through public praise and student-of-the-month awards.

Our instructors were exceptional not only because they got to 9
know us outside of school—in our neighborhoods and churches, and even at family picnics—but because they were obviously committed to us as students. Brighton cannot afford to pay its teachers competitive salaries, and many teachers take, without complaint, outside jobs during the school year.

Contrary to many assumptions about private education, the 10
student body at Brighton came from working-class and middle-

class families. Parents held monthly rummage sales. Students took after-school jobs to help pay their tuition.

Sadly, the most powerful lessons of my public school—listen to peers, not parents; disrespect authority; learn not to care about learning—directly undermined those I was taught at home. But my private school emphasized that parents are a child's primary moral teachers, and they did everything to support parents in this role. Parents were integrated into the school community via planning committees, monthly all-school meetings, student–teacher conferences, and invitations to all school functions. 11

I thank my teachers at this wonderful school who cared that I learned. Although they made less money than my public-school teachers, they awakened my love of learning, and they taught the principles—integrity, honesty, courage—that have enabled me to pursue my dreams. 12

Questions for Study and Discussion

1. Why is Inda's first sentence effective? (Glossary: *Beginnings and Endings*) Why do you think she makes it stand alone as the first paragraph?
2. Why was Inda's ethnic background an issue when she had trouble at her public school? How did it influence her public-school teachers' perception of her?
3. What *is* it about Brighton Academy that helped Inda succeed? Why did the faculty and administration at Brighton succeed in reaching her and rekindling her ardor for learning when their counterparts at the public school had failed?
4. What features of Brighton Academy made it unusual for a private school? Why does Inda consider such differences important to include in her essay? Does such detail make her essay less unified? (Glossary: *Unity*) Why or why not?
5. What were the most powerful lessons of Inda's public school? How did these "lessons" undermine her ability to get a good education?
6. What audience does Inda address in her essay? (Glossary: *Audience*) What does she assume about her audience? Explain your answer.

Vocabulary

Refer to your dictionary to define the following words as they are used in this selection. Then use each word in a sentence of your own.

lewd (2)
culminated (2)
ardor (5)
capitulate (8)
integrity (12)

Classroom Activity on Unity

A student wrote the following paragraphs for an essay using this thesis statement:

> In order to provide a good learning environment in school, the teachers and administrators need to be strong leaders.

Unfortunately, some of the sentences disrupt the unity of the essay. Find these sentences, eliminate them, and reread the essay.

> School administrators and teachers must do more than simply supply students with information and a school building. They must also provide students with an atmosphere that allows them to focus on learning within the walls of the school. Whether the walls are brick, steel, or cement, they are only walls, and they do not help to create an appropriate atmosphere. Strong leadership both inside and outside the classroom yields a school in which students are able to excel in their studies, because they know how to conduct themselves in their relationships with their teachers and fellow students.
>
> A recent change in the administration of Eastside High School demonstrated how important strong

leadership is to learning. Under the previous administration, parents and students complained that not enough emphasis was placed on studies. Most of the students lived in an impoverished neighborhood that had only one park for several thousand residents. Students were allowed to leave school at any time of the day, and little was done to curb the growing substance abuse problem. "What's the point of trying to teach algebra to students who are just going to get jobs as part-time sales clerks, anyway?" Vice Principal Iggy Norant said when questioned about his school's poor academic standards. Mr. Norant was known to students as Twiggy Iggy because of his tall, thin frame. Standardized test scores at the school lagged well behind the state average, and only 16% of the graduates attended college within two years.

Five years ago, the school board hired Mary Peña, former chair of the state educational standards committee, as principal. A cheerleader in college, Ms. Peña got her B.A. in recreation science before getting her masters in education. She immediately emphasized the importance of learning, replacing any faculty members who did not share her high expectations of the students. Among those she fired was Mr. Norant; she also replaced two social studies teachers, one math teacher, four English teachers, and a lab instructor who let students play Gameboy in lab. She also established a code of conduct, which clearly stated the rules all students had to follow. Students were allowed second chances, but those who continued to conduct themselves in a way that interfered with the other students' ability to learn were dealt with quickly and severely. "The attitude at Eastside has changed so much since Mary Peña arrived," said math teacher Jeremy Rifkin after Peña's second year. "Students come to class much more relaxed and ready to learn. I feel like I can teach again." Test scores at Eastside are now well above state averages, and 68% of the most recent graduating class went straight to college.

Suggested Writing Assignments

1. Inda states that "parents are a child's primary moral teachers, and they [the school staff] did everything to support parents in this role" (11). Write an essay in which you discuss how much of a role you think parents should play in a child's education. How can a school's policies encourage positive parental interaction? How might they discourage it? Base your answer on your own experience. If you have a child in school now or expect to in the future, how will you use your parents' example in handling your own child's education? What did they do that you might want to avoid doing yourself?
2. Think about the classes you had in high school. List two or three in which you learned a lot—classes that you enjoyed although they may not have been easy. In short, what classes encouraged an "ardor for learning" (5) within you? Write an essay in which you describe your ideal course, based on the experiences you had in the classes you listed. Would it be a lecture class, a discussion class, a "hands-on" class? What would characterize the teacher's relationship to the students in the class? How would you like your performance in the class evaluated?

The Meanings of a Word

Gloria Naylor

American novelist and essayist Gloria Naylor was born in 1950 in New York City, where she lives today. She worked first as a missionary for the Jehovah's Witnesses from 1967 to 1975, then as a telephone operator until 1981. That year she graduated from Brooklyn College of the City of New York and began graduate work in African American studies at Yale University. Naylor has taught writing and literature at George Washington University, New York University, and Cornell University, in addition to publishing several novels: The Women of Brewster Place *(1982),* Linden Hills *(1985),* Mama Day *(1988), and* Bailey's Cafe *(1992). The following essay first appeared in the* New York Times *in 1986. In it Naylor examines the ways in which words can take on meaning depending on who uses them and to what purpose. Notice how the paragraphs describing her experiences with the word* nigger *relate back to a clearly stated thesis at the end of paragraph 2.*

For Your Journal

Have you ever been called a derogatory name? What was the name, and how did you feel about it?

Language is the subject. It is the written form with which I've managed to keep the wolf away from the door and, in diaries, to keep my sanity. In spite of this, I consider the written word inferior to the spoken, and much of the frustration experienced by novelists is the awareness that whatever we manage to capture in even the most transcendent passages falls far short of the rich- 1 ness of life. Dialogue achieves its power in the dynamics of a fleeting moment of sight, sound, smell, and touch.

I'm not going to enter the debate here about whether it is lan- 2
guage that shapes reality or vice versa. That battle is doomed to be waged whenever we seek intermittent reprieve from the chicken and egg dispute. I will simply take the position that the spoken word, like the written word, amounts to a nonsensical arrangement of sounds or letters without a consensus that assigns "meaning." And building from the meanings of what we hear, we order reality. Words themselves are innocuous; it is the consensus that gives them true power.

I remember the first time I heard the word *nigger.* In my third- 3
grade class, our math tests were being passed down the rows, and as I handed the papers to a little boy in back of me, I remarked that once again he had received a much lower mark than I did. He snatched his test from me and spit out that word. Had he called me a nymphomaniac or a necrophiliac, I couldn't have been more puzzled. I didn't know what a nigger was, but I knew that whatever it meant, it was something he shouldn't have called me. This was verified when I raised my hand, and in a loud voice repeated what he had said and watched the teacher scold him for using a "bad" word. I was later to go home and ask the inevitable question that every black parent must face—"Mommy, what does *nigger* mean?"

And what exactly did it mean? Thinking back, I realize that 4
this could not have been the first time the word was used in my presence. I was part of a large extended family that had migrated from the rural South after World War II and formed a close-knit network that gravitated around my maternal grandparents. Their ground-floor apartment in one of the buildings they owned in Harlem was a weekend mecca for my immediate family, along with countless aunts, uncles, and cousins who brought along assorted friends. It was a bustling and open house with assorted neighbors and tenants popping in and out to exchange bits of gossip, pick up an old quarrel, or referee the ongoing checkers game in which my grandmother cheated shamelessly. They were all there to let down their hair and put up their feet after a week of labor in the factories, laundries, and shipyards of New York.

Amid the clamor, which could reach deafening proportions— 5
two or three conversations going on simultaneously, punctuated

by the sound of a baby's crying somewhere in the back rooms or out on the street—there was still a rigid set of rules about what was said and how. Older children were sent out of the living room when it was time to get into the juicy details about "you-know-who" up on the third floor who had gone and gotten herself "p-r-e-g-n-a-n-t!" But my parents, knowing that I could spell well beyond my years, always demanded that I follow the others out to play. Beyond sexual misconduct and death, everything else was considered harmless for our young ears. And so among the anecdotes of the triumphs and disappointments in the various workings of their lives, the word *nigger* was used in my presence, but it was set within contexts and inflections that caused it to register in my mind as something else.

In the singular, the word was always applied to a man who had distinguished himself in some situation that brought their approval for his strength, intelligence, or drive: 6

"Did Johnny *really* do that?" 7

"I'm telling you, that nigger pulled in $6,000 of overtime last year. Said he got enough for a down payment on a house." 8

When used with a possessive adjective by a woman—"my nigger"—it became a term of endearment for her husband or boyfriend. But it could be more than just a term applied to a man. In their mouths it became the pure essence of manhood—a disembodied force that channeled their past history of struggle and present survival against the odds into a victorious statement of being: "Yeah, that old foreman found out quick enough—you don't mess with a nigger." 9

In the plural, it became a description of some group within the community that had overstepped the bounds of decency as my family defined it. Parents who neglected their children, a drunken couple who fought in public, people who simply refused to look for work, those with excessively dirty mouths or unkempt households were all "trifling niggers." This particular circle could forgive hard times, unemployment, the occasional bout of depression—they had gone through all of that themselves—but the unforgivable sin was a lack of self-respect. 10

A woman could never be a "nigger" in the singular, with its connotation of confirming worth. The noun *girl* was its closest equivalent in that sense, but only when used in direct address and regardless of the gender doing the addressing. *Girl* was a token 11 of respect for a woman. The one-syllable word was drawn out to sound like three in recognition of the extra ounce of wit, nerve, or daring that the woman had shown in the situation under discussion.

"G-i-r-l, stop. You mean you said that to his face?" 12

But if the word was used in a third-person reference or short- 13
ened so that it almost snapped out of the mouth, it always involved some element of communal disapproval. And age became an important factor in these exchanges. It was only between individuals of the same generation, or from any older person to a younger (but never the other way around), that *girl* would be considered a compliment.

I don't agree with the argument that use of the word *nigger* at 14
this social stratum of the black community was an internalization of racism. The dynamics were the exact opposite: the people in my grandmother's living room took a word that whites used to signify worthlessness or degradation and rendered it impotent. Gathering there together, they transformed *nigger* to signify the varied and complex human beings they knew themselves to be. If the word was to disappear totally from the mouths of even the most liberal of white society, no one in that room was naive enough to believe it would disappear from white minds. Meeting the word head-on, they proved it had absolutely nothing to do with the way they were determined to live their lives.

So there must have been dozens of times that *nigger* was 15
spoken in front of me before I reached the third grade. But I didn't "hear" it until it was said by a small pair of lips that had already learned it could be a way to humiliate me. That was the word I went home and asked my mother about. And since she knew that I had to grow up in America, she took me in her lap and explained.

Questions for Study and Discussion

1. How does Naylor explain her preference for the spoken word over the written word? What does she mean by "context"?
2. What are the two meanings of the word "nigger" as Naylor uses it in her essay? Where in the essay is the clearest defi-

nition of each use of the word presented? (Glossary: *Definition*)

3. Naylor said she must have heard the word "nigger" many times while she was growing up; yet she "heard" it for the first time when she was in the third grade. How does she explain this seeming contradiction?
4. Naylor gives a detailed narration of her family and its lifestyle in paragraphs 4 and 5. What kinds of detail does she include in her brief story? (Glossary: *Narration* and *Details*) How does this narration contribute to your understanding of the word "nigger" as used by her family? Why do you suppose she offers so little in the way of a definition of the other use of the word "nigger"? What is the effect on you as a reader? Explain.
5. Would you characterize Naylor's tone as angry, objective, cynical, or something else? (Glossary: *Tone*) Cite examples of her diction to support your answer. (Glossary: *Diction*)
6. What is the meaning of Naylor's last sentence? How well does it work as an ending for her essay? (Glossary: *Beginnings and Endings*)

Vocabulary

Refer to your dictionary to define the following words as they are used in this selection. Then use each word in a sentence of your own.

transcendent (1)
consensus (2)
innocuous (2)
nymphomaniac (3)
necrophiliac (3)
mecca (4)
clamor (5)
anecdotes (5)
inflections (5)
unkempt (10)
trifling (10)
internalization (14)
impotent (14)

Classroom Activity on Unity

Carefully read the following five-paragraph sequence, paying special attention to how each paragraph relates to the writer's thesis. Identify the paragraph that disrupts the unity of the sequence, and explain why it doesn't belong.

> Though "experts" differ as to the best technique to follow when building a fire, one generally accepted method consists of first laying a generous amount of crumpled newspaper on the hearth between the andirons. Kindling wood is then spread generously over this layer of newspaper and one of the thickest logs is placed across the back of the andirons. This should be as close to the back of the fireplace as possible, but not quite touching it. A second log is then placed an inch or so in front of this, and a few additional sticks of kindling are laid across these two. A third log is then placed on top to form a sort of pyramid with air space between all logs so that flames can lick freely up between them.
>
> Roaring fireplace fires are particularly welcome during the winter months, especially after hearty outdoor activities. To avoid any mid-winter tragedies, care should be taken to have a professional inspect and clean the chimney before starting to use the fireplace in the fall. Also, be sure to clean out the fireplace after each use.
>
> A mistake frequently made is building the fire too far forward so that the rear wall of the fireplace does not get properly heated. A heated back wall helps increase the draft and tends to suck smoke and flames rearward with less chance of sparks or smoke spurting out into the room.
>
> Another common mistake often made by the inexperienced fire-tender is to try to build a fire with only one or two logs, instead of using at least three. A single log is difficult to ignite properly, and even two logs do not provide an efficient bed with adequate fuel-burning capacity.
>
> Use of too many logs, on the other hand, is also a common fault and can prove hazardous. Building too big a fire can create more smoke and draft than the chimney can safely handle, increasing the possibility of sparks or smoke being thrown out into the room. For best results, the homeowner should start with three medium-size logs as described above, then add additional logs as needed if the fire is to be kept burning.

The five paragraphs on "How to Build a Fire in a Fireplace" are taken from Bernard Gladstone's book *The New York Times Complete Manual of Home Repair.*

Suggested Writing Assignments

1. Write a short essay in which you define a word that has more than one meaning, depending on one's point of view. For example, wife, macho, liberal, success, and marriage.
2. Naylor disagrees with the notion that use of the word "nigger" in the African American community can be taken as an "internalization of racism." Reexamine her essay and discuss in what ways her definition of the word "nigger" affirms or denies her position. Draw on your own experiences, observations, and reading to add support to your answer.

3

ORGANIZATION

In an essay, ideas and information cannot be presented all at once; they have to be arranged in some order. That order is the essay's organization.

The pattern of organization in an essay should be suited to the writer's subject and purpose. For example, if you are writing about your experience working in a fast-food restaurant, and your purpose is to tell about the activities of a typical day, you might present those activities in chronological order. If, on the other hand, you wish to argue that working in a bank is an ideal summer job, you might proceed from the least rewarding to the most rewarding aspect of this job; this is called "climactic" order.

Some often-used patterns of organization are time order, space order, and logical order. Time order, or chronological order, is used to present events as they occurred. A personal narrative, a report of a campus incident, or an account of a historical event can be most naturally and easily related in chronological order. The description of a process, such as the refinishing of a table, the building of a stone wall, or the way to serve a tennis ball, almost always calls for a chronological organization. Of course, the order of events can sometimes be rearranged for special effect. For example, an account of an auto accident may begin with the collision itself and then go back in time to tell about the events leading up to it. One essay that is a model of chronological order is Dick Gregory's "Shame" (pp. 260–63).

Space order is used when describing a person, place, or thing. This organizational pattern begins at a particular point and moves in some direction, such as left to right, top to bottom, east to west, outside to inside, front to back, near to far, around, or over. In describing a house, for example, a writer could move from top to bottom, from outside to inside, or in a circle around the outside. One essay that is a model of spatial order is Gilbert Highet's "Subway Station" (pp. 287–88).

Logical order can take many forms depending on the writer's purpose. These include: general to specific, most familiar to least familiar, and smallest to biggest. Perhaps the most common type of logical order is order of importance. Notice how the writer uses this order in the following paragraph:

> The Egyptians have taught us many things. They were excellent farmers. They knew all about irrigation. They built temples which were afterwards copied by the Greeks and which served as the earliest models for the churches in which we worship nowadays. They invented a calendar which proved such a useful instrument for the purpose of measuring time that it has survived with few changes until today. But most important of all, the Egyptians learned how to preserve speech for the benefit of future generations. They invented the art of writing.

By organizing the material according to the order of increasing importance, the writer places special emphasis on the final sentence. In writing a descriptive essay you can move from the least striking to the most striking detail, so as to keep your reader interested and involved in the description. In an explanatory essay you can start with the point that readers will find least difficult to understand and move on to the most difficult; that's how teachers organize many courses. Or, in writing an argumentative essay, you can move from your least controversial point to the most controversial, preparing your reader gradually to accept your argument.

A simple way to check the organization of an essay is to outline it once you have a draft. Does the outline represent the organizational pattern—chronological, spatial, or logical—that you set out to use? Problems in outlining will naturally indicate areas where you will need to revise.

REACH OUT AND WRITE SOMEONE

Lynn Wenzel

Lynn Wenzel has been published in many major newspapers and magazines, including Ms., Newsweek, *the* New York Times, Newsday, *and* Down East: The Magazine of Maine. *Her book* I Hear America Singing: A Nostalgic Tour of Popular Sheet Music *appeared in 1989. Wenzel, who graduated magna cum laude from William Paterson College, makes her home in Maywood, New Jersey. In the essay below, she organizes her ideas chronologically, yet within that larger time-order arrangement she also establishes the relative importance of her reasons for writing letters, ending with the "most important of all."*

FOR YOUR JOURNAL

When is the last time you wrote a letter to a friend? Are you, like so many others, usually tempted to pick up the telephone instead of writing a letter when you need to communicate? Begin writing a letter to someone to whom you have something important to say. Remember that "important" does not have to mean "big news"; it may simply mean telling someone how important he or she is to you.

Everyone is talking about the breakup of the telephone company. Some say it will be a disaster for poor people and a bonanza for large companies while others fear a personal phone bill so exorbitant that—horror of horrors—we will all have to start writing letters again. 1

It's about time. One of the many talents lost in this increasingly technological age is that of putting pen to paper in order to communicate with family, friends and lovers. 2

Reading, and enjoying it, may not be the strong suit of our young but writing has truly become a lost art. I am not talking 3 about creative writing because this country still has its full share of fine fiction and poetry writers. There will always be those special few who need to transform experiences into short stories or poetry.

No, the skill we have lost is that of letter writing. When was the last time the mailbox contained anything more than bills, political and fund-raising appeals, advertisements, catalogs, magazines or junk mail? 4

Once upon a time, the only way to communicate from a distance was through the written word. As the country expanded and people moved west, they knew that when they left mother, father, sister, brother, it was very probably the last time they would see them again. So daughters, pioneering in Indiana or Michigan, wrote home with the news that their first son had been born dead, but the second child was healthy and growing and they also had a house and barn. By the time the letter reached east, another child might have been born, yet it was read over and over again, then smoothed out and slipped into the family Bible or keepsake box. 5

Letters were essential then. Imagine John Adams fomenting revolution and forming a new government without Abigail's letters to sustain him. Think of Elizabeth Barrett and Robert Browning without their written declarations of love; of all the lovers who, parted against their will, kept hope alive through letters often passed by hand or mailed in secret. 6

And what of history? Much of our knowledge of events and of the people who lived them is based on such commonplace communication. Harry Truman's letters to Bess, Mamie and Ike's correspondence and Eleanor Roosevelt's letters to some of her friends all illuminate actions and hint at intent. F. Scott Fitzgerald's letters to his daughter, Scottie, which were filled with melancholy over his wife's mental illness, suggest in part the reason why his last years were so frustratingly uncreative. Without letters we would have history—dry facts and dates of wars, treaties, elections, revolutions. But the causes and effects might be left unclear. 7

We would also know little about women's lives. History, until recently, neglected women's contributions to events. Much of what we now know about women in history comes from letters found, more often than not, in great-grandmother's trunk in the attic, carefully tied with ribbon, or stored, yellowed and boxed, in a 8 carton in the archives of a "women's college." These letters have helped immensely over the past ten years to create a verifiable women's history which is now taking its rightful place alongside weighty tomes about men's contributions to the changing world.

The story of immigration often begins with a letter. Millions of brave souls, carrying their worldly possessions in one bag, stepped off a ship and into American life on the strength of a note saying, "Come. It's better here." 9

To know how important the "art" of letter writing was, we have only to look at the accouterments our ancestors treasured and considered necessary: inkstands of silver, gold or glass, crafted to occupy a prominent place on the writing table; hot wax for a personal seal; the seals themselves, sometimes ornately carved in silver; quills, and then fountain pens. These were not luxuries but necessities. 10

Perhaps most important of all, letter writing required *thinking* before putting pen to paper. No hurried telephone call can ever replace the thoughtful, intelligent correspondence between two people, the patching up of a friendship, the formal request for the pleasure of someone's company, or a personal apology. Once written and sent, the writer can never declare, "But I never said that." Serious letter writing demands thought, logic, organization and sincerity because words, once written, cannot be taken back. These are qualities we must not lose, but ones we should polish and bring to luster. 11

What, after all, will we lose: our lover's letters tied with an old hair ribbon, written from somewhere far away; our children's first scribbled note from summer camp; the letters friends sent us as we scattered after college; letters we sent our parents telling them how much they meant to us? Without letters, what will we save, laugh about, read out loud to each other 20 years from now on a snowy afternoon in front of a fire? 12

Telephone bills. 13

And that is the saddest note of all. 14

Questions for Study and Discussion

1. What is Wenzel's thesis in this essay? Where is it stated? (Glossary: *Thesis*)

2. Why does Wenzel concentrate on letter writing in her essay and not on other kinds of writing?
3. What role has letter writing played in our understanding of history, according to Wenzel?
4. In what ways is writing a letter different from making a phone call? What can letter writing do to help us develop as human beings? (Glossary: *Comparison and Contrast*)
5. Which of the three patterns of organization has Wenzel used in presenting her examples of the importance of letter writing? Support your answer with examples.
6. How effective do you find the beginning and ending of Wenzel's essay? Explain. (Glossary: *Beginnings and Endings*)

Vocabulary

Refer to your dictionary to define the following words as they are used in this selection. Then use each word in a sentence of your own.

exorbitant (1)
fomenting (6)
tomes (8)
accouterments (10)
seal (10)

Classroom Activity on Organization

Carefully read the following descriptive paragraph from *Blue Highways* by William Least Heat Moon, and identify the organizational pattern that he has used to structure his description.

> The old store, lighted only by three fifty-watt bulbs, smelled of coal and baking bread. In the middle of the rectangular room, where the oak floor sagged a little, stood an iron stove. To the right was a wooden table with an unfinished game of checkers and a stool made from an apple-tree stump. On the shelves around the walls sat earthen jugs with corncob stoppers . . . , a few canned goods, and some of the two thousand old clocks and clockworks Thurmond Watts owned. Only one was ticking; the others he just looked at. I asked how long he'd been in the store.

Based upon Least Heat Moon's description, draw a sketch of the inside of Thurmond Watts's store. Compare your sketch with those of your classmates. Using the above paragraph as a model, describe a room or a place that you have strong feelings about.

Suggested Writing Assignments

1. Write a personal letter to a friend or relative with whom you haven't been in contact for some while. Draft and redraft the letter carefully, making it as thoughtful and interesting as you can. Send the letter and report back to your class or instructor on the response that the letter elicited.
2. Think of a commonplace subject that people might take for granted but that you find interesting. Write an essay on that subject, using one of the following types of logical order:

    least important to most important
    most familiar to least familiar
    smallest to biggest
    oldest to newest
    easiest to understand to most difficult to understand
    good news to bad news
    general to specific

Made to Order Babies

Geoffrey Cowley

Raised in Salt Lake City, Utah, Geoffrey Cowley earned a B.A. in English from Lewis & Clark College in Portland, Oregon, and an M.A. in English from the University of Washington in Seattle. A newspaper and feature writer, Cowley joined Newsweek *in 1988 and since 1990 has been the magazine's health and medicine editor. His medical cover stories have addressed such topics as AIDS, chronic fatigue syndrome, Prozac, Halcion, and tuberculosis. Cowley's August 1995 report on melatonin is credited with igniting a global run on the substance. In the following essay, which appeared in* Newsweek *in 1990, Cowley explores some of the moral and ethical dimensions of prenatal testing. He concludes that "failing to think, as a society, about the appropriate uses of the new tests would be a grave mistake." Note how he organizes his essay as a series of key ideas related to the practice of genetic screening, devoting two or three paragraphs to each, and leading logically to his conclusion in paragraph 18.*

For Your Journal

Every couple of months, it seems, scientists announce that they've made a new genetic discovery, linking a disease or human characteristic to a particular gene. Genetic research opens new frontiers for exploration and poses new questions to ponder. Take a few minutes to list as many of your genetically determined traits as you can. If it were possible for you to change just one of these traits, what would it be and why?

For centuries, Jewish communities lived Job-like with the knowledge that many of their babies would thrive during in- 1 fancy, grow demented and blind as toddlers and die by the age of 5. Joseph Ekstein, a Hasidic rabbi in Brooklyn, lost four children to Tay-Sachs disease over three decades, and his experience was not unusual. Some families were just unlucky.

Today, the curse of Tay-Sachs is being lifted—not through better treatments (the hereditary disease is as deadly as ever) but through a new cultural institution called Chevra Dor Yeshorim, the "Association of an Upright Generation." Thanks largely to Rabbi Ekstein's efforts, Orthodox teenagers throughout the world now line up at screening centers to have their blood tested for evidence of the Tay-Sachs gene. Before getting engaged, prospective mates simply call Chevra Dor Yeshorim and read off the code numbers assigned to their test results. 2

If the records show that neither person carries the gene, or that just one does, the match is judged sound. But if both happen to be carriers (meaning any child they conceive will have a one-in-four chance of suffering the fatal disease), marriage is virtually out of the question. Even if two carriers wanted to wed, few rabbis would abet them. "It's a rule of thumb that engagements won't occur until compatibility is established," says Rabbi Jacob Horowitz, codirector of the Brooklyn-based program. "Each day, we could stop many marriages worldwide." 3

Marriage isn't the only institution being reshaped by modern genetics; a host of new diagnostic tests could soon change every aspect of creating a family. Physicians can now identify some 250 genetic defects, not only in the blood of a potential parent but in the tissue of a developing fetus. The result is that, for the first time in history, people are deciding, rather than wondering, what kind of children they will bear. 4

Choosing to avoid a horrible disease may be easy, at least in principle, but that's just one of many options 21st-century parents could face. Already, conditions far less grave than Tay-Sachs have been linked to specific genes, and the science is still exploding. Researchers are now at work on a massive $3 billion project to decipher the entire human genetic code. By the turn of the century, knowledge gained through this Human Genome Initiative could enable doctors to screen fetuses—even test-tube embryos—for traits that have nothing to do with disease. "Indeed," says one geneticist, "we should be able to locate which [gene] combinations affect kinky hair, olive skin and pointy teeth." 5

How will such knowledge be handled? How should it be handled? Are we headed for an age in which having a child is morally analogous to buying a car? There is already evidence that couples are using prenatal tests to identify and abort fetuses on the basis of sex, and there is no reason to assume the trend will stop there. "We should be worried about the future and where this might take us," says George Annas, a professor of health law at Boston University's School of Medicine. "The whole definition of normal could well be changed. The issue becomes not the ability of the child to be happy but rather our ability to be happy with the child." 6

So far, at least, the emphasis has been on combating serious hereditary disorders. Everyone carries four to six genes that are harmless when inherited from one parent but can be deadly when inherited from both. Luckily, most of these mutations are rare enough that carriers are unlikely to cross paths. But some have become common within particular populations. Five percent of all whites carry the gene for cystic fibrosis, for example, and one in 2,000 is born with the disease. Seven percent of all blacks harbor the mutation for sickle-cell anemia, and one in 500 is afflicted. Asian and Mediterranean people are particularly prone to the deadly blood disease thalassemia, just as Jews are to Tay-Sachs. 7

When accommodating the disability means watching a toddler die of Tay-Sachs or thalassemia, few couples hesitate to abort, and only the most adamant pro-lifer would blame them. But few of the defects for which fetuses can be screened are so devastating. Consider Huntington's disease, the hereditary brain disorder that killed the folk singer Woody Guthrie. Huntington's relentlessly destroys its victim's mind, and anyone who inherits the gene eventually gets the disease. Yet Huntington's rarely strikes anyone under 40, and it can remain dormant into a person's 70s. What does a parent do with the knowledge that a fetus has the gene? Is some life better than none? 8

Most carriers think not. . . . 9

As more abnormalities are linked to genes, the dilemmas can only get stickier. Despite all the uncertainties, a positive test for Down or Huntington's leaves no doubt that the condition will set in. But not every disease-related gene guarantees ill health. Those associated with conditions like alcoholism, Alzheimer's disease and manic-depressive illness signal only a susceptibility. Prevent- 10 ing such conditions would thus require aborting kids who might never have suffered. And because one gene can have more than one effect, the effort could have unintended consequences. There is considerable evidence linking manic-depressive illness to artistic genius, notes Dr. Melvin Konner, an anthropologist and non-practicing physician at Emory University. "Doing away with the gene would destroy the impetus for much human creativity."

The future possibilities are even more troubling when you con- 11
sider that mere imperfections could be screened for as easily as serious diseases. Stuttering, obesity and reading disorders are all traceable to genetic markers, notes Dr. Kathleen Nolan of The Hastings Center, a biomedical think tank in suburban New York. And many aspects of appearance and personality are under fairly simple genetic control. Are we headed for a time when straight teeth, a flat stomach and a sense of humor are standards for admission into some families? It's not inconceivable. "I see people in my clinic occasionally who have a sort of new-car mentality," says Dr. Francis Collins, a University of Michigan geneticist who recently helped identify the gene for cystic fibrosis. "It's got to be perfect, and if it isn't you take it back to the lot and get a new one."

At the moment, gender is the only nonmedical condition for 12
which prenatal tests are widely available. There are no firm figures on how often people abort to get their way, but physicians say many patients use the tests for that purpose. The requests have traditionally come from Asians and East Indians expressing a cultural preference for males. But others are now asking, too. "I've found a high incidence of sex selection coming from doctors' families in the last two years," says Dr. Lawrence D. Platt, a geneticist at the University of Southern California—"much higher than ethnic requests. Once there is public awareness about the technology, other people will use the procedure as well."

Those people will find their physicians increasingly willing to 13
help. A 1973 survey of American geneticists found that only 1 percent considered it morally acceptable to help parents identify and abort fetuses of the undesired sex. Last year University of Virginia ethicist John C. Fletcher and Dr. Mark I. Evans, a geneticist at Wayne State University, conducted a similar poll and found that nearly 20 percent approved. Meanwhile, 62 percent of the geneticists questioned in a 1985 survey said they would screen

fetuses for a couple who had four healthy daughters and wanted a son.

Right or wrong, the new gender option has set an important precedent. If parents will screen babies for one nonmedical condition, there is no reason to assume they won't screen them for others. Indeed, preliminary results from a recent survey of 200 New England couples showed that while only 1 percent would abort on the basis of sex, 11 percent would abort to save a child from obesity. As Dr. Robin Dawn Clark, head of clinical genetics at Loma Linda Medical Center observes, the temptation will be to select for "other features that are honored by society." 14

The trend toward even greater control could lead to bizarre, sci-fi scenarios. But it seems unlikely that prenatal swimsuit competitions will sweep the globe anytime soon: most of the globe has yet to reap the benefits of 19th-century medicine. Even in America, many prospective parents are still struggling to obtain basic health insurance. If the masses could suddenly afford cosmetic screening tests, the trauma of abortion would remain a powerful deterrent. And while [geneticist] John Buster's dream of extracting week-old embryos for a quick gene check could ease the trauma, it seems a safe bet many women would still opt to leave their embryos alone. 15

The more immediate danger is that the power to predict children's medical futures will diminish society's tolerance for serious defects. Parents have already sued physicians for "wrongful life" after giving birth to disabled children, claiming it was the doctor's responsibility to detect the defect in the womb. The fear of such suits could prompt physicians to run every available test, however remote the possibility of spotting a medical problem. Conversely, parents who are content to forgo all the genetic fortune-telling could find themselves stigmatized for their backward ways. When four-cell embryos can be screened for hereditary diseases, failing to ensure a child's future health could become the same sort of offense that declining heroic measures for a sick child is today. 16

In light of all the dangers, some critics find the very practice of prenatal testing morally questionable. "Even at the beginning of the journey the eugenics question looms large," says Jeremy Rifkin, a Washington activist famous for his opposition to genetic 17 tinkering. "Screening is eugenics." Perhaps, but its primary effect so far has been to bring fewer seriously diseased children into the world. In Britain's Northeast Thames region, the number of Indian and Cypriot children born with thalassemia fell by 78 percent after prenatal tests became available in the 1970s. Likewise, carrier and prenatal screening have virtually eliminated Tay-Sachs from the United States and Canada.

Failing to think, as a society, about the appropriate uses of the 18
new tests would be a grave mistake. They're rife with potential for abuse, and the coming advances in genetic science will make them more so. But they promise some control over diseases that have caused immense suffering and expense. Society need only remember that there are no perfect embryos but many ways to be a successful human being.

Questions for Study and Discussion

1. To study the organization of Cowley's essay, it is useful to divide it into three-paragraph blocks. Summarize what Cowley says in each block (1–3, 4–6, and so on). What form of organization does Cowley use? Is it effective? Why or why not?
2. How does Cowley's title affect the way you read the essay? (Glossary: *Title*) Do you think it is an appropriate title? Explain.
3. What is Cowley's purpose? (Glossary: *Purpose*) How does he organize his essay to communicate his purpose?
4. Note where Cowley inserts quotes from medical experts into his essay. Comment on his choice of placement of the quotes. What does he gain by using them?
5. Summarize the benefits and dangers of prenatal testing.
6. What does Cowley accomplish in the fifth block (paragraphs 13–15)? What is its importance relative to the rest of the essay? Why does Cowley place it near the end?
7. What is Cowley's tone? (Glossary: *Tone*) Support your answer.

Vocabulary

Refer to your dictionary to define the following words as they are used in this selection. Then use each word in a sentence of your own.

abet (3)
analogous (6)
prenatal (6)
adamant (8)
impetus (10)
ethicist (13)
stigmatized (16)
eugenics (17)
rife (18)

Classroom Activity on Organization

Consider the ways in which you might organize a discussion of the seven states listed below. For each state, we have provided you with some basic information: the date it entered the Union, population, land area, and number of electoral votes in a presidential election.

MAINE
March 15, 1820
1,240,209 people
30,865 sq. miles
4 electoral votes

ARIZONA
February 14, 1912
4,075,052 people
113,642 sq. miles
8 electoral votes

OREGON
February 14, 1859
3,086,188 people
96,002 sq. miles
7 electoral votes

MONTANA
November 8, 1889
856,047 people
145,556 sq. miles
3 electoral votes

FLORIDA
March 3, 1845
13,952,714 people
53,937 sq. miles
25 electoral votes

MISSOURI
August 10, 1821
5,277,640 people
68,898 sq. miles
11 electoral votes

ALASKA
January 3, 1959
606,276 people
570,374 sq. miles
3 electoral votes

Suggested Writing Assignments

1. Write a short, well-organized essay in which you either support or oppose the use of prenatal testing of fetuses for all

but the most severe conditions. Organize your essay by beginning with the point that you believe is of the least importance or has the least impact and ending with your strongest point.

2. Imagine you are writing in the year 2050. How have eugenics developed in the past fifty years or so? What procedures have gained widespread acceptance? Has there been a backlash if "cosmetic" eugenics has increased? Have genetic diseases been wiped out? Is human cloning being practiced in 2050? How have the prenuptial proceedings changed for couples? Write an essay, organized chronologically, in which you discuss the five most important changes in eugenics since 2000. Use your creativity, but make sure your essay makes chronological sense.

THE CORNER STORE

Eudora Welty

Eudora Welty is one of the most honored and respected writers at work today. She was born in 1909 in Jackson, Mississippi, where she has lived most of her life. Her published works include many short stories, now available as her Collected Stories *(1980); a collection of her essays, in* The Eye of the Story *(1975); collected book reviews, in* The Writer's Eye *(1994); five novels; and a memoir,* One Writer's Beginnings *(1987). Her novel* The Optimist's Daughter *won the Pulitzer Prize for fiction in 1973. Welty's description of the corner store, taken from an essay about growing up in Jackson, recalls for many readers the neighborhood store in the town or city where they grew up. As you read, pay particular attention to what effect Welty's spatial arrangement of descriptive details has on the dominant impression of the store.*

FOR YOUR JOURNAL

Write about a store you frequented as a child. Maybe it was the local supermarket, the hardware store, or the corner quick-stop. Using your five senses (sight, smell, taste, touch, and hearing), describe what you remember about the place.

Our Little Store rose right up from the sidewalk; standing in a street of family houses, it alone hadn't any yard in front, any tree or flower bed. It was a plain frame building covered over with brick. Above the door, a little railed porch ran across on an upstairs level and four windows with shades were looking out. But I didn't catch on to those. 1

Running in out of the sun, you met what seemed total obscurity inside. There were almost tangible smells—licorice recently 2 sucked in a child's cheek, dill pickle brine that had leaked through a paper sack in a fresh trail across the wooden floor, ammonia-loaded ice that had been hoisted from wet croker sacks and slammed into the icebox with its sweet butter at the door, and perhaps the smell of still untrapped mice.

Then through the motes of cracker dust, cornmeal dust, the Gold Dust of the Gold Dust Twins that the floor had been swept out with, the realities emerged. Shelves climbed to high reach all the way around, set out with not too much of any one thing but a lot of things—lard, molasses, vinegar, starch, matches, kerosene, Octagon soap (about a year's worth of octagon-shaped coupons cut out and saved brought a signet ring addressed to you in the mail). It was up to you to remember what you came for, while your eye traveled from cans of sardines to tin whistles to ice-cream salt to harmonicas to flypaper (over your head, batting around on a thread beneath the blades of the ceiling fan, stuck with its testimonial catch). 3

Its confusion may have been in the eye of its beholder. Enchantment is cast upon you by all those things you weren't supposed to have need for, to lure you close to wooden tops you'd outgrown, boys' marbles and agates in little net pouches, small rubber balls that wouldn't bounce straight, frail, frazzly kite string, clay bubble pipes that would snap off in your teeth, the stiffest scissors. You could contemplate those long narrow boxes of sparklers gathering dust while you waited for it to be the Fourth of July or Christmas, and noisemakers in the shape of tin frogs for somebody's birthday party you hadn't been invited to yet, and see that they were all marvelous. 4

You might not have even looked for Mr. Sessions when he came around his store cheese (as big as a doll's house) and in front of the counter looking for you. When you'd finally asked him for, and received from him in its paper bag, whatever single thing it was that you had been sent for, the nickel that was left over was yours to spend. 5

Down at a child's eye level, inside those glass jars with mouths in their sides through which the grocer could run his scoop or a child's hand might be invited to reach for a choice, were wine-balls, all-day suckers, gumdrops, peppermints. Making a row under the glass of a counter were the Tootsie Rolls, Hershey bars, Goo Goo Clusters, Baby Ruths. And whatever was the name of 6 those pastilles that came stacked in a cardboard cylinder with a cardboard lid? They were thin and dry, about the size of tiddledy-winks, and in the shape of twisted rosettes. A kind of chocolate dust came out with them when you shook them out in your hand. Were they chocolate? I'd say, rather, they were brown. They didn't taste of anything at all, unless it was wood. Their attraction was the number you got for a nickel.

Making up your mind, you circled the store around and around, 7
around the pickle barrel, around the tower of Crackerjack boxes; Mr. Sessions had built it for us himself on top of a packing case like a house of cards.

If it seemed too hot for Crackerjacks, I might get a cold drink. 8
Mr. Sessions might have already stationed himself by the cold-drinks barrel, like a mind reader. Deep in ice water that looked black as ink, murky shapes—that would come up as Coca-Colas, Orange Crushes, and various flavors of pop—were all swimming around together. When you gave the word, Mr. Sessions plunged his bare arm in to the elbow and fished out your choice, first try. I favored a locally bottled concoction called Lake's Celery. (What else could it be called? It was made by a Mr. Lake out of celery. It was a popular drink here for years but was not known universally, as I found out when I arrived in New York and ordered one in the Astor bar.) You drank on the premises, with feet set wide apart to miss the drip, and gave him back his bottle and your nickel.

But he didn't hurry you off. A standing scales was by the door, 9
with a stack of iron weights and a brass slide on the balance arm, that would weigh you up to three hundred pounds. Mr. Sessions, whose hands were gentle and smelled of carbolic, would lift you up and set your feet on the platform, hold your loaf of bread for you, and taking his time while you stood still for him, he would make certain of what you weighed today. He could even remember what you weighed the last time, so you could subtract and announce how much you'd gained. That was goodbye.

Questions for Study and Discussion

1. Which of the three patterns of organization has Welty used in this essay: chronological, spatial, or logical? If she has used more than one, where precisely has she used each type?

2. What is the dominant impression that Welty creates in her description of the corner store? (Glossary: *Dominant Impression*) How does Welty create this dominant impression?
3. What does Welty mean when she writes that the store's "confusion may have been in the eye of its beholder" (4)? What factors might lead one to become confused?
4. What impression of Mr. Sessions does Welty create? What details contribute to this impression? (Glossary: *Details*)
5. Welty places certain pieces of information in parentheses in this essay. Why are they in parentheses? What, if anything, does this information add to our understanding of the corner store? Might this information be left out? Explain.
6. Comment on Welty's ending. Is it too abrupt? Why or why not? (Glossary: *Beginnings and Endings*)

Vocabulary

Refer to your dictionary to define the following words as they are used in this selection. Then use each word in a sentence of your own.

frame (1)	signet (3)
tangible (2)	agates (4)
brine (2)	concoction (8)
motes (3)	scales (9)

Classroom Activity on Organization

Yesterday, while cleaning out the center drawer of his desk, a student found the following items:

2 no. 2 pencils	2 pairs of scissors
3 rubber bands	1 book mailing bag
1 roll of Scotch tape	1 mechanical pencil
1 plastic comb	3 first-class postage stamps
25 3 × 5 cards	5 postcards
3 ballpoint pens	2 clasps
1 eraser	2 8 × 10 manila envelopes
6 paper clips	7 thumbtacks
1 nail clipper	1 bottle of Wite Out

1 highlighting marker
1 bottle of glue
3 business envelopes
6 postcard stamps
1 nail file
1 toothbrush
1 felt-tip pen
2 airmail stamps

In order to organize the student's drawer, into what categories would you divide these items? Explain which items you would place in each category.

Suggested Writing Assignments

1. Describe your neighborhood store or supermarket. Gather a large quantity of detailed information from memory and from an actual visit to the store if that is still possible. Once you have gathered your information, try to select those details that will help you create a dominant impression of the store. Finally, organize your examples and illustrations according to some clear organizational pattern.
2. Write an essay on one of the following topics:

   local restaurants
   reading materials
   television shows
   ways of financing a college education
   types of summer employment

   Be sure to use an organizational pattern that is well thought out and suited to both your material and your purpose.

4

BEGINNINGS AND ENDINGS

"Begin at the beginning and go on till you come to the end: then stop," advised the King of Hearts in *Alice in Wonderland.* "Good advice, but more easily said than done," you might be tempted to reply. Certainly, no part of writing essays can be more daunting than coming up with effective beginnings and endings. In fact, many writers feel these are the most important parts of any piece of writing regardless of its length. Even before coming to your introduction proper, your readers will usually know something about your intentions from your title. Titles like "The Case against Euthanasia," "How to Buy a Used Car," or "What Is a Migraine Headache?" indicate both your subject and approach and prepare your readers for what is to follow.

But what makes for an effective beginning? Not unlike a personal greeting, a good beginning should catch a reader's interest and then hold it. The experienced writer realizes that most readers would rather do almost anything than make a commitment to read, so the opening or "lead," as journalists refer to it, requires a lot of thought and much revising to make it right and to keep the reader's attention from straying. The inexperienced writer, on the other hand, knows that the beginning is important but tries to write it first and to perfect it before moving on to the rest of the essay. Although there are no "rules" for writing introductions, we can offer one bit of general advice: wait until the writing process is well underway or almost completed before focusing on your lead. Following this advice will keep you from spending too much time on an introduction that you will probably revise. More important, once you actually see how your essay develops, you will know better how to introduce it to your reader.

Often a particularly striking paragraph somewhere within the body of your essay can be moved to the beginning to serve as your introduction. Be aware, however, that such a change may require a slight revision to make the paragraph fit or may, in fact, alter the structure or direction of the essay itself.

In addition to capturing your reader's attention, a good beginning frequently introduces your thesis and either suggests or actually reveals the structure of the composition. Keep in mind that the best beginning is not necessarily the most catchy or the most shocking but the one most appropriate for the job you are trying to do.

Beginnings

The following examples from published essays show you some effective beginnings:

Short Generalization

It is a miracle that New York works at all.

E. B. White

Startling Claim

It is possible to stop most drug addiction in the United States within a very short time.

Gore Vidal

Rhetorical Questions

Just how interconnected *is* the animal world? Is it true that if we change any part of that world we risk unduly damaging life in other, larger parts of it?

Matthew Douglas

Humor/Apt Quotation

"Amid the quotidian trials of suburban life," wrote *Newsweek* in appreciation of Erma Bombeck, "she found a way to make us laugh."

Paradoxically, *quotidian* is just the sort of word that the late humorist would never use. She dispensed simple wisdom in plain style: "Never go to a doctor whose office plants have died." Highfalutin language was not in her.

William Safire

Startling Fact

Charles Darwin and Abraham Lincoln were born on the same day—February 12, 1809. They are also linked in another curious way—for both must simultaneously play, and for similar reasons, the role of man and legend.

Stephen Jay Gould

Dialogue

"This would be excellent, to go in the ocean with this thing," says Dave Gembutis, fifteen.

He is looking at a $170 Sea Cruiser raft.

"Great," says his companion, Dan Holmes, also fifteen.

This is at Herman's World of Sporting Goods, in the middle of the Woodfield Mall in Schaumburg, Illinois.

Bob Greene

Statistics/Question

In the 40 years from 1939 to 1979 white women who work full time have with monotonous regularity made slightly less than 60 percent as much as white men. Why?

Lester C. Thurow

Irony

In Moulmein, in lower Burma, I was hated by large numbers of people—the only time in my life that I have been important enough for this to happen to me.

George Orwell

There are many more excellent ways to begin an essay, but there are also some ways of beginning that should be avoided. Some of these follow:

Apology

I am a college student and do not consider myself an expert on the computer industry, but I think that many computer companies make false claims about just how easy it is to learn to use a computer.

Complaint

> I'd rather write about a topic of my own choice than the one that is assigned, but here goes.

Webster's Dictionary

> *Webster's New Collegiate Dictionary* defines the verb *to snore* as follows: "to breathe during sleep with a rough hoarse noise due to vibration of the soft palate."

Platitude

> America is the land of opportunity and no one knows it better than Madonna.

Reference to Title

> As you can see from my title, this essay is about why we should continue to experiment with human heart transplants.

Endings

An effective ending does more than simply indicate where the writer stopped writing. A conclusion may summarize; may inspire the reader to further thought or even action; may return to the beginning by repeating key words, phrases, or ideas; or may surprise the reader by providing a particularly convincing example to support a thesis. Indeed, there are, as with beginnings, many ways to write a conclusion, but the effectiveness of any choice really must be measured by how appropriately it fits what has gone before it. In the following conclusion to a long chapter on weasel words, a form of deceptive advertising language, writer Paul Stevens summarizes the points that he has made:

> A weasel word is a word that's used to imply a meaning that cannot be truthfully stated. Some weasels imply meanings that are not the same as their actual definition, such as "help," "like," or "fortified." They can act as qualifiers and/or comparatives. Other weasels, such as "taste" and "flavor," have no definite meanings, and are simply subjective opin-

> ions offered by the manufacturer. A weasel of omission is one that implies a claim so strongly that it forces you to supply the bogus fact. Adjectives are weasels used to convey feelings and emotions to a greater extent than the product itself can.
>
> In dealing with weasels, you must strip away the innuendos and try to ascertain the facts, if any. To do this, you need to ask questions such as: How? Why? How many? How much? Stick to basic definitions of words. Look them up if you have to. Then, apply the strict definition to the text of the advertisement or commercial. "Like" means similar to, but not the same as. "Virtually" means the same in essence, but not in fact.
>
> Above all, never underestimate the devious qualities of a weasel. Weasels twist and turn and hide in dark shadows. You must come to grips with them, or advertising will rule you forever.
>
> My advice to you is: Beware of weasels. They are nasty and untrainable, and they attack pocketbooks.

If you are having trouble with your conclusion—and this is not an uncommon problem—it may be because of problems with your essay itself. Frequently, writers do not know when to end because they are not sure about their overall purpose in the first place. For example, if you are taking a trip and your purpose is to go to Chicago, you'll know when you get there and will stop. But if you don't really know where you are going, it's very difficult to know when to stop.

It's usually a good idea in your conclusion to avoid such overworked expressions as "In conclusion," "In summary," "I hope I have shown," or "Finally." Your conclusion should also do more than simply repeat what you've said in your opening paragraph. The most satisfying essays are those in which the conclusion provides an interesting way of wrapping up ideas introduced in the beginning and developed throughout.

You might find it revealing as your course progresses to read with special attention the beginnings and endings of the essays throughout *Models for Writers.* Take special note of the varieties of beginnings and endings, the possible relationship between a beginning and an ending, and the general appropriateness of these elements to the writer's subject and purpose.

Of My Friend Hector and My Achilles Heel

Michael T. Kaufman

The former writer of the "About New York" column for the New York Times, *Michael T. Kaufman was born in 1938 in Paris and grew up in the United States. He studied at the Bronx High School of Science, City College of New York, and Columbia University. He began his career at the* New York Times *as a reporter and feature writer, and before assuming his position as columnist, he served as bureau chief in Ottawa and Warsaw. The experience in Warsaw is evident in his book about Poland,* Mad Dreams, Saving Graces, *published in 1989. Kaufman is also a past winner of the George Polk Award for International Reporting. In the following selection, which appeared in the* New York Times *in 1992, Kaufman uses the story of his childhood friend Hector Elizondo to reflect on his own "prejudice and stupidity." Take note of how the two very brief sentences at the beginning establish the chronological and narrative structure of what follows.*

For Your Journal

Many schools "track" students by intellectual ability into such categories as "honors," "college bound," "vocational," "remedial," or "terminal." Did you go to a high school that "tracked" its students? How did the tracking system work? How did you feel about your placement? What did you think about classmates who were on tracks higher or lower than yours?

This story is about prejudice and stupidity. My own. 1

It begins in 1945 when I was a 7-year-old living on the fifth 2
floor of a tenement walkup on 107th Street between Columbus

and Manhattan Avenues in New York City. The block was almost entirely Irish and Italian, and I believe my family was the only Jewish one around.

One day a Spanish-speaking family moved into one of the four 3
apartments on our landing. They were the first Puerto Ricans I had met. They had a son who was about my age named Hector, and the two of us became friends. We played with toy soldiers and I particularly remember how, using rubber bands and wood from orange crates, we made toy pistols that shot off little squares we cut from old linoleum.

We visited each other's home and I know that at the time I 4
liked Hector and I think he liked me. I may even have eaten my first avocado at his house.

About a year after we met, my family moved to another part 5
of Manhattan's West Side and I did not see Hector again until I entered Booker T. Washington Junior High School as an 11-year-old.

The Special Class

The class I was in was called 7SP-1; the SP was for special. 6
Earlier, I recall, I had been in the IGC class, for "intellectually gifted children." The SP class was to complete the seventh, eighth and ninth grades in two years and almost all of us would then go to schools like Bronx Science, Stuyvesant or Music and Art, where admission was based on competitive exams. I knew I was in the SP class and the IGC class. I guess I also knew that other people were not.

Hector was not. He was in some other class, maybe even 7-2, 7
the class that was held to be the next-brightest, or maybe 7-8. I remember I was happy to see him whenever we would meet, and sometimes we played punchball during lunch period. Mostly, of course, I stayed with my own classmates, with other Intellectually Gifted Children.

Sometimes children from other classes, those presumably not 8
so intellectually gifted, would tease and taunt us. At such times I was particularly proud to have Hector as a friend. I assumed that he was tougher than I and my classmates and I guess I thought that if necessary he would come to my defense.

Different High Schools

For high school, I went uptown to Bronx Science. Hector, I think, went downtown to Commerce. Sometimes I would see him in Riverside Park, where I played basketball and he worked out on the parallel bars. We would acknowledge each other, but by this time the conversations we held were perfunctory—sports, families, weather. 9

After I finished college, I would see him around the neighborhood pushing a baby carriage. He was the first of my contemporaries to marry and to have a child. 10

A few years later, in the 60's, married and with children of my own, I was once more living on the West Side, working until late at night as a reporter. Some nights as I took the train home I would see Hector in the car. A few times we exchanged nods, but more often I would pretend that I didn't see him, and maybe he also pretended he didn't see me. Usually he would be wearing a knitted watch cap, and from that I deduced that he was probably working on the docks as a longshoreman. 11

I remember quite distinctly how I would sit on the train and think about how strange and unfair fate had been with regard to the two of us who had once been playmates. Just because I had become an intellectually gifted adult or whatever and he had become a longshoreman or whatever, was that any reason for us to have been left with nothing to say to each other? I thought it was wrong and unfair, but I also thought that conversation would be a chore or a burden. That is pretty much what I thought about Hector, if I thought about him at all, until one Sunday in the mid-70's, when I read in the drama section of this newspaper that my childhood friend, Hector Elizondo, was replacing Peter Falk in the leading role in "The Prisoner of Second Avenue." 12

Since then, every time I have seen this versatile and acclaimed actor in movies or on television I have blushed for my assumptions. I have replayed the subway rides in my head and tried to fathom why my thoughts had led me where they did. 13

In retrospect it seems far more logical that the man I saw on the train, the man who had been my friend as a boy, was coming home from an Off Broadway theater or perhaps from a job as a waiter while taking acting classes. So why did I think he was a longshoreman? Was it just the cap? Could it be that his being 14

Puerto Rican had something to do with it? Maybe that reinforced the stereotype I concocted, but it wasn't the root of it.

When It Got Started

No, the foundation was laid when I was 11, when I was in 7SP-1 and he was not, when I was in the IGC class and he was not. 15

I have not seen him since I recognized how I had idiotically kept tracking him for years and decades after the school system had tracked both of us. I wonder now if my experience was that unusual, whether social categories conveyed and absorbed before puberty do not generally tend to linger beyond middle age. And I wonder, too, that if they affected the behavior of someone like myself who had been placed on the upper track, how much more damaging it must have been for someone consigned to the lower. 16

I have at times thought of calling him, but kept from doing it because how exactly does one apologize for thoughts that were never expressed? And there was still the problem of what to say. "What have you been up to for the last 40 years?" Or "Wow, was I wrong about you!" Or maybe just, "Want to come over and help me make a linoleum gun?" 17

Questions for Study and Discussion

1. If you are unfamiliar with the Greek myth of Hector and Achilles, look it up in a book on mythology. Why does Kaufman allude to Hector and Achilles in his title? (Glossary: *Allusion*)
2. How do Kaufman's first two sentences affect how the reader views the rest of the essay? Did they catch your attention? Why or why not?
3. How does Kaufman organize his essay? (Glossary: *Organization*)
4. What is Kaufman's purpose in the essay? How does his organization of the essay help him express his purpose? (Glossary: *Purpose*)

5. Why did Kaufman ignore Hector after he graduated from college? What does this tell him about society in general?
6. Why is Kaufman's ending effective? What point does he want to emphasize with the ending he uses?

Vocabulary

Refer to your dictionary to define the following words as they are used in this selection. Then use each word in a sentence of your own.

intellectually (6)	acclaimed (13)
perfunctory (9)	concocted (14)
contemporaries (10)	

Classroom Activity on Beginnings and Endings

Carefully read the following three beginnings for an essay on the world's most famous practical joker, Hugh Troy. What are the advantages and disadvantages of each? Which one would you select as an opening paragraph? Why?

> Whether questioning the values of American society or simply relieving the monotony of daily life, Hugh Troy always managed to put a little of himself into each of his stunts. One day he attached a plaster hand to his shirt sleeve and took a trip through the Holland Tunnel. As he approached the tollbooth, with his toll ticket between the fingers of the artificial hand, Troy left both ticket and hand in the grasp of the stunned tollbooth attendant and sped away.

> Nothing seemed unusual. In fact, it was a rather common occurrence in New York City. Five men dressed in overalls roped off a section of busy Fifth Avenue in front of the old Rockefeller residence, hung out MEN WORKING signs, and began ripping up the pavement. By the time they stopped for lunch, they had dug quite a hole in the street. This crew was different, however, from all the others that had descended upon the streets of the city. It was led by Hugh Troy—the world's greatest practical joker.

Hugh Troy was born in Ithaca, New York, where his father was a professor at Cornell University. After graduating from Cornell, Troy left for New York City, where he became a successful illustrator of children's books. When World War II broke out, he went into the army and eventually became a captain in the 21st Bomber Command, 20th Air Force, under General Curtis LeMay. After the war he made his home in Garrison, New York, for a short while before finally settling in Washington, D.C., where he lived until his death.

Suggested Writing Assignments

1. Kaufman's essay is a deeply personal one. Use it as a model to write an essay about a time or an action in your life that you are not proud of. What happened? Why did it happen? What would you do differently if you could? Be sure to catch the reader's attention in the beginning and to end your essay with a thought-provoking conclusion.
2. Everyone has childhood friends that we either have lost track of or don't communicate with as often as we would like. Choose an old friend whom you have lost track of and would like to see again. Write an essay about your relationship. What made your friend special to you as a child? Why did you lose touch? What does the future hold? Organize your essay chronologically.

Even You Can Get It

Bruce Lambert

Bruce Lambert was born in 1943, in Albany, New York, and attended Hamilton College, where he prepared for a career in journalism. Lambert covered government and political issues for several New York newspapers until 1984, when he began to focus on the issue of AIDS. In 1988 the New York Times *assigned Lambert to cover the AIDS story exclusively. He first published the following selection on March 11 and 12, 1989. In it he alerts heterosexuals that they should not become complacent about the need to protect themselves from the dangers of AIDS. The subject of the piece, Alison Gertz, fought a courageous battle to live and to inform others before finally succumbing to AIDS. A TV movie about her, entitled* Something to Live For, *generated more responses to the AIDS Hotline than even Magic Johnson's announcement that he is HIV positive. As you read Lambert's essay, notice how his surprising, and perhaps controversial, opening line catches a reader's attention, while his conclusion conveys the "determined optimism" of Alison's struggle.*

For Your Journal

Since the 1980s, Americans have been bombarded with news about AIDS. What do you think about this disease? Has anyone you know tested HIV positive or been stricken with AIDS? How did you feel when you first heard this news?

Alison L. Gertz wasn't supposed to get AIDS. 1

She has never injected drugs or had a blood transfusion, and 2
she describes herself as "not at all promiscuous." But she does

say she had a single sexual encounter—seven years ago—with a male acquaintance who, she has since learned, has died of AIDS.

Though AIDS has hit hardest among gay men and poor intra- 3
venous drug users, it also afflicts people like Ms. Gertz.

"People think this can't happen to them," she said in an interview 4
at her Manhattan apartment. "I never thought I could have AIDS."

Going Public

She is 23 years old, affluent, college-educated and a profes- 5
sional from a prominent family. She grew up on Park Avenue.

Now Ms. Gertz and her family are going public because they 6
have a message. A message for heterosexuals who could make a potentially fatal mistake if they dismiss the threat of AIDS. A message for doctors who may miss a diagnosis; she spent three weeks undergoing exhaustive hospital tests for all other conceivable causes of her illness before AIDS was discovered. And a message asking for greater public support on AIDS issues.

"I decided when I was in the hospital I would give as much 7
time as I can to help people who are going through this, and warn others of the danger," she said. "I want to make a condom commercial, do speaking engagements, whatever I can.

"All the AIDS articles are about homosexuals or poor people 8
on drugs, and unfortunately a lot of people just flip by them," she said. "They think it doesn't apply to them."

But she added: "They can't turn the page on me. I could be 9
one of them, or their daughter. They have to deal with this."

Statistics show that the number of AIDS cases is rising alarm- 10
ingly among heterosexuals who get the virus by sharing needles for drugs and then pass it to their sex partners and babies.

Although there is no evidence that AIDS is spreading rampantly 11
among other heterosexuals in this country—as it is in Haiti and parts of Africa—cases like Ms. Gertz's do exist. About four percent of all newly reported AIDS cases stem from heterosexual intercourse, and that rate has been remaining steady.

New York City has recorded 524 cases in which women got ac- 12
quired immune deficiency syndrome through sexual intercourse. The men they were with were infected through either drug use or sexual contact with other men. Another 83 cases were of women from Haiti or Africa.

"It Took Only One Time for Me"

"I want to talk to these kids who think they're immortal," Ms. Gertz said. "I want to tell them: I'm heterosexual, and it took only one time for me." 13

Ms. Gertz is certain how it happened. "It was one romantic night," she said. "There were roses and champagne and everything. That was it. I only slept with him once." 14

Ms. Gertz has since learned that the man was bisexual and that he has died of AIDS. Had she known his past then, she said, she doubts it would have made a difference. "At that point they weren't publicizing AIDS," she said. "It wasn't an issue then." 15

AIDS is no respecter of wealth or social status. Ms. Gertz is a granddaughter of a founder of the old Gertz department stores in Queens and on Long Island. Her father, Jerrold E. Gertz, is a real-estate executive; her mother, Carol, is the co-founder of Tennis Lady, a national chain of high-fashion shops. Ms. Gertz went to Horace Mann, an exclusive private school in the Bronx, then studied art at Parsons School of Design in Manhattan. 16

"Probably Just a Bug"

When AIDS struck, Ms. Gertz said, "I was just, as they say, starting out in life." Her goals had been simple: "I wanted a house and kids and animals and to paint my paintings." 17

She had recently signed on with an art agent, embarking on a career as an illustrator. She had also quit her pack-a-day smoking habit and joined a health club "to get really healthy," she said. 18

Then fever and a spell of diarrhea hit last summer. A doctor told her it was "probably just a bug," she said. But the symptoms persisted, so she checked into Lenox Hill Hospital. 19

When her doctor told her the diagnosis, he had tears in his eyes. "I said 'Oh, my God. I'm going to die,'" she recalled. "And as I said it, I thought to myself, 'No I'm not. Why am I saying this?' I thought my life was over. 'I'm 22, I'm never going to have sex again. I'm never going to have children.'" 20

Determined to Keep Going

From that initial shock, Ms. Gertz bounced back with the ebullience so well known to her friends—they call her Ali for short— 21 and with the fervor of activism that runs in the family. Recovering from her first treatment, she returned to her apartment, her pets (a dog, Saki; a cat, Sambucca; and tropical fish) and a new course in life.

"It's a dreadful disease, but it's also a gift," she said. "I've always been positive, optimistic. I thought, 'What can I do with it?' I like to think I'm here for a purpose. If I die, I would like to have left something, to make the world a little bit better before I go, to help people sick like me and prevent others from getting this. It would make it all worthwhile." 22

She and friends are organizing a fall theater performance and dinner-dance to raise money for an AIDS newsletter and other AIDS services. Her parents and their friends are planning a spring benefit for an organization they are forming called Concerned Parents and Friends for AIDS Research. 23

To keep her functioning normally, Ms. Gertz each day takes AZT, Acyclovir and Bactrim pills, which fight the virus and opportunistic diseases. "We just have to keep her healthy until there's a breakthrough and they find a cure," her mother said. 24

"I Started to Cry Softly"

"I'm not afraid of death, but I am afraid of pain," Ms. Gertz said. She is learning psychological and behavioral techniques to withstand it, and doctors have promised medication if she needs it. "As far as dying goes, it's okay," she said. "There's no point in thinking about it now." 25

But her frequent high spirits do not erase her pain. While watching a soap opera love scene one day, she said, "I started to cry softly." 26

"I've made a conscious effort not to cry in front of people," she added. "But I do give myself a certain amount of time each month to be miserable, to cry and to vent." 27

Ms. Gertz is an only child. Her illness "was an enormous shock," her father said. "AIDS was the furthest thing from my mind. I used to suspect they magnified the statistics to get research money." Now he's giving and raising money himself and feels "anger at AIDS happening to anyone." 28

"It certainly turned our lives around," Mrs. Gertz said. "It changes your perspective on what's important." For her, every 29 day starts with a morning call to her daughter's apartment, a block away.

One of Ms. Gertz's first concerns was not for herself. "I was worried about my previous boyfriends," she said. "I didn't want them to be sick." Two past boyfriends have been tested, she said, and "both of them are O.K." 30

Her current boyfriend "is wonderful," she said. "He's stood by me." But AIDS has changed their relationship. "Yes, you can have safe sex. I know all the facts, and so does he. But still, in the back of his mind, he is scared, so we don't sleep together any more, and that's rough." 31

Ms. Gertz has not felt ostracized as many AIDS patients have. But there have been a few exceptions. 32

"The nurses told me this one resident doctor, a woman, insisted that I must have used IV drugs or must have had anal sex," Ms. Gertz said. She interprets the doctor's comment as a denial of her own possible risk by regarding the patient as different. 33

Loss of a Friend

"And one friend I lost," Ms. Gertz said. "She left. She deserted me." That, too, she understands. "She was with me at Studio 54 during those earlier years, and she was much more sexually active than I was. It wasn't my mortality she was facing; it was her own. She just couldn't handle it." 34

Health insurance is a problem that has made her financially dependent on her parents. "I think the insurance company owes me about $50,000," she said. "I haven't gotten one dime. They're trying to prove I knew I had this before I signed up for the policy two years before." 35

That angers Ms. Gertz because of the dozens of exhaustive, sometimes painful, tests she underwent to find what was wrong. 36

The Gertz family praises the hospital staff and their doctors, but it does regret that AIDS wasn't checked earlier. Mrs. Gertz said, "Because of her background, nobody thought this was a possibility." 37

"It stands to reason you're going to see more people like Ali," her mother said, since AIDS symptoms may not show up for 10 or 12 years. 38

Indeed, such cases are appearing. 39

Dr. Jody Robinson, an internist in Washington who has written on AIDS, said that other cases like Ms. Gertz's are "out there." 40

"How many is a tremendous unknown," he said. "It may not be an overwhelming number, but what will it be five or six years from now?" 41

The danger, he said, is that because experts have said there has not been an explosive outbreak among heterosexuals, people have become complacent. 42

"The common wisdom has gone back to the idea that AIDS is really the gay plague and disease of IV drug users that it was set out to be in the first place, and the warning on heterosexual spread was a false alarm," he said. 43

Alison Gertz struggles against AIDS with the benefit of a number of factors unknown to most patients—she has a determined optimism bolstered by the love of family and friends, financial aid and first-class medical care. 44

Gathered on a sofa for photographs, the Gertz family was all hugs and smiles. "I never felt from the beginning that this was anything to be hidden or ashamed of," Mrs. Gertz said. After a few pictures were taken, she wondered aloud, "Should we be looking so happy for such a serious subject?" 45

For a few seconds the family managed sober expressions for the camera. But soon, for at least one more day, the smiles broke through again. 46

Questions for Study and Discussion

1. How would you describe Lambert's beginning? How did you react to it? Did you think his beginning was effective? Why or why not?
2. How did Alison Gertz get AIDS? Did it surprise you that a heterosexual female contracted AIDS?
3. In paragraph 22 Alison Gertz says, "It's a dreadful disease, but it's also a gift." What does Alison mean by this?
4. Who is Alison Gertz's audience? (Glossary: *Audience*) What is her message for this audience? How likely is her audience to hear her message? Explain.

5. What is Lambert's attitude toward AIDS? (Glossary: *Attitude*) What in his essay led you to this conclusion?
6. How has Lambert organized his essay? What function do the running titles serve in his overall organizational plan? (Glossary: *Organization*)

Vocabulary

Refer to your dictionary to define the following words as they are used in this selection. Then use each word in a sentence of your own.

promiscuous (2)	fervor (21)
affluent (5)	optimistic (22)
rampant (11)	opportunistic (24)
embark (18)	ostracized (32)
ebullience (21)	bolster (44)

Classroom Activity on Beginnings and Endings

Choose one of the essays you have been writing for your course, and write at least two different beginnings for it. If you are having trouble coming up with two, check to see whether or not one of the paragraphs in the body of your essay is appropriate, or consult the list of effective beginnings in the introduction to this chapter. After you have finished, have several classmates read your beginnings and select their favorite. Do any of your new beginnings suggest ways that you can improve the focus, the organization, or the ending of your essay? Explain these revision possibilities to your partners.

Suggested Writing Assignments

1. How knowledgeable is the American public about AIDS? Do you think we know all the facts? How have the media worked to inform society of hazards and untruths about AIDS? Write an essay in which you discuss what responsibility you believe the media have to keep the public informed.

2. American pop singer Madonna has come under fire for the "lurid" content of some of her videos and stage shows. Madonna explains that her sexual overtones will encourage children to go to their parents and discuss things such as safe sex and premarital sex. How do you react to her reasoning? Is her approach for bringing these topics into the open a reasonable one? Write an essay in which you discuss the role of sex education in our fight against AIDS.

How to Take a Job Interview

Kirby W. Stanat

Formerly a personnel recruiter and placement officer at the University of Wisconsin–Milwaukee, and presently an executive search consultant in Milwaukee, Kirby W. Stanat has helped thousands of people get jobs. His book Job Hunting Secrets and Tactics *(1977) tells readers what they need to know in order to get the jobs they want. In this selection Stanat analyzes the campus interview, a process that hundreds of thousands of college students undergo each year as they seek to enter the job market. Notice how he establishes an effective and engaging context with his brief opening paragraph, and how the "snap" of his ending echoes back through the essay.*

For Your Journal

While seeking summer employment or selecting a college or university to attend, you may have had the experience of being interviewed. What do you remember most about the interviewer? What kinds of questions did this person ask you? If you could take the interview over again, what would you change?

To succeed in campus job interviews, you have to know where that recruiter is coming from. The simple answer is that he is coming from corporate headquarters. 1

That may sound obvious, but it is a significant point that too many students do not consider. The recruiter is not a free spirit as he flies from Berkeley to New Haven, from Chapel Hill to Boulder. He's on an invisible leash to the office, and if he is worth his salary, he is mentally in corporate headquarters all the time he's on the road. 2

If you can fix that in your mind—that when you walk into that bare-walled cubicle in the placement center you are walking into a branch office of Sears, Bendix or General Motors—you can avoid a lot of little mistakes and maybe some big ones. 3

If, for example, you assume that because the interview is on campus the recruiter expects you to look and act like a student, you're in for a shock. A student is somebody who drinks beer, wears blue jeans and throws a Frisbee. No recruiter has jobs for student Frisbee whizzes. 4

A cool spring day in late March, Sam Davis, a good recruiter who has been on the college circuit for years, is on my campus talking to candidates. He comes out to the waiting area to meet the student who signed up for an 11 o'clock interview. I'm standing in the doorway of my office taking in the scene. 5

Sam calls the candidate: "Sidney Student." There sits Sidney. He's at a 45-degree angle, his feet are in the aisle, and he's almost lying down. He's wearing well-polished brown shoes, a tasteful pair of brown pants, a light brown shirt, and a good-looking tie. Unfortunately, he tops off this well-coordinated outfit with his Joe's Tavern Class A Softball Championship jacket, which has a big woven emblem over the heart. 6

If that isn't bad enough, in his left hand is a cigarette and in his right hand is a half-eaten apple. 7

When Sam calls his name, the kid is caught off guard. He ditches the cigarette in an ashtray, struggles to his feet, and transfers the apple from the right to the left hand. Apple juice is everywhere, so Sid wipes his hand on the seat of his pants and shakes hands with Sam. 8

Sam, who by now is close to having a stroke, gives me that what-do-I-have-here look and has the young man follow him into the interviewing room. 9

The situation deteriorates even further—into pure Laurel and Hardy. The kid is stuck with the half-eaten apple, doesn't know what to do with it, and obviously is suffering some discomfort. He carries the apple into the interviewing room with him and places it in the ashtray on the desk—right on top of Sam's freshly lit cigarette. 10

The interview lasts five minutes. . . . 11

Let us move in for a closer look at how the campus recruiter operates. 12

Let's say you have a 10 o'clock appointment with the recruiter 13
from the XYZ Corporation. The recruiter gets rid of the candidate in front of you at about 5 minutes to 10, jots down a few notes about what he is going to do with him or her, then picks up your résumé or data sheet (which you have submitted in advance). . . .

Although the recruiter is still in the interview room and you 14
are still in the lobby, your interview is under way. You're on. The recruiter will look over your sheet pretty carefully before he goes out to call you. He develops a mental picture of you.

He thinks, "I'm going to enjoy talking with this kid," or "This 15
one's going to be a turkey." The recruiter has already begun to make a screening decision about you.

His first impression of you, from reading the sheet, could come 16
from your grade point. It could come from misspelled words. It could come from poor erasures or from the fact that necessary information is missing. By the time the recruiter has finished reading your sheet, you've already hit the plus or minus column.

Let's assume the recruiter got a fairly good impression from 17
your sheet.

Now the recruiter goes out to the lobby to meet you. He almost 18
shuffles along, and his mind is somewhere else. Then he calls your name, and at that instant he visibly clicks into gear. He just went to work.

As he calls your name he looks quickly around the room, wait- 19
ing for somebody to move. If you are sitting on the middle of your back, with a book open and a cigarette going, and if you have to rebuild yourself to stand up, the interest will run right out of the recruiter's face. You, not the recruiter, made the appointment for 10 o'clock, and the recruiter expects to see a young professional come popping out of that chair like today is a good day and you're anxious to meet him.

At this point, the recruiter does something rude. He doesn't 20
walk across the room to meet you halfway. He waits for you to come to him. Something very important is happening. He wants to see you move. He wants to get an impression about your posture, your stride, and your briskness.

If you slouch over to him, sidewinderlike, he is not going to be 21
impressed. He'll figure you would probably slouch your way through your workdays. He wants you to come at him with lots

of good things going for you. If you watch the recruiter's eyes, you can see the inspection. He glances quickly at shoes, pants, coat, shirt; dress, blouse, hose—the whole works.

After introducing himself, the recruiter will probably say, 22
"Okay, please follow me," and he'll lead you into his interviewing room.

When you get to the room, you may find that the recruiter will 23
open the door and gesture you in—with him blocking part of the doorway. There's enough room for you to get past him, but it's a near thing.

As you scrape past, he gives you a closeup inspection. He 24
looks at your hair; if it's greasy, that will bother him. He looks at your collar; if it's dirty, that will bother him. He looks at your shoulders; if they're covered with dandruff, that will bother him. If you're a man, he looks at your chin. If you didn't get a close shave, that will irritate him. If you're a woman, he checks your makeup. If it's too heavy, he won't like it.

Then he smells you. An amazing number of people smell bad. 25
Occasionally a recruiter meets a student who smells like a canal horse. That student can expect an interview of about four or five minutes.

Next the recruiter inspects the back side of you. He checks 26
your hair (is it combed in front but not in back?), he checks your heels (are they run down?), your pants (are they baggy?), your slip (is it showing?), your stockings (do they have runs?).

Then he invites you to sit down. 27

At this point, I submit, the recruiter's decision on you is 75 to 28
80 percent made.

Think about it. The recruiter has read your résumé. He knows 29
who you are and where you are from. He knows your marital status, your major and your grade point. And he knows what you have done with your summers. He has inspected you, exchanged greetings with you and smelled you. There is very little additional hard information that he must gather on you. From now on it's mostly body chemistry.

Many recruiters have argued strenuously with me that they 30
don't make such hasty decisions. So I tried an experiment. I told several recruiters that I would hang around in the hall outside the interview room when they took candidates in.

I told them that as soon as they had definitely decided not to 31 recommend (to department managers in their companies) the candidate they were interviewing, they should snap their fingers loud enough for me to hear. It went like this.

First candidate: 38 seconds after the candidate sat down: Snap! 32

Second candidate: 1 minute, 42 seconds: Snap! 33

Third candidate: 45 seconds: Snap! 34

One recruiter was particularly adamant, insisting that he didn't 35
rush to judgment on candidates. I asked him to participate in the snapping experiment. He went out in the lobby, picked up his first candidate of the day, and headed for an interview room.

As he passed me in the hall, he glared at me. And his fingers 36
went "Snap!"

Questions for Study and Discussion

1. Explain the appropriateness of the beginning and ending of Stanat's essay.
2. What are Stanat's purpose and thesis in telling the reader how the recruitment process works? (Glossary: *Purpose* and *Thesis*)
3. In paragraphs 12–29 Stanat explains how the campus recruiter works. Make a list of the steps in that process. (Glossary: *Process Analysis*)
4. Why do recruiters pay so much attention to body language when they interview job candidates?
5. What specifically have you learned from reading Stanat's essay? Do you feel that the essay is useful in preparing someone for a job interview? Explain.
6. Stanat's tone—his attitude toward his subject and audience—in this essay is informal. What in his sentence structure and diction creates this informality? (Glossary: *Diction*) Cite examples. How might the tone be made more formal for a different audience? (Glossary: *Tone*)

Vocabulary

Refer to your dictionary to define the following words as they are used in this selection. Then use each word in a sentence of your own.

cubicle (3)	résumé (13)
deteriorates (10)	adamant (35)

Classroom Activity on Beginnings and Endings

Stanat could have ended his essay with paragraph 29. What are the advantages of ending with this paragraph? What are the advantages of ending with the anecdote of his experiment with recruiters? Which ending do you prefer? Why?

Suggested Writing Assignments

1. Stanat's purpose is to offer practical advice to students interviewing for jobs. Determine a subject about which you could offer advice to a specific audience. Present your advice in the form of an essay, being careful to provide an attention-grabbing beginning and a convincing conclusion.
2. Stanat gives us an account of the interview process from the viewpoint of the interviewer. If you have ever been interviewed and remember the experience well, write an essay on your feelings and thoughts as the interview took place. What were the circumstances of the interview? What questions were asked of you, how did you feel about them, and how comfortable was the process? How did the interview turn out? What precisely, if anything, did you learn from the experience? What advice would you give someone about to be interviewed? You may find it helpful to review the journal entry that you wrote for this selection before beginning your essay.

It's Not Just a Phase

Katherine E. Zondlo

Katherine E. Zondlo, a student at Morgantown High School in West Virginia, published the following essay as a "My Turn" column in Newsweek *in June 1996. After graduating from high school, Zondlo hopes to attend Smith College in Massachusetts and pursue a degree in women's studies. Her ultimate goal is to become a women's rights activist. As you read her essay, consider how the title phrase helps to establish Zondlo's purpose and tone right from the start, and then serves as a reinforcing echo in the essay itself.*

For Your Journal

What does the noun "grown-up" mean to you? Does it have a positive or negative connotation for you? Why?

A few weeks ago my mother invited a friend and her son, a 5-year-old named Joseph, to dinner at our house. Very mature and intelligent for his age, Joseph seemed to have an endless supply of comments that, when spoken in his earnest little voice, kept most of our dinner guests in stitches. Sitting at the table, I was suddenly visited by a flood of childhood memories—memories of having been laughed at for speaking my mind, often using "big words" as Joseph was. I remembered the shame and humiliation I felt, worrying that I had said something wrong or stupid. What a mixed message: adults using sophisticated words around kids and then laughing when they experiment with them. Suddenly, my heart went out to the little boy sitting next to me, looking at us with wide eyes like video cameras, capturing all of our responses on tape to be played over and over again. For all I know, the footage that Joseph gathered at dinner that night could stay 1 with him forever, a reminder that sometimes, even if you speak the truth and do so sincerely, someone may laugh at you.

The adults did not mean to diminish a child's self-esteem or 2
scar him for life. They just wanted to have pleasant conversation. Unfortunately, it was at Joseph's expense. They were suffering from the "how cute" syndrome: adults making light of kids' opinions. They can't effectively put themselves in young people's shoes. As a result, many do not know how to treat us with respect.

Another nasty symptom of the "how cute" syndrome is mak- 3
ing an unnecessary issue of young people's age. Many magazines and newspapers print a young person's age after a letter in the reader-response section. This suggests to children that adults don't care what kids have to say. Adults just think it's charming that they would write in at all, cute that they have opinions on world issues, adorable that they think of the world past their own backyards. If questioned, the adults would likely say they're simply recognizing and respecting the fact that a young person took the time to write a letter, an act that deserves notice. But publishing a young person's age makes it the central issue and deflects from the writer's point of view.

"How cute" is an easy put-down adults use for children. For 4
teens who've grown beyond the cute stage, there's the "it's just a phase" brushoff. "It's just a phase" is a belittling and harmful remark, but one that adolescents hear almost every day to dismiss behavior that adults simply don't (want to) understand. And there are many different ways of saying it. When I got my nose pierced in November, for instance, my parents' first remark was "*When* you decide to take that thing out, will the hole close up?" It didn't occur to them that I might not ever take it out. When I chose to become vegetarian, I heard, "You'll give this up as soon as you get hungry for a pepperoni pizza."

As a young person, I am very excited about the world, my fu- 5
ture and the endless possibilities both offer. I want to make a positive difference, live a happy life and be true to myself. In college, I'd like to major in women's studies and use this knowledge to improve the status of women and girls in our society. I'm saddened by adults who say "it's just a phase" when I speak of my hopes and dreams. They smile wryly, thinking, "Just wait, young lady, when you enter the real world you'll wake up and realize

that one person can't make that much difference." The adults I am drawn to are those who have not completely forgotten their adolescence and its open-mindedness. They believe in me and my abilities, and encourage me to attain my goals.

Adults can learn a lot from young people. Children are born 6 with a clean slate, free from hatred, racism, sexism, homophobia and all of their nasty cousins. Kids cooperate and share, skills requiring attitudes that many nations today seem to be lacking. Maybe the United Nations should watch a few episodes of "Sesame Street" and "Mister Rogers' Neighborhood" at their next meeting. From teens, adults can learn to renew their radical ideas and activist thoughts lost through life and their experiences. They can learn it is never too late to switch gears. They can learn that stubbornness and conviction are actually admirable qualities when compared with being passive and unquestioning.

Perhaps if kids and teens took over the government, or at least 7 if we had a voice, the quality of life in this country might well begin to improve. Don't laugh or dismiss this as nonsense. Just think about it.

I know I'm not perfect. As a teen, I have already lost much of 8 the innocence and open-mindedness of my childhood. So, in a sense, I'm already jaded. But I'm determined not to lose sight of my future plans. I'm going to cherish my hopes and dreams, hang on to my enthusiasm and keep my belief in the possibilities life has to offer. I'm determined I'll not trade in my idealism for a good job, a fat paycheck and a nice house.

Some adults surprise and inspire me. It heartens me when I 9 see them switching gears in middle age, choosing a job or lifestyle that they genuinely enjoy. My mother, for example, decided to return to college when I was 5 to pursue her dream of becoming a physician. Teachers can be a source of motivation, too, especially those who enjoy their career and teach their classes with energy and innovation. Unfortunately, they are few and far between.

Little Joseph made an impact on me that night at dinner be- 10 cause his lively conversation was free of inhibitions. The adults at the party were not so spontaneous, and I realized that I, too, will probably soon be watching my words. Adults can still realize their dreams of adolescence if their present path makes them unhappy. Dreams are important to keep and work on. Grown-ups should make themselves look at young people—and that's what we are, young people—in a new light. Respect and try to understand us, love and learn from us. As Robert Frost said, "I go to school, to youth, to learn the future."

And by the way, if you're interested in my age, just leave it to your imagination. 11

Questions for Study and Discussion

1. What is Zondlo's purpose in telling the story of Joseph? (Glossary: *Purpose*) Why is her experience with Joseph an effective way to introduce her essay? (Glossary: *Illustration*)
2. Why is "It's just a phase" a "belittling and harmful remark" (4) according to Zondlo? What are the different ways in which it can be said?
3. How are children's ages used to undermine what they have to say? Do you agree with Zondlo's interpretation of this practice?
4. Zondlo asserts that if teens and children had more of a voice in national affairs, "the quality of life in this country might well begin to improve" (7). Based on her essay, how would she say our quality of life would benefit from such a change? What might be some potential problems?
5. What do people lose on their path from childhood to adulthood? What can adults learn by listening to children?
6. What does Zondlo's last sentence indicate about her intent? Does this statement get you thinking about her or about what she has said in the essay? How effective do you find this ending?

Vocabulary

Refer to your dictionary to define the following words as they are used in this selection. Then use each word in a sentence of your own.

earnest (1)
self-esteem (2)
wryly (5)
homophobia (6)
radical (6)
activist (6)

Classroom Activity on Beginnings and Endings

Pick two of the eight methods discussed in the introduction to this section and use each to write alternative opening sentences or paragraphs for Zondlo's essay.

Suggested Writing Assignments

1. Zondlo boldly states: "I'm determined I'll not trade in my idealism for a good job, a fat paycheck and a nice house" (8). It would be interesting to contact her in fifteen years to see what has become of her determination—whether she is still pursuing her ideals or whether she has "sold out." Write an essay in which you propose an idealistic course of action in your life. What kind of life do you want to lead? What is your dream job? How do you propose getting it? What, if anything, will you have to sacrifice to achieve it? What might get in the way of your dreams? Why do you think many adults have given up their ideals and become, as Zondlo scornfully asserts, "passive and unquestioning"?
2. Every year a literary contest awards a prize for the writer of the worst possible opening sentence for a novel. Reread the "don'ts" listed in the introduction to this section and write the worst opening paragraph you can come up with for an essay on a topic of your choice. Make it at least four sentences long. Then write an analysis of the paragraph, explaining why it is bad and what could be done to fix it.

5

PARAGRAPHS

Within an essay, the paragraph is the most important unit of thought. Like the essay, it has its own main idea, often stated directly in a topic sentence. Like a good essay, a good paragraph is unified: it avoids digressions and develops its main idea. Paragraphs use many of the rhetorical techniques that essays use, techniques such as classification, comparison and contrast, and cause and effect. Consider the following three paragraphs:

> I've learned from experience that good friendships are based on a delicate balance. When friends are on a par, professionally and personally, it's easier for them to root for one another. It's taken me a long time to realize that not all my "friends" wish me well. Someone who wants what you have may not be able to handle your good fortune: If you find yourself apologizing for your hard-earned raise or soft-pedaling your long-awaited promotion, it's a sure sign that the friendship is off balance. Real friends are secure enough in their own lives to share each other's successes—not begrudge them.
>
> Stephanie Mansfield

> Most stories of illegal drugs overshadow Americans' struggles with alcohol, tobacco, food, and nonprescription drugs—our so-called legal addictions. The problem of substance abuse is far more complex and far more pervasive than any of us really knows or is willing to admit. In 1990, for example, 14,000 deaths were attributed to cocaine and heroin. In that same year, 390,000 deaths were attributed to tobacco and 90,000 to alcohol. It's not surprising then that many sociologists believe we are a nation of substance abusers—drinkers, smokers, eaters, and pill poppers. Although the statistics are alarming, they do not begin to suggest the heavy toll of substance abuse on Americans and their families. Loved ones die, relationships are fractured, children are abandoned, job productivity falters, and the dreams of young people are extinguished.
>
> Alfred Rosa and Paul Eschholz

> Many rock musicians consciously work to maintain the aura of mystery surrounding themselves. Typically, they walk on stage and proceed to sneer at or completely ignore the audience. If a star is especially articulate, he may yell, "A-a-all ri-i-ight! Gonna rock to-o-ni-i-ight!" He cannot use the vocabulary of the common man, for fear of being mistakenly identified as such. Besides, a few well-timed thrusts of the hips communicate the message just as well. The audience responds wildly to this invitation, and the concert is off to a good start. The performer has successfully gauged the mood of the spectators; now his task is to manipulate it, through his choice of material and through such actions as dancing, prancing, foot-stomping, and unearthly screaming. His movements, gestures, and often, his bizarre clothing, high heels, and make-up deliberately violate accepted standards of conduct and appearance. He can afford to take chances and to risk offending people; after all, as every good student of mythology knows, deities are not bound by the same restrictions as mere mortals. The Dionysus figure on the stage tempts us to follow him into the never-never land where inhibitions are nonexistent.
>
> Jennifer McBride Young

Many writers find it helpful to think of the paragraph as a very small, compact essay. Here is a paragraph from an essay on testing:

> Multiple-choice questions distort the purposes of education. Picking one answer among four is very different from thinking a question through to an answer of one's own, and far less useful in life. Recognition of vocabulary and isolated facts makes the best kind of multiple-choice questions, so these dominate the tests, rather than questions that test the use of knowledge. Because schools want their children to perform well, they are often tempted to teach the limited sorts of knowledge most useful on the tests.

This paragraph, like all well-written paragraphs, has several distinguishing characteristics: it is unified, coherent, and adequately developed. It is unified in that every sentence and every idea relates to the main idea, stated in the topic sentence, "Multiple-choice questions distort the purposes of education." It is coherent in that the sentences and ideas are arranged logically and the relationships among them are made clear by the use of effective transitions. Finally, the paragraph is adequately developed in that it presents a short but persuasive argument supporting its main idea.

How much development is "adequate" development? The answer depends on many things: how complicated or controversial the main idea is; what readers already know and believe; how much space the writer is permitted. Everyone, or nearly everyone, agrees that the earth circles around the sun; a single sentence would be enough to make that point. A writer trying to argue that affirmative action has outlived its usefulness, however, would need many sentences, indeed many paragraphs, to develop that idea convincingly.

Here is another model of an effective paragraph. As you read this paragraph about the resourcefulness of pigeons in evading attempts to control them, pay particular attention to its controlling idea, unity, development, and coherence.

> Pigeons (and their human friends) have proved remarkably resourceful in evading nearly all the controls, from birth-control pellets to carbide shells to pigeon apartment complexes, that pigeon-haters have devised. One of New York's leading museums once put large black rubber owls on its wide ledges to discourage the large number of pigeons that roosted there. Within the day the pigeons had gotten over their fear of owls and were back perched on the owls' heads. A few years ago San Francisco put a sticky coating on the ledges of some public buildings, but the pigeons got used to the goop and came back to roost. The city then tried trapping, using electric owls, and periodically exploding carbide shells outside a city building, hoping the noise would scare the pigeons away. It did, but not for long, and the program was abandoned. More frequent explosions probably would have distressed the humans in the area more than the birds. Philadelphia tried a feed that makes pigeons vomit, and then, they hoped, go away. A New York firm claimed it had a feed that made a pigeon's nervous system send "danger signals" to the other members of its flock.

The controlling idea is stated at the beginning in a topic sentence. Other sentences in the paragraph support the controlling idea with examples. Since all the separate examples illustrate how pigeons have evaded attempts to control them, the paragraph is unified. Since there are enough examples to convince the reader of the truth of the topic statement, the paragraph is adequately developed. Finally, the regular use of transitional words and phrases such as *once, within the day, a few years ago,* and *then* lends the paragraph coherence.

How long should a paragraph be? In modern essays most paragraphs range from 50 to 250 words, but some run a full page or more and others may be only a few words long. The best answer is that a paragraph should be long enough to develop its main idea adequately. Some authors, when they find a paragraph running very long, may break it into two or more paragraphs so that readers can pause and catch their breath. Other writers forge ahead, relying on the unity and coherence of their paragraph to keep their readers from getting lost.

Articles and essays that appear in magazines and newspapers often have relatively short paragraphs, some of only one or two sentences. Short paragraphs are a convention in journalism because of the narrow columns, which make paragraphs of average length appear very long. But often you will find that these journalistic "paragraphs" could be joined together into a few longer, more normal paragraphs. Longer, more normal paragraphs are the kind you should use in all but journalistic writing.

ZEN AND THE ART OF OLYMPIC SUCCESS

Adam Rogers

Adam Rogers is a science, technology, and medicine reporter for Newsweek *magazine. He was born in England in 1970 but grew up in Los Angeles. After receiving his bachelor's degree from Pomona College in 1992, Rogers went on to Boston University, where he obtained a master's degree in science journalism. Prior to joining* Newsweek, *he worked at* The Harvard Health Letter *and as a freelance associate producer for video projects. As you read the selection below, which appeared in* Newsweek *in July 1996, pay particular attention to how Rogers connects the sentences within his paragraphs, often repeating words and ideas to achieve coherence.*

FOR YOUR JOURNAL

There's an old saying that sports are 90 percent mental and 10 percent physical. Based on your own experience or observations, do you agree with this saying? Why, or why not?

Here's how Rebecca Snyder remembers it: she was walking past the other air-gun shooters to take her place on the firing range. At stake was a spot on the national team and, perhaps, an Olympic berth. She felt good, strong—almost cocky. Her mouth was filled with a chunk of watermelon bubble gum. She sighted down the barrel of her gun and started firing. A solid 90 out of 100. Then a 92, a 93 and a 96. In the finals, where they count tenths, a near-perfect 98.1. "Every time I put the gun up I expected to shoot a bull's-eye," she says. "I was telling myself, 'This is so easy, it's just there today.'" 1

Every athlete knows the feeling. The ball looks bigger. The game slows down. They have different names for it, of course: the zone, 2 flow, harmony, the Zen moment. At the Olympics, the physical condition of the athletes is as close to perfect as human beings can get. The difference between a trip to the medal stand and a quiet plane ride home may be all in the mind.

A mind "in flow" can make an athlete seem invincible, but getting there isn't easy. "It seems to be the result of total concentration on a doable task, which can be physical, intellectual or even emotional," says Mihaly Csikszentmihalyi, a psychologist at the University of Chicago and author of *Flow: The Psychology of Optimal Experience.* 3

Csikszentmihalyi started calling this state of mind "flow" 25 years ago as part of his research on happiness. But sports psychologists soon recognized that athletes describing how they felt when they were at their best sounded very much as if they'd been in flow. So why should a blissed-out state of mind enhance performance? The key is the type and amount of attention an athlete pays to the task. In a series of studies, sports scientists at Arizona State University have looked at the brain waves of archers, shooters and golfers in the seconds before they release a motion. The researchers found decreases in activity in the left hemisphere of the brain, the hemisphere thought to handle rational thought. The decline in left-hemisphere activity represents less attention to the mechanics of the action and more on how it feels. And only certain ratios of left-to-right-hemisphere activity correlate with peak performance, suggesting that there is an ideal frame of mind. 4

Fear Factor

Olympians have practiced their events much of their lives, but repetition guarantees only know-how. Psychological factors such as stress or fear can intervene, throwing execution off. Almost every sport now consults psychologists to help athletes integrate mental focus with physical ability. Visualization, self-hypnosis, even tapes of simulated competitions with the voices of the Olympic announcers all hone the mind–body link. Foil fencer Felicia Zimmermann repeats key words to keep herself focused. Backstroker Tripp Schwenk envisions every stroke of a race. 5

The athletes want to connect mind with body because performing perfectly requires the synchronization of literally mil- 6 lions of neural and muscular events. Visualization may cue the body to launch that optimal set of movements. A high-definition mental TV is especially important in events like weight lifting, where lifters have no way of knowing what a record weight will actually feel like, or canoe/kayak, where the paddlers don't get to try out their course. Says Dragomir Cioroslan, coach of the U.S. Weightlifting team: "We train for imagery just as we train for muscles and technique."

Though the psychologists might not be sure what's going on in flow, they know a few things about how to get there. In a beautiful irony, the harder athletes try to win, the less likely they are to find their zone. "Any time you get into that state where you're thinking about the result instead of what you're doing, you're pretty much screwed, to use a scientific term," says Shane Murphy, a sports psychologist and consultant. That's an ancient notion—since the 13th century, students of kyudo, Japanese Zen archery, have been forbidden to even aim at a target until they perfect their drawing and firing. Even today, says Janet Dykman, a U.S. archer, "I try to have no emotion about what happens to the arrow. I just concentrate on my form." And the arrow lands smack in the bull's-eye of harmony. 7

Questions for Study and Discussion

1. How did you react to the title of the essay? (Glossary: *Title*) Do you think it's appropriate? Propose an alternative title that is less literary. Explain your choice of words.
2. Why does Rogers begin his essay with the story of Rebecca Snyder? (Glossary: *Beginnings and Endings*) In what way is a specific example more effective than a general statement?
3. According to Rogers, what happens in the minds of athletes when they perform well? How does this affect their physical performance? (Glossary: *Cause and Effect*)
4. Athletes get their minds "in flow" by achieving a state of mind that allows them to focus on feeling rather than mechanics. Why is this state of mind so difficult to achieve in competition? Are practice and repetition by athletes enough to ensure that they are able to get in flow?

5. What must athletes avoid doing to get in flow? How do psychologists explain the apparent contradiction of this situation? (Glossary: *Paradox*)

Vocabulary

Refer to your dictionary to define the following words as they are used in this selection. Then use each word in a sentence of your own.

invincible (3)
optimal (3)
correlate (4)
integrate (5)
neural (6)

Classroom Activity on Paragraphs

Rearrange the following sentences to create an effective paragraph. Be ready to explain why you chose the order that you did.

1. PGA golfer Fred Divot learned the hard way what overtraining could do.
2. Divot's case is typical, and most researchers believe that too much repetition makes it difficult for the athlete to reduce left-hemisphere brain activity.
3. Athletes who overtrain find it very difficult to get in flow.
4. "Two weeks later, all I could think about was mechanics, and I couldn't hit a fairway to save my life!"
5. Athletes think about mechanics (left hemisphere) rather than feel (right hemisphere), and they lose the ability to achieve peak performance.
6. "I was playing well, so I thought with a bit more practice, I could start winning on tour," Divot recalls.

Suggested Writing Assignments

1. Talk to three students who excel at a sport at your school. If you participate in a sport yourself, you can use personal experience as well. How do the athletes define being "in the

zone"? When they are in the zone, what do they feel like? What do they think about? Write an essay in which you report your findings.

2. Look up *Zen* in a reference book. Based on what it says, write an essay in which you discuss how Zen might relate to athletics. How might Zen teachings help an athlete perform at his or her best? Focus your essay on the specific sport that you have played or watched most frequently.

SIMPLICITY

William Zinsser

William Zinsser was born in New York City in 1922. After graduating from Princeton University, he worked for the New York Herald Tribune, *first as a feature writer and later as its drama editor and film critic. Zinsser has also taught writing at Yale University and served as general editor of the Book-of-the-Month Club. He is currently the series editor for The Writer's Craft Series, which publishes talks by writers and is cosponsored by the Book-of-the-Month Club and the New York Public Library. Zinsser's own published works cover many aspects of contemporary American culture, but he is best known as the author of lucid and accessible books about writing, including* Writing with a Word Processor *(1983),* Writing to Learn *(1988), and* On Writing Well *(1976), a perennial favorite for college-writing courses as well as the general population. Zinsser now teaches at the New School for Social Research in New York. In the following piece, he reminds us, as did Thoreau before him, to "simplify, simplify." As you read each paragraph, notice the clarity with which Zinsser presents its main idea, and how he develops that idea with adequate and logically related supporting information. You should also note that he follows his own advice about simplicity.*

FOR YOUR JOURNAL

Sometimes we get so caught up in what's going on around us that we start to feel frantic, and we lose sight of what is really important or meaningful to us. At such times it's a good idea to take stock of what we are doing and to simplify our lives by dropping activities that are no longer rewarding. Write about a time when you've felt the need to simplify your life.

Clutter is the disease of American writing. We are a society strangling in unnecessary words, circular constructions, pompous frills and meaningless jargon. 1

Who can understand the viscous language of everyday American commerce: the memo, the corporation report, the business letter, the notice from the bank explaining its latest "simplified" statement? What member of an insurance or medical plan can decipher the brochure explaining his costs and benefits? What father or mother can put together a child's toy from the instructions on the box? Our national tendency is to inflate and thereby sound important. The airline pilot who announces that he is presently anticipating experiencing considerable precipitation wouldn't think of saying it may rain. The sentence is too simple—there must be something wrong with it. 2

But the secret of good writing is to strip every sentence to its cleanest components. Every word that serves no function, every long word that could be a short word, every adverb that carries the same meaning that's already in the verb, every passive construction that leaves the reader unsure of who is doing what—these are the thousand and one adulterants that weaken the strength of a sentence. And they usually occur in proportion to education and rank. 3

During the 1960s the president of my university wrote a letter to mollify the alumni after a spell of campus unrest. "You are probably aware," he began, "that we have been experiencing very considerable potentially explosive expressions of dissatisfaction on issues only partially related." He meant the students had been hassling them about different things. I was far more upset by the president's English than by the students' potentially explosive expressions of dissatisfaction. I would have preferred the presidential approach taken by Franklin D. Roosevelt when he tried to convert into English his own government's memos, such as this blackout order of 1942: 4

> Such preparations shall be made as will completely obscure all Federal buildings and non-Federal buildings occupied by the Federal government during an air raid for any period of time from visibility by reason of internal or external illumination.

"Tell them," Roosevelt said, "that in buildings where they have to keep the work going to put something across the windows."

Simplify, simplify. Thoreau said it, as we are so often reminded, 5
and no American writer more consistently practiced what he preached. Open *Walden* to any page and you will find a man saying in a plain and orderly way what is on his mind:

> I went to the woods because I wished to live deliberately, to front only the essential facts of life, and see if I could not learn what it had to teach, and not, when I came to die, discover that I had not lived.

How can the rest of us achieve such enviable freedom from 6
clutter? The answer is to clear our heads of clutter. Clear thinking becomes clear writing; one can't exist without the other. It's impossible for a muddy thinker to write good English. You may get away with it for a paragraph or two, but soon the reader will be lost, and there's no sin so grave, for the reader will not easily be lured back.

Who is this elusive creature, the reader? The reader is some- 7
one with an attention span of about 30 seconds—a person assailed by other forces competing for attention. At one time these forces weren't so numerous: newspapers, radio, spouse, home, children. Today they also include a "home entertainment center" (TV, VCR, tapes, CDs), pets, a fitness program, a yard and all the gadgets that have been bought to keep it spruce, and that most potent of competitors, sleep. The person snoozing in a chair with a magazine or a book is a person who was being given too much unnecessary trouble by the writer.

It won't do to say that the reader is too dumb or too lazy to keep 8
pace with the train of thought. If the reader is lost, it's usually because the writer hasn't been careful enough. The carelessness can take any number of forms. Perhaps a sentence is so excessively cluttered that the reader, hacking through the verbiage, simply doesn't know what it means. Perhaps a sentence has been so shoddily constructed that the reader could read it in several ways. Perhaps the writer has switched pronouns in midsentence, or has switched tenses, so the reader loses track of who is talking or when the action took place. Perhaps Sentence B is not a logical sequel to Sentence A—the writer, in whose head the connection is clear, hasn't bothered to provide the missing link. Perhaps the writer has used an important word incorrectly by not taking the trouble to look it up. The writer may think "sanguine" and "sanguinary" mean the same thing, but the difference is a bloody

big one. The reader can only infer (speaking of big differences) what the writer is trying to imply.

Faced with such obstacles, readers are at first tenacious. They 9 blame themselves—they obviously missed something, and they go back over the mystifying sentence, or over the whole paragraph, piecing it out like an ancient rune, making guesses and moving on. But they won't do this for long. The writer is making them work too hard, and they will look for one who is better at the craft.

Writers must therefore constantly ask: What am I trying to say? 10 Surprisingly often they don't know. Then they must look at what they have written and ask: Have I said it? Is it clear to someone encountering the subject for the first time? If it's not, some fuzz has worked its way into the machinery. The clear writer is someone clearheaded enough to see this stuff for what it is: fuzz.

I don't mean that some people are born clearheaded and are 11 therefore natural writers, whereas others are naturally fuzzy and will never write well. Thinking clearly is a conscious act that writers must force upon themselves, just as if they were working on any other project that requires logic: adding up a laundry list or doing an algebra problem. Good writing doesn't come naturally, though most people obviously think it does. The professional writer is constantly being bearded by strangers who say they'd like to "try a little writing sometime"—meaning when they retire from their real profession, which is difficult, like insurance or real estate. Or they say, "I could write a book about that." I doubt it.

Writing is hard work. A clear sentence is no accident. Very few 12 sentences come out right the first time, or even the third time. Remember this in moments of despair. If you find that writing is hard, it's because it *is* hard. It's one of the hardest things people do.

Questions for Study and Discussion

1. What exactly does Zinsser mean by clutter? How does Zinsser believe we can free ourselves of clutter?
2. In paragraph 3 Zinsser lists a number of "adulterants" that weaken English sentences and claims that "they usually occur in proportion to education and rank." Why do you suppose this is true?

3. What is the relationship between thinking and writing for Zinsser?
4. In paragraph 10, Zinsser says that writers must constantly ask themselves some questions. What are these and why are they important?
5. How do Zinsser's first and last paragraphs serve to introduce and conclude his essay? (Glossary: *Beginnings and Endings*)
6. What is the function of paragraphs 4 and 5 in the context of the essay? (Glossary: *Illustration*)
7. How do the questions in paragraph 2 further Zinsser's purpose? (Glossary: *Rhetorical Question*)

Vocabulary

Refer to your dictionary to define the following words as they are used in this selection. Then use each word in a sentence of your own.

pompous (1)	enviable (6)
decipher (2)	tenacious (9)
adulterants (3)	bearded (11)
mollify (4)	

Classroom Activity on Paragraphs

The following pages show a passage from the manuscript for Zinsser's essay. Carefully study the manuscript and Zinsser's changes, and be prepared to discuss how his changes enhance his paragraphs' unity, coherence, and logical development.

is too dumb or too lazy to keep pace with the ~~writer's~~ train of thought. My sympathies are ~~entirely~~ with him. ~~He's not so dumb.~~ If the reader is lost, it is generally because the writer ~~of the article~~ has not been careful enough to keep him on the ~~proper~~ path.

This carelessness can take any number of ~~different~~ forms. Perhaps a sentence is so excessively ~~long and~~ cluttered that the reader, hacking his way through ~~all~~ the verbiage, simply doesn't know what it ~~the writer~~ means. Perhaps a sentence has been so shoddily constructed that the reader could read it in any of several ~~two or three different~~ ways. ~~He thinks he knows what the writer is trying to say, but he's not sure.~~ Perhaps the writer has switched pronouns in mid-sentence, or ~~perhaps he~~ has switched tenses, so the reader loses track of who is talking ~~to whom~~ or ~~exactly~~ when the action took place. Perhaps Sentence B is not a logical sequel to Sentence A -- the writer, in whose head the connection is ~~perfectly~~ clear, has not bothered to provide ~~given enough thought to providing~~ the missing link. Perhaps the writer has used an important word incorrectly by not taking the trouble to look it up. ~~and make sure~~. He may think that "sanguine" and "sanguinary" mean the same thing, but ~~I can assure you that~~ the difference is a bloody big one. ~~to the reader~~. The reader ~~He~~ can only ~~try to~~ infer ~~abxx~~ (speaking of big differences) what the writer is trying to imply.

Faced with these ~~such a variety of~~ obstacles, the reader is at first a remarkably tenacious bird. He ~~tends to~~ blames himself. He obviously missed something, ~~he thinks,~~ and he goes back over the mystifying sentence, or over the whole paragraph, piecing it out like an ancient rune, making guesses and moving on. But he won't do this for long. ~~He will soon run out of patience.~~ The writer is making him work too hard, ~~– harder than he should have to work –~~ and the reader will look for ~~a writer~~ one who is better at his craft.

The writer must therefore constantly ask himself: What am I trying to say? ~~in this sentence?~~ (Surprisingly often, he doesn't know.) ~~And~~ Then he must look at what he has ~~just~~ written and ask: Have I said it? Is it clear to someone encountering ~~who is coming upon~~ the subject for the first time? If it's not, ~~clear,~~ it is because some fuzz has worked its way into the machinery. The clear writer is a person ~~who is~~ clear-headed enough to see this stuff for what it is: fuzz.

I don't mean ~~to suggest~~ that some people are born clear-headed and are therefore natural writers, whereas others ~~other people~~ are naturally fuzzy and will ~~therefore~~ never write well. Thinking clearly is a ~~an entirely~~ conscious act that the writer must force ~~keep forcing~~ upon himself, just as if he were embarking ~~starting out~~ on any other ~~kind of~~ project that requires ~~calls for~~ logic: adding up a laundry list or doing an algebra problem ~~or playing chess.~~ ⊙ Good writing doesn't ~~just~~ come naturally, though most people obviously think it does. ~~it's as easy as walking.~~ The professional

Suggested Writing Assignments

1. Using some of the ideas you explored in your journal entry for this selection, write a brief essay analyzing your need to simplify some aspect of your life. For example, are you involved in too many extracurricular activities, taking too many courses, working too many hours on an off-campus job, or not making sensible choices with regard to your social life?
2. If what Zinsser writes about clutter is an accurate assessment, we should easily be able to find numerous examples of clutter all around us. During the next few days, make a point of looking for clutter in the written materials you come across. Choose one example that you find—an article, an essay, a form letter, or a chapter from a textbook, for example—and write an extended analysis explaining how it might have been written more simply. Develop your paragraphs well, make sure they are coherent, and try not to "clutter" your own writing.

"I Just Wanna Be Average"

Mike Rose

Born in Altoona, Pennsylvania, to immigrant parents, Mike Rose moved to California in the early 1950s. A graduate of Loyola University in Los Angeles, Rose is now a professor at the UCLA Graduate School of Education and Information Studies. He has written a number of books and articles on language and literacy. His best-known book, Lives on the Boundary: The Struggles and Achievements of America's Underprepared, *was recognized by the National Council of Teachers of English with its highest award in 1989. More recently he published* Possible Lives: The Promise of Public Education *(1995). In the following selection from* Lives on the Boundary, *Rose explains how his high-school English teacher, Jack MacFarland, picked him up out of the doldrums of "scholastic indifference." As you read, notice that although his paragraphs are fairly lengthy, Rose never digresses from the main point of each.*

For Your Journal

Often our desire to get more out of school and to go on to college can be traced back to the influence of a single teacher. Which teacher turned you on to learning? Describe what that person did to stimulate change in you.

Jack MacFarland couldn't have come into my life at a better time. My father was dead, and I had logged up too many years of scholastic indifference. Mr. MacFarland had a master's degree from Columbia and decided, at twenty-six, to find a little school and teach his heart out. He never took any credentialing 1 courses, couldn't bear to, he said, so he had to find employment in a private system. He ended up at Our Lady of Mercy teaching five sections of senior English. He was a beatnik who was born too late. His teeth were stained, he tucked his sorry tie in between the third and fourth buttons of his shirt, and his pants were chronically wrinkled. At first, we couldn't believe this guy, thought he slept in his car. But within no time, he had us so startled with work that we didn't much worry about where he slept or if he slept at all. We wrote three or four essays a month. We read a book every two to three weeks, starting with the *Iliad* and ending up with Hemingway. He gave us a quiz on the reading every other day. He brought a prep school curriculum to Mercy High.

MacFarland's lectures were crafted, and as he delivered them 2
he would pace the room jiggling a piece of chalk in his cupped hand, using it to scribble on the board the names of all the writers and philosophers and plays and novels he was weaving into his discussion. He asked questions often, raised everything from Zeno's paradox to the repeated last line of Frost's "Stopping by Woods on a Snowy Evening." He slowly and carefully built up our knowledge of Western intellectual history—with facts, with connections, with speculations. We learned about Greek philosophy, about Dante, the Elizabethan world view, the Age of Reason, existentialism. He analyzed poems with us, had us reading sections from John Ciardi's *How Does a Poem Mean?,* making a potentially difficult book accessible with his own explanations. We gave oral reports on poems Ciardi didn't cover. We imitated the styles of Conrad, Hemingway, and *Time* magazine. We wrote and talked, wrote and talked. The man immersed us in language.

Even MacFarland's barbs were literary. If Jim Fitzsimmons, 3
hung over and irritable, tried to smart-ass him, he'd rejoin with a flourish that would spark the indomitable Skip Madison—who'd lost his front teeth in a hapless tackle—to flick his tongue through the gap and opine, "good chop," drawing out the single "o" in stinging indictment. Jack MacFarland, this tobacco-stained intellectual, brandished linguistic weapons of a kind I hadn't encountered before. Here was this *egghead,* for God's sake, keeping some pretty difficult people in line. And from what I heard, Mike Dweetz and Steve Fusco and all the notorious Voc. Ed. crowd settled down as well when MacFarland took the podium. Though

a lot of guys groused in the schoolyard, it just seemed that giving trouble to this particular teacher was a silly thing to do. Tomfoolery, not to mention assault, had no place in the world he was trying to create for us, and instinctively everyone knew that. If nothing else, we all recognized MacFarland's considerable intelligence and respected the hours he put into his work. It came to this: The troublemaker would look foolish rather than daring. Even Jim Fitzsimmons was reading *On the Road* and turning his incipient alcoholism to literary ends.

There were some lives that were already beyond Jack MacFarland's ministrations, but mine was not. I started reading again as I hadn't since elementary school. I would go into our gloomy little bedroom or sit at the dinner table while, on the television, Danny McShane was paralyzing Mr. Moto with the atomic drop, and work slowly back through *Heart of Darkness,* trying to catch the words in Conrad's sentences. I certainly was not MacFarland's best student; most of the other guys in College Prep, even my fellow slackers, had better backgrounds than I did. But I worked very hard, for MacFarland had hooked me. He tapped my old interest in reading and creating stories. He gave me a way to feel special by using my mind. And he provided a role model that wasn't shaped on physical prowess alone, and something inside me that I wasn't quite aware of responded to that. Jack MacFarland established a literacy club, to borrow a phrase of Frank Smith's, and invited me—invited all of us—to join. 4

There's been a good deal of research and speculation suggesting that the acknowledgment of school performance with extrinsic rewards—smiling faces, stars, numbers, grades—diminishes the intrinsic satisfaction children experience by engaging in reading or writing or problem solving. While it's certainly true that we've created an educational system that encourages our best and brightest to become cynical grade collectors and, in general, have developed an obsession with evaluation and assessment, I must tell you that venal though it may have been, I loved getting good grades from MacFarland. I now know how subjective grades can be, but then they came tucked in the back of essays like bits of scientific data, some sort of spectroscopic readout that said, objectively and publicly, that I had made something of value. I suppose I'd been mediocre for too long and enjoyed a public redefinition. 5

And I suppose the workings of my mind, such as they were, had been private for too long. My linguistic play moved into the world; like the intergalactic stories I told years before on Frank's berry-splattered truck bed, these papers with their circled, red B-pluses and A-minuses linked my mind to something outside it. I carried them around like a club emblem.

One day in the December of my senior year, Mr. MacFarland asked me where I was going to go to college. I hadn't thought much about it. Many of the students I teach today spent their last year in high school with a physics text in one hand and the Stanford catalog in the other, but I wasn't even aware of what "entrance requirements" were. My folks would say that they wanted me to go to college and be a doctor, but I don't know how seriously I ever took that; it seemed a sweet thing to say, a bit of supportive family chatter, like telling a gangly daughter she's graceful. The reality of higher education wasn't in my scheme of things: No one in the family had gone to college; only two of my uncles had completed high school. I figured I'd get a night job and go to the local junior college because I knew that Snyder and Company were going there to play ball. But I hadn't even prepared for that. When I finally said, "I don't know," MacFarland looked down at me—I was seated in his office—and said, "Listen, you can write." 6

My grades stank. I had A's in biology and a handful of B's in a few English and social science classes. All the rest were C's—or worse. MacFarland said I would do well in his class and laid down the law about doing well in the others. Still, the record for my first three years wouldn't have been acceptable to any four-year school. To nobody's surprise, I was turned down flat by USC and UCLA. But Jack MacFarland was on the case. He had received his bachelor's degree from Loyola University, so he made calls to old professors and talked to somebody in admissions and wrote me a strong letter. Loyola finally accepted me as a probationary student. I would be on trial for the first year, and if I did okay, I would be granted regular status. MacFarland also intervened to get me a loan, for I could never have afforded a private college without it. Four more years of religion classes and four more years of boys at one school, girls at another. But at least I was going to college. Amazing. 7

Questions for Study and Discussion

1. Why do you think Rose chose the title "I Just Wanna Be Average"? (Glossary: *Title*) How does it relate to the essay?
2. Describe Jack MacFarland. How does his appearance contrast with his ability as a teacher?
3. Rose's paragraphs are long and full of information, but they are very coherent. Summarize in one sentence the topics of each of the seven paragraphs.
4. Analyze the transitions between paragraphs 2 and 3 and between 3 and 4. (Glossary: *Transitions*) What techniques does Rose use to smoothly introduce the reader to different aspects of his relationship with Jack MacFarland?
5. Rose introduces the reader to some of his classmates, quickly establishes their personalities, and names them in full: Jim Fitzsimmons, Skip Madison, Mike Dweetz. Why does he do this? How does it help him describe MacFarland?
6. Why does Rose have difficulty getting into college? How does he finally make it?

Vocabulary

Refer to your dictionary to define the following words as they are used in this selection. Then use each word in a sentence of your own.

beatnik (1)	linguistic (3)
curriculum (1)	incipient (3)
paradox (2)	ministrations (4)
existentialism (2)	extrinsic (5)
rejoin (3)	spectroscopic (5)
indomitable (3)	gangly (6)

Classroom Activity on Paragraphs

Write a unified, coherent, and adequately developed paragraph using one of the following topic sentences. Be sure to select details that clearly demonstrate/support the general statement you chose.

1. It was the noisiest place I had ever visited.
2. I was terribly frightened.
3. Signs of the sanitation strike were evident everywhere.
4. It was the best meal I've ever eaten.
5. Even though we lost, our team earned an "A" for effort.

Suggested Writing Assignments

1. Pick a good teacher whom you have had. Identify what about him or her was of importance and how he or she influenced your life. Write an essay about the teacher using this essay as a model. Make sure that each paragraph accomplishes a specific purpose and that each paragraph is coherent enough to be readily summarized.
2. Write an essay about the process you went through to get into college. Did you visit different schools? Did your parents pressure you to go? Have you always wanted to go to college, or did you make the decision later in high school, like Rose? Did any particular teacher(s) help you? Make sure that you develop your paragraphs fully and that you have effective transitions between paragraphs.

6

TRANSITIONS

Transitions are words and phrases that are used to signal the relationships between ideas in an essay and to join the various parts of an essay together. Writers use transitions to relate ideas within sentences, between sentences, and between paragraphs. Perhaps the most common type of transition is the so-called transitional expression. Following is a list of transitional expressions categorized according to their functions.

ADDITION: and, again, too, also, in addition, further, furthermore, moreover, besides

CAUSE AND EFFECT: therefore, consequently, thus, accordingly, as a result, hence, then, so

COMPARISON: similarly, likewise, by comparison

CONCESSION: to be sure, granted, of course, it is true, to tell the truth, certainly, with the exception of, although this may be true, even though, naturally

CONTRAST: but, however, in contrast, on the contrary, on the other hand, yet, nevertheless, after all, in spite of

EXAMPLE: for example, for instance

PLACE: elsewhere, here, above, below, farther on, there, beyond, nearby, opposite to, around

RESTATEMENT: that is, as I have said, in other words, in simpler terms, to put it differently, simply stated

SEQUENCE: first, second, third, next, finally

SUMMARY: in conclusion, to conclude, to summarize, in brief, in short

TIME: afterward, later, earlier, subsequently, at the same time, simultaneously, immediately, this time, until now, before, meanwhile, shortly, soon, currently, when, lately, in the meantime, formerly

Besides transitional expressions, there are two other important ways to make transitions: by using pronoun reference and by repeating key words and phrases. This paragraph begins with the phrase "Besides transitional expressions": the phrase contains the transitional word *besides* and also repeats an earlier idea. Thus the reader knows that this discussion is moving toward a new but related idea. Repetition can also give a word or idea emphasis: "Foreigners look to America as a land of freedom. Freedom, however, is not something all Americans enjoy."

Pronoun reference avoids monotonous repetition of nouns and phrases. Without pronouns, these two sentences are wordy and tiring to read: "Jim went to the concert, where he heard Beethoven's Ninth Symphony. Afterwards, Jim bought a recording of the Ninth Symphony." A more graceful and readable passage results if two pronouns are substituted in the second sentence: "Afterwards, he bought a recording of it." The second version has another advantage in that it is now more tightly related to the first sentence. The transition between the two sentences is smoother.

In the following example, notice how Rachel Carson uses transitional expressions, repetition of words and ideas, and pronoun reference:

> Under primitive agricultural conditions the farmer had few insect problems. *These* arose with the intensification of agriculture—the devotion of immense acreages to a single crop. *Such a system* set the stage for explosive increases in specific insect populations. Single-crop farming does not take advantage of the principles by which nature works; *it* is agriculture as an engineer might conceive it to be. Nature has introduced great variety into the landscape, but man has displayed a passion for simplifying *it. Thus he* undoes the built-in checks and balances by which nature holds the species within bounds. One important natural *check* is a limit on the amount of suitable habitat for each species. *Obviously then,* an insect that lives on wheat can build up its population to much higher levels on a farm de-

repeated key idea

pronoun reference

repeated key word

pronoun reference

pronoun reference

transitional expression; pronoun reference

transitional expression

voted to wheat than on one in which wheat is intermingled with other crops to which the insect is not adapted.

repeated key idea

The same thing happens in other situations. A generation or more ago, the towns of large areas of the United States lined their streets with the noble elm tree. *Now* the beauty *they* hopefully created is threatened with complete destruction as disease sweeps through the elms, carried by a beetle that would have only limited chance to build up large populations and to spread from tree to tree if the elms were only occasional trees in a richly diversified planting.

transitional expression; pronoun reference

Carson's transitions in this passage enhance its *coherence*—that quality of good writing that results when all sentences, paragraphs, and longer divisions of an essay are effectively and naturally connected.

Why I Want to Have a Family

Lisa Brown

When she wrote the following essay, Lisa Brown was a junior majoring in American studies at the University of Texas. In the essay, which was published as a "My Turn" column in the October 1984 issue of Newsweek on Campus, *she uses a variety of transitional devices to put together a coherent argument—that many women in their drive to succeed have overlooked the potential for fulfillment inherent in good relationships and family life. As you read, pay particular attention to the way Brown begins many of her sentences by establishing a clear and direct relationship to the sentences immediately preceding.*

For Your Journal

How do you feel about the idea of becoming a parent someday? What aspects of having children appeal to you most? Appeal to you least? In what ways will your career choice affect your decision to have a family?

For years the theory of higher education operated something like this: men went to college to get rich, and women went to college to marry rich men. It was a wonderful little setup, almost mathematical in its precision. To disturb it would have been to rock an American institution. 1

During the '60s, though, this theory lost much of its luster. As the nation began to recognize the idiocy of relegating women to a secondary role, women soon joined men in what once were male-only pursuits. This rebellious decade pushed women toward independence, showed them their potential and compelled them to take charge of their lives. Many women took the oppor- 2 tunity and ran with it. Since then feminine autonomy has been the rule, not the exception, at least among college women.

That's the good news. The bad news is that the invisible push 3 has turned into a shove. Some women are downright obsessive about success, to the point of becoming insular monuments to selfishness and fierce bravado, the condescending sort that hawks: "I don't need *anybody.* So there." These women dismiss children and marriage as unbearably outdated and potentially harmful to their up-and-coming careers. This notion of independence smacks of egocentrism. What do these women fear? Why can't they slow down long enough to remember that relationships and a family life are not inherently awful things?

Granted that for centuries women were on the receiving end 4 of some shabby treatment. Now, in an attempt to liberate college women from the constraints that forced them almost exclusively into teaching or nursing as a career outside the home—always subject to the primary career of motherhood—some women have gone too far. Any notion of motherhood seems to be regarded as an unpleasant reminder of the past, when homemakers were imprisoned by husbands, tots and household chores. In short, many women consider motherhood a time-consuming obstacle to the great joy of working outside the home.

The rise of feminism isn't the only answer. Growing up has 5 something to do with it, too. Most people find themselves in a bind as they hit their late 20s: they consider the ideals they grew up with and find that these don't necessarily mix with the ones they've acquired. The easiest thing to do, it sometimes seems, is to throw out the precepts their parents taught. Growing up, my friends and I were enchanted by the idea of starting new traditions. We didn't want self-worth to be contingent upon whether there was a man or child around the house to make us feel wanted.

I began to reconsider my values after my sister and a friend had 6 babies. I was entertained by their pregnancies and fascinated by the births; I was also thankful that I wasn't the one who had to change the diapers every day. I was a doting aunt only when I wanted to be. As my sister's and friend's lives changed, though, my attitude changed. I saw their days flip-flop between frustration and joy. Though these two women lost the freedom to run off to the beach or to a bar, they gained something else—an abstract happiness that reveals itself when they talk about Jessica's or

Amanda's latest escapade or vocabulary addition. Still in their 20s, they shuffle work and motherhood with the skill of poker players. I admire them, and I marvel at their kids. Spending time with the Jessicas and Amandas of the world teaches us patience and sensitivity and gives us a clue into our own pasts. Children are also reminders that there is a future and that we must work to ensure its quality.

Now I feel challenged by the idea of becoming a parent. I want 7
to decorate a nursery and design Halloween costumes; I want to answer my children's questions and help them learn to read. I want to be unselfish. But I've spent most of my life working in the opposite direction: toward independence, no emotional or financial strings attached. When I told a friend—one who likes kids but never, ever wants them—that I'd decided to accommodate motherhood, she accused me of undermining my career, my future, my life. "If that's all you want, then why are you even in college?" she asked.

The answer's simple: I want to be a smart mommy. I have solid 8
career plans and look forward to working. I make a distinction between wanting kids and wanting nothing but kids. And I've accepted that I'll have to give up a few years of full-time work to allow time for being pregnant and buying Pampers. As for undermining my life, I'm proud of my decision because I think it's evidence that the women's movement is working. While liberating women from the traditional childbearing role, the movement has given respectability to motherhood by recognizing that it's not a brainless task like dishwashing. At the same time, women who choose not to have children are not treated as oddities. That certainly wasn't the case even 15 years ago. While the graying, middle-aged bachelor was respected, the female equivalent—tagged a spinster—was automatically suspect.

Today, women have choices: about careers, their bodies, chil- 9
dren. I am grateful that women are no longer forced into motherhood as a function of their biology; it's senseless to assume that having a uterus qualifies anyone to be a good parent. By the same token, it is ridiculous for women to abandon all maternal desire because it might jeopardize personal success. Some women make the decision to go childless without ever analyzing their true needs or desires. They forget that motherhood can add to personal fulfillment.

I wish those fiercely independent women wouldn't look down 10
upon those of us who, for whatever reason, choose to forgo much of the excitement that runs in tandem with being single, liberated and educated. Excitement also fills a family life; it just comes in different ways.

I'm not in college because I'll learn how to make tastier pot 11
roast. I'm a student because I want to make sense of the world and of myself. By doing so, I think I'll be better prepared to be a mother to the new lives that I might bring into the world. I'll also be a better me. It's a package deal I don't want to turn down.

Questions for Study and Discussion

1. What is Brown arguing for in this essay? What does she say prompted a change in her attitude? (Glossary: *Attitude*)
2. Against what group is Brown arguing? What does she find wrong with the beliefs of that group? (Glossary: *Argument*)
3. What reasons does she provide for wanting to have a family?
4. Identify Brown's use of transitions in paragraphs 2, 3, 4, 6, 8, and 9. How do these help you as a reader to follow her point?
5. What are the implications of Brown's last two sentences in paragraph 6: "Spending time with the Jessicas and Amandas of the world teaches us patience and sensitivity and gives us a clue into our own pasts. Children are also reminders that there is a future and that we must work to ensure its quality"?
6. For what audience do you think this essay is intended? Do you think men would be as interested as women in the author's viewpoint? Explain. (Glossary: *Audience*)

Vocabulary

Refer to your dictionary to define the following words as they are used in this selection. Then use each word in a sentence of your own.

relegating (2)	precepts (5)
autonomy (2)	contingent (5)
insular (3)	doting (6)
bravado (3)	tandem (10)

Classroom Activity on Transitions

The following sentences, which make up the first paragraph of E. B. White's essay "Once More to the Lake," have been rearranged. Place the sentences in what seems to you a coherent sequence by relying on language signals such as transitions, repeated words, pronouns, and temporal references. Be prepared to explain your reasons for the placement of each sentence.

1. I have since become a salt-water man, but sometimes in summer there are days when the restlessness of the tides and the fearful cold of the sea water and the incessant wind which blows across the afternoon and into the evening make me wish for the placidity of a lake in the woods.
2. We all got ringworm from some kittens and had to rub Pond's Extract on our arms and legs night and morning, and my father rolled over in a canoe with all his clothes on; but outside of that the vacation was a success and from then on none of us ever thought there was any place in the world like that lake in Maine.
3. A few weeks ago this feeling got so strong I bought myself a couple of bass hooks and a spinner and returned to the lake where we used to go for a week's fishing and to revisit old haunts.
4. One summer, along about 1904, my father rented a camp on a lake in Maine and took us all there for the month of August.
5. We returned summer after summer—always on August 1st for one month.

Suggested Writing Assignments

1. Write an essay in which you argue any one of the following positions with regard to the women's movement: it has gone

too far; it is out of control; it is misdirected; it hasn't gone far enough or done enough; it needs to reach more women and men; it should lower its sights; a position of your own different from the above. Whichever position you argue, be sure that you provide sufficient evidence to support your point of view.

2. Complete the following statement and write an argument in support of it:

   The purpose of a college education is to ____________________
   ____ .

How I Got Smart

Steve Brody

Steve Brody is a retired high-school English teacher who enjoys writing about the lighter side of teaching. He was born in Chicago in 1915 and received his bachelor's degree in English from Columbia University. In addition to his articles in educational publications, Brody has published many newspaper articles on travel and a humorous book about golf, How to Break Ninety before You Reach It *(1979). As you read his account of how love made him smart, notice the way he uses transitional words and expressions to unify his essay and make it a seamless whole.*

For Your Journal

Motivation is a difficult topic about which to generalize. What motivates one person to act often will not work on another person. How do you get motivated to work, to join extracurricular activities, or to take care of yourself? Are you able to motivate yourself, or do you need to have someone else give you a push?

A common misconception among youngsters attending school is that their teachers were child prodigies. Who else but a bookworm, prowling the libraries and disdaining the normal youngster's propensity for play rather than study, would grow up to be a teacher anyway? 1

I tried desperately to explain to my students that the image they had of me as an ardent devotee of books and homework during my adolescence was a bit out of focus. Au contraire! I hated compulsory education with a passion. I could never quite accept the notion of having to go to school while the fish were biting. 2

Consequently, my grades were somewhat bearish. That's how my father, who dabbled in the stock market, described them. Presenting my report card for my father to sign was like serving him a subpoena. At midterm and other sensitive periods, my father kept a low profile. 3

But in my sophomore year, something beautiful and exciting happened. Cupid aimed his arrow and struck me squarely in the heart. All at once, I enjoyed going to school, if only to gaze at the lovely face beneath the raven tresses in English II. My princess sat near the pencil sharpener, and that year I ground up enough pencils to fuel a campfire. 4

Alas, Debbie was far beyond my wildest dreams. We were separated not only by five rows of desks, but by about 50 I.Q. points. She was the top student in English II, the apple of Mrs. Larrivee's eye. I envisioned how eagerly Debbie's father awaited her report card. 5

Occasionally, Debbie would catch me staring at her, and she would flash a smile—an angelic smile that radiated enlightenment and quickened my heartbeat. It was a smile that signaled hope and made me temporarily forget the intellectual gulf that separated us. 6

I schemed desperately to bridge that gulf. And one day, as I was passing the supermarket, an idea came to me. 7

A sign in the window announced that the store was offering the first volume of a set of encyclopedias at the introductory price of 29 cents. The remaining volumes would cost $2.49 each, but it was no time to be cynical. 8

I purchased Volume I—Aardvark to Asteroid—and began my venture into the world of knowledge. I would henceforth become a seeker of facts. I would become chief egghead in English II and sweep the princess off her feet with a surge of erudition. I had it all planned. 9

My first opportunity came one day in the cafeteria line. I looked behind me and there she was. 10

"Hi," she said. 11

After a pause, I wet my lips and said, "Know where anchovies come from?" 12

She seemed surprised. "No, I don't." 13

I breathed a sigh of relief. "The anchovy lives in salt water and is rarely found in fresh water." I had to talk fast, so that I could get all the facts in before we reached the cash register. "Fishermen 14 catch anchovies in the Mediterranean Sea and along the Atlantic coast near Spain and Portugal."

15 "How fascinating," said Debbie.

16 "The anchovy is closely related to the herring. It is thin and silvery in color. It has a long snout and a very large mouth."

17 "Incredible."

18 "Anchovies are good in salads, mixed with eggs, and are often used as appetizers before dinner, but they are salty and cannot be digested too rapidly."

19 Debbie shook her head in disbelief. It was obvious that I had made quite an impression.

20 A few days later, during a fire drill, I sidled up to her and asked, "Ever been to the Aleutian Islands?"

21 "Never have," she replied.

22 "Might be a nice place to visit, but I certainly wouldn't want to live there," I said.

23 "Why not?" said Debbie, playing right into my hands.

24 "Well, the climate is forbidding. There are no trees on any of the 100 or more islands in the group. The ground is rocky and very little plant life can grow on it."

25 "I don't think I'd even care to visit," she said.

26 The fire drill was over and we began to file into the building, so I had to step it up to get the natives in. "The Aleuts are short and sturdy and have dark skin and black hair. They subsist on fish, and they trap blue fox, seal and otter for their valuable fur."

27 Debbie's hazel eyes widened in amazement. She was undoubtedly beginning to realize that she wasn't dealing with an ordinary lunkhead. She was gaining new and valuable insights instead of engaging in the routine small talk one would expect from most sophomores.

28 Luck was on my side, too. One day I was browsing through the library during my study period. I spotted Debbie sitting at a table, absorbed in a crossword puzzle. She was frowning, apparently stumped on a word. I leaned over and asked if I could help.

29 "Four-letter word for Oriental female servant," Debbie said.

30 "Try *amah,*" I said, quick as a flash.

31 Debbie filled in the blanks, then turned to stare at me in amazement. "I don't believe it," she said. "I just don't believe it."

32 And so it went, that glorious, amorous, joyous sophomore year. Debbie seemed to relish our little conversations and hung on my every word. Naturally, the more I read, the more my confi-

dence grew. I expatiated freely on such topics as adenoids, air brakes, and arthritis.

In the classroom, too, I was gradually making my presence felt. 33
Among my classmates, I was developing a reputation as a wheeler-dealer in data. One day, during a discussion of Coleridge's "The Ancient Mariner," we came across the word *albatross*.

"Can anyone tell us what an albatross is?" asked Mrs. Larrivee. 34

My hand shot up. "The albatross is a large bird that lives mostly 35
in the ocean regions below the equator, but may be found in the north Pacific as well. The albatross measures as long as four feet and has the greatest wingspread of any bird. It feeds on the surface of the ocean, where it catches shellfish. The albatross is a very voracious eater. When it is full it has trouble getting into the air again."

There was a long silence in the room. Mrs. Larrivee couldn't 36
quite believe what she had just heard. I sneaked a peek at Debbie and gave her a big wink. She beamed proudly and winked back.

It was a great feeling, having Debbie and Mrs. Larrivee and my 37
peers according me respect and paying attention when I spoke.

My grades edged upward and my father no longer tried to avoid 38
me when I brought home my report card. I continued reading the encyclopedia diligently, packing more and more into my brain.

What I failed to perceive was that Debbie all this while was 39
going steady with a junior from a neighboring school—a hockey player with a C+ average. The revelation hit me hard, and for a while I felt like disgorging and forgetting everything I had learned. I had saved enough money to buy Volume II—Asthma to Bullfinch—but was strongly tempted to invest in a hockey stick instead.

How could she lead me on like that—smiling and concurring 40
and giving me the impression that I was important?

I felt not only hurt, but betrayed. Like Agamemnon, but with 41
less dire consequences, thank God.

In time I recovered from my wounds. The next year Debbie 42
moved from the neighborhood and transferred to another school. Soon she became no more than a fleeting memory.

Although the original incentive was gone, I continued poring 43
over the encyclopedias, as well as an increasing number of other books. Having savored the heady wine of knowledge, I could not now alter my course. For:

"A little knowledge is a dangerous thing:
Drink deep, or taste not the Pierian spring."

So wrote Alexander Pope, Volume XIV, Paprika to Pterodactyl. 44

Questions for Study and Discussion

1. Why didn't Brody stop reading the volumes of the encyclopedias when he discovered that Debbie had a steady boyfriend?
2. If you find Brody's narrative humorous, try to explain the sources of his humor. For example, what humor resides in the choice of examples Brody uses?
3. How are paragraphs 2 and 3, 3 and 4, 5 and 6, 31 and 32, and 43 and 44 linked? Identify the transitions that Brody uses in paragraph 35.
4. Brody refers to Coleridge's "The Ancient Mariner" in paragraph 33 and to Agamemnon in paragraph 41, and he quotes Alexander Pope in paragraph 43. Use an encyclopedia to explain Brody's allusions. (Glossary: *Allusion*)
5. Comment on the effectiveness of the beginning and ending of Brody's essay. (Glossary: *Beginnings and Endings*)
6. Brody could have told his story using far less dialogue than he did. What, in your opinion, would have been gained or lost had he done so? (Glossary: *Dialogue)*

Vocabulary

Refer to your dictionary to define the following words as they are used in this selection. Then use each word in a sentence of your own.

misconception (1)
prodigies (1)
devotee (2)
bearish (3)
dabbled (3)
surge (9)
erudition (9)
snout (16)
sidled (20)
forbidding (24)
subsist (26)
amorous (32)
expatiated (32)
adenoids (32)
voracious (35)
disgorging (39)
savored (43)

Classroom Activity on Transitions

In *The New York Times Complete Manual of Home Repair,* Bernard Gladstone gives directions for applying blacktop sealer to a driveway. His directions appear below in scrambled order. First read all of Gladstone's sentences carefully. Next, arrange the sentences in what seems to you to be the logical sequence. Finally, identify places where Gladstone has used transitional expressions, the repetition of words and ideas, and pronoun reference to give coherence to his paragraph.

1. A long-handled pushbroom or roofing brush is used to spread the coating evenly over the entire area.
2. Care should be taken to make certain the entire surface is uniformly wet, though puddles should be swept away if water collects in low spots.
3. Greasy areas and oil slicks should be scraped up, then scrubbed thoroughly with a detergent solution.
4. With most brands there are just three steps to follow.
5. In most cases one coat of sealer will be sufficient.
6. The application of blacktop sealer is best done on a day when the weather is dry and warm, preferably while the sun is shining on the surface.
7. This should not be applied until the first coat is completely dry.
8. First sweep the surface absolutely clean to remove all dust, dirt and foreign material.
9. To simplify spreading and to assure a good bond, the surface of the driveway should be wet down thoroughly by sprinkling with a hose.
10. However, for surfaces in poor condition a second coat may be required.
11. The blacktop sealer is next stirred thoroughly and poured on while the surface is still damp.
12. The sealer should be allowed to dry overnight (or longer if recommended by the manufacturer) before normal traffic is resumed.

Suggested Writing Assignments

1. One serious thought that arises as a result of reading Brody's essay is that perhaps we learn best when we are sufficiently motivated to do so. And once we are motivated, the desire to learn seems to feed on itself: "Having savored the heady wine of knowledge, I could not now alter my course" (43). Write an essay in which you explore this same subject using your own experiences.
2. Relationships can influence our lives either positively or negatively. Even the appearance of a relationship can have an effect, as we saw in Brody's infatuation with Debbie during his sophomore year in high school. By trying to impress Debbie with his knowledge, Brody got hooked on learning and chose a career in education. Write a brief essay in which you explore the effects that a relationship had on your life.

Becoming a Writer

Russell Baker

Russell Baker has had a long and distinguished career as a newspaper reporter and columnist. He was born in Virginia and attended Johns Hopkins University. In 1947 he got his first newspaper job with the Baltimore Sun, *then moved to the* New York Times *in 1954, where he covered national politics and has been writing the "Observer" column since 1962. His columns have been collected in numerous books over the years. In 1979 he received the George Polk Award for commentary and the Pulitzer Prize for distinguished commentary. Baker's memoir* Growing Up *also received a Pulitzer in 1983. His autobiographical follow-up,* The Good Times, *appeared in 1989. In addition to performing his writing duties, Baker has served as host of* Masterpiece Theatre *on PBS, succeeding Alistair Cooke in that role. As you read Baker's account of how he discovered his abilities as a writer, note how effectively he uses repetition of key words and ideas to achieve coherence and to emphasize his emotional responses to the events he describes.*

For Your Journal

Life is full of moments that change us, for better or worse, in major and minor ways. We decide what hobbies we like and dislike, whom we want to date and, perhaps, eventually marry, what we want to study in school, what career we eventually pursue. Identify an event that changed your life or helped you to make an important decision. How did it clarify your situation? How might your life be different if the event had never happened?

The notion of becoming a writer had flickered off and on in my head . . . but it wasn't until my third year in high school that the possibility took hold. Until then I'd been bored by everything associated with English courses. I found English grammar dull and baffling. I hated the assignments to turn out "compositions," and went at them like heavy labor, turning out laden, lackluster paragraphs that were agonies for teachers to read and for me to write. The classics thrust on me to read seemed as deadening as chloroform. 1

When our class was assigned to Mr. Fleagle for third-year English I anticipated another grim year in that dreariest of subjects. Mr. Fleagle was notorious among City students for dullness and inability to inspire. He was said to be stuffy, dull, and hopelessly out of date. To me he looked to be sixty or seventy and prim to a fault. He wore primly severe eyeglasses, his wavy hair was primly cut and primly combed. He wore prim vested suits with neckties blocked primly against the collar buttons of his primly starched white shirts. He had a primly pointed jaw, a primly straight nose, and a prim manner of speaking that was so correct, so gentlemanly, that he seemed a comic antique. 2

I anticipated a listless, unfruitful year with Mr. Fleagle and for a long time was not disappointed. We read *Macbeth*. Mr. Fleagle loved *Macbeth* and wanted us to love it too, but he lacked the gift of infecting others with his own passion. He tried to convey the murderous ferocity of Lady Macbeth one day by reading aloud the passage that concludes 3

> . . . I have given suck, and know
> How tender 'tis to love the babe that milks me.
> I would, while it was smiling in my face,
> Have plucked my nipple from his boneless gums . . .

The idea of prim Mr. Fleagle plucking his nipple from boneless gums was too much for the class. We burst into gasps of irrepressible snickering. Mr. Fleagle stopped.

"There is nothing funny, boys, about giving suck to a babe. It is the—the very essence of motherhood, don't you see." 4

He constantly sprinkled his sentences with "don't you see." It wasn't a question but an exclamation of mild surprise at our ignorance. "Your pronoun needs an antecedent, don't you see," he 5 would say, very primly. "The purpose of the Porter's scene, boys, is to provide comic relief from the horror, don't you see."

Late in the year we tackled the informal essay. "The essay, don't you see, is the. . . ." My mind went numb. Of all forms of writing, none seemed so boring as the essay. Naturally we would have to write informal essays. Mr. Fleagle distributed a homework sheet offering us a choice of topics. None was quite so simpleminded as "What I Did on My Summer Vacation," but most seemed to be almost as dull. I took the list home and dawdled until the night before the essay was due. Sprawled on the sofa, I finally faced up to the grim task, took the list out of my notebook, and scanned it. The topic on which my eye stopped was "The Art of Eating Spaghetti." 6

This title produced an extraordinary sequence of mental images. Surging up from the depths of memory came a vivid recollection of a night in Belleville when all of us were seated around the supper table—Uncle Allen, my mother, Uncle Charlie, Doris, Uncle Hal—and Aunt Pat served spaghetti for supper. Spaghetti was an exotic treat in those days. Neither Doris nor I had ever eaten spaghetti, and none of the adults had enough experience to be good at it. All the good humor of Uncle Allen's house reawoke in my mind as I recalled the laughing arguments we had that night about the socially respectable method for moving spaghetti from plate to mouth. 7

Suddenly I wanted to write about that, about the warmth and good feeling of it, but I wanted to put it down simply for my own joy, not for Mr. Fleagle. It was a moment I wanted to recapture and hold for myself. I wanted to relive the pleasure of an evening at New Street. To write it as I wanted, however, would violate all the rules of formal composition I'd learned in school, and Mr. Fleagle would surely give it a failing grade. Never mind. I would write something else for Mr. Fleagle after I had written this thing for myself. 8

When I finished it the night was half gone and there was no time left to compose a proper, respectable essay for Mr. Fleagle. There was no choice next morning but to turn in my private reminiscence of Belleville. Two days passed before Mr. Fleagle returned the graded papers, and he returned everyone's but mine. I was bracing myself for a command to report to Mr. Fleagle immediately after school for discipline when I saw him lift my paper from his desk and rap for the class's attention. 9

"Now, boys," he said, "I want to read you an essay. This is titled 'The Art of Eating Spaghetti.'" 10

And he started to read. My words! He was reading *my words* out loud to the entire class. What's more, the entire class was listening. Listening attentively. Then somebody laughed, then the entire class was laughing, and not in contempt and ridicule, but with openhearted enjoyment. Even Mr. Fleagle stopped two or three times to repress a small prim smile. 11

I did my best to avoid showing pleasure, but what I was feeling was pure ecstasy at this startling demonstration that my words had the power to make people laugh. In the eleventh grade, at the eleventh hour as it were, I had discovered a calling. It was the happiest moment of my entire school career. When Mr. Fleagle finished he put the final seal on my happiness by saying, "Now that, boys, is an essay, don't you see. It's—don't you see—it's of the very essence of the essay, don't you see. Congratulations, Mr. Baker." 12

For the first time, light shone on a possibility. It wasn't a very heartening possibility, to be sure. Writing couldn't lead to a job after high school, and it was hardly honest work, but Mr. Fleagle had opened a door for me. After that I ranked Mr. Fleagle among the finest teachers in the school. 13

Questions for Study and Discussion

1. How does Baker describe his English teacher, Mr. Fleagle, in the second paragraph? (Glossary: *Description*) Why does he repeat the word "prim" throughout the paragraph? Why is the vivid description important to the essay as a whole? (Glossary: *Dominant Impression*)
2. Baker gives Mr. Fleagle an identifiable voice. What is ironic about what Mr. Fleagle says? (Glossary: *Irony*) In what way does this irony contribute to Baker's purpose in writing the essay? (Glossary: *Purpose*)
3. What does Baker write about in his informal essay for Mr. Fleagle? Why does he write about this subject? Why doesn't he want to turn the essay in?
4. Baker's passage about Mr. Fleagle's choosing to read his essay to the class is critical to the impact of "Becoming a Writer."

Baker writes (paragraph 12): "And he started to read. My words! He was reading *my words* out loud to the entire class." Why do you think Baker repeats himself? Why is his wording more effective than a simple "And he started to read my essay to the class" would be?

5. Identify the transitions Baker uses between paragraphs from paragraph 4 to the end. Explain how they work to make the paragraphs flow smoothly from one to another.
6. What door had Mr. Fleagle opened for Baker? Why is Baker reluctant to pursue the opportunity that Mr. Fleagle provided to him?

Vocabulary

Refer to your dictionary to define the following words as they are used in this selection. Then use each word in a sentence of your own.

laden (1)
chloroform (1)
irrepressible (5)
antecedent (7)
reminiscence (11)

Classroom Activity on Transitions

Read the following three paragraphs. Provide transitions between paragraphs so that the narrative flows smoothly.

> In the late 1950s, I got lost on a camping trip in the Canadian wilderness. My only thought was to head south, towards warmth and civilization. My perilous journey was exhausting—the cold sapped my strength, and there were few places to find shelter and rest.
>
> There I found friendly faces and a warm fire. As I built my strength, I tried to communicate with the villagers, but they did not understand me. I came to the conclusion that I could stay in the village and wait—perhaps forever—for help to come, or I could strike out on my own again.
>
> I heard a gurgling sound. It was running water. Running water! Spring was here at last. Perhaps I would survive after all. I picked up my pack, squared my shoulders, and marched,

the afternoon sun a beautiful sight, still ahead, but starting to drift to my right.

Suggested Writing Assignments

1. Using as a model Baker's effort to write about eating spaghetti, write something from your own experience that you would like to record for yourself, not necessarily for the teacher. Don't worry about writing a formal essay; simply use language with which you are comfortable to convey why the event or experience is important to you.
2. Write an essay in which you describe how your perception of someone important in your life changed. How did you feel about the person at first? How do you feel now? What brought about the change? What impact did the transition have on you? Make sure your essay is coherent and flows well—use transitional expressions to help the reader follow the story of *your* transition.

7

Effective Sentences

Each of the following paragraphs describes the city of Vancouver. Although the content of both paragraphs is essentially the same, the first paragraph is written in sentences of nearly the same length and pattern and the second paragraph in sentences of varying length and pattern.

> Water surrounds Vancouver on three sides. The snow-crowned Coast Mountains ring the city on the northeast. Vancouver has a floating quality of natural loveliness. There is a curved beach at English Bay. This beach is in the shape of a half moon. Residential high rises stand behind the beach. They are in pale tones of beige, blue, and ice-cream pink. Turn-of-the-century houses of painted wood frown upward at the glitter of office towers. Any urban glare is softened by folds of green lawns, flowers, fountains, and trees. Such landscaping appears to be unplanned. It links Vancouver to her ultimate treasure of greenness. That treasure is thousand-acre Stanley Park. Surrounding stretches of water dominate. They have image-evoking names like False Creek and Lost Lagoon. Sailboats and pleasure craft skim blithely across Burrard Inlet. Foreign freighters are out in English Bay. They await their turn to take on cargoes of grain.

> Surrounded by water on three sides and ringed to the northeast by the snow-crowned Coast Mountains, Vancouver has a floating quality of natural loveliness. At English Bay, the half-moon curve of beach is backed by high rises in pale tones of beige, blue, and ice-cream pink. Turn-of-the-century houses of painted wood frown upward at the glitter of office towers. Yet any urban glare is quickly softened by folds of green lawns, flowers, fountains, and trees that in a seemingly unplanned fashion link Vancouver to her ultimate treasure of greenness—thousand-acre Stanley Park. And always it is the surrounding stretches of water that dominate, with their image-evoking names like False Creek and Lost Lagoon. Sailboats and pleasure craft skim blithely across Burrard Inlet,

> while out in English Bay foreign freighters await their turn to take on cargoes of grain.

The difference between these two paragraphs is dramatic. The first is monotonous because of the sameness of the sentences and because the ideas are not related to one another in a meaningful way. The second paragraph is much more interesting and readable; its sentences vary in length and are structured to clarify the relationships among the ideas. Sentence variety, an important aspect of all good writing, should not be used for its own sake, but rather to express ideas precisely and to emphasize the most important ideas within each sentence. Sentence variety includes the use of subordination, the periodic and loose sentence, the dramatically short sentence, the active and passive voice, and coordination.

Subordination, the process of giving one idea less emphasis than another in a sentence, is one of the most important characteristics of an effective sentence and a mature prose style. Writers subordinate ideas by introducing them either with subordinating conjunctions *(because, if, as though, while, when, after, in order that)* or with relative pronouns *(that, which, who, whomever, what).* Subordination not only deemphasizes some ideas, but also highlights others that the writer feels are more important.

Of course, there is nothing about an idea—*any* idea—that automatically makes it primary or secondary in importance. The writer decides what to emphasize, and he or she may choose to emphasize the less profound or noteworthy of two ideas. Consider, for example, the following sentence: "Melissa was reading a detective story the night TWA Flight 800 crashed into Long Island Sound." Everyone, including the author of the sentence, knows that the crash of Flight 800 is a more noteworthy event than Melissa's reading of the detective story. But the sentence concerns Melissa, not the plane crash, and so the fact that she was reading is stated in the main clause, while the crash is subordinated in a dependent clause.

Generally, writers place the ideas they consider important in main clauses, and other ideas go into dependent clauses. For example:

> When she was thirty years old, she made her first solo flight across the Atlantic.

> When she made her first solo flight across the Atlantic, she was thirty years old.

The first sentence emphasizes the solo flight; in the second, the emphasis is on the pilot's age.

Another way to achieve emphasis is to place the most important words, phrases, and clauses at the beginning or end of a sentence. The ending is the most emphatic part of a sentence; the beginning is less emphatic; and the middle is the least emphatic of all. The two sentences about the pilot put the main clause at the end, achieving special emphasis. The same thing occurs in a much longer kind of sentence, called a *periodic sentence.* Here is an example from John Updike:

> On the afternoon of the first day of spring, when the gutters were still heaped high with Monday's snow but the sky itself had been swept clean, we put on our galoshes and walked up the sunny side of Fifth Avenue to Central Park.

By holding the main clause back, Updike keeps his readers in suspense and so puts the most emphasis possible on his main idea.

A *loose sentence,* on the other hand, states its main idea at the beginning and then adds details in subsequent phrases and clauses. Rewritten as a loose sentence, Updike's sentence might read like this:

> We put on our galoshes and walked up the sunny side of Fifth Avenue to Central Park on the afternoon of the first day of spring, when the gutters were still heaped high with Monday's snow but the sky itself had been swept clean.

The main idea still gets plenty of emphasis, since it is contained in a main clause at the beginning of the sentence. Yet a loose sentence resembles the way people talk: it flows naturally and is easy to understand.

Another way to create emphasis is to use a *dramatically short sentence.* Especially following a long and involved sentence, a short declarative sentence helps drive a point home. Here are two examples, the first from Edwin Newman and the second from David Wise:

> Meaning no disrespect, I suppose there is, if not general rejoicing, at least some sense of relief when the football season ends. It's a long season.

> The executive suite on the thirty-fifth floor of the Columbia Broadcasting System skyscraper in Manhattan is a tasteful

> blend of dark wood paneling, expensive abstract paintings, thick carpets, and pleasing colors. It has the quiet look of power.

Finally, since the subject of a sentence is automatically emphasized, writers may choose to use the *active voice* when they want to emphasize the doer of an action and the *passive voice* when they want to downplay or omit the doer completely. Here are two examples:

> High winds pushed our sailboat onto the rocks, where the force of the waves tore it to pieces.

> Our sailboat was pushed by high winds onto the rocks, where it was torn to pieces by the force of the waves.

The first sentence emphasizes the natural forces that destroyed the boat, while the second sentence focuses attention on the boat itself. The passive voice may be useful in placing emphasis, but it has important disadvantages. As the examples show, and as the terms suggest, active-voice verbs are more vigorous and vivid than the same verbs in the passive voice. Then, too, some writers use the passive voice to hide or evade responsibility. "It has been decided" conceals who did the deciding, whereas "I have decided" makes all clear. So the passive voice should be used only when necessary—as it is in this sentence.

Often, a writer wants to place equal emphasis on several facts or ideas. One way to do this is to give each its own sentence. For example:

> Nancy Lopez selected her club. She lined up her shot. She chipped the ball to within a foot of the pin.

But a long series of short, simple sentences quickly becomes tedious. Many writers would combine these three sentences by using *coordination*. The coordinating conjunctions *and, but, or, nor, for, so,* and *yet* connect words, phrases, and clauses of equal importance:

> Nancy Lopez selected her club, lined up her shot, *and* chipped the ball to within a foot of the pin.

By coordinating three sentences into one, the writer not only makes the same words easier to read, but also shows that Lopez's three actions are equally important parts of a single process.

When parts of a sentence are not only coordinated but also grammatically the same, they are *parallel.* Parallelism in a sentence is created by balancing a word with a word, a phrase with a phrase, or a clause with a clause. Here is one example from the beginning of Mark Twain's *The Adventures of Huckleberry Finn:*

> Persons attempting to find a motive in this narrative will be prosecuted; persons attempting to find a moral in it will be banished; persons attempting to find a plot in it will be shot.

Parallelism is also often found in speeches. For example, in the last sentence of the Gettysburg Address Lincoln proclaims his hope that "government of the people, by the people, for the people, shall not perish from the earth."

Hitting Pay Dirt

Annie Dillard

Annie Dillard was born in 1945 in Pennsylvania and attended Hollins College in Virginia. Although she is known primarily as an essayist for such works as Pilgrim at Tinker Creek *(1974), which won a Pulitzer Prize, and* Teaching a Stone to Talk *(1982), she has demonstrated an impressive versatility in her publications:* Tickets for a Prayer Wheel *(1974), poetry;* Holy the Firm *(1977), a prose narrative;* Living by Fiction *(1982), literary theory;* An American Childhood *(1987), autobiography; and* The Living *(1992), a novel. In* The Writing Life *(1989), Dillard explores the processes of writing itself. As you read the selection below, taken from* An American Childhood, *pay particular attention to the way Dillard's active verbs give her sentences strength and emphasis. There is also a good example of parallel sentence structure in paragraph 5.*

For Your Journal

What was your favorite possession in your preteen years? How did you get it? Why was it special to you?

After I read *The Field Book of Ponds and Streams* several times, I longed for a microscope. Everybody needed a microscope. 1 Detectives used microscopes, both for the FBI and at Scotland Yard. Although usually I had to save my tiny allowance for things I wanted, that year for Christmas my parents gave me a microscope kit.

2 In a dark basement corner, on a white enamel table, I set up the microscope kit. I supplied a chair, a lamp, a batch of jars, a candle, and a pile of library books. The microscope kit supplied a blunt black three-speed microscope, a booklet, a scalpel, a

dropper, an ingenious device for cutting thin segments of fragile tissue, a pile of clean slides and cover slips, and a dandy array of corked test tubes.

One of the test tubes contained "hay infusion." Hay infusion was a wee brown chip of grass blade. You added water to it, and after a week it became a jungle in a drop, full of one-celled animals. This did not work for me. All I saw in the microscope after a week was a wet chip of dried grass, much enlarged. 3

Another test tube contained "diatomaceous earth." This was, I believed, an actual pinch of the white cliffs of Dover. On my palm it was an airy, friable chalk. The booklet said it was composed of the siliceous bodies of diatoms—one-celled creatures that lived in, as it were, small glass jewelry boxes with fitted lids. Diatoms, I read, come in a variety of transparent geometrical shapes. Broken and dead and dug out of geological deposits, they made chalk, and a fine abrasive used in silver polish and toothpaste. What I saw in the microscope must have been the fine abrasive—grit enlarged. It was years before I saw a recognizable, whole diatom. The kit's diatomaceous earth was a bust. 4

All that winter I played with the microscope. I prepared slides from things at hand, as the books suggested. I looked at the transparent membrane inside an onion's skin and saw the cell. I looked at a section of cork and saw the cells, and at scrapings from the inside of my cheek, ditto. I looked at my blood and saw not much; I looked at my urine and saw a long iridescent crystal, for the drop had dried. 5

All this was very well, but I wanted to see the wildlife I had read about. I wanted especially to see the famous amoeba, who had eluded me. He was supposed to live in the hay infusion, but I hadn't found him there. He lived outside in warm ponds and streams, too, but I lived in Pittsburgh, and it had been a cold winter. 6

Finally late that spring I saw an amoeba. The week before, I had gathered puddle water from Frick Park; it had been festering in a jar in the basement. This June night after dinner I figured I had waited long enough. In the basement at my microscope table I spread a scummy drop of Frick Park puddle water on a slide, peeked in, and lo, there was the famous amoeba. He was as blobby and grainy as his picture; I would have known him anywhere. 7

8 Before I had watched him at all, I ran upstairs. My parents were still at table, drinking coffee. They, too, could see the famous amoeba. I told them, bursting, that he was all set up, that they should hurry before his water dried. It was the chance of a lifetime.

9 Father had stretched out his long legs and was tilting back in his chair. Mother sat with her knees crossed, in blue slacks, smoking a Chesterfield. The dessert dishes were still on the table. My sisters were nowhere in evidence. It was a warm evening; the big dining-room windows gave onto blooming rhododendrons.

10 Mother regarded me warmly. She gave me to understand that she was glad I had found what I had been looking for, but that she and Father were happy to sit with their coffee, and would not be coming down.

11 She did not say, but I understood at once, that they had their pursuits (coffee?) and I had mine. She did not say, but I began to understand then, that you do what you do out of your private passion for the thing itself.

12 I had essentially been handed my own life. In subsequent years my parents would praise my drawings and poems, and supply me with books, art supplies, and sports equipment, and listen to my troubles and enthusiasms, and supervise my hours, and discuss and inform, but they would not get involved with my detective work, nor hear about my reading, nor inquire about my homework or term papers or exams, nor visit the salamanders I caught, nor listen to me play the piano, nor attend my field hockey games, nor fuss over my insect collection with me, or my poetry collection or stamp collection or rock collection. My days and nights were my own to plan and fill.

13 When I left the dining room that evening and started down the dark basement stairs, I had a life. I sat down to my wonderful amoeba, and there he was, rolling his grains more slowly now, extending an arc of his edge for a foot and drawing himself along by that foot, and absorbing it again and rolling on. I gave him some more pond water.

14 I had hit pay dirt. For all I knew, there were paramecia, too, in that pond water, or daphniae, or stentors, or any of the many other creatures I had read about and never seen: volvox, the spherical algal colony; euglena with its one red eye; the elusive,

glassy diatom; hydra, rotifers, water bears, worms. Anything was possible. The sky was the limit.

Questions for Study and Discussion

1. In her second sentence, Dillard says "Everybody needed a microscope." This confident yet naive statement indicates that she is writing from the point of view of herself as a child. (Glossary: *Point of View*) Why does she write her essay from this point of view?
2. Analyze the sentences in the first four paragraphs. How would you describe Dillard's use of sentence variety? Identify her very short sentences—those with eight or fewer words. What does each contribute to the essay?
3. Why does the microscope appeal to Dillard? How does she react to her early disappointments?
4. What do her parents do when Dillard sees the amoeba? Explain their response.
5. Is Dillard's diction appropriate for the essay's content and point of view? (Glossary: *Diction*) Defend your answer with specific examples from the essay.
6. Dillard says that she had been handed her own life. What does she mean? How did her parents communicate this transaction to her?
7. Why does Dillard say that she had hit pay dirt? In what way was the sky the limit in the drop of pond water?

Vocabulary

Refer to your dictionary to define the following words as they are used in this selection. Then use each word in a sentence of your own.

infusion (3)	iridescent (5)
friable (4)	festering (7)
siliceous (4)	

Classroom Activity on Effective Sentences

Rewrite the following paragraph, presenting the information in any order you choose. Use sentence variety and subordination as discussed in the chapter introduction to make the paragraph more interesting to read.

> When Billy saw the crime, he was in a grocery store buying hot dog buns for the barbecue he had scheduled for the next weekend. The crime was a burglary, and the criminal was someone you would never expect to see commit a crime. His basketball shoes squeaked as he ran away, and he looked no more than fifteen years old with a fresh, eager face that was the picture of innocence. Billy watched the youth steal a purse right off a woman's shoulder, and the bright sun reflected off the thief's forehead as he ran away, although the weather was quite chilly and had been for a week. The policeman who caught the thief tripped him and handcuffed him as Billy paid for the hot dog buns, got in his car, and drove away.

Suggested Writing Assignments

1. Write an essay about a particularly memorable experience you had with one or both of your parents. It can be a special trip, a conversation, a conflict, a quiet moment, or any time that was important to you. Pay close attention to your sentences and use them to emphasize what stands out in your mind about the experience.
2. Write a brief essay using one of the following sentences to focus and control the descriptive details you select. Place the sentence in the essay wherever it will have the greatest emphasis.

   The music stopped.
   It was broken glass.
   I started to sweat.
   Tears filled his eyes.
   I could see nothing.

SALVATION

Langston Hughes

Born in Joplin, Missouri, Langston Hughes (1902–1967), became an important figure in the African American cultural movement of the 1920s known as the Harlem Renaissance. He wrote poetry, fiction, and plays, and contributed columns to the New York Post *and the African American weekly the* Chicago Defender. *He is best known for* The Weary Blues *(1926) and other books of poetry that express his racial pride, his familiarity with African American traditions, and his understanding of blues and jazz rhythms. In the following selection from his autobiography* The Big Sea *(1940), note how Hughes varies the length and types of sentences he uses for the sake of emphasis. The impact of the dramatically short sentence in paragraph 12, for instance, derives from the variety of sentences preceding it.*

FOR YOUR JOURNAL

What role does religion play in your family? Do you consider yourself a religious person? Have you ever felt pressure from others to participate in religious activities? How did that make you feel?

I was saved from sin when I was going on thirteen. But not really saved. It happened like this. There was a big revival at my Auntie Reed's church. Every night for weeks there had been much preaching, singing, praying, and shouting, and some very hardened sinners had been brought to Christ, and the membership of the church had grown by leaps and bounds. Then just before the revival ended, they held a special meeting for children, "to bring the young lambs to the fold." My aunt spoke of it for 1 days ahead. That night I was escorted to the front row and placed on the mourners' bench with all the other young sinners, who had not yet been brought to Jesus.

My aunt told me that when you were saved you saw a light, and something happened to you inside! And Jesus came into your life! And God was with you from then on! She said you could see and hear and feel Jesus in your soul. I believed her. I had heard a great many old people say the same thing and it seemed to me they ought to know. So I sat there calmly in the hot, crowded church, waiting for Jesus to come to me. 2

The preacher preached a wonderful rhythmical sermon, all moans and shouts and lonely cries and dire pictures of hell, and then he sang a song about the ninety and nine safe in the fold, but one little lamb was left out in the cold. Then he said: "Won't you come? Won't you come to Jesus? Young lambs, won't you come?" And he held out his arms to all us young sinners there on the mourners' bench. And the little girls cried. And some of them jumped up and went to Jesus right away. But most of us just sat there. 3

A great many old people came and knelt around us and prayed, old women with jet-black faces and braided hair, old men with work-gnarled hands. And the church sang a song about the lower lights are burning, some poor sinners to be saved. And the whole building rocked with prayer and song. 4

Still I kept waiting to *see* Jesus. 5

Finally all the young people had gone to the altar and were saved, but one boy and me. He was a rounder's son named Westley. Westley and I were surrounded by sisters and deacons praying. It was very hot in the church, and getting late now. Finally Westley said to me in a whisper: "God damn! I'm tired o' sitting here. Let's get up and be saved." So he got up and was saved. 6

Then I was left all alone on the mourners' bench. My aunt came and knelt at my knees and cried, while prayers and songs swirled all around me in the little church. The whole congregation prayed for me alone, in a mighty wail of moans and voices. And I kept waiting serenely for Jesus, waiting, waiting—but he didn't come. I wanted to see him, but nothing happened to me. Nothing! I wanted something to happen to me, but nothing happened. 7

I heard the songs and the minister saying: "Why don't you come? My dear child, why don't you come to Jesus? Jesus is wait- 8 ing for you. He wants you. Why don't you come? Sister Reed, what is this child's name?"

"Langston," my aunt sobbed. 9

"Langston, why don't you come? Why don't you come and be 10
saved? Oh, Lamb of God! Why don't you come?"

Now it was really getting late. I began to be ashamed of myself, 11
holding everything up so long. I began to wonder what God thought about Westley, who certainly hadn't seen Jesus either, but who was now sitting proudly on the platform, swinging his knickerbockered legs and grinning down at me, surrounded by deacons and old women on their knees praying. God had not struck Westley dead for taking his name in vain or for lying in the temple. So I decided that maybe to save further trouble, I'd better lie, too, and say that Jesus had come, and get up and be saved.

So I got up. 12

Suddenly the whole room broke into a sea of shouting, as they 13
saw me rise. Waves of rejoicing swept the place. Women leaped in the air. My aunt threw her arms around me. The minister took me by the hand and led me to the platform.

When things quieted down, in a hushed silence, punctuated 14
by a few ecstatic "Amens," all the new young lambs were blessed in the name of God. Then joyous singing filled the room.

That night, for the last time in my life but one—for I was a big 15
boy twelve years old—I cried. I cried, in bed alone, and couldn't stop. I buried my head under the quilts, but my aunt heard me. She woke up and told my uncle I was crying because the Holy Ghost had come into my life, and because I had seen Jesus. But I was really crying because I couldn't bear to tell her that I had lied, that I had deceived everybody in the church, that I hadn't seen Jesus, and that now I didn't believe there was a Jesus any more, since he didn't come to help me.

Questions for Study and Discussion

1. What is salvation? Is it important to young Langston Hughes that he be saved? Why is it important to Langston's aunt that he be saved?
2. Why does young Langston expect to be saved at the revival meeting? Once the children are in church, what appeals are made to them to encourage them to seek salvation?

3. Why does young Langston cry on the night of his being "saved"? Why is the story of his being saved so ironic? (Glossary: *Irony*)
4. What would be gained or lost if the essay began with the first two sentences combined as follows: "I was saved from sin when I was going on thirteen, but I was not really saved"?
5. Identify the coordinating conjunctions in paragraph 3. Rewrite the paragraph without them. Compare your paragraph with the original, and explain what Hughes gains by using coordinating conjunctions. (Glossary: *Coordination*)
6. Identify the subordinating conjunctions in paragraph 15. What is it about the ideas in this last paragraph that makes it necessary for Hughes to use these subordinating conjunctions? (Glossary: *Subordination*)
7. How does Hughes's choice of words, or diction, help to establish a realistic atmosphere for a religious revival meeting? (Glossary: *Diction*)

Vocabulary

Refer to your dictionary to define the following words as they are used in this selection. Then use each word in a sentence of your own.

dire (3)
gnarled (4)
vain (11)
punctuated (14)
ecstatic (14)

Classroom Activity on Effective Sentences

Using coordination or subordination, rewrite each set of short sentences as a single sentence.

FOR EXAMPLE: This snow is good for Colorado's economy. Tourists are now flocking to ski resorts.

REVISED: This snow is good for Colorado's economy because tourists are now flocking to ski resorts.

1. I can take the 6:30 express train. I can catch the 7:00 bus.
2. Miriam worked on her research paper. She interviewed five people for the paper. She worked all weekend. She was tired.
3. Juan's new job kept him busy every day. He did not have time to work out at the gym for over a month.
4. The Statue of Liberty welcomes newcomers to America. It was a gift of the French government. It was completely restored for the nation's 200th birthday. It is over 120 years old.
5. Carla is tall. She is strong. She is a team player. She was the starting center on the basketball team.
6. Betsy loves Bach's music. She also likes Scott Joplin.

Suggested Writing Assignments

1. Like the young Langston Hughes, we sometimes find ourselves in situations in which, for the sake of conformity, we do things we do not believe in. Consider one such experience you have had, and write an essay about it. What is it about human nature that makes us occasionally act in ways that contradict our inner feelings? As you write, pay particular attention to your sentence variety.
2. Reread the introduction to this chapter. Then review one of the essays that you have written, paying particular attention to sentence structure. Recast sentences as necessary in order to make your writing more interesting and effective.

Playing to Win

Margaret A. Whitney

Margaret A. Whitney is a writer by profession. In the following piece, first published in 1988 in the New York Times Magazine, *she describes how her daughter overcame gender stereotypes in the face of social resistance against women in sports. As you read Whitney's account of her daughter Ann's love for sports, notice how the varied structures of her sentences enhance her descriptions. Pay particular attention to how she balances long and short sentences, as well as how she subordinates or coordinates ideas within sentences depending on what she wishes to emphasize.*

For Your Journal

Think about the role sports have played in your life and what they mean to you. Do you like to participate in a particular sport, or do you prefer the role of spectator?

My daughter is an athlete. Nowadays, this statement won't strike many parents as unusual, but it does me. Until her freshman year in high school, Ann was only marginally interested in sports of any kind. When she played, she didn't swing hard, often dropped the ball, and had an annoying habit of tittering on field or court. 1

Indifference combined with another factor that did not bode well for a sports career. Ann was growing up to be beautiful. By the eighth grade, nature and orthodontics had produced a 5-foot-8-inch, 125-pound, brown-eyed beauty with a wonderful smile. People told her, too. And, as many young women know, it is considered a satisfactory accomplishment to be pretty and stay pretty. Then you can simply sit still and enjoy the unconditional positive regard. Ann loved the attention too, and didn't consider it 2 demeaning when she was awarded "Best Hair," female category, in the eighth-grade yearbook.

So it came as a surprise when she became a jock. The first indication that athletic indifference had ended came when she joined the high-school cross-country team. She signed up in early September and ran third for the team within three days. Not only that. After one of those 3.1-mile races up hill and down dale on a rainy November afternoon, Ann came home muddy and bedraggled. Her hair was plastered to her head, and the mascara she had applied so carefully that morning ran in dark circles under her eyes. This is it, I thought. Wait until Lady Astor sees herself. But the kid with the best eighth-grade hair went on to finish the season and subsequently letter in cross-country, soccer, basketball and softball. 3

I love sports, she tells anyone who will listen. So do I, though my midlife quest for a doctorate leaves me little time for either playing or watching. My love of sports is bound up with the goals in my life and my hopes for my three daughters. I have begun to hear the message of sports. It is very different from many messages that women receive about living, and I think it is good. 4

My husband, for example, talked to Ann differently when he realized that she was a serious competitor and not just someone who wanted to get in shape so she'd look good in a prom dress. Be aggressive, he'd advise. Go for the ball. Be intense. 5

Be intense. She came in for some of the most scathing criticism from her dad, when, during basketball season, her intensity waned. You're pretending to play hard, he said. You like it on the bench? Do you like to watch while your teammates play? 6

I would think, how is this kid reacting to such advice? For years, she'd been told at home, at school, by countless advertisements, "Be quiet, Be good, Be still." When teachers reported that Ann was too talkative, not obedient enough, too flighty. When I dressed her up in frilly dresses and admonished her not to get dirty. When ideals of femininity are still, quiet, cool females in ads whose vacantness passes for sophistication. How can any adolescent girl know what she's up against? Have you ever really noticed intensity? It is neither quiet nor good. And it's definitely not pretty. 7

In the end, her intensity revived. At halftime, she'd look for her father, and he would come out of the bleachers to discuss tough 8 defense, finding the open player, squaring up on her jump shot. I'd watch them at the edge of the court, a tall man and a tall girl, talking about how to play.

Of course I'm particularly sensitive at this point in my life to messages about trying hard, being active, getting better through individual and team effort. Ann, you could barely handle a basketball two years ago. Now you're bringing the ball up against the press. Two defenders are after you. You must dribble, stop, pass. We're depending on you. We need you to help us. I wonder if my own paroxysms of uncertainty would be eased had more people urged me—be active, go for it! 9

Not that dangers don't lurk for the females of her generation. I occasionally run this horror show in my own mental movie theater: an unctuous but handsome lawyer-like drone of a young man spies my Ann. Hmmm, he says unconsciously to himself, good gene pool, and wouldn't she go well with my BMW and the condo? Then I see Ann with a great new hairdo kissing the drone goodbyehoney and setting off to the nearest mall with splendid-looking children to spend money. 10

But the other night she came home from softball tryouts at 6 in the evening. The dark circles under her eyes were from exhaustion, not makeup. I tried too hard today, she says. I feel like I'm going to puke. 11

After she has revived, she explains. She wants to play a particular position. There is competition for it. I can't let anybody else get my spot, she says, I've got to prove that I can do it. Later we find out that she has not gotten the much-wanted third-base position, but she will start with the varsity team. My husband talks about the machinations of coaches and tells her to keep trying. You're doing fine, he says. She gets that I-am-going-to-keep-trying look on her face. The horror-show vision of Ann-as-Stepford-Wife fades. 12

Of course, Ann doesn't realize the changes she has wrought, the power of her self-definition. I'm an athlete, Ma, she tells me when I suggest participation in the school play or the yearbook. But she has really caused us all to rethink our views of existence: her younger sisters who consider sports a natural activity for females, her father whose advocacy of women has increased, and me. Because when I doubt my own abilities, I say to myself, Get intense, Margaret. Do you like to sit on the bench? 13

And my intensity revives. 14

I am not suggesting that participation in sports is the answer 15
for all young women. It is not easy—the losing, jealousy, raw competition and intense personal criticism of performance.

And I don't wish to imply that the sports scene is a morality 16
play either. Girls' sports can be funny. You can't forget that out on that field are a bunch of people who know the meaning of the word cute. During one game, I noticed that Ann had a blue ribbon tied on her ponytail, and it dawned on me that every girl on the team had an identical bow. Somehow I can't picture the Celtics gathered in the locker room of the Boston Garden agreeing to wear the same color sweatbands.

No, what has struck me, amazed me and made me hold my 17
breath in wonder and in hope is both the ideal of sport and the reality of a young girl not afraid to do her best.

I watch her bringing the ball up the court. We yell encourage- 18
ment from the stands, though I know she doesn't hear us. Her face is red with exertion, and her body is concentrated on the task. She dribbles, draws the defense to her, passes, runs. A teammate passes the ball back to her. They've beaten the press. She heads toward the hoop. Her father watches her, her sisters watch her, I watch her. And I think, drive, Ann, drive.

Questions for Study and Discussion

1. Why was Whitney surprised that Ann became interested in sports? What social attitudes worked against Ann's becoming a good athlete? How does the author feel about these attitudes? How do you feel about these attitudes?
2. In paragraph 7 Whitney says, "ideals of femininity are still, quiet, cool females in ads whose vacantness passes for sophistication." Do you agree? Find some ads to support your answer.
3. Why does the author wish she had been told to "go for it" when she was younger? How does Whitney believe this would have changed her life? Do you agree with her reasoning?
4. Would you describe Whitney's tone (Glossary: *Tone*) as angry, frustrated, resigned, or something else? Is her tone different at different points in the essay or does it remain

consistent? Cite examples of her diction (Glossary: *Diction*) to support your answer.

5. Whitney mixes short, dramatic sentences with longer, more detailed ones. Choose several instances of this and comment on the possible reasons for this strategy. (Glossary: *Emphasis*)

Vocabulary

Refer to your dictionary to define the following words as they are used in this selection. Then use each word in a sentence of your own.

marginally (1)
titter (1)
bode (2)
bedraggled (3)
scathing (6)
wane (6)
admonish (7)
paroxysm (9)
unctuous (10)
machinations (12)
wrought (13)

Classroom Activity on Effective Sentences

Rewrite the following sets of sentences to combine short, simple sentences and to reduce repetition wherever possible.

FOR EXAMPLE: Angelo's team won the championship. He pitched a two-hitter. He struck out ten batters. He hit a home run.

REVISED: Angelo's team won the championship, because he pitched a two-hitter, struck out ten batters, and hit a home run.

1. Bonnie wore shorts. The shorts were red. The shorts had pockets.
2. The deer hunter awoke at 5:00 a.m. He ate a quick breakfast. The breakfast consisted of coffee, juice, and cereal. He was in the woods before the sun came up.
3. My grandparents played golf every weekend for years. Last year they stopped playing. They miss the game now.

4. Fly over any major city. Look out the airplane's window. You will be appalled at the number of tall smokestacks you will see.
5. It did not rain for over three months. Most crops in the region failed. Some farmers were on the brink of declaring bankruptcy.
6. Every weekday I go to work. I exercise. I shower and relax. I eat a light low-fat dinner.

Suggested Writing Assignments

1. Read or reread Langston Hughes's essay, "Salvation" (pp. 160–62). Write an essay in which you compare and contrast Whitney's variety of sentence structures with that of Hughes.
2. Without changing the meaning, rewrite the following paragraph using a variety of sentence structures to add interest and emphasis. When you have finished, add another paragraph to finish the idea, again paying attention to sentence structure.

    The score was 8 to 10. Allied was down. Allied was at bat. It was the bottom of the seventh inning. The bases were loaded. There were two strikes. There were two outs. Ronson's pitcher was throwing all strikes. Sweat was pouring from the batter's forehead. It was hot. The batter was nervous. This game determined the state champs. The state champs would go to the national tournament. The national tournament was in Washington, D.C. The batter took some practice swings. The batter pivoted the ball of her foot into the ground. The dirt was dusty. Dust flew into the umpire's face. The batter was ready. The batter nodded to the pitcher.

38 Who Saw Murder Didn't Call Police

Martin Gansberg

Martin Gansberg (1920–1995) was born in Brooklyn, New York, and graduated from St. John's University. A long-time reporter, Gansberg wrote the following essay for the New York Times *two weeks after the early morning events he so poignantly narrates. Once you've finished reading the essay, you will understand why it has been so often reprinted and why the name Kitty Genovese is still invoked whenever questions of public apathy arise. Gansberg uses dialogue effectively to emphasize his point. Pay particular attention to how he constructs the sentences that incorporate dialogue and to how subordination and coordination often determine where quoted material appears.*

For Your Journal

Have you ever witnessed an accident or a crime? How did you react to the situation—did you come forward and testify, or did you choose not to get involved? Why do you think you reacted the way you did? How do you feel about your behavior?

For more than half an hour 38 respectable, law-abiding citizens in Queens watched a killer stalk and stab a woman in three separate attacks in Kew Gardens. 1

Twice their chatter and the sudden glow of their bedroom lights interrupted him and frightened him off. Each time he returned, sought her out, and stabbed her again. Not one person telephoned the police during the assault; one witness called after the woman was dead. 2

That was two weeks ago today. 3

Still shocked is Assistant Chief Inspector Frederick M. Lussen, 4
in charge of the borough's detectives and a veteran of 25 years of homicide investigations. He can give a matter-of-fact recitation on many murders. But the Kew Gardens slaying baffles him—not because it is a murder, but because the "good people" failed to call the police.

"As we have reconstructed the crime," he said, "the assailant 5
had three chances to kill this woman during a 35-minute period. He returned twice to complete the job. If we had been called when he first attacked, the woman might not be dead now."

This is what the police say happened beginning at 3:20 A.M. in 6
the staid, middle-class, tree-lined Austin Street area:

Twenty-eight-year-old Catherine Genovese, who was called 7
Kitty by almost everyone in the neighborhood, was returning home from her job as manager of a bar in Hollis. She parked her red Fiat in a lot adjacent to the Kew Gardens Long Island Rail Road Station, facing Mowbray Place. Like many residents of the neighborhood, she had parked there day after day since her arrival from Connecticut a year ago, although the railroad frowns on the practice.

She turned off the lights of her car, locked the door, and started 8
to walk the 100 feet to the entrance of her apartment at 82-70 Austin Street, which is in a Tudor building, with stores in the first floor and apartments on the second.

The entrance to the apartment is in the rear of the building be- 9
cause the front is rented to retail stores. At night the quiet neighborhood is shrouded in the slumbering darkness that marks most residential areas.

Miss Genovese noticed a man at the far end of the lot, near a 10
seven-story apartment house at 82-40 Austin Street. She halted. Then, nervously, she headed up Austin Street toward Lefferts Boulevard, where there is a call box to the 102nd Police Precinct in nearby Richmond Hill.

She got as far as a street light in front of a bookstore before 11
the man grabbed her. She screamed. Lights went on in the 10-story apartment house at 82-67 Austin Street, which faces the bookstore. Windows slid open and voices punctuated the early-morning stillness.

Miss Genovese screamed: "Oh, my God, he stabbed me! Please 12
help me! Please help me!"

From one of the upper windows in the apartment house, a 13
man called down: "Let that girl alone!"

The assailant looked up at him, shrugged, and walked down 14
Austin Street toward a white sedan parked a short distance away. Miss Genovese struggled to her feet.

Lights went out. The killer returned to Miss Genovese, now try- 15
ing to make her way around the side of the building by the parking lot to get to her apartment. The assailant stabbed her again.

"I'm dying!" she shrieked. "I'm dying!" 16

Windows were opened again, and lights went on in many apart- 17
ments. The assailant got into his car and drove away. Miss Genovese staggered to her feet. A city bus, O-10, the Lefferts Boulevard line to Kennedy International Airport, passed. It was 3:35 A.M.

The assailant returned. By then, Miss Genovese had crawled 18
to the back of the building, where the freshly painted brown doors to the apartment house held out hope for safety. The killer tried the first door; she wasn't there. At the second door, 82-62 Austin Street, he saw her slumped on the floor at the foot of the stairs. He stabbed her a third time—fatally.

It was 3:50 by the time the police received their first call, from 19
a man who was a neighbor of Miss Genovese. In two minutes they were at the scene. The neighbor, a 70-year-old woman, and another woman were the only persons on the street. Nobody else came forward.

The man explained that he had called the police after much de- 20
liberation. He had phoned a friend in Nassau County for advice and then he had crossed the roof of the building to the apartment of the elderly woman to get her to make the call.

"I didn't want to get involved," he sheepishly told the police. 21

Six days later, the police arrested Winston Moseley, a 29-year- 22
old business-machine operator, and charged him with homicide. Moseley had no previous record. He is married, has two children and owns a home at 133-19 Sutter Avenue, South Ozone Park, Queens. On Wednesday, a court committed him to Kings County Hospital for psychiatric observation.

When questioned by the police, Moseley also said that he had 23
slain Mrs. Annie May Johnson, 24, of 146-12 133d Avenue, Jamaica, on Feb. 29 and Barbara Kralik, 15, of 174-17 140th Ave-

nue, Springfield Gardens, last July. In the Kralik case, the police are holding Alvin L. Mitchell, who is said to have confessed to that slaying.

The police stressed how simple it would have been to have got- 24
ten in touch with them. "A phone call," said one of the detectives, "would have done it." The police may be reached by dialing "O" for operator or SPring 7-3100.

Today witnesses from the neighborhood, which is made up of 25
one-family homes in the $35,000 to $60,000 range with the exception of the two apartment houses near the railroad station, find it difficult to explain why they didn't call the police.

A housewife, knowingly if quite casually, said, "We thought it 26
was a lovers' quarrel." A husband and wife both said, "Frankly, we were afraid." They seemed aware of the fact that events might have been different. A distraught woman, wiping her hands in her apron, said, "I didn't want my husband to get involved."

One couple, now willing to talk about that night, said they heard 27
the first screams. The husband looked thoughtfully at the bookstore where the killer first grabbed Miss Genovese.

"We went to the window to see what was happening," he said, 28
"but the light from our bedroom made it difficult to see the street." The wife, still apprehensive, added: "I put out the light and we were able to see better."

Asked why they hadn't called the police, she shrugged and re- 29
plied: "I don't know."

A man peeked out from a slight opening in the doorway to his 30
apartment and rattled off an account of the killer's second attack. Why hadn't he called the police at the time? "I was tired," he said without emotion. "I went back to bed."

It was 4:25 A.M. when the ambulance arrived to take the body 31
of Miss Genovese. It drove off. "Then," a solemn police detective said, "the people came out."

Questions for Study and Discussion

1. What is the author's purpose in this selection? What are the advantages or disadvantages in using narration to accomplish this purpose? Explain. (Glossary: *Purpose*)

2. Where does the narrative actually begin? What is the function of the material that precedes the beginning of the narrative proper? (Glossary: *Narration*)
3. What reasons did Kitty Genovese's neighbors give for not calling the police when they first heard her calls for help? What, in your opinion, do their reasons say about contemporary American society? Explain.
4. How would you describe Gansberg's tone? Is the tone appropriate for the story Gansberg narrates? Explain. (Glossary: *Tone*)
5. Gansberg uses dialogue throughout his essay. How many people does he quote? What does he accomplish by using dialogue? (Glossary: *Dialogue)*
6. What do you think Gansberg achieves by giving the addresses of the other victims in paragraph 23? (Glossary: *Details*)
7. Reflect on Gansberg's ending. What would be lost or gained by adding a paragraph that analyzed the meaning of the narrative for the reader? (Glossary: *Beginnings and Endings*)

Vocabulary

Refer to your dictionary to define the following words as they are used in this selection. Then use each word in a sentence of your own.

stalk (1)
recitation (4)
assailant (5)
staid (6)
shrouded (9)
sheepishly (21)
apprehensive (28)

Classroom Activity on Effective Sentences

Repetition can be an effective writing device to emphasize important points and to enhance coherence. Unless it is handled carefully, however, it can often result in a tedious piece of writing. Rewrite the following paragraph, either eliminating repetition or reworking the repetitions to improve coherence and to emphasize important information.

Day care centers should be available to all women who work and have no one to care for their children. Day care centers should not be available only to women who are raising their children alone or to families whose income is below the poverty level. All women who work should have available to them care for their children that is reliable, responsible, convenient, and that does not cost an exorbitant amount. Women who work need and must demand more day care centers. No woman should be prevented from working because of the lack of convenient and reliable facilities for child care.

Suggested Writing Assignments

1. Gansberg's essay is about public apathy and fear. What is your own experience with the public? Modeling an essay after Gansberg's, narrate another event or series of events that you personally know about. Or, write a narration about public involvement, one that contradicts Gansberg's essay.
2. It is common when using narration to tell about firsthand experience and to tell the story in the first person. It is good practice, however, to try writing a narration about something you don't know about firsthand but must learn about, much as a newspaper reporter gathers information for a story. For several days, be attentive to events occurring around you—in your neighborhood, school, community, region—events that would be appropriate for a narrative essay. Interview the principal characters involved in your story, take detailed notes, and then write your narration.

8

DICTION AND TONE

Diction

Diction refers to a writer's choice and use of words. Good diction is precise and appropriate—the words mean exactly what the writer intends, and the words are well suited to the writer's subject, purpose, and intended audience.

For careful writers it is not enough merely to come close to saying what they want to say; they select words that convey their exact meaning. Perhaps Mark Twain put this best when he said, "The difference between the right word and the almost right word is the difference between lightning and the lightning bug." Inaccurate, imprecise, or inappropriate diction not only fails to convey the writer's intended meaning but also may cause confusion and misunderstanding for the reader.

Connotation and Denotation

Both connotation and denotation refer to the meanings of words. Denotation is the dictionary meaning of a word, the literal meaning. Connotative meanings are the associations or emotional overtones that words have acquired gradually. For example, the word *home* denotes a place where someone lives, but it connotes warmth, security, family, comfort, affection, and other more private thoughts and images. The word *residence* also denotes a place where someone lives, but its connotations are colder and more formal.

Many words in English have synonyms, words with very similar denotations—for example, *mob, crowd, multitude,* and *bunch.* Deciding which to use depends largely on the connotations that each synonym has and the context in which the word is to be used. For example, you might say, "There was a crowd at the lecture," but not "There was a mob at the lecture." Good writers are sensitive to both the denotations and the connotations of words.

Abstract and Concrete Words

Abstract words name ideas, conditions, emotions—things nobody can touch, see, or hear. Some abstract words are *love, wisdom, cowardice, beauty, fear,* and *liberty.* People often disagree about abstract things. You may find a forest beautiful, while someone else might find it frightening, and neither of you would be wrong. Beauty and fear are abstract ideas; they exist in your mind, not in the forest along with the trees and the owls. Concrete words refer to things we can touch, see, hear, smell, and taste, such as *sandpaper, soda, birch trees, smog, cow, sailboat, rocking chair,* and *pancake.* If you disagree with someone on a concrete issue—say, you claim that the forest is mostly birch trees, while the other person says it is mostly pine—only one of you can be right, and both of you can be wrong; what kinds of trees grow in the forest is a concrete fact, not an abstract idea.

Good writing balances ideas and facts, and it also balances abstract and concrete diction. If the writing is too abstract, with too few concrete facts and details, it will be unconvincing and tiresome. If the writing is too concrete, devoid of ideas and emotions, it can seem pointless and dry.

General and Specific Words

General and *specific* do not necessarily refer to opposites. The same word can often be either general or specific, depending on the context: *dessert* is more specific than *food,* but more general than *chocolate cream pie.* Being very specific is like being concrete: *chocolate cream pie* is something you can see and taste. Being general, on the other hand, is like being abstract. *Food, dessert,* and even *pie* are general classes of things that bring no particular taste or image to mind.

Good writing moves back and forth from the general to the specific. Without specific words, generalities can be unconvincing and even confusing: the writer's idea of "good food" may be very different from the reader's. But writing that does not relate specifics to each other by generalization often lacks focus and direction.

Clichés

Some words, phrases, and expressions have become trite through overuse. Let's assume your roommate has just returned from an evening out. You ask her "How was the concert?" She responds, "The concert was okay, but they had us *packed in* there *like sardines.* How was your evening?" And you reply, "Well, I finished my term paper, but the noise here is enough to *drive me crazy.* The dorm is a real *zoo.*" At one time the italicized expressions were vivid and colorful, but through constant use they have grown stale and ineffective. The experienced writer always tries to avoid such clichés as *believe it or not, doomed to failure, hit the spot, let's face it, sneaking suspicion, step in the right direction,* and *went to great lengths.*

Jargon

Jargon, or technical language, is the special vocabulary of a trade or profession. Writers who use jargon do so with an awareness of their audience. If their audience is a group of coworkers or professionals, jargon may be used freely. If the audience is more general, jargon should be used sparingly and carefully so that readers can understand it. Jargon becomes inappropriate when it is overused, used out of context, or used pretentiously. For example, computer terms such as *input, output,* and *feedback* are sometimes used in place of *contribution, result,* and *response* in other fields, especially in business. If you think about it, the terms suggest that people are machines, receiving and processing information according to a program imposed by someone else.

Formal and Informal Diction

Diction is appropriate when it suits the occasion for which it is intended. If the situation is informal—a friendly letter, for example—the writing may be colloquial; that is, its words may be chosen to suggest the way people talk with each other. If, on the other hand, the situation is formal—a term paper or a research report, for example—then the words should reflect this formality. Informal writing tends to be characterized by slang, contractions, references to the reader, and concrete nouns. Formal writing tends to be impersonal, abstract, and free of contractions and references to the reader. Formal writing and informal writing are, of course, the extremes. Most writing falls between these two extremes and is a blend of those formal and informal elements that best fit the context.

Tone

Tone is the attitude a writer takes toward the subject and the audience. The tone may be friendly or hostile, serious or humorous, intimate or distant, enthusiastic or skeptical.

As you read the following paragraphs, notice how each writer has created a different tone and how that tone is supported by the diction—the writer's particular choice and use of words.

Nostalgic

> My generation is special because of what we missed rather than what we got, because in a certain sense we are the first and the last. The first to take technology for granted. (What was a space shot to us, except an hour cut from Social Studies to gather before a TV in the gym as Cape Canaveral counted down?) The first to grow up with TV. My sister was 8 when we got our set, so to her it seemed magic and always somewhat foreign. She had known books already and would never really replace them. But for me, the TV set was, like the kitchen sink and the telephone, a fact of life.
>
> Joyce Maynard, "An 18-Year-Old Looks Back on Life"

Angry

> Cans. Beer cans. Glinting on the verges of a million miles of roadways, lying in scrub, grass, dirt, leaves, sand, mud, but never hidden. Piels, Rheingold, Ballantine, Schaefer, Schlitz, shining in the sun or picked by moon or the beams of headlights at night; washed by rain or flattened by wheels, but

never dulled, never buried, never destroyed. Here is the mark of savages, the testament of wasters, the stain of prosperity.

Marya Mannes, "Wasteland"

Humorous

In perpetrating a revolution, there are two requirements: someone or something to revolt against and someone to actually show up and do the revolting. Dress is usually casual and both parties may be flexible about time and place but if either faction fails to attend the whole enterprise is likely to come off badly. In the Chinese Revolution of 1650 neither party showed up and the deposit on the hall was forfeited.

Woody Allen, "A Brief, Yet Helpful Guide to Civil Disobedience"

Resigned

I make my living humping cargo for Seaboard World Airlines, one of the big international airlines at Kennedy Airport. They handle strictly all cargo. I was once told that one of the Rockefellers is the major stockholder for the airline, but I don't really think about that too much. I don't get paid to think. The big thing is to beat that race with the time clock every morning of your life so the airline will be happy. The worst thing a man could ever do is to make suggestions about building a better airline. They pay people $40,000 a year to come up with better ideas. It doesn't matter that these ideas never work; it's just that they get nervous when a guy from South Brooklyn or Ozone Park acts like he has a brain.

Patrick Fenton, "Confessions of a Working Stiff"

Ironic

Once upon a time there was a small, beautiful, green and graceful country called Vietnam. It needed to be saved. (In later years no one could remember exactly what it needed to be saved from, but that is another story.) For many years Vietnam was in the process of being saved by France, but the French eventually tired of their labors and left. Then America took on the job. America was well equipped for country-saving. It was the richest and most powerful nation on earth. It had, for example, nuclear explosives on hand and ready to

> use equal to six tons of TNT for every man, woman, and child in the world. It had huge and very efficient factories, brilliant and dedicated scientists, and most (but not everybody) would agree, it had good intentions. Sadly, America had one fatal flaw—its inhabitants were in love with technology and thought it could do no wrong. A visitor to America during the time of this story would probably have guessed its outcome after seeing how its inhabitants were treating their own country. The air was mostly foul, the water putrid, and most of the land was either covered with concrete or garbage. But Americans were never much on introspection, and they didn't foresee the result of their loving embrace on the small country. They set out to save Vietnam with the same enthusiasm and determination their forefathers had displayed in conquering the frontier.
>
> The Sierra Club, "A Fable for Our Times"

The diction and tone of an essay are subtle forces, but they exert a tremendous influence on readers. They are instrumental in determining how we will feel while reading the essay and what attitude we will have toward its argument or the points that it makes. Of course, readers react in a variety of ways. An essay written informally but with a largely angry tone may make one reader defensive and unsympathetic; another may feel that the author is being unusually honest and courageous, and may admire these qualities and feel moved by them. Either way, the diction and tone of the piece have made a strong emotional impression. As you read the essays in this chapter and throughout this book, see if you can analyze how the diction and tone are shaping your reactions.

On Being 17, Bright, and Unable to Read

David Raymond

When the following article appeared in the New York Times *in 1976, David Raymond was a high-school student in Connecticut. In 1981 Raymond graduated from Curry College outside of Boston, one of the few colleges with learning-disability programs at the time. He and his family now live in Fairfield, Connecticut, where he works as a builder. In his essay he poignantly discusses the great difficulties he had with reading because of his dyslexia and the many problems he experienced in school as a result. As you read, pay particular attention to the natural quality of the words he uses to convey his ideas, and how that naturalness of diction contributes to the essay's informal yet sincere tone.*

For Your Journal

One of the fundamental skills that we are supposed to learn in school is how to read. How would you rate yourself as a reader? Would you like to be able to read better? How important is reading in your everyday life?

One day a substitute teacher picked me to read aloud from the textbook. When I told her "No, thank you," she came unhinged. She thought I was acting smart, and told me so. I kept calm, and that got her madder and madder. We must have spent 10 minutes trying to solve the problem, and finally she got so red in the face I thought she'd blow up. She told me she'd see me after class. 1

Maybe someone like me was a new thing for that teacher. But she wasn't new to me. I've been through scenes like that all my life. You see, even though I'm 17 and a junior in high school, I 2 can't read because I have dyslexia. I'm told I read "at a fourth-grade level," but from where I sit, that's not reading. You can't know what that means unless you've been there. It's not easy to tell how it feels when you can't read your homework assignments or the newspaper or a menu in a restaurant or even notes from your own friends.

My family began to suspect I was having problems almost 3
from the first day I started school. My father says my early years in school were the worst years of his life. They weren't so good for me, either. As I look back on it now, I can't find the words to express how bad it really was. I wanted to die. I'd come home from school screaming, "I'm dumb. I'm dumb—I wish I were dead!"

I guess I couldn't read anything at all then—not even my own 4
name—and they tell me I didn't talk as good as other kids. But what I remember about those days is that I couldn't throw a ball where it was supposed to go, I couldn't learn to swim, and I wouldn't learn to ride a bike, because no matter what anyone told me, I knew I'd fail.

Sometimes my teachers would try to be encouraging. When I 5
couldn't read the words on the board they'd say, "Come on, David, you know that word." Only I didn't. And it was embarrassing. I just felt dumb. And dumb was how the kids treated me. They'd make fun of me every chance they got, asking me to spell "cat" or something like that. Even if I knew how to spell it, I wouldn't; they'd only give me another word. Anyway, it was awful, because more than anything I wanted friends. On my birthday when I blew out the candles I didn't wish I could learn to read; what I wished for was that the kids would like me.

With the bad reports coming from school, and with me moan- 6
ing about wanting to die and how everybody hated me, my parents began looking for help. That's when the testing started. The school tested me, the child-guidance center tested me, private psychiatrists tested me. Everybody knew something was wrong—especially me.

It didn't help much when they stuck a fancy name onto it. I 7
couldn't pronounce it then—I was only in second grade—and I was ashamed to talk about it. Now it rolls off my tongue, because I've been living with it for a lot of years—dyslexia.

All through elementary school it wasn't easy. I was always hav- 8
ing to do things that were "different," things the other kids didn't have to do. I had to go to a child psychiatrist, for instance.

One summer my family forced me to go to a camp for children with reading problems. I hated the idea, but the camp turned out pretty good, and I had a good time. I met a lot of kids who couldn't read and somehow that helped. The director of the camp said I had a higher I.Q. than 90 percent of the population. I didn't believe him. 9

About the worst thing I had to do in fifth and sixth grade was go to a special education class in another school in our town. A bus picked me up, and I didn't like that at all. The bus also picked up emotionally disturbed kids and retarded kids. It was like going to a school for the retarded. I always worried that someone I knew would see me on that bus. It was a relief to go to the regular junior high school. 10

Life began to change a little for me then, because I began to feel better about myself. I found the teachers cared; they had meetings about me and I worked harder for them for a while. I began to work on the potter's wheel, making vases and pots that the teachers said were pretty good. Also, I got a letter for being on the track team. I could always run pretty fast. 11

At high school the teachers are good and everyone is trying to help me. I've gotten honors some marking periods and I've won a letter on the cross-country team. Next quarter I think the school might hold a show of my pottery. I've got some friends. But there are still some embarrassing times. For instance, every time there is writing in the class, I get up and go to the special education room. Kids ask me where I go all the time. Sometimes I say, "to Mars." 12

Homework is a real problem. During free periods in school I go into the special ed room and staff members read assignments to me. When I get home my mother reads to me. Sometimes she reads an assignment into a tape recorder, and then I go into my room and listen to it. If we have a novel or something like that to read, she reads it out loud to me. Then I sit down with her and we do the assignment. She'll write, while I talk my answers to her. Lately I've taken to dictating into a tape recorder, and then someone—my father, a private tutor or my mother—types up what I've dictated. Whatever homework I do takes someone else's time, too. That makes me feel bad. 13

We had a big meeting in school the other day—eight of us, four from the guidance department, my private tutor, my parents and me. The subject was me. I said I wanted to go to college, and 14 they told me about colleges that have facilities and staff to handle people like me. That's nice to hear.

15 As for what happens after college, I don't know and I'm worried about that. How can I make a living if I can't read? Who will hire me? How will I fill out the application form? The only thing that gives me any courage is the fact that I've learned about well-known people who couldn't read or had other problems and still made it. Like Albert Einstein, who didn't talk until he was 4 and flunked math. Like Leonardo da Vinci, who everyone seems to think had dyslexia.

16 I've told this story because maybe some teacher will read it and go easy on a kid in the classroom who has what I've got. Or, maybe some parent will stop nagging his kid, and stop calling him lazy. Maybe he's not lazy or dumb. Maybe he just can't read and doesn't know what's wrong. Maybe he's scared, like I was.

Questions for Study and Discussion

1. What is dyslexia? Is it essential for an understanding of the essay that we know more about dyslexia than Raymond tells us? Explain.
2. What does Raymond say his purpose is in telling his story? (Glossary: *Purpose*)
3. What does Raymond's story tell us about the importance of our early childhood experiences, especially within our educational system?
4. Raymond uses many colloquial and idiomatic expressions, such as "she got so red in the face I thought she'd blow up" and "she came unhinged" (1). Identify other examples of such diction and tell how they affect your reaction to the essay. (Glossary: *Colloquial Expressions*)
5. In the context of the essay, comment on the appropriateness of each of the following possible choices of diction. Which word is better in each case? Why?
   a. *selected* for *picked* (1)
   b. *experience* for *thing* (2)
   c. *speak as well* for *talk as good* (4)

d. *negative* for *bad* (6)
e. *important* for *big* (14)
f. *failed* for *flunked* (15)
g. *frightened* for *scared* (16)

6. How would you describe Raymond's tone in this essay?

Vocabulary

Refer to your dictionary to define the following words as they are used in this selection. Then use each word in a sentence of your own.

dyslexia (2) psychiatrists (6)

Classroom Activity on Diction and Tone

Many menus use connotative language to persuade customers that they are about to have an exceptional eating experience. Phrases like the following are commonplace: "skillfully seasoned and basted with lime juice," "festive red cranberry sauce," "a bed of crisp baby vegetables," and "freshly ground coffee." Imagine that you are creating a menu. Use connotative language to describe the following basic foods. Try to make them sound as attractive and inviting as possible.

a. tomato juice
b. onion soup
c. ground beef
d. chicken
e. peas
f. potatoes
g. salad
h. bread and butter
i. teas
j. cake

Suggested Writing Assignments

1. Imagine that you are away at school. Recently you were caught in a radar speed trap—you were going 70 miles per hour in a 55-mile-per-hour zone—and have just lost your license; you will not be able to go home this coming weekend, as you had planned. Write two letters in which you explain why you will not be able to go home, one to your

parents and the other to your best friend. Your audience is different in each case, so be sure to choose your diction accordingly.

2. Select an essay you have already completed for this course, and rewrite it in a different tone. If the essay was originally formal or serious, lighten it so that it is now informal and humorous. Pay special attention to diction. Actually think in terms of a different reader as your audience—not your instructor but perhaps your classmates, your clergyman, your sister, or the state environmental protection board. Reshape your essay as necessary.

La Vida Loca (The Crazy Life): Two Generations of Gang Members

Luis J. Rodriguez

Luis Rodriguez managed to walk away from his vida loca *in the gangs of Los Angeles. Since then he has published several volumes of poetry, including* Poems across the Pavement *(1991),* The Concrete River *(1991), and* Am Erica Is Her Name *(1996). He is also the author of* Always Running: Gang Days in L.A. *(1993) and has produced a video entitled* The Breeding of Impotence: Perspectives on the Crisis in Our Communities and Schools *(1993). In the following selection, Rodriguez uses vivid language to describe his gang experiences and the anguish he feels when he sees his son repeating some of his own mistakes. As you read, take note of how he supports general statements with specific and startlingly concrete descriptive details.*

For Your Journal

Membership in street gangs has grown rapidly in recent years, especially in America's large cities. Have you had any experience with street gangs? Were there gangs in your high school or hometown, or have you only read about them or seen them on television or in the movies? Why do you think people join gangs?

Late winter, Chicago, 1991: The once-white snow that fell in December has turned into a dark scum, an admixture of salt, car oil and decay; icicles hang from rooftops and window sills like the whiskers of old men. The bone-chilling temperatures force my family to stay inside a one-and-a-half bedroom apartment in 1 a three-flat building in Humboldt Park. My third wife, Trini, our child Ruben and my 15-year-old son Ramiro from a previous marriage huddle around the television set. Tensions build up like a fever.

One evening, words of anger bounce back and forth between the walls of our gray-stone flat. Two-year-old Ruben, confused and afraid, crawls up to my leg and hugs it. Trini and I had jumped on Ramiro's case for coming in late following weeks of trouble: Ramiro had joined the Insane Campbell Boys, a group of Puerto Rican and Mexican youth allied with the Spanish Cobras and Dragons. 2

Within moments, Ramiro runs out of the house, entering the freezing Chicago night. I go after him, sprinting down the gangway leading to a debris-strewn alley. I see Ramiro's fleeing figure, his breath rising in quickly dissipating clouds. 3

I follow him toward Division Street, the neighborhood's main drag. People yell out of windows and doorways: *"Que pasa, hombre?"** This is not an unfamiliar sight—a father or mother chasing some child down the street. 4

Watching my son's escape, it is as though he enters the waters of a distant time, back to my youth, back to when I ran, to when I jumped over fences, fleeing *vato locos,*** the police or my own shadow, in some drug-induced hysteria. 5

As Ramiro speeds off, I see my body enter the mouth of darkness, my breath cut the frigid flesh of night—my voice crack open the night sky. 6

We are a second-generation gang family. I was involved in gangs in Los Angeles in the late 1960s and early 1970s. When I was 2 years old, in 1956, my family emigrated from Mexico to Watts. I spent my teen years in a barrio called Las Lomas, east of Los Angeles. 7

I was arrested on charges ranging from theft, assaulting an officer to attempted murder. As a teenager, I did some time. I began using drugs at age 12—including pills, weed and heroin. I had a near-death experience at 16 from sniffing toxic spray. After being kicked out of three high schools, I dropped out at 15. 8

---

*"What's happening, man?"

**Crazy guys

By the time I turned 18, some 25 friends had been killed by rival gangs, the police, overdoses, car crashes and suicides. 9

Three years ago, I brought Ramiro to Chicago to escape the violence. If I barely survived all this, it appeared unlikely my son would make it. But in Chicago, we found kindred conditions. 10

I had to cut Ramiro's bloodline to the street before it became too late. I had to begin the long, intense struggle to save his life from the gathering storm of street violence—some 20 years after I had sneaked out of the 'hood in the dark of night and removed myself from the death fires of *La Vida Loca*. 11

What to do with those whom society cannot accommodate? Criminalize them. Outlaw their actions and creations. Declare them the enemy, then wage war. Emphasize the differences—the shade of skin, the accent or manner of clothes. Like the scapegoat of the Bible, place society's ills on them, then "stone them" in absolution. It's convenient, it's logical. 12

It doesn't work. 13

Gangs are not alien powers. They begin as unstructured groupings, our children who desire the same as any young person. Respect. A sense of belonging. Protection. This is no different than the YMCA, Little League or the Boy Scouts. It wasn't any more than what I wanted. 14

When I entered 109th Street School in Watts, I spoke perfect Spanish. But teachers punished me for speaking it on the playground. I peed in my pants a few times because I was unable to say in English that I had to go. One teacher banished me to a corner, to build blocks for a year. I learned to be silent within the walls of my body. 15

The older boys who lived on 103rd Street would take my money or food. They chased me through alleys and side streets. Fear compelled my actions. 16

The police, I learned years later, had a strategy: They picked up as many 7-year-old boys as they could—for loitering, throwing dirt clods, curfew—whatever. By the time a boy turned 13, and had been popped for something like stealing, he had accumulated a detention record, and was bound for "juvey." 17

One felt besieged, under intense scrutiny. If you spoke out, dared to resist, you were given a "jacket" of troublemaker; I'd tried many times to take it off, but somebody always put it back on. 18

Soon after my family moved to South San Gabriel, a local group, Thee Mystics, rampaged through the school. They carried bats, chains, pipes and homemade zip guns. They terrorized teachers and students alike. I was 12. 19

I froze as the head stomping came dangerously my way. But I was intrigued. I wanted this power. I wanted to be able to bring a whole school to its knees. All my school life until then had been poised against me. I was broken and shy. I wanted what Thee Mystics had. I wanted to hurt somebody. 20

Police sirens broke the spell. Thee Mystics scattered in all directions. But they had done their damage. They had left their mark on the school—and on me. 21

Gangs flourish when there's a lack of social recreation, decent education or employment. Today, many young people will never know what it is to work. They can only satisfy their needs through collective strength—against the police, who hold the power of life and death, against poverty, against idleness, against their impotence in society. 22

Without definitive solutions, it's easy to throw blame. George Bush and Dan Quayle, for example, say the lack of family values is behind our problems. 23

But "family" is a farce among the propertyless and disenfranchised. Too many families are wrenched apart, as even children are forced to supplement meager incomes. At age 9, my mother walked me to the door and, in effect, told me: Now go forth and work. 24

People can't just consume; they have to sell something, including their ability to work. If so-called legitimate work is unavailable, people will do the next best thing—sell sex or dope. 25

You'll find people who don't care about whom they hurt, but nobody I know *wants* to sell death to their children, their neighbors, friends. If there was a viable, productive alternative, they would stop. 26

At 18, I had grown tired. I felt like a war veteran with a kind of post-traumatic syndrome. I had seen too many dead across the pavement; I'd walk the aisles in the church wakes as if in a daze; I'd often watched my mother's weary face in hospital corridors, outside of courtrooms and cells, refusing, finally, to have anything to do with me. 27

In addition, I had fallen through the cracks of two languages; unable to communicate well in any. 28

I wanted the pain to end, the self-consuming hate to wither in the sunlight. With the help of those who saw potential in me, perhaps for some poetry, I got out: No more heroin, spray or pills; no more jails; no more trying to hurt somebody until I stopped hurting—which never seemed to pass. 29

There is an aspect of suicide in gang involvement for those whose options have been cut off. They stand on street corners, flash hand signs and invite the bullets. It's life as stance, as bravado. They say "You can't touch this," but "Come kill me" is the inner cry. It's either *la torcida** or death, a warrior's path, where even self-preservation doesn't make a play. If they murder, the targets are the ones who look like them, walk like them, those closest to who they are—the mirror reflection. They murder and they are killing themselves, over and over. 30

Ramiro stayed away for two weeks the day he ran off. When he returned, we entered him into a psychotherapy hospital. After three months, he was back home. Since then, I've had to pull everyone into the battle for my son. I've spent hours with teachers. I've involved therapists, social workers, the police. 31

We all have some responsibility: Schools, the law, parents. But at the same time, there are factors beyond our control. It's not a simple matter of "good" or "bad" values, or even of choices. If we all had a choice, I'm convinced nobody would choose *la vida loca,* the "insane nation"—to gangbang. But it's going to take collective action and a plan. 32

Recently, Ramiro got up at a Chicago poetry event and read a piece about being physically abused by a stepfather. It stopped everyone cold. He later read the poem at Chicago's Poetry Festival. Its title: "Running Away." 33

The best way to deal with your children is to help construct the conditions for free and healthy development of all, but it's also true you can't be for all children if you can't be for your own. 34

There's a small but intense fire burning in my son. Ramiro has just turned 17; he's made it thus far, but it's day by day. Now I tell him: You have an innate value outside of your job, outside the "jacket" imposed on you since birth. Draw on your expressive powers. 35

Stop running. 36

*Deceit

Questions for Study and Discussion

1. Identify several words in the first paragraph that Rodriguez uses to describe the conditions that led to Ramiro's running away. What do they add to the selection? Why didn't Rodriguez simply say that it was cold and his family was getting cabin fever?
2. Why had Rodriguez brought Ramiro to Chicago? How did the move relate to his own gang experiences?
3. What do gangs offer their members? How did Rodriguez's experiences make him susceptible to the lure of gang life?
4. Reread paragraphs 27–29. What is the tone of the paragraphs? How does Rodriguez's choice of words contribute to his tone?
5. What does "You can't touch this" often mean for gang members? Why are gang murders often a reflection of gang members' suicidal tendencies?
6. What does Rodriguez suggest as ways to solve the problem of gang violence? Is his ending optimistic? (Glossary: *Beginnings and Endings*) Why, or why not?

Vocabulary

Refer to your dictionary to define the following words as they are used in this selection. Then use each word in a sentence of your own.

admixture (1)
dissipating (3)
kindred (10)
absolution (12)
impotence (22)
disenfranchised (24)
innate (35)

Classroom Activity on Diction and Tone

Good writers rely on strong verbs—verbs that contribute significantly to what is being said. Because they must repeatedly describe similar situations, sportswriters, for example, are acutely aware of the need for strong action verbs. It is not enough for them to say that a team wins or loses; they must describe the type of win or loss more precisely. As a result, such verbs as *beats, buries, edges, shocks,* and *trounces* are common in the headlines on the sports page. Each of these verbs, in addition to describing the act of winning, makes a statement about the quality of the victory. Like sportswriters, all of us write about actions that are performed daily. If we were restricted only to the verbs *eat, drink, sleep,* and *work* for each of these activities, for example, our writing would be repetitious and monotonous. List as many verbs as you can that you could use in place of these four. What connotative differences do you find in your lists of alternatives? What is the importance of these connotative differences for you as a writer?

Suggested Writing Assignments

1. Write an essay about a group that you joined as a teenager. It can be a sports team, a school club, scouts, a band, a gang—any group that made you feel like a member. Why did you first join the group? How did you feel being a member of the group? Was it an ultimately positive or negative experience? Why? Make sure your diction and tone communicate the feelings you had toward the group.
2. What do your parents do for a living? Would you like to follow one or the other in their career choice? Write an objective essay in which you consider the pros and cons of one parent's career, and explain why you would or would not wish to follow in his or her footsteps. Choose your words carefully in order to maintain your objectivity.

THE FOURTH OF JULY

Audre Lorde

Audre Lorde (1934–1992) was a professor of English at Hunter College in New York City. Born in New York, she studied at Hunter and at Columbia University. Her published works include several volumes of poetry, such as Undersong: Chosen Poems Old and New *(1982), which was revised in 1992; essay collections such as* Sister Outsider *(1984) and* Burst of Light *(1988); and an autobiography,* Zami: A New Spelling of My Name *(1982). Her book of poems,* The Arithmetics of Distance, *appeared posthumously in 1993. The following selection from* Zami *eloquently communicates the tragedy of racism. Take special note of Lorde's tone as you read, particularly the way it intensifies as the essay continues and culminates in the anger of the final paragraph.*

FOR YOUR JOURNAL

Think about the Fourth of July or some other national holiday like Memorial Day or Thanksgiving. Perhaps you celebrate Cinco de Mayo or Bastille Day. What are your memories of celebrating that holiday? What meaning does the holiday have for you?

The first time I went to Washington, D.C., was on the edge of the summer when I was supposed to stop being a child. At least that's what they said to us all at graduation from the eighth grade. My sister Phyllis graduated at the same time from high school. I don't know what she was supposed to stop being. But as graduation presents for us both, the whole family took a Fourth of July trip to Washington, D.C., the fabled and famous capital of our country. 1

It was the first time I'd ever been on a railroad train during the 2
day. When I was little, and we used to go to the Connecticut shore, we always went at night on the milk train, because it was cheaper.

Preparations were in the air around our house before school 3
was even over. We packed for a week. There were two very large suitcases that my father carried, and a box filled with food. In fact, my first trip to Washington was a mobile feast; I started eating as soon as we were comfortably ensconced in our seats, and did not stop until somewhere after Philadelphia. I remember it was Philadelphia because I was disappointed not to have passed by the Liberty Bell.

My mother had roasted two chickens and cut them up into 4
dainty bite-size pieces. She packed slices of brown bread and butter and green pepper and carrot sticks. There were little violently yellow iced cakes with scalloped edges called "marigolds," that came from Cushman's Bakery. There was a spice bun and rock-cakes from Newton's, the West Indian bakery across Lenox Avenue from St. Mark's School, and iced tea in a wrapped mayonnaise jar. There were sweet pickles for us and dill pickles for my father, and peaches with the fuzz still on them, individually wrapped to keep them from bruising. And, for neatness, there were piles of napkins and a little tin box with a washcloth dampened with rosewater and glycerine for wiping sticky mouths.

I wanted to eat in the dining car because I had read all about 5
them, but my mother reminded me for the umpteenth time that dining car food always cost too much money and besides, you never could tell whose hands had been playing all over that food, nor where those same hands had been just before. My mother never mentioned that Black people were not allowed into railroad dining cars headed south in 1947. As usual, whatever my mother did not like and could not change, she ignored. Perhaps it would go away, deprived of her attention.

I learned later that Phyllis's high school senior class trip had 6
been to Washington, but the nuns had given her back her deposit in private, explaining to her that the class, all of whom were white, except Phyllis, would be staying in a hotel where Phyllis "would not be happy," meaning, Daddy explained to her, also in private, that they did not rent rooms to Negroes. "We will take among-you to Washington, ourselves," my father had avowed, "and not just for an overnight in some measly fleabag hotel."

American racism was a new and crushing reality that my parents had to deal with every day of their lives once they came to this country. They handled it as a private woe. My mother and father believed that they could best protect their children from the realities of race in america and the fact of american racism by never giving them name, much less discussing their nature. We were told we must never trust white people, but *why* was never explained, nor the nature of their ill will. Like so many other vital pieces of information in my childhood, I was supposed to know without being told. It always seemed like a very strange injunction coming from my mother, who looked so much like one of those people we were never supposed to trust. But something always warned me not to ask my mother why she wasn't white, and why Auntie Lillah and Auntie Etta weren't, even though they were all that same problematic color so different from my father and me, even from my sisters, who were somewhere in-between. 7

In Washington, D.C., we had one large room with two double beds and an extra cot for me. It was a back-street hotel that belonged to a friend of my father's who was in real estate, and I spent the whole next day after Mass squinting up at the Lincoln Memorial where Marian Anderson had sung after the D.A.R. refused to allow her to sing in their auditorium because she was Black. Or because she was "Colored," my father said as he told us the story. Except that what he probably said was "Negro," because for his times, my father was quite progressive. 8

I was squinting because I was in that silent agony that characterized all of my childhood summers, from the time school let out in June to the end of July, brought about by my dilated and vulnerable eyes exposed to the summer brightness. 9

I viewed Julys through an agonizing corolla of dazzling whiteness and I always hated the Fourth of July, even before I came to realize the travesty such a celebration was for Black people in this country. 10

My parents did not approve of sunglasses, nor of their expense. 11

I spent the afternoon squinting up at monuments to freedom and past presidencies and democracy, and wondering why the light and heat were both so much stronger in Washington, D.C., than back home in New York City. Even the pavement on the streets was a shade lighter in color than back home. 12

Late that Washington afternoon my family and I walked back down Pennsylvania Avenue. We were a proper caravan, mother bright and father brown, the three of us girls step-standards in-between. Moved by our historical surroundings and the heat of early evening, my father decreed yet another treat. He had a great sense of history, a flair for the quietly dramatic and the sense of specialness of an occasion and a trip. 13

"Shall we stop and have a little something to cool off, Lin?" 14

Two blocks away from our hotel, the family stopped for a dish of vanilla ice cream at a Breyer's ice cream and soda fountain. Indoors, the soda fountain was dim and fan-cooled, deliciously relieving to my scorched eyes. 15

Corded and crisp and pinafored, the five of us seated ourselves one by one at the counter. There was I between my mother and father, and my two sisters on the other side of my mother. We settled ourselves along the white mottled marble counter, and when the waitress spoke at first no one understood what she was saying, and so the five of us just sat there. 16

The waitress moved along the line of us closer to my father and spoke again. "I said I kin give you to take out, but you can't eat here. Sorry." Then she dropped her eyes looking very embarrassed, and suddenly we heard what it was she was saying all at the same time, loud and clear. 17

Straight-backed and indignant, one by one, my family and I got down from the counter stools and turned around and marched out of the store, quiet and outraged, as if we had never been Black before. No one would answer my emphatic questions with anything other than a guilty silence. "But we hadn't done anything!" This wasn't right or fair! Hadn't I written poems about Bataan and freedom and democracy for all? 18

My parents wouldn't speak of this injustice, not because they had contributed to it, but because they felt they should have anticipated it and avoided it. This made me even angrier. My fury was not going to be acknowledged by a like fury. Even my two sisters copied my parents' pretense that nothing unusual and anti-american had occurred. I was left to write my angry letter to the president of the united states all by myself, although my father did promise I could type it out on the office typewriter next week, after I showed it to him in my copybook diary. 19

The waitress was white, and the counter was white, and the 20
ice cream I never ate in Washington, D.C., that summer I left childhood was white, and the white heat and the white pavement and the white stone monuments of my first Washington summer made me sick to my stomach for the whole rest of that trip and it wasn't much of a graduation present after all.

Questions for Study and Discussion

1. Lorde takes great care in describing the food her family took on the train with them to Washington. What is Lorde's purpose in describing the food? (Glossary: *Purpose*)
2. Why did Lorde dislike the Fourth of July as a child? Why does she dislike it as an adult?
3. Do you see any irony in Lorde's title? (Glossary: *Irony*) In what way? Do you think it is an appropriate title for her essay?
4. Lorde's essay is not long or hyperbolic, but it is a very effective indictment of racism. Identify some of the words Lorde uses to communicate her outrage when she writes of the racism that she and her family faced. How does her choice of words contribute to her message?
5. What is the tone of Lorde's essay? Identify passages to support your answer.
6. Why do you think Lorde's family deals with racism by ignoring it? In what way is Lorde different?

Vocabulary

Refer to your dictionary to define the following words as they are used in this selection. Then use each word in a sentence of your own.

ensconced (3)
measly (6)
injunction (7)
corolla (10)
travesty (10)
pinafored (16)
emphatic (18)

Classroom Activity on Diction and Tone

Writers create and control tone in their writing in part through the words they choose. For example, words like *laugh, cheery, dance,* and *melody* help to create a tone of celebration. Make a list of the words that come to mind for each of the following tones:

humorous
angry
authoritative
tentative
triumphant

Compare your lists of words with those of others in the class. What generalizations can you make about the connotations associated with each of these words?

Suggested Writing Assignments

1. When read with the ideals of the American Revolution and the Constitution in mind, Lorde's essay is strongly ironic. What does the Fourth of July mean to you? Why? How do your feelings relate to the stated ideals of our forebears? Choose your words carefully, and use specific personal experiences to support your general statements.
2. Imagine that you are Audre Lorde in 1947. Write a letter to Harry Truman in which you protest the reception you received in the nation's capital on the Fourth of July. Do not overstate your case. Show the president in what way you and your family were treated unfairly rather than merely stating that you were discriminated against, and carefully choose words that will help President Truman see the irony of your experience.

The Dance within My Heart

Pat Mora

Poet, essayist, and children's book author Pat Mora was born in El Paso, Texas, in 1942. After receiving degrees from Texas Western College and the University of Texas at El Paso, she worked as a teacher and administrator and served as director of the University Museum at UTEP. Mora is also host of a radio show, "Voices: The Mexican-American Perspective," at a National Public Radio affiliate in El Paso. Her published works include books of poems such as Chants *(1984) and* Borders *(1986); a collection of essays,* Nepantla: Essays from the Land in the Middle *(1993); and the children's story* Pablo's Tree *(1994). As you read the following essay, pay particular attention to the way Mora moves back and forth between abstract concepts such as* strength, inventiveness, beauty, *and* grandeur, *and more concrete and detailed depictions of what she means by those terms.*

For Your Journal

Of the museums you have visited, which succeeded best in capturing your attention? Why? Describe the exhibit or exhibits that had the greatest impact on you.

For a Southwesterner, early spring in the Midwest is a time for jubilation. Another winter survived. Why, then, on a soft spring Saturday would I choose to leave the dogwoods and daffodils and spend my day inside museums? 1

Certainly, I didn't spend my youth enduring trips through solemn rooms, being introduced to "culture." There was only one small art museum in my hometown, and I'm not sure how comfortable my parents would have felt there. My father worked 2 evenings and weekends to support the four of us and to give us what he and my mother hadn't had, a youth without financial worries. And my mother not only helped him in his optical business but was our willing chauffeur in addition to assisting the grandmother and aunt who lived with us, our extended Mexican American family.

But as an adult I began to visit those echoing buildings. A fel- 3
lowship allowed trips to modest and grand museums in New York, Paris, Washington, Mexico, Hawaii, and the Dominican Republic. And much to my surprise, I even found myself directing a small university museum for a time, having the opportunity to convince people of all ages and backgrounds that indeed the museum was theirs. I was hooked for life.

For me, museums are pleasure havens. When I enter, my 4
breathing changes just as it does when I visit aquariums, zoos, botanical gardens. These latter sites offer a startling array of living species. Unless we have become totally desensitized to nature's grandeur, to its infinite variations, arboretums and nature centers inspire us to treat our planet with more care, to be more attentive to the life around us, no matter how minute. I stand entranced by the spriteliness of glass shrimp, the plushness of the jaguar, the haughtiness of birds of paradise in bloom. Parrots make me laugh, fins spin my blood, ferns hush my doubts. I leave refreshed.

When they were younger, my children could far more easily 5
understand my desire to visit displays of living creatures than they could my penchant for natural history and art museums, for gazing at baskets and pottery, at sculpture and flashing neon. It sounded like work walking through room after room, up and down stairs, being relatively quiet, not eating, reading small cards of text, staring at "weird" objects. This is fun?

But museums remind me of the strength and inventiveness of 6
the human imagination through time. They remind me that offering beauty to a community is a human habit, a needed reminder in a society with little time for observing, listening, appreciating. I gaze at African masks crusted with cowrie shells, at drums and carvings of old, wrinkled wood, at the serenity of Buddha. I watch my fellow visitors, drawn to cases both by the beauty and craft but also as a kind of testimony to humans who once sat under our sun and moon and with rough hands graced our world.

I walk on to see the sturdy pre-Columbian female figures from Nayarit, Mexico, women of broad dimensions who occupy space rather than shrink as we sometimes do. I see pan pipes and bone flutes from Peru, 180 B.C., back then, high in the Andes, hear a man transforming his breath into music. 7

Room after room I watch light and shadow play on sandstone, silver, wood, bronze, earthenware, copper, ivory, hemp, oil, acrylic, watercolor, straw, gold. I study toenails on a headless marble statue, watch light stroke the soft curves, wish I could touch her outstretched Roman hand. The next room, or turning a corner, can yield surprise, the halls and rooms a pleasure maze. I stand in Chagall's blue light, see his glass bird poised to fly from room to room. 8

I ignore the careful museum maps, enjoying the unexpected, the independence of viewing at will, the private pleasure of letting myself abandon order and logic room to room. Purposeless wandering? Not really, for I now know I come not only for the intellectual and sensory stimulation but for comfort. I come to be with humans I admire, with those who produced these drums and breathing dancers, who through the ages added beauty to this world. Their work gives me hope, reminds me that art is not a luxury: it nourishes our parched spirits. It is essential. 9

I think again of how privileged I am to be in these quiet rooms, not having to wait for a free day, having time to spend wandering these galleries rather than having to care for someone else's children while mine are alone, or having to iron clothes that I will never wear. 10

And certainly free days and increased public programming—the democratization of museums—are an improvement from past eras, an acknowledgment, although sometimes grudging, that not only the "washed and worthy" deserve entrance. Museums are slowly changing, realizing that artifacts and art belong to all people, not some people. Museums are even becoming a bit embarrassed about how they acquired what they own, about why they arrogantly ushered certain groups past their polished doors. The faces viewing with me have been more varied in recent years. 11

I walk on. I, who can barely sew a button, study an array of quilts, glad that such women's art is now displayed, think of the careful fingers—stitch, stitch, stitch—and probably careful voices 12 that produced these works. The text of a bronze of Shiva says that her dance takes place within her heart. I study her and think of that dance, of the private nature of that spring of emotion. I watch a group of teenage girls walk by and wonder if they can hear or feel their private dance in a world that equates noise and brutality with entertainment.

The contemporary art halls most baffled my children when they were young. "Why, I could do that!" they would scoff staring at a Jackson Pollock. I smile secretly when my youngest, now taller than I am, asks, "Where are our favorite rooms?" meaning, yes, those rooms with massive canvases, with paint everywhere, the rooms that loosen me up inside, that provide escape from the confines of the predictable. 13

I walk outside glad to breathe in sky and wind but also brimming with all I saw and felt, hearing the dance within my heart. 14

Questions for Study and Discussion

1. What word or words would you use to describe the prevailing tone of Mora's essay? How is this tone achieved? Identify a paragraph that you feel exemplifies it.
2. Mora offers a number of reasons to explain her love of museums. What are they? Notice the order in which these reasons are presented. Why does she write about exhibits of living things first, before moving on to human art and artifacts?
3. Throughout the essay, Mora cites many examples of museum exhibits that have attracted her. To describe them she chooses descriptive words rich in connotation. For example, in paragraph 4 she employs the phrase "the plushness of the jaguar." Plushness *denotes* furry softness; it *connotes* luxury, richness, majesty. In the same paragraph appears the phrase "the spriteliness of glass shrimp." In a dictionary, look up *sprightliness* and *sprite.* What connotations arise from combining these two words? Find other examples of words or phrases with connotations that add depth to the meaning of the essay.

4. "Museums are slowly changing," Mora says in paragraph 11. Why and in what ways are they changing? Why does she take a positive view of the changes?
5. At the conclusion of the opening paragraph, Mora leads the reader into the essay with a rhetorical question instead of the more usual thesis statement. (Glossary: *Rhetorical Question*) Is this an effective organizational strategy? (Glossary: *Strategy*) Why, or why not? Where in the essay is the thesis located? Is it implied or stated directly?
6. What is the meaning of the title? (Glossary: *Title*) How does the title serve both to introduce and to reinforce the central idea of the essay?

Vocabulary

Refer to your dictionary to define the following words as they are used in this selection. Then use each word in a sentence of your own.

havens (4)	penchant (5)
grandeur (4)	cowrie (6)
arboretums (4)	parched (9)

Classroom Activity on Diction and Tone

Writers use different sorts of diction to communicate with different audiences of readers. (Glossary: *Audience*) Recall a fairground activity or amusement-park ride that you have enjoyed. Write a paragraph in which you describe this ride or activity to an older relative. Then rewrite the paragraph to appeal to a ten-year-old.

Suggested Writing Assignments

1. What sort of public institution do you like to visit? Perhaps you enjoy visiting libraries, county fairs, cathedrals, movie theaters, or sports arenas. Write an essay in which you describe the characteristics of a public place you enjoy visiting

and explain the reasons it pleases you. Like Mora, be sure to include sensory details that evoke a vivid impression of this pleasurable setting for the reader.

2. Mora says that "art is not a luxury" (9). Do you agree or disagree with her opinion? There is much debate over this issue within American society today. Write an essay using one of these thesis statements: "Art is a luxury" or "Art is not a luxury." Each paragraph in the body of the essay should contain a topic sentence that clearly states one of your reasons. Make sure your tone is appropriate and consistent with your attitude toward the subject.

9

FIGURATIVE LANGUAGE

Figurative language is language used in an imaginative rather than a literal sense. Although it is most often associated with poetry, figurative language is used widely in our daily speech and in our writing. Prose writers have long known that figurative language not only brings freshness and color to writing, but also helps to clarify ideas.

Two of the most commonly used figures of speech are the simile and the metaphor. A *simile* is an explicit comparison between two essentially different ideas or things that uses the words *like* or *as* to link them.

> Canada geese sweep across the hills and valleys like a formation of strategic bombers.
>
> Benjamin B. Bachman

> I walked toward her and hailed her as a visitor to the moon might salute a survivor of a previous expedition.
>
> John Updike

A *metaphor,* on the other hand, makes an implicit comparison between dissimilar ideas or things without using *like* or *as.*

> She was very old and small and she walked slowly in the dark pine shadows, moving a little from side to side in her steps, with the balanced heaviness and lightness of a pendulum in a grandfather clock.
>
> Eudora Welty

> Charm is the ultimate weapon, the supreme seduction, against which there are few defenses.
>
> Laurie Lee

In order to take full advantage of the richness of a particular comparison, writers sometimes use several sentences or even a whole paragraph to develop a metaphor. Such a comparison is called an *extended metaphor.*

> The point is that you have to strip down your writing before you can build it back up. You must know what the essential tools are and what job they were designed to do. If I may belabor the metaphor on carpentry, it is first necessary to be able to saw wood neatly and to drive nails. Later you can bevel the edges or add elegant finials, if that is your taste. But you can never forget that you are practicing a craft that is based on certain principles. If the nails are weak, your house will collapse. If your verbs are weak and your syntax is rickety, your sentences will fall apart.
>
> William Zinsser

Another frequently used figure of speech is *personification.* In personification the writer attributes human qualities to animals or inanimate objects.

> Blond October comes striding over the hills wearing a crimson shirt and faded green trousers.
>
> Hal Borland

> Indeed, haste can be the assassin of elegance.
>
> T. H. White

In the preceding examples, the writers have, through the use of figurative language, both enlivened their prose and emphasized their ideas. Keep in mind that figurative language should never be used merely to "dress up" writing; above all, it should help you to develop your ideas and to clarify your meaning for the reader.

The Barrio

Robert Ramirez

Robert Ramirez has worked as a cameraman, reporter, anchorman, and producer for the news team at KGBT-TV in Edinburg, Texas, and in the Latin American division of the Northern Trust Bank in Chicago. In the following essay, Ramirez uses figurative language, particularly metaphors, to awaken the reader's senses to the sights, smells, and sounds that are the essense of the barrio.

For Your Journal

Where did you grow up? What do you remember most about your childhood neighborhood? How did it feel as a young person to live in this world? Do you still call this neighborhood "home"? Explain.

The train, its metal wheels squealing as they spin along the silvery tracks, rolls slower now. Through the gaps between the cars blinks a streetlamp, and this pulsing light on a barrio streetcorner beats slower, like a weary heartbeat, until the train shudders to a halt, the light goes out, and the barrio is deep asleep. 1

Throughout Aztlán (the Nahuatl term meaning "land to the north"), trains grumble along the edges of a sleeping people. From Lower California, through the blistering Southwest, down the Rio Grande to the muddy Gulf, the darkness and mystery of dreams engulf communities fenced off by railroads, canals, and expressways. Paradoxical communities, isolated from the rest of the town by concrete columned monuments of progress, and yet stranded in the past. They are surrounded by change. It eludes their reach, in their own backyards, and the people, unable and unwilling to see the future, or even touch the present, perpetuate the past. 2

Leaning from the expressway or jolting across the tracks, one enters a different physical world permeated by a different attitude. 3

The physical dimensions are impressive. It is a large section of town which extends for fifteen blocks north and south along the tracks, and then advances eastward, thinning into nothingness beyond the city limits. Within the invisible (yet sensible) walls of the barrio are many, many people living in too few houses. The homes, however, are much more numerous than on the outside.

Members of the barrio describe the entire area as their home. It is a home, but it is more than this. The barrio is a refuge from the harshness and the coldness of the Anglo world. It is a forced refuge. The leprous people are isolated from the rest of the community and contained in their section of town. The stoical pariahs of the barrio accept their fate, and from the angry seeds of rejection grow the flowers of closeness between outcasts, not the thorns of bitterness and the mad desire to flee. There is no want to escape, for the feeling of the barrio is known only to its inhabitants, and the material needs of life can also be found here. 4

The *tortillería* [tortilla factory] fires up its machinery three times a day, producing steaming, round, flat slices of barrio bread. In the winter, the warmth of the tortilla factory is a wool *sarape* [blanket] in the chilly morning hours, but in the summer, it unbearably toasts every noontime customer. 5

The *panadería* [bakery] sends its sweet messenger aroma down the dimly lit street, announcing the arrival of fresh, hot sugary *pan dulce* [sweet rolls]. 6

The small corner grocery serves the meal-to-meal needs of customers, and the owner, a part of the neighborhood, willingly gives credit to people unable to pay cash for foodstuffs. 7

The barbershop is a living room with hydraulic chairs, radio, and television, where old friends meet and speak of life as their salted hair falls aimlessly about them. 8

The pool hall is a junior level country club where *'chucos* [young men], strangers in their own land, get together to shoot pool and rap, while veterans, unaware of the cracking, popping balls on the green felt, complacently play dominoes beneath rudely hung *Playboy* foldouts. 9

The *cantina* [canteen or snackbar] is the night spot of the barrio. It is the country club and the den where the rites of puberty are enacted. Here the young become men. It is in the taverns that a young dude shows his *machismo* through the quantity of beer he can hold, the stories of *rucas* [women] he has had, and 10 his willingness and ability to defend his image against hardened and scarred old lions.

No, there is no frantic wish to flee. It would be absurd to leave the familiar and nervously step into the strange and cold Anglo community when the needs of the Chicano can be met in the barrio. 11

The barrio is closeness. From the family living unit, familial relationships stretch out to immediate neighbors, down the block, around the corner, and to all parts of the barrio. The feeling of family, a rare and treasurable sentiment, pervades and accounts for the inability of the people to leave. The barrio is this attitude manifested on the countenances of the people, on the faces of their homes, and in the gaiety of their gardens. 12

The color-splashed homes arrest your eyes, arouse your curiosity, and make you wonder what life scenes are being played out in them. The flimsy, brightly colored, wood-frame houses ignore no neon-brilliant color. Houses trimmed in orange, chartreuse, lime-green, yellow, and mixtures of these and other hues beckon the beholder to reflect on the peculiarity of each home. Passing through this land is refreshing like Brubeck,* not narcoticizing like revolting rows of similar houses, which neither offend nor please. 13

In the evenings, the porches and front yards are occupied with men calmly talking over the noise of children playing baseball in the unpaved extension of the living room, while the women cook supper or gossip with female neighbors as they water the *jardines* [gardens]. The gardens mutely echo the expressive verses of the colorful houses. The denseness of multicolored plants and trees gives the house the appearance of an oasis or a tropical island hide-away, sheltered from the rest of the world. 14

Fences are common in the barrio, but they are fences and not the walls of the Anglo community. On the western side of town, the high wooden fences between houses are thick, impenetrable walls, built to keep the neighbors at bay. In the barrio, the fences may be rusty, wire contraptions or thick green shrubs. In either case you can see through them and feel no sense of intrusion when you cross them. 15

Many lower-income families of the barrio manage to maintain a comfortable standard of living through the communal action 16

*Dave Brubeck, pianist, composer, and conductor of "cool" modern jazz of family members who contribute their wages to the head of the family. Economic need creates interdependence and closeness. Small barefooted boys sell papers on cool, dark Sunday mornings, deny themselves pleasantries, and give their earnings to *mamá.* The older the child, the greater the responsibility to help the head of the household provide for the rest of the family.

17 There are those, too, who for a number of reasons have not achieved a relative sense of financial security. Perhaps it results from too many children too soon, but it is the homes of these people and their situation that numbs rather than charms. Their houses, aged and bent, oozing children, are fissures in the horn of plenty. Their wooden homes may have brick-pattern asbestos tile on the outer walls, but the tile is not convincing.

18 Unable to pay city taxes or incapable of influencing the city to live up to its duty to serve all the citizens, the poorer barrio families remain trapped in the nineteenth century and survive as best they can. The backyards have well-worn paths to the outhouses, which sit near the alley. Running water is considered a luxury in some parts of the barrio. Decent drainage is usually unknown, and when it rains, the water stands for days, an incubator of health hazards and an avoidable nuisance. Streets, costly to pave, remain rough, rocky trails. Tires do not last long, and the constant rattling and shaking grind away a car's life and spread dust through screen windows.

19 The houses and their *jardines,* the jollity of the people in an adverse world, the brightly feathered alarm clock pecking away at supper and cautiously eyeing the children playing nearby, produce a mystifying sensation at finding the noble savage alive in the twentieth century. It is easy to look at the positive qualities of life in the barrio, and look at them with a distantly envious feeling. One wishes to experience the feelings of the barrio and not the hardships. Remembering the illness, the hunger, the feeling of time running out on you, the walls, both real and imagined, reflecting on living in the past, one finds his envy becoming more elusive, until it has vanished altogether.

20 Back now beyond the tracks, the train creaks and groans, the cars jostle each other down the track, and as the light begins its pulsing, the barrio, with all its meanings, greets a new dawn with yawns and restless stretchings.

Questions for Study and Discussion

1. What is the barrio? Where is it? What does Ramirez mean when he says that "There is no want to escape, for the feeling of the barrio is known only to its inhabitants, and the material needs of life can also be found here" (4)?
2. Ramirez uses Spanish phrases throughout his essay. Why do you suppose he uses them? What is their effect on the reader? He also uses the words "home," "refuge," "family," and "closeness." What do they connote in the context of this essay? (Glossary: *Connotation/Denotation*) In what ways, if any, are they essential to his purpose? (Glossary: *Purpose*)
3. Identify several of the metaphors Ramirez uses in his essay and explain why they are particularly appropriate for this essay.
4. Explain Ramirez's use of the imagery of walls and fences to describe a sense of cultural isolation. What might this imagery be symbolic of? (Glossary: *Symbol*)
5. Ramirez goes into some detail about the many groups in the barrio. (Glossary: *Details*) Identify those groups. In what ways do they participate in the unity of life in the barrio?
6. Ramirez begins his essay with a relatively positive picture of the barrio, but ends on a more disheartening note. Why has he organized his essay this way? What might the effect have been if he had reversed these images? (Glossary: *Beginnings and Endings*)

Vocabulary

Refer to your dictionary to define the following words as they are used in this selection. Then use each word in a sentence of your own.

paradoxical (2)
eludes (2)
permeated (3)
stoical (4)
pariahs (4)
complacently (9)
Chicano (11)
countenances (12)
fissures (17)
adverse (19)
elusive (19)

Classroom Activity on Figurative Language

Create a metaphor or simile that would be helpful in describing each item on the following list. The first one has been completed for you to illustrate the process.

1. a skyscraper: The skyscraper sparkled like a huge glass needle.
2. the sound of an explosion
3. an intelligent student
4. a crowded bus
5. a slow-moving car
6. a pillow
7. a narrow alley
8. greasy french fries
9. hot sun
10. a dull knife

Compare your metaphors and similes with those written by other members of your class. Which metaphors and similes for each item on the list seem to work best? Why? Do any seem tired or clichéd?

Suggested Writing Assignments

1. Write a brief essay in which you describe your own neighborhood.
2. In paragraph 19 of his essay Ramirez says, "One wishes to experience the feelings of the barrio and not the hardships." Explore his meaning in light of what you have just read and of other experience or knowledge you may have of "ghetto" living. In what way can it be said that the hardships of such living are a necessary part of its "feelings"? How might barrio life change, for better or worse, if the city were to "live up to its duty to serve all the citizens" (18)?

POLAROIDS

Anne Lamott

Born in San Francisco in 1954, Anne Lamott is a graduate of Goucher College in Baltimore and the author of four novels; Crooked Little Heart *(1997) is the most recent of them. She has also written a food-review column for* California *magazine and a book-review column for* Mademoiselle. *In 1993 she published* Operating Instructions: A Journal of My Son's First Year, *in which she describes her own adventures as a single parent. The selection below is from Lamott's popular book about writing,* Bird by Bird *(1994). The entire essay is built around the analogy of a developing Polaroid photograph. As you read, notice how effectively Lamott weaves in references to the Polaroid to clarify points she wishes to make about the process of writing.*

FOR YOUR JOURNAL

Do you or does someone in your family enjoy taking photographs? Do the pictures always come out just the way you expected (or hoped) they would, or do they sometimes contain surprises? Perhaps they made you laugh, or disappointed you, or revealed something of value—some new insight into a familiar person, scene, or relationship. Describe a photograph or photographs that literally developed into something unexpected.

Writing a first draft is very much like watching a Polaroid develop. You can't—and, in fact, you're not supposed to— 1
know exactly what the picture is going to look like until it has finished developing. First you just point at what has your attention and take the picture. In the last chapter, for instance, what had my attention were the contents of my lunch bag. But as the

picture developed, I found I had a really clear image of the boy against the fence. Or maybe *your* Polaroid was supposed to be a picture of that boy against the fence, and you didn't notice until the last minute that a family was standing a few feet away from him. Now, maybe it's his family, or the family of one of the kids in his class, but at any rate these people are going to be in the photograph, too. Then the film emerges from the camera with a grayish green murkiness that gradually becomes clearer and clearer, and finally you see the husband and wife holding their baby with two children standing beside them. And at first it all seems very sweet, but then the shadows begin to appear, and then you start to see the animal tragedy, the baboons baring their teeth. And then you see a flash of bright red flowers in the bottom left quadrant that you didn't even know were in the picture when you took it, and these flowers evoke a time or a memory that moves you mysteriously. And finally, as the portrait comes into focus, you begin to notice all the props surrounding these people, and you begin to understand how props define us and comfort us, and show us what we value and what we need, and who we think we are.

You couldn't have had any way of knowing what this piece of work would look like when you first started. You just knew that there was something about these people that compelled you, and you stayed with that something long enough for it to show you what it was about. 2

Watch this Polaroid develop: 3

Six or seven years ago I was asked to write an article on the Special Olympics. I had been going to the local event for years, partly because a couple of friends of mine compete. Also, I love sports, and I love to watch athletes, special or otherwise. So I showed up this time with a great deal of interest but no real sense of what the finished article might look like. 4

Things tend to go very, very slowly at the Special Olympics. It is not like trying to cover the Preakness. Still, it has its own exhilaration, and I cheered and took notes all morning. 5

The last track-and-field event before lunch was a twenty-five-yard race run by some unusually handicapped runners and walkers, many of whom seemed completely confused. They lumped and careened along, one man making a snail-slow break for the stands, one heading out toward the steps where the winners re- 6 ceive their medals; both of them were shepherded back. The race took just about forever. And here it was nearly noon and we were all so hungry. Finally, though, everyone crossed over the line, and those of us in the stands got up to go—when we noticed that way down the track, four or five yards from the starting line, was another runner.

She was a girl of about sixteen with a normal-looking face 7
above a wracked and emaciated body. She was on metal crutches, and she was just plugging along, one tiny step after another, moving one crutch forward two or three inches, then moving a leg, then moving the other crutch two or three inches, then moving the other leg. It was just excruciating. Plus, I was starving to death. Inside I was going, Come on, come on, come on, swabbing at my forehead with anxiety, while she kept taking these two- or three-inch steps forward. What felt like four hours later, she crossed the finish line, and you could see that she was absolutely stoked, in a shy, girlish way.

A tall African American man with no front teeth fell into step 8
with me as I left the bleachers to go look for some lunch. He tugged on the sleeve of my sweater, and I looked up at him, and he handed me a Polaroid someone had taken of him and his friends that day. "Look at us," he said. His speech was difficult to understand, thick and slow as a warped record. His two friends in the picture had Down's syndrome. All three of them looked extremely pleased with themselves. I admired the picture and then handed it back to him. He stopped, so I stopped, too. He pointed to his own image. "That," he said, "is one cool man."

And this was the image from which an article began forming, 9
although I could not have told you exactly what the piece would end up being about. I just knew that something had started to emerge.

After lunch I wandered over to the auditorium, where it turned 10
out a men's basketball game was in progress. The African American man with no front teeth was the star of the game. You could tell that he was because even though no one had made a basket yet, his teammates almost always passed him the ball. Even the people on the *other* team passed him the ball a lot. In lieu of any scoring, the men stampeded in slow motion up and down the court, dribbling the ball thunderously. I had never heard such a loud game. It was all sort of crazily beautiful. I imagined de-

scribing the game for my article and then for my students: the loudness, the joy. I kept replaying the scene of the girl on crutches making her way up the track to the finish line—and all of a sudden my article began to appear out of the grayish green murk. And I could see that it was about tragedy transformed over the years into joy. It was about the beauty of sheer effort. I could see it almost as clearly as I could the photograph of that one cool man and his two friends.

The auditorium bleachers were packed. Then a few minutes later, still with no score on the board, the tall black man dribbled slowly from one end of the court to the other, and heaved the ball up into the air, and it dropped into the basket. The crowd roared, and all the men on both teams looked up wide-eyed at the hoop, as if it had just burst into flames. 11

You would have loved it, I tell my students. You would have felt like you could write all day. 12

Questions for Study and Discussion

1. This entire essay is based on one broad analogy. (Glossary: *Analogy*) What is the analogy? How does it serve to clarify Lamott's central idea?
2. Besides the extended analogy, Lamott uses several figures of speech in this essay. Find at least one metaphor and one simile. How does each contribute to the impact of the piece on the reader?
3. Lamott uses the phrase "grayish green murkiness" in the first paragraph and refers again to "grayish green murk" near the end of the essay, in paragraph 10. Why does she repeat these words? What does this phrase mean to a photographer? To a writer? For which of them does it function as a metaphor?
4. In paragraph 1, Lamott identifies four elements in "*your* Polaroid" that you didn't expect to find. What are they? Why does she include them?
5. Although the diction of this essay is simple and informal (Glossary: *Diction*), the structure is quite complicated. It is

almost like an essay within an essay. What purpose is served by the long embedded narrative about the Special Olympics? (Glossary: *Example*) How does Lamott succeed in achieving unity? (Glossary: *Unity*)

6. In what way does the African American man's perception of himself in the Polaroid picture help Lamott with her writing assignment?

Vocabulary

Refer to your dictionary to define the following words as they are used in this selection. Then use each word in a sentence of your own.

quadrant (1)	emaciated (7)
props (1)	excruciating (7)
wracked (7)	

Classroom Activity on Figurative Language

Carefully read the following descriptions of October. Identify the figures of speech that each writer uses. Did you find one description more effective than the other? Why, or why not? Compare your reactions with those of others in the class.

The Fading Season

October's lyrics are spilled in scarlet syllables on shadowed paths that bend with the wind as they wander through field and forest to heights where foliate hills commune with azure skies in the last golden moments of the autumns of our days.

Where a wisp of the wind tingles with the cidery essences of vagrant apples, fluttering leaflets bear bittersweet messages of another season's passing and warnings of harsh moments yet to be. Caught for a breath of a moment in the fingers of slim sunbeams, they glisten and gleam in a saffron splendor before they settle gently into the dappled pattern on the forest floor.

Walk slowly in October and you can savor the scents of cedar and pine, the musky odor of the earth before it dozes off for another winter, and the crackling leaves beneath your feet will snap and echo in the silences that only woods contain. Stop for a moment and you will sense scurryings in the underbrush where squirrels dash to and fro in a frenetic race to hoard as much as they can before winter sets in. A whirr of sudden wings will tell you that you have invaded the partridge's exclusive territory.

In the dusk of an October day when the sun's last crimson embers have slipped behind the hills, the crisp chill in the air signals fall's coming surrender to the approaching winter's legions.

The Burlington Free Press

October

Blond October comes striding over the hills wearing a crimson shirt and faded green trousers. His morning breath is the mist in the valleys, and at evening there are stars in his eyes, a waxing moon over his shoulder, and the cool whisper of a valley breeze in his voice. He comes this way to light the fires of autumn in the maple groves, to put a final polish on the late winesaps, to whistle a farewell to summer and set the foxes to barking and tell the owls that now they can ask their eternal questions.

October might be called a god of travel, if we were to fashion a new mythology; for now come the perfect days to get out and wander the hills and valleys of these latitudes. The scene changes from day to day, as though all the color in the spectrum were being spilled across the landscape—radiant blue of the sky and the lakes and ponds reflecting it, green of every tone in the conifers and in the reluctant oaks, yellows verging from the sun simmer to moon orange in the elms, the beeches, the maples, and reds that range to purplish browns, sumac and dogwood and maple and oak and sour gum and sassafras and viburnum. There is the indigo of fox grapes, if you know where to find them.

October is colorful, it is exuberant, it is full of lively spirit. Spring fever can't hold a candle to October fever, when it comes to inner restlessness. The birds are on the wing, the leaves are footloose and eager for a breeze, the horizon is a challenge that amounts to an insidious summons. Listen closely and you can hear October, that fellow in the crimson shirt, whistling a soft melody that is as old as autumn upon this earth.

Hal Borland, *The New York Times*

Suggested Writing Assignments

1. With sudden insight, Lamott understands what the Special Olympics meant to her: "it was about tragedy transformed over the years into joy. It was about the beauty of sheer effort" (10). Everyone has experiences in life that take on special meaning. Look back on a significant event that you have witnessed or in which you took part, one that has come to represent to you some important truth about life. Write a narrative essay describing the event. Wait until you are at or approaching the end of your narrative to reveal explicitly your insight into its meaning.
2. When we think about our daily activities, we often clarify our understanding of some aspect of them by seeing one activity in terms of another. Not everyone's perceptions will be the same: a good horseback rider, for example, might come back from a relaxing day on the trail thinking, "Riding a horse is a form of meditation," while the novice bumping around in the saddle thinks, "Riding a horse is a form of torture." A computer expert finds that surfing the Web is like traveling on a magic carpet, while someone else might find it more like being lost in a labyrinth. Choose an activity in your daily life that suggests such a simile or metaphor. Write an essay about the activity that begins with a figure of speech and explores its implications.

A Hanging

George Orwell

Although probably best known for his novels Animal Farm *(1945) and* 1984 *(1949), George Orwell was also a renowned essayist on language and politics. Two of his most famous essays, "Shooting an Elephant" and "Politics and the English Language," are among the most frequently reprinted. Orwell was born in Bengal, India, and educated in England. He traveled a great deal during his life and spent five years serving with the British colonial police in Burma. The following essay is a product of that experience. In it, Orwell relies consistently on similes to help convey and emphasize his attitude about the events he describes, events in which he is both an observer and a participant.*

For Your Journal

Throughout history, we read that people have gone out of their way to witness events in which someone was certain to be killed, such as fights between gladiators, jousting tournaments, and public executions. What fascinates people about such events?

It was in Burma, a sodden morning of the rains. A sickly light, like yellow tinfoil, was slanting over the high walls into the 1
jail yard. We were waiting outside the condemned cells, a row of sheds fronted with double bars, like small animal cages. Each cell measured about ten feet by ten and was quite bare within except for a plank bed and a pot of drinking water. In some of them brown silent men were squatting at the inner bars, with their blankets draped round them. These were the condemned men, due to be hanged within the next week or two.

One prisoner had been brought out of his cell. He was a Hindu, a puny wisp of a man, with a shaven head and vague liquid eyes. He had a thick, sprouting moustache, absurdly too big for his body, rather like the moustache of a comic man in the films. Six tall Indian warders were guarding him and getting him ready for the gallows. Two of them stood by with rifles with fixed bayonets, while the others handcuffed him, passed a chain through his handcuffs and fixed it to their belts, and lashed his arms tight to his sides. They crowded very close about him, with their hands always on him in a careful, caressing grip, as though all the while feeling him to make sure he was there. It was like men handling a fish which is still alive and may jump back into the water. But he stood quite unresisting, yielding his arms limply to the ropes, as though he hardly noticed what was happening. 2

Eight o'clock struck and a bugle call, desolately thin in the wet air, floated from the distant barracks. The superintendent of the jail, who was standing apart from the rest of us, moodily prodding the gravel with his stick, raised his head at the sound. He was an army doctor, with a grey toothbrush moustache and a gruff voice. "For God's sake hurry up, Francis," he said irritably. "The man ought to have been dead by this time. Aren't you ready yet?" 3

Francis, the head jailer, a fat Dravidian in a white drill suit and gold spectacles, waved his black hand. "Yes sir, yes sir," he bubbled. "All iss satisfactorily prepared. The hangman iss waiting. We shall proceed." 4

"Well, quick march, then. The prisoners can't get their breakfast till this job's over." 5

We set out for the gallows. Two warders marched on either side of the prisoner, with their files at the slope; two others marched close against him, gripping him by arm and shoulder, as though at once pushing and supporting him. The rest of us, magistrates and the like, followed behind. Suddenly, when we had gone ten yards, the procession stopped short without any order or warning. A dreadful thing had happened—a dog, come goodness knows whence, had appeared in the yard. It came bounding among us with a loud volley of barks, and leapt round us wagging its whole body, wild with glee at finding so many human beings together. It was a large woolly dog, half Airedale, half pariah. For a moment it pranced round us, and then, before anyone could stop it, 6 it had made a dash for the prisoner, and jumping up tried to lick his face. Everyone stood aghast, too taken aback even to grab at the dog.

7 "Who let that bloody brute in here?" said the superintendent angrily. "Catch it, someone!"

8 A warder, detached from the escort, charged clumsily after the dog, but it danced and gambolled just out of his reach, taking everything as part of the game. A young Eurasian jailer picked up a handful of gravel and tried to stone the dog away, but it dodged the stones and came after us again. Its yaps echoed from the jail walls. The prisoner, in the grasp of the two warders, looked on incuriously, as though this was another formality of the hanging. It was several minutes before someone managed to catch the dog. Then we put my handkerchief through its collar and moved off once more, with the dog still straining and whimpering.

9 It was about forty yards to the gallows. I watched the bare brown back of the prisoner marching in front of me. He walked clumsily with his bound arms, but quite steadily, with that bobbing gait of the Indian who never straightens his knees. At each step his muscles slid neatly into place, the lock of hair on his scalp danced up and down, his feet printed themselves on the wet gravel. And once, in spite of the men who gripped him by each shoulder, he stepped slightly aside to avoid a puddle on the path.

10 It is curious, but till that moment I had never realised what it means to destroy a healthy, conscious man. When I saw the prisoner step aside to avoid the puddle, I saw the mystery, the unspeakable wrongness, of cutting a life short when it is in full tide. This man was not dying, he was alive just as we were alive. All the organs of his body were working—bowels digesting food, skin renewing itself, nails growing, tissues forming—all toiling away in solemn foolery. His nails would still be growing when he stood on the drop, when he was falling through the air with a tenth of a second to live. His eyes saw the yellow gravel and the grey walls, and his brain still remembered, foresaw, reasoned—reasoned even about puddles. He and we were a party of men walking together, seeing, hearing, feeling, understanding the same world; and in two minutes, with a sudden snap, one of us would be gone—one mind less, one world less.

11 The gallows stood in a small yard, separate from the main grounds of the prison, and overgrown with tall prickly weeds. It

was a brick erection like three sides of a shed, with planking on top, and above that two beams and a crossbar with the rope dangling. The hangman, a grey-haired convict in the white uniform of the prison, was waiting beside his machine. He greeted us with a servile crouch as we entered. At a word from Francis the two warders, gripping the prisoner more closely than ever, half led, half pushed him to the gallows and helped him clumsily up the ladder. Then the hangman climbed up and fixed the rope round the prisoner's neck.

We stood waiting, five yards away. The warders had formed in 12
a rough circle round the gallows. And then, when the noose was fixed, the prisoner began crying out to his god. It was a high, reiterated cry of "Ram! Ram! Ram! Ram!," not urgent and fearful like a prayer or a cry for help, but steady, rhythmical, almost like the tolling of a bell. The dog answered the sound with a whine. The hangman, still standing on the gallows, produced a small cotton bag like a flour bag and drew it down over the prisoner's face. But the sound, muffled by the cloth, still persisted, over and over again: "Ram! Ram! Ram! Ram! Ram!"

The hangman climbed down and stood ready, holding the 13
lever. Minutes seemed to pass. The steady, muffled crying from the prisoner went on and on, "Ram! Ram! Ram!" never faltering for an instant. The superintendent, his head on his chest, was slowly poking the ground with his stick; perhaps he was counting the cries, allowing the prisoner a fixed number—fifty, perhaps, or a hundred. Everyone had changed colour. The Indians had gone grey like bad coffee, and one or two of the bayonets were wavering. We looked at the lashed, hooded man on the drop, and listened to his cries—each cry another second of life; the same thought was in all our minds: oh, kill him quickly, get it over, stop that abominable noise!

Suddenly the superintendent made up his mind. Throwing up 14
his head he made a swift motion with his stick. "Chalo!" he shouted almost fiercely.

There was a clanking noise, and then dead silence. The pris- 15
oner had vanished, and the rope was twisting on itself. I let go of the dog, and it galloped immediately to the back of the gallows; but when it got there it stopped short, barked, and then retreated into a corner of the yard, where it stood among the weeds, looking timorously out at us. We went round the gallows to inspect

the prisoner's body. He was dangling with his toes pointed straight downwards, very slowly revolving, as dead as a stone.

The superintendent reached out with his stick and poked the 16
bare body; it oscillated, slightly. "*He's* all right," said the superintendent. He backed out from under the gallows, and blew out a deep breath. The moody look had gone out of his face quite suddenly. He glanced at his wristwatch. "Eight minutes past eight. Well, that's all for this morning, thank God."

The warders unfixed bayonets and marched away. The dog, 17
sobered and conscious of having misbehaved itself, slipped after them. We walked out of the gallows yard, past the condemned cells with their waiting prisoners, into the big central yard of the prison. The convicts, under the command of warders armed with lathis, were already receiving their breakfast. They squatted in long rows, each man holding a tin pannikin, while two warders with buckets marched round ladling out rice; it seemed quite a homely, jolly scene, after the hanging. An enormous relief had come upon us now that the job was done. One felt an impulse to sing, to break into a run, to snigger. All at once everyone began chattering gaily.

The Eurasian boy walking beside me nodded towards the way 18
we had come, with a knowing smile: "Do you know, sir, our friend (he meant the dead man), when he heard his appeal had been dismissed, he pissed on the floor of his cell. From fright.—Kindly take one of my cigarettes, sir. Do you not admire my new silver case, sir? From the boxwallah, two rupees eight annas. Classy European style."

Several people laughed—at what, nobody seemed certain. 19

Francis was walking by the superintendent, talking garru- 20
lously: "Well, sir, all hass passed off with the utmost satisfactoriness. It wass all finished—flick! like that. It iss not always so—oah, no! I have known cases where the doctor wass obliged to go beneath the gallows and pull the prisoner's legs to ensure decease. Most disagreeable!"

"Wriggling about, eh? That's bad," said the superintendent. 21

"Ach, sir, it iss worse when they become refractory! One man, 22
I recall, clung to the bars of hiss cage when we went to take him out. You will scarcely credit, sir, that it took six warders to dislodge him, three pulling at each leg. We reasoned with him. 'My dear fellow,' we said, 'think of all the pain and trouble you are

causing to us!' But no, he would not listen! Ach, he wass very troublesome!"

I found that I was laughing quite loudly. Everyone was laughing. Even the superintendent grinned in a tolerant way. "You'd better all come out and have a drink," he said quite genially. "I've got a bottle of whisky in the car. We could do with it." 23

We went through the big double gates of the prison, into the road. "Pulling at his legs!" exclaimed a Burmese magistrate suddenly, and burst into a loud chuckling. We all began laughing again. At that moment Francis's anecdote seemed extraordinarily funny. We all had a drink together, native and European alike, quite amicably. The dead man was a hundred yards away. 24

Questions for Study and Discussion

1. In paragraph 6, why is the appearance of the dog "a dreadful thing"? From whose point of view is it dreadful? Why?
2. The role of the narrator of this essay (Glossary: *Narration*) is never clearly defined, nor is the nature of the prisoner's transgression. Why does Orwell deliberately withhold this information?
3. In paragraphs 9 and 10, the prisoner steps aside to avoid a puddle, and Orwell considers the implications of this action. What understanding does he reach? In paragraph 10, what is the meaning of the phrase "one mind less, one world less"?
4. In paragraph 22, what is ironic about Francis's story of the "troublesome" prisoner? (Glossary: *Irony*)
5. Throughout this essay, Orwell uses figurative language, primarily similes, to bring a strange foreign experience closer to the reader's understanding. Find and explain three or four similes that clarify the event for a modern American reader.
6. Orwell goes to some pains to identify the multicultural nature of the group participating in the hanging scene: Hindu, Dravidian, Eurasian, European, Burmese. Even the dog is "half Airedale, half pariah." What is a pariah, and why is its inclusion appropriate? Why is the variety of backgrounds of the participants important to the central idea of the essay?

7. What word or words would you use to describe the mood of the group that observed the hanging before the event? Afterward? Cite specific details to support your word choice. Why are the moods so extreme?

Vocabulary

Refer to your dictionary to define the following words as they are used in this selection. Then use each word in a sentence of your own.

magistrates (6)	timorously (15)
volley (6)	oscillated (16)
gambolled (8)	garrulously (20)
erection (11)	refractory (22)
servile (11)	genially (23)
abominable (13)	amicably (24)

Classroom Activity on Figurative Language

Think of a time when you were one of a group of people assembled to do something most or all of you didn't really want to do. People in such a situation behave in various ways to show their discomfort. One might stare steadily at the ground, for example. An author describing the scene could use a metaphor to make it more vivid for the reader: "With his gaze he drilled a hole in the ground between his feet."

Other people in the situation might fidget, lace their fingers together, breathe rapidly, squirm, or tap an object, such as a pen or a key. Create a simile or metaphor to describe each of these behaviors.

Suggested Writing Assignments

1. Are the men who carry out the hanging in Orwell's essay cruel? Are they justified in their actions, following orders from others better able to judge? Or should they question their assigned role as executioners? Who has the right to take the life of another? Write an essay in which you either

condemn or support Orwell's role in the hanging of the Hindu. Was it appropriate for him to have participated, even as a spectator? What, if anything, should or could he have done when he "saw the mystery, the unspeakable wrongness, of cutting a life short when it is in full tide" (10)?

2. Recall and narrate an event in your life when you or someone you know underwent some sort of punishment. You may have been a participant or a spectator in the event. How did you react when you learned what the punishment was to be? When it was administered? After it was over? Use figurative language to make vivid the scene during which the punishment was imposed.

10

ILLUSTRATION

Illustration is the use of examples to make ideas more concrete and to make generalizations more specific and detailed. Examples enable writers not just to tell but to show what they mean. For instance, an essay about recently developed alternative sources of energy becomes clear and interesting with the use of some examples—say, solar energy or the heat from the earth's core. The more specific the example, the more effective it is. Along with general statements about solar energy, the writer might offer several examples of how the home building industry is promoting the installation of solar collectors instead of conventional oil, gas, or electric systems, and is suggesting the building of solar greenhouses to replace conventional central heating.

In an essay a writer uses examples to clarify or support the thesis; in a paragraph, to clarify or support the main idea. Sometimes a single striking example suffices; sometimes a whole series of related examples is necessary. The following paragraph presents a single extended example—an anecdote, or story—that illustrates the author's point about cultural differences:

> Whenever there is a great cultural distance between two people, there are bound to be problems arising from differences in behavior and expectations. An example is the American couple who consulted a psychiatrist about their marital problems. The husband was from New England and had been brought up by reserved parents who taught him to control his emotions and to respect the need for privacy. His wife was from an Italian family and had been brought up in close contact with all the members of her large family, who were extremely warm, volatile and demonstrative. When the husband came home after a hard day at the office, dragging his feet and longing for peace and quiet, his wife would rush to him and smother him. Clasping his hands, rubbing his brow, crooning over his weary head, she never left him alone. But when the wife was upset or anxious about her day, the husband's response was to withdraw completely and leave her

> alone. No comforting, no affectionate embrace, no attention—just solitude. The woman became convinced her husband didn't love her and, in desperation, she consulted a psychiatrist. Their problem wasn't basically psychological but cultural.
>
> Edward T. Hall

This single example is effective because it is *representative*—that is, essentially similar to other such problems Hall might have described and familiar to many readers. Hall tells the story with enough detail that readers can understand the couple's feelings and so better understand the point he is trying to make.

In contrast, Edwin Way Teale supports his topic sentence about country superstitions with ten examples:

> In the folklore of the country, numerous superstitions relate to winter weather. Back-country farmers examine their corn husks—the thicker the husk, the colder the winter. They watch the acorn crop—the more acorns, the more severe the season. They observe where white-faced hornets place their paper nests—the higher they are, the deeper will be the snow. They examine the size and shape and color of the spleens of butchered hogs for clues to the severity of the season. They keep track of the blooming of dogwood in the spring—the more abundant the blooms, the more bitter the cold in January. When chipmunks carry their tails high and squirrels have heavier fur and mice come into country houses early in the fall, the superstitious gird themselves for a long, hard winter. Without any scientific basis, a wider-than-usual black band on a woolly-bear caterpillar is accepted as a sign that winter will arrive early and stay late. Even the way a cat sits beside the stove carries its message to the credulous. According to a belief once widely held in the Ozarks, a cat sitting with its tail to the fire indicates very cold weather is on the way.
>
> Edwin Way Teale

Teale uses numerous examples because he is writing about various superstitions. Also, putting all those strange beliefs side by side in a kind of catalogue makes the paragraph fun to read as well as informative.

Illustration is often found in effective writing; every essay in this book uses examples. Likewise, in this introduction we have used examples to clarify our ideas about illustration.

A Crime of Compassion

Barbara Huttmann

Barbara Huttmann received her nursing degree in 1976. After obtaining a master's degree in nursing administration, she cofounded a health-care consulting firm for hospitals, nursing organizations, and consumers. Her interest in patients' rights is clearly evident in her two books, The Patient's Advocate *and* Code Blue. *In the following essay, which first appeared in* Newsweek *in 1983, Huttmann narrates the final months of the life of Mac, one of her favorite patients. By using emotional and graphic detail, Huttmann hopes the example of Mac will convince her audience of the need for new legislation that would permit terminally ill patients to choose to die rather than suffer great pain and indignity. As you read about Mac, consider the degree to which his experience seems representative of what patients often endure because medical technology is now able to keep them alive longer than they would be able to survive on their own.*

For Your Journal

For most people, being sick is at best an unpleasant experience. Reflect on an illness you have had, whether you were sick with a simple common cold or with an affliction that required you to be hospitalized for a time. What were your concerns, your fears? For what were you most thankful?

"Murderer," a man shouted. "God help patients who get *you* for a nurse." 1

"What gives you the right to play God?" another one asked. 2

It was the Phil Donahue show where the guest is a fatted calf and the audience a 200-strong flock of vultures hungering to pick 3 at the bones. I had told them about Mac, one of my favorite cancer patients. "We resuscitated him 52 times in just one month. I refused to resuscitate him again. I simply sat there and held his hand while he died."

There wasn't time to explain that Mac was a young, witty, 4
macho cop who walked into the hospital with 32 pounds of attack equipment, looking as if he could single-handedly protect the whole city, if not the entire state. "Can't get rid of this cough," he said. Otherwise, he felt great.

Before the day was over, tests confirmed that he had lung can- 5
cer. And before the year was over, I loved him, his wife, Maura, and their three kids as if they were my own. All the nurses loved him. And we all battled his disease for six months without ever giving death a thought. Six months isn't such a long time in the whole scheme of things, but it was long enough to see him lose his youth, his wit, his macho, his hair, his bowel and bladder control, his sense of taste and smell, and his ability to do the slightest thing for himself. It was also long enough to watch Maura's transformation from a young woman into a haggard, beaten old lady.

When Mac had wasted away to a 60-pound skeleton kept alive 6
by liquid food we poured down a tube, IV solutions we dripped into his veins, and oxygen we piped to a mask on his face, he begged us: "Mercy . . . for God's sake, please just let me go."

The first time he stopped breathing, the nurse pushed the but- 7
ton that calls a "code blue" throughout the hospital and sends a team rushing to resuscitate the patient. Each time he stopped breathing, sometimes two or three times in one day, the code team came again. The doctors and technicians worked their miracles and walked away. The nurses stayed to wipe the saliva that drooled from his mouth, irrigate the big craters of bedsores that covered his hips, suction the lung fluids that threatened to drown him, clean the feces that burned his skin like lye, pour the liquid food down the tube attached to his stomach, put pillows between his knees to ease the bone-on-bone pain, turn him every hour to keep the bedsores from getting worse, and change his gown and linen every two hours to keep him from being soaked in perspiration.

At night I went home and tried to scrub away the smell of de- 8
caying flesh that seemed woven into the fabric of my uniform. It was in my hair, the upholstery of my car—there was no washing it away. And every night I prayed that Mac would die, that his agonized eyes would never again plead with me to let him die.

Every morning I asked his doctor for a "no-code" order. Without that order, we had to resuscitate every patient who stopped breathing. His doctor was one of several who believe we must extend life as long as we have the means and knowledge to do it. To not do it is to be liable for negligence, at least in the eyes of many people, including some nurses. I thought about what it would be like to stand before a judge, accused of murder, if Mac stopped breathing and I didn't call a code. 9

And after the fifty-second code, when Mac was still lucid enough to beg for death again, and Maura was crumbled in my arms again, and when no amount of pain medication stilled his moaning and agony, I wondered about a spiritual judge. Was all this misery and suffering supposed to be building character or infusing us all with the sense of humility that comes from impotence? 10

Had we, the whole medical community, become so arrogant that we believed in the illusion of salvation through science? Had we become so self-righteous that we thought meddling in God's work was our duty, our moral imperative and our legal obligation? Did we really believe that we had the right to force "life" on a suffering man who had begged for the right to die? 11

Such questions haunted me more than ever early one morning when Maura went home to change her clothes and I was bathing Mac. He had been still for so long, I thought he at last had the blessed relief of coma. Then he opened his eyes and moaned, "Pain . . . no more . . . Barbara . . . do something . . . God, let me go." 12

The desperation in his eyes and voice riddled me with guilt. "I'll stop," I told him as I injected the pain medication. 13

I sat on the bed and held Mac's hands in mine. He pressed his bony fingers against my hand and muttered, "Thanks." Then there was one soft sigh and I felt his hands go cold in mine. "Mac?" I whispered, as I waited for his chest to rise and fall again. 14

A clutch of panic banded my chest, drew my finger to the code button, urged me to do something, anything . . . but sit there alone with death. I kept one finger on the button, without pressing it, as a waxen pallor slowly transformed his face from person to empty shell. Nothing I've ever done in my 47 years has taken so much effort as it took *not* to press that code button. 15

Eventually, when I was as sure as I could be that the code team would fail to bring him back, I entered the legal twilight zone 16 and pushed the button. The team tried. And while they were trying, Maura walked into the room and shrieked, "No . . . don't let them do this to him . . . for God's sake . . . please, no more."

Cradling her in my arms was like cradling myself, Mac, and all those patients and nurses who had been in this place before, who do the best they can in a death-denying society. 17

So a TV audience accused me of murder. Perhaps I am guilty. 18
If a doctor had written a no-code order, which is the only *legal* alternative, would he have felt any less guilty? Until there is legislation making it a criminal act to code a patient who has requested the right to die, we will all of us risk the same fate as Mac. For whatever reason, we developed the means to prolong life, and now we are forced to use it. We do not have the right to die.

Questions for Study and Discussion

1. Why did people in the audience of the *Phil Donahue Show* call Huttmann a "murderer"? Is there any sense in which their accusation is justified? In what ways do you think Huttmann might agree with them?
2. In paragraph 15, Huttmann says, "Nothing I've ever done in my 47 years has taken so much effort as it took *not* to press that code button." How effectively does she describe her struggle against pressing the button? What steps led to her ultimate decision not to press the code button?
3. What, according to Huttmann, is the "only legal alternative" to her action? What does she find hypocritical about that choice?
4. Huttmann makes a powerfully emotional appeal for a patient's right to die. Some readers might even find some of her story shocking or offensive. Cite examples of some of the graphic scenes Huttmann describes and discuss their impact on you as a reader. (Glossary: *Example*) Did they help persuade you to Huttmann's point of view or did you find them overly unnerving? What would have been gained or lost had she left them out?

5. The story in Huttmann's example covers a period of six months. In paragraphs 4–6, she describes the first five months of Mac's illness; in paragraphs 7–10, the sixth month; and in paragraphs 12–17, the final morning. What important point about narration does her use of time in this sequence demonstrate?
6. Huttmann concludes her essay with the statement, "We do not have the right to die." What does she mean by this? In your opinion, is she exaggerating, or simply stating the facts? Does her example of Mac adequately illustrate Huttmann's concluding point?

Vocabulary

Refer to your dictionary to define the following words as they are used in this selection. Then use each word in a sentence of your own.

resuscitate (3)	imperative (11)
irrigate (7)	waxen (15)
lucid (10)	pallor (15)

Classroom Activity Using Illustration

Barbara Huttmann illustrates her thesis by using the single example of Mac's experience in the hospital. For each of the following potential thesis statements, what single example might be used to best illustrate each one:

Seat belts save lives. (*Possible answer:* The example of an automobile accident in which a relative's life was saved because she was wearing her seat belt.)
Friends can be very handy.
Having good study skills can improve a student's grades.
Loud music can damage your hearing.
Reading the directions for a new product you have just purchased can save time and aggravation.
Humor can often make a bad situation more tolerable.
American manufacturers can make their products safer.

Suggested Writing Assignments

1. Write a letter to the editor of *Newsweek* in which you respond to Huttmann's essay. Would you be for or against legislation that would give terminally ill patients the right to die? Give examples from your personal experience or from your reading to support your opinion.
2. Using one of the following sentences as your thesis statement, write an essay giving examples from personal experience or from reading to support your opinion.

   Consumers have more power than they realize.
   Most products do/do not measure up to the claims of their advertisements.
   Religion is/is not alive and well in America.
   Our government works far better than its critics claim.
   Being able to write well is more than a basic skill.
   The seasons for professional sports are too long.
   Today's college students are serious minded when it comes to academics.

The Case for Short Words

Richard Lederer

Richard Lederer has been a prolific and popular writer about language. He is the vice president of S.P.E.L.L. (the Society for the Preservation of English Literature and Language) and the author of numerous books about how Americans use language, including Anguished English *(1987),* The Play of Words *(1990),* The Miracle of Language *(1991),* More Anguished English *(1993),* Adventures of a Verbivore *(1994), and his most recent,* Fractured English *(1996). In addition to writing books, Lederer pens a weekly column called "Looking at Language" for newspapers and magazines all over the United States. He is also the Grammar Grappler for* Writer's Digest *and language commentator for National Public Radio. After spending many years as an English teacher at St. Paul's School in Concord, New Hampshire, Lederer now lives in Las Vegas, Nevada. In the essay below, pay particular attention to the different ways he uses examples to illustrate. The title and first four paragraphs serve as an extended example of his point about small words, while later in the essay he incorporates examples from his students' writing to illustrate that point more deliberately.*

For Your Journal

We all carry with us a vocabulary of short, simple-looking words that possess a special personal meaning. For example, to some the word *rose* represents not just a flower, but a whole array of gardens, ceremonies, and romantic occasions. What are a few little words that have special meaning for you? What images do they bring to mind?

When you speak and write, there is no law that says you have to use big words. Short words are as good as long ones, and short, old words—like *sun* and *grass* and *home*—are best of all. A lot of small words, more than you might think, can meet your needs with a strength, grace, and charm that large words do not have. 1

Big words can make the way dark for those who read what you write and hear what you say. Small words cast their clear light on big things—night and day, love and hate, war and peace, and life and death. Big words at times seem strange to the eye and the ear and the mind and the heart. Small words are the ones we seem to have known from the time we were born, like the hearth fire that warms the home. 2

Short words are bright like sparks that glow in the night, prompt like the dawn that greets the day, sharp like the blade of a knife, hot like salt tears that scald the cheek, quick like moths that flit from flame to flame, and terse like the dart and sting of a bee. 3

Here is a sound rule: Use small, old words where you can. If a long word says just what you want to say, do not fear to use it. But know that our tongue is rich in crisp, brisk, swift, short words. Make them the spine and the heart of what you speak and write. Short words are like fast friends. They will not let you down. 4

The title of this chapter and the four paragraphs that you have just read are wrought entirely of words of one syllable. In setting myself this task, I did not feel especially cabined, cribbed, or confined. In fact, the structure helped me to focus on the power of the message I was trying to put across. 5

One study shows that twenty words account for twenty-five percent of all spoken English words, and all twenty are monosyllabic. In order of frequency they are: *I, you, the, a, to, is, it, that, of, and, in, what, he, this, have, do, she, not, on,* and *they*. Other studies indicate that the fifty most common words in written English are each made of a single syllable. 6

For centuries our finest poets and orators have recognized and employed the power of small words to make a straight point between two minds. A great many of our proverbs punch home their points with pithy monosyllables: "Where there's a will, there's a way," "A stitch in time saves nine," "Spare the rod and spoil the child," "A bird in the hand is worth two in the bush." 7

Nobody used the short word more skillfully than William Shakespeare, whose dying King Lear laments: 8

> And my poor fool is hang'd! No, no, no life!
> Why should a dog, a horse, a rat have life,
> And thou no breath at all? . . .
> Do you see this? Look on her, look, her lips.
> Look there, look there!

Shakespeare's contemporaries made the King James Bible a centerpiece of short words—"And God said, Let there be light: and there was light. And God saw the light, that it was good." The descendants of such mighty lines live on in the twentieth century. When asked to explain his policy to Parliament, Winston Churchill responded with these ringing monosyllables: "I will say: it is to wage war, by sea, land, and air, with all our might and with all the strength that God can give us." In his "Death of the Hired Man" Robert Frost observes that "Home is the place where, when you have to go there,/They have to take you in." And William H. Johnson uses ten two-letter words to explain his secret of success: "If it is to be,/It is up to me." 9

You don't have to be a great author, statesman, or philosopher to tap the energy and eloquence of small words. Each winter I ask my ninth graders at St. Paul's School to write a composition composed entirely of one-syllable words. My students greet my request with obligatory moans and groans, but, when they return to class with their essays, most feel that, with the pressure to produce high-sounding polysyllables relieved, they have created some of their most powerful and luminous prose. Here are submissions from two of my ninth graders: 10

> What can you say to a boy who has left home? You can say that he has done wrong, but he does not care. He has left home so that he will not have to deal with what you say. He wants to go as far as he can. He will do what he wants to do.
>
> This boy does not want to be forced to go to church, to comb his hair, or to be on time. A good time for this boy does not lie in your reach, for what you have he does not want. He dreams of ripped jeans, shorts with no starch, and old socks.
>
> So now this boy is on a bus to a place he dreams of, a place with no rules. This boy now walks a strange street, his long hair blown back by the wind. He wears no coat or tie,

just jeans and an old shirt. He hates your world, and he has left it.

Charles Shaffer

For a long time we cruised by the coast and at last came to a wide bay past the curve of a hill, at the end of which lay a small town. Our long boat ride at an end, we all stretched and stood up to watch as the boat nosed its way in.

The town climbed up the hill that rose from the shore, a space in front of it left bare for the port. Each house was a clean white with sky blue or grey trim; in front of each one was a small yard, edged by a white stone wall strewn with green vines.

As the town basked in the heat of noon, not a thing stirred in the streets or by the shore. The sun beat down on the sea, the land, and the back of our necks, so that, in spite of the breeze that made the vines sway, we all wished we could hide from the glare in a cool, white house. But, as there was no one to help dock the boat, we had to stand and wait.

At last the head of the crew leaped from the side and strode to a large house on the right. He shoved the door wide, poked his head through the gloom, and roared with a fierce voice. Five or six men came out, and soon the port was loud with the clank of chains and creak of planks as the men caught ropes thrown by the crew, pulled them taut, and tied them to posts. Then they set up a rough plank so we could cross from the deck to the shore. We all made for the large house while the crew watched, glad to be rid of us.

Celia Wren

You too can tap into the vitality and vigor of compact expression. Take a suggestion from the highway department. At the boundaries of your speech and prose place a sign that reads "Caution: Small Words at Work." 11

Questions for Study and Discussion

1. Lederer says in paragraph 1 that "short, old words—like *sun* and *grass* and *home*—are best of all." What are the attributes of these words that make them "best"? Why are short old words superior to short newer words? (Glossary: *Connotation/Denotation*)

2. In this essay, written to encourage the use of short words, Lederer himself employs many polysyllabic words, especially in paragraphs 5 through 9. What is his purpose in doing so?
3. Lederer quotes a wide variety of passages to illustrate the effectiveness of short words. For example, he quotes from famous, universally familiar old sources such as Shakespeare and the King James Bible, and from unknown contemporary sources such as his own ninth-grade students. How does the variety of his illustrations serve to inform his readers? (Glossary: *Exposition*) How does each example gain impact from the inclusion of the others?
4. To make clear to the reader why short words are effective, Lederer relies heavily on metaphor and simile, especially in the first four paragraphs. (Glossary: *Figures of Speech*) Choose at least one metaphor and one simile from these paragraphs and explain the comparison implicit in each.
5. In paragraph 10, Lederer refers to the relief his students feel when released from "the pressure to produce high-sounding polysyllables." Where does this pressure come from? How does it relate to the central purpose of this essay?
6. How does the final paragraph serve to close the essay effectively? (Glossary: *Beginnings and Endings*)
7. This essay abounds with examples of striking sentences and passages consisting entirely of words of one syllable. Choose four of the single-sentence examples or a section of several sentences from one of the longer examples and rewrite them, using only words of two or more syllables. Notice how the effect differs from the original.

Vocabulary

Refer to your dictionary to define the following words as they are used in this selection. Then use each word in a sentence of your own.

cabined (5)
cribbed (5)
monosyllabic (6)
proverbs (7)
eloquence (10)
obligatory (10)
vitality (11)

Classroom Activity Using Illustration

In your opinion, what is the finest sort of present to give or receive? Why? Define the ideal gift. Illustrate by describing one or more of the best gifts you have received or given, making it clear how each fits the ideal.

Suggested Writing Assignments

1. Follow the assignment Lederer gives his own students: "Write a composition composed entirely of one-syllable words." Make your piece about the length of his student examples or of his own four-paragraph opening.
2. A chief strength of Lederer's essay is his use of a broad variety of examples to illustrate his thesis that short words are the most effective. Choose a subject about which you are knowledgeable, and find as wide a range of examples as you can to illustrate its appeal. For example, if you are enthusiastic about water, you could explore the relative attractions of puddles, ponds, lakes, and oceans; if a music lover, you might consider why Bach and/or the Beatles became popular far beyond the boundaries of the musical tastes of their eras.

A Read-Only Man in an Interactive Age

George Felton

George Felton lives in Columbus, Ohio, and is an associate professor of English at the Columbus College of Art and Design, where he teaches writing and copywriting. His textbook, Advertising: Concept and Copy, *was published in 1994. He has also contributed essays on popular culture, the media, and his own perplexities to* Newsweek, *the* New York Times, Advertising Age, *and the* Los Angeles Times. *In the following selection, first published in the* Wall Street Journal *in May 1995, Felton relies on numerous examples to emphasize how pervasive the notion of interactivity has become in regard to what we read, view, or listen to. As you read, take note of the way he uses examples within his paragraphs to support and clarify his topic sentences.*

For Your Journal

Have you ever voted by telephone in a TV poll or sent a customer survey back to a company? If so, why did you choose to participate? If not, why didn't you participate?

America's obsession with interactivity is going too far. Recently my CBS affiliate, WBNS-TV, wanted me to tell them what the news would be: "The future of television news is in your hands. You pick the story you want to see tonight at 11." I was given three options, each with an 800 number: 1. foods that make you nuts, 2. cabbies—is the fare fair? 3. things to know before you sign a house contract. I was supposed to jump to the phone and vote. 1

This is just a gimmick, of course. It's condescending, overhyped, and irrelevant all at once, but none of that bothers me; local news as a genre is virtually defined by such terms. What does 2 bother me is the growing demand that I stick my finger into the middle of every experience I have, no matter with whom or what. In this instance, I want WBNS to pick the news. I've been doing my job all day. Let them do theirs.

Everywhere I turn I'm being urged to dial, punch, vote, fax, e-mail, double click, or simply stand up, grab the microphone, and let loose with my comment, my question, my need, my self. It's our new, interactive way of being, and if it's all about control, I don't think I want that much. 3

Interactivity's key premise is that, at long last, I get to direct the action: I point and click or stand up and fire my salvo, after which the thing viewed changes its course for me. I'm told I'll soon be able to sit in my living room and press a button routing the movie/book/video/CD/experience-mechanism in the direction I want it to go. Why let Thoreau lead me around by the nose if I can hypertext my own way across Walden? Why move my lips if I can press a button and have James Earl Jones move them for me? Why suffer Walden's dreary, gray type at all if I can punch up on CD-ROM a video of the more recent, more dramatic fight to preserve the pond from developers, or better yet, watch a Don Henley benefit concert that makes me feel noble about what I just quit reading? 4

Which gets me to one of my problems with the interactive future: When I'm finally free to direct where *everything* goes, I'll never go anywhere I don't intend. In fact, I'll never learn anything new, just keep recycling a few of my favorite things. I do enough of this already. I don't need invitations to spiral even deeper into my own black holes. 5

Nor do I need to have a "conversation" with Thoreau in which I determine what's interesting and get appropriate text bytes in response. If it took him two years to live the book, nine years to write it, and six drafts to get it right, I can at least shut up and let him determine what's interesting. But this has become an old-fashioned idea, very out of tune with the noisy, nosy I-Me-My-isms of interactive life. 6

My Lutheran church, for example, no longer finds the call and refrain of its own liturgy sufficiently interactive. Now the pastor opens with a warm-up monologue during which he invites comment. We interrupt the service to stand, shake hands, and exchange greetings. The kids are trooped up front for an interac- 7 tive mini-sermon—the pastor telling them a parable and asking questions, during which they fidget and mumble. I wonder if next week they'll be asked to field questions from us.

I go to an art exhibit, only to discover it's nothing without me. 8
I must help create the art by intersecting it, walking into the viewerscope of a camera, spinning a globe and making videos reel, sticking my nose in a little hole and having a woman in there talk back to me. As one art critic said about the show, it's hard to know what to make of it, but it sure is noisy.

At home my newspaper thinks if I'm just reading it, I'm not 9
doing enough. I've got to say how the mayor's doing, call the tax hot line with my Schedule C problems, fill in today's clip-out quiz about O.J. I turn on the radio, but it turns on me. Ron Barr's "Sports Byline USA" has a line open and needs a call. Our local NPR station is schmoozing with P. J. O'Rourke and wants me to make it a three-way. I click on TV—and not a moment too soon. VH-1 says it's now or never if I want good Tom Petty tickets for the summer tour. Bob Berkowitz needs some fast answers about masturbation. NBC's "Dateline" doesn't know what to make of the latest news scandal. Can I take a quick gut check and give them a call, send a fax, maybe an e-mail?

I reach for a beer, but even it wants to hear from me. It says so 10
on the little paper band around its neck, the band I love to rake off with my thumbnail while drinking, the one that used to say "the champagne of bottled beer" or some other satisfyingly dumb advertising slogan. But now I look down and see an 800 number. I am being urged to speak with my beer, which is entirely different from mumbling in its presence, a far more traditional interaction and, these days, perhaps a more meaningful one.

Questions for Study and Discussion

1. What is Felton's thesis? (Glossary: *Thesis*) Where does he state it?
2. Why does Felton feel that TV news is condescending, overhyped, and irrelevant? Do you agree with this rather critical assessment? Why, or why not?

3. Identify three examples Felton uses to illustrate his thesis. In what way does each example help Felton make his point?
4. Why doesn't Felton like the increased control that interactivity offers him? When, in his opinion, is it better to "shut up" and accept what's presented to him?
5. What is the tone of Felton's essay? (Glossary: *Tone*) Support your answer with examples of his diction. (Glossary: *Diction*)
6. Felton's concluding sentence is an obviously sarcastic comment. How effective is it as an ending? (Glossary: *Beginnings and Endings*) Why do you suppose he chose to end his essay in this way?

Vocabulary

Refer to your dictionary to define the following words as they are used in this selection. Then use each word in a sentence of your own.

interactivity (1)
genre (2)
salvo (4)
hypertext (5)
liturgy (7)

Classroom Activity Using Illustration

Think about the following thesis: "Computers and electronic devices play a large role in my life every day." Write four sentences that provide examples that effectively illustrate this thesis. For example, "The computer chip in my car makes it more fuel efficient, which saves me money."

Suggested Writing Assignments

1. Felton suggests that the interactive future will stifle his inclination to learn anything new. He says, "I don't need invitations to spiral even deeper into my own black holes" (5). Write an essay in which you argue for or against this assessment. Will technology stimulate or stifle learning and curi-

osity? Illustrate your essay with examples from your own experience with our current technology.

2. Spend a week collecting and recording every customer survey, request for viewer feedback, and other request that involves what Felton would call interactivity. What kinds of information are these surveys and requests looking for? Come up with a thesis statement that is either for or against the "control" such interactivity gives you. Write an essay in which you argue your thesis, illustrating your points with examples of interactivity that you found.

DON'T LET STEREOTYPES WARP YOUR JUDGMENTS

Robert L. Heilbroner

The economist Robert L. Heilbroner was educated at Harvard and at the New School for Social Research, where he has been the Norman Thomas Professor of Economics since 1972. His many books over the past few decades include The Future as History *(1960),* A Primer of Government Spending: Between Capitalism and Socialism *(1970),* An Inquiry into the Human Prospect *(1974), and, more recently,* Visions of the Future *(1995). "Don't Let Stereotypes Warp Your Judgments" first appeared in* Reader's Digest, *and is particularly timely for people seeking understanding and respect for all in a culturally diverse, pluralistic society. In the essay, Heilbroner relies on the authority of questionnaires, university studies, and the findings of criminologists to bolster his own opinions. He also uses quotes from people known for their observations about human behavior to support and illustrate his statements about stereotypes and prejudice.*

FOR YOUR JOURNAL

"Stereotypes are a kind of gossip about the world, a gossip that makes us prejudge people before we ever lay eyes on them," writes Robert L. Heilbroner. Do you find yourself relying on stereotypes? What are they? Are they helpful to you in any way?

Is a girl called Gloria apt to be better-looking than one called Bertha? Are criminals more likely to be dark than blond? Can you tell a good deal about someone's personality from hearing his voice briefly over the phone? Can a person's nationality be 1 pretty accurately guessed from his photograph? Does the fact that someone wears glasses imply that he is intelligent?

The answer to all these questions is obviously, "No." 2

Yet, from all the evidence at hand, most of us believe these 3 things. Ask any college boy if he'd rather take his chances with a Gloria or a Bertha, or ask a college girl if she'd rather blind-date a Richard or a Cuthbert. In fact, you don't have to ask: college students in questionnaires have revealed that names conjure up the same images in their minds as they do in yours—and for as little reason.

Look into the favorite suspects of persons who report "suspi- 4 cious characters" and you will find a large percentage of them to be "swarthy" or "dark and foreign-looking"—despite the testimony of criminologists that criminals do *not* tend to be dark, foreign or "wild-eyed." Delve into the main asset of a telephone stock swindler and you will find it to be a marvelously confidence-inspiring telephone "personality." And whereas we all think we know what an Italian or a Swede looks like, it is the sad fact that when a group of Nebraska students sought to match faces and nationalities of 15 European countries, they were scored wrong in 93 percent of their identifications. Finally, for all the fact that horn-rimmed glasses have now become the standard television sign of an "intellectual," optometrists know that the main thing that distinguishes people with glasses is just bad eyes.

Stereotypes are a kind of gossip about the world, a gossip that 5 makes us prejudge people before we ever lay eyes on them. Hence it is not surprising that stereotypes have something to do with the dark world of prejudice. Explore most prejudices (note that the word means prejudgment) and you will find a cruel stereotype at the core of each one.

For it is the extraordinary fact that once we have typecast the 6 world, we tend to see people in terms of our standardized pictures. In another demonstration of the power of stereotypes to affect our vision, a number of Columbia and Barnard students were shown 30 photographs of pretty but unidentified girls, and asked to rate each in terms of "general liking," "intelligence," "beauty" and so on. Two months later, the same group were shown the same photographs, this time with fictitious Irish, Italian, Jewish and "American" names attached to the pictures. Right away the ratings changed. Faces which were now seen as representing a national group went down in looks and still farther down in likability, while the "American" girls suddenly looked decidedly prettier and nicer.

Why is it that we stereotype the world in such irrational and 7
harmful fashion? In part, we begin to type-cast people in our childhood years. Early in life, as every parent whose child has watched a TV Western knows, we learn to spot the Good Guys from the Bad Guys. Some years ago, a social psychologist showed very clearly how powerful these stereotypes of childhood vision are. He secretly asked the most popular youngsters in an elementary school to make errors in their morning gym exercises. Afterwards, he asked the class if anyone had noticed any mistakes during gym period. Oh, yes, said the children. But it was the *unpopular* members of the class—the "bad guys"—they remembered as being out of step.

We not only grow up with standardized pictures forming in- 8
side of us, but as grown-ups we are constantly having them thrust upon us. Some of them, like the half-joking, half-serious stereotypes of mothers-in-law, or country yokels, or psychiatrists, are dinned into us by the stock jokes we hear and repeat. In fact, without such stereotypes, there would be a lot fewer jokes. Still other stereotypes are perpetuated by the advertisements we read, the movies we see, the books we read.

And finally, we tend to stereotype because it helps us make 9
sense out of a highly confusing world, a world which William James once described as "one great, blooming, buzzing confusion." It is a curious fact that if we don't *know* what we're looking at, we are often quite literally unable to *see* what we're looking at. People who recover their sight after a lifetime of blindness actually cannot at first tell a triangle from a square. A visitor to a factory sees only noisy chaos where the superintendent sees a perfectly synchronized flow of work. As Walter Lippmann has said, "For the most part we do not first see, and then define; we define first, and then we see."

Stereotypes are one way in which we "define" the world in or- 10
der to see it. They classify the infinite variety of human beings into a convenient handful of "types" towards whom we learn to act in stereotyped fashion. Life would be a wearing process if we had to start from scratch with each and every human contact. Stereotypes economize on our mental effort by covering up the

blooming, buzzing confusion with big recognizable cut-outs. They save us the "trouble" of finding out what the world is like—they give it its accustomed look.

Thus the trouble is that stereotypes make us mentally lazy. As S. I. Hayakawa, the authority on semantics, has written: "The danger of stereotypes lies not in their existence, but in the fact that they become for all people some of the time, and for some people all the time, *substitutes for observation.*" Worse yet, stereotypes get in the way of our judgment, even when we do observe the world. Someone who has formed rigid preconceptions of all Latins as "excitable," or all teenagers as "wild," doesn't alter his point of view when he meets a calm and deliberate Genoese, or a serious-minded high school student. He brushes them aside as "exceptions that prove the rule." And, of course, if he meets someone true to type, he stands triumphantly vindicated. "They're all like that," he proclaims, having encountered an excited Latin, an ill-behaved adolescent. 11

Hence, quite aside from the injustice which stereotypes do to others, they impoverish ourselves. A person who lumps the world into simple categories, who type-casts all labor leaders as "racketeers," all businessmen as "reactionaries," all Harvard men as "snobs," and all Frenchmen as "sexy," is in danger of becoming a stereotype himself. He loses his capacity to be himself—which is to say, to see the world in his own absolutely unique, inimitable and independent fashion. 12

Instead, he votes for the man who fits his standardized picture of what a candidate "should" look like or sound like, buys the goods that someone in his "situation" in life "should" own, lives the life that others define for him. The mark of the stereotyped person is that he never surprises us, that we do indeed have him "typed." And no one fits this strait-jacket so perfectly as someone whose opinions about *other people* are fixed and inflexible. 13

Impoverishing as they are, stereotypes are not easy to get rid of. The world we type-cast may be no better than a Grade B movie, but at least we know what to expect of our stock characters. When we let them act for themselves in the strangely unpredictable way that people do act, who knows but that many of our fondest convictions will be proved wrong? 14

Nor do we suddenly drop our standardized pictures for a blinding vision of the Truth. Sharp swings of ideas about people often 15 just substitute one stereotype for another. The true process of change is a slow one that adds bits and pieces of reality to the pictures in our heads, until gradually they take on some of the blurriness of life itself. Little by little, we learn not that Jews and Negroes and Catholics and Puerto Ricans are "just like everybody else"—for that, too, is a stereotype—but that each and every one of them is unique, special, different and individual. Often we do not even know that we have let a stereotype lapse until we hear someone saying, "all so-and-so's are like such-and-such," and we hear ourselves saying, "Well—maybe."

Can we speed the process along? Of course we can. 16

First, we can become *aware* of the standardized pictures in 17 our heads, in other people's heads, in the world around us.

Second, we can become suspicious of all judgments that we 18 allow exceptions to "prove." There is no more chastening thought than that in the vast intellectual adventure of science, it takes but one tiny exception to topple a whole edifice of ideas.

Third, we can learn to be chary of generalizations about people. 19 As F. Scott Fitzgerald once wrote: "Begin with an individual, and before you know it you have created a type; begin with a type, and you find you have created—nothing."

Most of the time, when we type-cast the world, we are not in 20 fact generalizing about people at all. We are only revealing the embarrassing facts about the pictures that hang in the gallery of stereotypes in our own heads.

Questions for Study and Discussion

1. What is Heilbroner's main point, or thesis, in this essay? (Glossary: *Thesis*)
2. Study paragraphs 6, 8, and 15. Each paragraph illustrates Heilbroner's thesis. How? What does each paragraph contribute to support the thesis?
3. Transitional devices indicate relationships between paragraphs and thus help to unify the essay. Identify three transitions in this essay. Explain how they help to unify the essay. (Glossary: *Transitions*)

4. What are the reasons Heilbroner gives for why we stereotype individuals? What are some of the dangers of stereotypes, according to Heilbroner? How does he say we can rid ourselves of stereotypes?
5. Heilbroner uses the word *picture* in his discussion of stereotypes. Why is this an appropriate word in this discussion? (Glossary: *Diction*)

Vocabulary

Refer to your dictionary to define the following words as they are used in this selection. Then use each word in a sentence of your own.

irrational (7)
perpetuated (8)
infinite (10)
preconceptions (11)
vindicated (11)
impoverish (12)
chastening (18)
edifice (18)
chary (19)

Classroom Activity Using Illustration

In order to present a good example you need to provide details, and to collect telling details you must be observant. To test your powers of observation, try listing the features or qualities of an ordinary object—a soft drink can, a Styrofoam coffee cup, a ballpoint pen—something everyone in the class has access to. Compare your list of characteristics with those of other members of the class. Discuss whether having a label for something—soft drink can, coffee cup, or ballpoint pen—is a help or a hindrance in describing it.

Suggested Writing Assignments

1. Write an essay in which you attempt to convince your readers that it is not in their best interests to perform a particular act—for example, smoke, take stimulants to stay awake, go on a crash diet, or make snap judgments. In writing your

essay, follow Heilbroner's lead: first identify the issue; then explain why it is a problem; and, finally, offer a solution or some advice. Remember to unify the various parts of your essay.

2. Have you ever been stereotyped—as a student, or a member of a particular class, ethnic, national, or racial group? Write a unified essay that examines how stereotyping has affected you, how it has perhaps changed you, and how you regard the process.

11

NARRATION

To *narrate* is to tell a story or to tell what happened. Whenever you relate an incident or use an anecdote to make a point, you use narration. In its broadest sense, narration is any account of any event or series of events. We all love to hear stories; some people believe that sharing stories is a part of what defines us as human beings. Good stories are interesting, sometimes suspenseful—we need to know "how things turn out"—and always instructive because they give us insights into the human condition. Although most often associated with fiction, narration is effective and useful in all kinds of writing. For example, in "Even You Can Get It," author Bruce Lambert narrates the poignant story of Alison Gertz to alert heterosexuals to the fact that they should not become complacent about the need to protect themselves from AIDS.

Good narration has five essential features: a clear context; well-chosen and thoughtfully emphasized details; a logical, often chronological organization; an appropriate and consistent point of view; and a meaningful point or purpose. Consider, for example, the following paragraph from Willie Morris's "On a Commuter Train":

> One afternoon in late August, as the summer's sun streamed into the [railroad] car and made little jumping shadows on the windows, I sat gazing out at the tenement-dwellers, who were themselves looking out of their windows from the gray crumbling buildings along the tracks of upper Manhattan. As we crossed into the Bronx, the train unexpectedly slowed down for a few miles. Suddenly from out of my window I saw a large crowd near the tracks, held back by two policemen. Then, on the other side from my window, I saw a sight I would never be able to forget: a little boy almost severed in halves, lying at an incredible angle near the track. The ground was covered with blood, and the boy's eyes were opened wide, strained and disbelieving in his sudden oblivion. A policeman stood next to him, his arms folded, staring straight ahead at the windows of our train. In the orange glow of late after-

> noon the policemen, the crowd, the corpse of the boy were for a brief moment immobile, motionless, a small tableau to violence and death in the city. Behind me, in the next row of seats, there was a game of bridge. I heard one of the four men say as he looked out at the sight, "God, that's horrible." Another said, in a whisper, "Terrible, terrible." There was a momentary silence, punctuated only by the clicking of the wheels on the track. Then, after the pause, I heard the first man say: "Two hearts."
>
> Willie Morris

This paragraph contains all the elements of good narration. At the beginning Morris establishes a clear context for his narrative, telling when, where, and to whom the action happened. He has chosen details well, including enough detail so that we know what is happening but not so much that we become overwhelmed, confused, or bored. Morris organizes his narration logically, with a beginning that sets the scene, a middle that paints the picture, and an end that makes his point, all arranged chronologically. He tells the story from the first-person point of view: We experience the event directly through the writer's eyes and ears, as if we too had been on the scene of the action. Finally, Morris reveals the purpose of his narration: the comfortably well-off respond coolly to the tragedies of the ghetto.

Morris could have told his story from the third-person point of view. In this point of view, the narrator is not a participant in the action, and does not use the pronoun *I.* In the following example, William Allen White narrates his daughter's fatal accident:

> The last hour of her life was typical of its happiness. She came home from a day's work at school, topped off by a hard grind with the copy on the High School Annual, and felt that a ride would refresh her. She climbed into her khakis, chattering to her mother about the work she was doing, and hurried to get her horse and be out on the dirt roads for the country air and the radiant green fields of the spring. As she rode through the town on an easy gallop she kept waving at passers-by. She knew everyone in town. For a decade the little figure with the long pig-tail and the red hair ribbon has been familiar on the streets of Emporia, and she got in the way of speaking to those who nodded at her. She passed the Kerrs, walking the horse, in front of the Normal Library, and waved at them; passed another friend a few hundred feet fur-

> ther on, and waved at her. The horse was walking and, as she turned into North Merchant street she took off her cowboy hat, and the horse swung into a lope. She passed the Tripletts and waved her cowboy hat at them, still moving gaily north on Merchant street. A Gazette carrier passed—a High School boy friend—and she waved at him, but with her bridle hand: the horse veered quickly, plunged into the parking area where the low-hanging limb faced her, and, while she still looked back waving the blow came. But she did not fall from the horse; she slipped off, dazed a bit, staggered and fell in a faint. She never quite recovered consciousness.
>
> William Allen White

As you begin to write your own narration, take time to ask yourself why you are telling your story. Your purpose in writing will influence which events and details you include and which you leave out. You should include enough detail about the action and its context so that your readers can understand what's going on. You should not get so carried away with details that your readers become confused or bored by an excess of information. In good storytelling, deciding what to include is as important as deciding what to leave out.

Be sure to give some thought to the organization of your narrative. While chronological organization is natural in narration because it is a reconstruction of the original order of events, it is not always the most interesting. To add interest to your storytelling, try using a technique common in the movies and theater called *flashback*. Begin your narration midway through the story with an important or exciting event and then use flashback to fill in what happened earlier.

Shame

Dick Gregory

Dick Gregory, the well-known comedian and nutrition expert, has long been active in the civil-rights movement. During the 1960s Gregory was also an outspoken critic of America's involvement in Vietnam. In the following episode from his autobiography Nigger *(1964), he narrates the story of a childhood experience that taught him the meaning of shame. Through his use of realistic dialogue and vivid details, he dramatically re-creates the experience for readers. Notice also how he uses the first three paragraphs to establish a context for the events that follow.*

For Your Journal

We all learn many things in school beyond the lessons we study formally. Some of the extracurricular truths we learn stay with us for the rest of our lives. Write about something you learned in school that you still find very useful—something that has made life easier or more understandable for you.

I never learned hate at home, or shame. I had to go to school for that. I was about seven years old when I got my first big lesson. I was in love with a little girl named Helene Tucker, a light-complexioned little girl with pigtails and nice manners. She was always clean and she was smart in school. I think I went to school then mostly to look at her. I brushed my hair and even got me a little old handkerchief. It was a lady's handkerchief, but I didn't want Helene to see me wipe my nose on my hand. The pipes were frozen again, there was no water in the house, but I washed my socks and shirt every night. I'd get a pot, and go over to Mister Ben's grocery store, and stick my pot down into his soda machine. 1

Scoop out some chopped ice. By evening the ice melted to water for washing. I got sick a lot that winter because the fire would go out at night before the clothes were dry. In the morning I'd put them on, wet or dry, because they were the only clothes I had.

Everybody's got a Helene Tucker, a symbol of everything you 2
want. I loved her for her goodness, her cleanness, her popularity. She'd walk down my street and my brothers and sisters would yell, "Here comes Helene," and I'd rub my tennis sneakers on the back of my pants and wish my hair wasn't so nappy and the white folks' shirt fit me better. I'd run out on the street. If I knew my place and didn't come too close, she'd wink at me and say hello. That was a good feeling. Sometimes I'd follow her all the way home, and shovel the snow off her walk and try to make friends with her Momma and her aunts. I'd drop money on her stoop late at night on my way back from shining shoes in the taverns. And she had a Daddy, and he had a good job. He was a paper hanger.

I guess I would have gotten over Helene by summertime, but 3
something happened in that classroom that made her face hang in front of me for the next twenty-two years. When I played the drums in high school it was for Helene and when I broke track records in college it was for Helene and when I started standing behind microphones and heard applause I wished Helene could hear it, too. It wasn't until I was twenty-nine years old and married and making money that I finally got her out of my system. Helene was sitting in that classroom when I learned to be ashamed of myself.

It was on a Thursday. I was sitting in the back of the room, in 4
a seat with a chalk circle drawn around it. The idiot's seat, the troublemaker's seat.

The teacher thought I was stupid. Couldn't spell, couldn't read, 5
couldn't do arithmetic. Just stupid. Teachers were never interested in finding out that you couldn't concentrate because you were so hungry, because you hadn't had any breakfast. All you could think about was noontime, would it ever come? Maybe you could sneak into the cloakroom and steal a bite of some kid's lunch out of a coat pocket. A bite of something. Paste. You can't really make a meal of paste, or put it on bread for a sandwich, but sometimes I'd scoop a few spoonfuls out of the paste jar in the back of the room. Pregnant people get strange tastes. I was pregnant with poverty. Pregnant with dirt and pregnant with smells that made

people turn away, pregnant with cold and pregnant with shoes that were never bought for me, pregnant with five other people in my bed and no Daddy in the next room, and pregnant with hunger. Paste doesn't taste too bad when you're hungry.

The teacher thought I was a troublemaker. All she saw from 6
the front of the room was a little black boy who squirmed in his idiot's seat and made noises and poked the kids around him. I guess she couldn't see a kid who made noises because he wanted someone to know he was there.

It was on a Thursday, the day before the Negro payday. The 7
eagle always flew on Friday. The teacher was asking each student how much his father would give to the Community Chest. On Friday night, each kid would get the money from his father, and on Monday he would bring it to the school. I decided I was going to buy me a Daddy right then. I had money in my pocket from shining shoes and selling papers, and whatever Helene Tucker pledged for her Daddy I was going to top it. And I'd hand the money right in. I wasn't going to wait until Monday to buy me a Daddy.

I was shaking, scared to death. The teacher opened her book 8
and started calling out names alphabetically.

"Helene Tucker?" 9

"My daddy said he'd give two dollars and fifty cents." 10

"That's very nice, Helene. Very, very nice indeed." 11

That made me feel pretty good. It wouldn't take too much to 12
top that. I had almost three dollars in dimes and quarters in my pocket. I stuck my hand in my pocket and held onto the money, waiting for her to call my name. But the teacher closed her book after she called everybody else in the class.

I stood up and raised my hand. 13

"What is it now?" 14

"You forgot me." 15

She turned toward the blackboard. "I don't have time to be 16
playing with you, Richard."

"My Daddy said he'd . . ." 17

"Sit down, Richard, you're disturbing the class." 18

"My Daddy said he'd give . . . fifteen dollars." 19

She turned around and looked mad. "We are collecting this 20
money for you and your kind, Richard Gregory. If your Daddy can give fifteen dollars you have no business being on relief."

"I got it right now, I got it right now, my Daddy gave it to me 21
to turn in today, my Daddy said . . ."

"And furthermore," she said, looking right at me, her nostrils 22
getting big and her lips getting thin and her eyes opening wide, "we know you don't have a Daddy."

Helene Tucker turned around, her eyes full of tears. She felt 23
sorry for me. Then I couldn't see her too well because I was crying, too.

"Sit down, Richard." 24

And I always thought the teacher kind of liked me. She always 25
picked me to wash the blackboard on Friday, after school. That was a big thrill, it made me feel important. If I didn't wash it, come Monday the school might not function right.

"Where are you going, Richard?" 26

I walked out of school that day, and for a long time I didn't go 27
back very often. There was shame there.

Now there was shame everywhere. It seemed like the whole 28
world had been inside that classroom, everyone had heard what the teacher had said, everyone had turned around and felt sorry for me. There was shame in going to the Worthy Boys Annual Christmas Dinner for you and your kind, because everybody knew what a worthy boy was. Why couldn't they just call it the Boys Annual Dinner; why'd they have to give it a name? There was shame in wearing the brown and orange and white plaid mackinaw the welfare gave to three thousand boys. Why'd it have to be the same for everybody so when you walked down the street the people could see you were on relief? It was a nice warm mackinaw and it had a hood, and my Momma beat me and called me a little rat when she found out I stuffed it in the bottom of a pail full of garbage way over on Cottage Street. There was shame in running over to Mister Ben's at the end of the day and asking for his rotten peaches, there was shame in asking Mrs. Simmons for a spoonful of sugar, there was shame in running out to meet the relief truck. I hated that truck, full of food for you and your kind. I ran into the house and hid when it came. And then I started to sneak through alleys, to take the long way home so the people going into White's Eat Shop wouldn't see me. Yeah, the whole world heard the teacher that day, we all know you don't have a Daddy.

Questions for Study and Discussion

1. What does Gregory mean by "shame"? What precisely was he ashamed of, and what in particular did he learn from the incident? (Glossary: *Definition*)
2. How do the first three paragraphs of the essay help to establish a context for the narrative that follows?
3. Why do you think Gregory narrates this episode from the first-person point of view? What would be gained or lost if he instead wrote it from the third-person point of view? (Glossary: *Point of View*)
4. What is the teacher's attitude toward Gregory? Consider her own words and actions as well as Gregory's opinion in arriving at your answer.
5. What role does money play in Gregory's narrative? How does money relate to his sense of shame?
6. Specific details can enhance the reader's understanding and appreciation of a narrative. (Glossary: *Details*) Gregory's description of Helene Tucker's manners or the plaid of his mackinaw, for example, makes his account vivid and interesting. Cite several other specific details he gives, and consider how the narrative would be different without them.
7. Effective narration often depends on establishing an accurate sense of the chronology of the events discussed as well as carefully adhering to this chronology even if one chooses to reorder the events. Make a list of the chronological references Dick Gregory makes in his essay. Compare your list with those made by others in your class.

Vocabulary

Refer to your dictionary to define the following words as they are used in this selection. Then use each word in a sentence of your own.

nappy (2)   mackinaw (28)

Classroom Activity Using Narration

Dick Gregory tells his story from the first-person point of view. Rewrite his first paragraph in the third person. In a class discussion, compare notes on what you did to change the point of view. What problems did you have? How did you solve them? Which version do you like better? Why?

Suggested Writing Assignments

1. Using Dick Gregory's essay as a model, write an essay narrating an experience that made you especially afraid, angry, surprised, embarrassed, or proud. Include sufficient detail so that your readers will know exactly what happened.
2. Most of us have had frustrating experiences with mechanical objects that seem to have perverse minds of their own. Write a brief narrative recounting one such experience with a vending machine, television set, computer, pay telephone, or any other such machine. Be sure to establish a clear context for your narrative.

THE DARE

Roger Hoffmann

Born in 1948, Roger Hoffmann is a freelance writer and the author of The Complete Software Marketplace *(1984). In "The Dare," first published in the* New York Times Magazine *in 1986, Hoffmann recounts how in his youth he accepted a friend's challenge to dive under a moving freight train and to roll out on the other side. As an adult, Hoffmann appreciates the act for what it was—a crazy, dangerous childhood stunt. But he also remembers what the episode meant to him as a seventh-grader trying to prove himself to his peers. As you read the essay, pay particular attention to how Hoffman incorporates both of these perspectives into his point of view concerning "I-dare-you's."*

FOR YOUR JOURNAL

Most of us when we are growing up want more than anything to be a part of a group. Was being part of a group something you cherished as a youngster? Or did you have a desire to be independent, to be your own person? Why do you think young people in particular worry about the issue of independence versus belonging?

The secret to diving under a moving freight train and rolling out the other side with all your parts attached lies in picking the right spot between the tracks to hit with your back. Ideally, you want soft dirt or pea gravel, clear of glass shards and railroad spikes that could cause you instinctively, and fatally, to sit up. Today, at thirty-eight, I couldn't be threatened or baited enough to attempt that dive. But as a seventh grader struggling to make the cut in a tough Atlanta grammar school, all it took was a dare. 1

I coasted through my first years of school as a fussed-over smart kid, the teacher's pet who finished his work first and then strutted around the room tutoring other students. By the seventh grade, I had more A's than friends. Even my old cronies, Dwayne and O.T., made it clear I'd never be one of the guys in junior high if I didn't dirty up my act. They challenged me to break the rules, and I did. The I-dare-you's escalated: shoplifting, sugaring teachers' gas tanks, dropping lighted matches into public mailboxes. Each guerrilla act won me the approval I never got for just being smart. 2

Walking home by the railroad tracks after school, we started playing chicken with oncoming trains. O.T., who was failing that year, always won. One afternoon he charged a boxcar from the side, stopping just short of throwing himself between the wheels. I was stunned. After the train disappeared, we debated whether someone could dive under a moving car, stay put for a 10-count, then scramble out the other side. I thought it could be done and said so. O.T. immediately stepped in front of me and smiled. Not by me, I added quickly, I certainly didn't mean that I could do it. "A smart guy like you," he said, his smile evaporating, "you could figure it out easy." And then, squeezing each word for effect, "I . . . DARE . . . you." I'd just turned twelve. The monkey clawing my back was Teacher's Pet. And I'd been dared. 3

As an adult, I've been on both ends of life's implicit business and social I-dare-you's, although adults don't use those words. We provoke with body language, tone of voice, ambiguous phrases. I dare you to: argue with the boss, tell Fred what you think of him, send the wine back. Only rarely are the risks physical. How we respond to dares when we are young may have something to do with which of the truly hazardous male inner dares—attacking mountains, tempting bulls at Pamplona—we embrace or ignore as men. 4

For two weeks, I scouted trains and tracks. I studied moving boxcars close up, memorizing how they squatted on their axles, never getting used to the squeal or the way the air fell hot from the sides. I created an imaginary, friendly train and ran next to it. I mastered a shallow, head-first dive with a simple half-twist. I'd land on my back, count to ten, imagine wheels and, locking both hands on the rail to my left, heave myself over and out. Even under pure sky, though, I had to fight to keep my eyes open and my shoulders between the rails. 5

The next Saturday, O.T., Dwayne and three eighth graders met me below the hill that backed up to the lumberyard. The track followed a slow bend there and opened to a straight, slightly uphill climb for a solid third of a mile. My run started two hundred yards after the bend. The train would have its tongue hanging out. 6

The other boys huddled off to one side, a circle on another planet, and watched quietly as I double-knotted my shoelaces. My hands trembled. O.T. broke the circle and came over to me. He kept his hands hidden in the pockets of his jacket. We looked at each other. BB's of sweat appeared beneath his nose. I stuffed my wallet in one of his pockets, rubbing it against his knuckles on the way in, and slid my house key, wired to a red-and-white fishing bobber, into the other. We backed away from each other, and he turned and ran to join the four already climbing up the hill. 7

I watched them all the way to the top. They clustered together as if I were taking their picture. Their silhouette resembled a round-shouldered tombstone. They waved down to me, and I dropped them from my mind and sat down on the rail. Immediately, I jumped back. The steel was vibrating. 8

The train sounded like a cow going short of breath. I pulled my shirttail out and looked down at my spot, then up the incline of track ahead of me. Suddenly the air went hot, and the engine was by me. I hadn't pictured it moving that fast. A man's bare head leaned out and stared at me. I waved to him with my left hand and turned into the train, burying my face in the incredible noise. When I looked up, the head was gone. 9

I started running alongside the boxcars. Quickly, I found their pace, held it, and then eased off, concentrating on each thick wheel that cut past me. I slowed another notch. Over my shoulder, I picked my car as it came off the bend, locking in the image of the white mountain goat painted on its side. I waited, leaning forward like the anchor in a 440-relay, wishing the baton up the track behind me. Then the big goat fired by me, and I was flying and then tucking my shoulder as I dipped under the train. 10

A heavy blanket of red dust settled over me. I felt bolted to the earth. Sheet-metal bellies thundered and shook above my face. Count to ten, a voice said, watch the axles and look to your left for daylight. But I couldn't count, and I couldn't find left if my life depended on it, which it did. The colors overhead went from brown to red to black to red again. Finally, I ripped my hands 11 free, forced them to the rail, and, in one convulsive jerk, threw myself into the blue light.

I lay there face down until there was no more noise, and I could feel the sun against the back of my neck. I sat up. The last ribbon of train was slipping away in the distance. Across the tracks, O.T. was leading a cavalry charge down the hill, five very small, galloping boys, their fists whirling above them. I pulled my knees to my chest. My corduroy pants puckered wet across my thighs. I didn't care. 12

Questions for Study and Discussion

1. Why did Hoffmann accept O.T.'s dare when he was twelve years old? Would he accept the same dare today? Why, or why not?
2. How does paragraph 4 function in the context of Hoffmann's narrative?
3. How has Hoffmann organized his essay? (Glossary: *Organization*) What period of time is covered in paragraphs 2–5? In paragraphs 6–12? What conclusions about narrative time can you draw from what Hoffmann has done?
4. What were Hoffmann's feelings on the day of his dive under the moving freight train? Do you think he was afraid? How do you know?
5. Identify four figures of speech that Hoffmann uses in his essay. (Glossary: *Figures of Speech*) What does each figure add to his narrative?
6. Hoffmann tells his story in the first person: the narrator is the principal actor. What would have been gained or lost had Hoffmann used the third person, with O.T. or Dwayne telling the story? Explain. (*Glossary: Point of View*)

Vocabulary

Refer to your dictionary to define the following words as they are used in this selection. Then use each word in a sentence of your own.

shards (1)
baited (1)
cronies (2)
escalated (2)
guerrilla (2)
evaporating (3)
implicit (4)
ambiguous (4)
convulsive (11)

Classroom Activity Using Narration

At the heart of Hoffmann's narrative in paragraph 11 is a very detailed depiction of the precise movements he made as he threw himself under the train and swung himself out to the other side of the tracks. Spend 10 or 15 minutes trying to depict a simple sequence of movements, using this paragraph as a model. You might try, for example, to capture a movement in gymnastics, a classic ballet step, a turn at bat in baseball, a skateboarding stunt, or any action of your own choosing. Share your narration with classmates to see how successful you have been.

Suggested Writing Assignments

1. Can you remember any dares that you made or accepted while growing up? What were the consequences of these dares? Did you and your peers find dares a way to test or prove yourselves? Write a narrative essay about a dare that you made, accepted, or simply witnessed.
2. Each of us can tell of an experience that has been unusually significant for us. Think about your past, identify one experience that has been especially important for you, and write an essay about it. In preparing to write your narrative, you may find it helpful to ask such questions as: Why is the experience important for me? What details are necessary in order for me to re-create the experience in an interesting and engaging way? How can my narrative of the experience be most effectively organized? Over what period of time did the experience occur? What point of view will work best?

MOMMA, THE DENTIST, AND ME

Maya Angelou

Maya Angelou is best known as the author of I Know Why the Caged Bird Sings *(1970), the first book in a series that constitutes her autobiography, and for "On the Pulse of the Morning," a characteristically optimistic poem on the need for personal and national renewal that she read at President Clinton's inauguration on January 20, 1993. Starting with her beginnings in St. Louis in 1928, Angelou's autobiography presents a life of joyful triumph over hardships that test her courage and threaten her spirit. The most recent chapter in that life story,* Wouldn't Take Nothing for My Journey Now, *appeared in 1993. Angelou is also a successful and respected poet. Her several volumes of poetry were collected in* Complete Collected Poems of Maya Angelou *in 1994. Trained as a dancer, Angelou has also acted in the television series* Roots, *and, at the request of Martin Luther King, Jr., served as a coordinator of the Southern Christian Leadership Conference. In the following excerpt from* I Know Why the Caged Bird Sings, *Angelou narrates what happened, and what might have happened, when her grandmother, the "Momma" of the story, took her to the local dentist. As you read, consider how vital first-person narration is to the essay's success, particularly as you gauge the effect of the italicized paragraphs.*

FOR YOUR JOURNAL

When you were growing up, did one or both of your parents ever come to your defense over a principle that you little appreciated at the time? What were the circumstances? For example, did your school have a dress code that you disagreed with, or were you not allowed to participate in some activity that your parents found objectionable? Narrate the events that brought about the controversy and how it was resolved. Were you embarrassed by their actions or happy that they had intervened on your behalf?

The angel of the candy counter had found me out at last, and was exacting excruciating penance for all the stolen Milky Ways, Mounds, Mr. Goodbars and Hersheys with Almonds. I had two cavities that were rotten to the gums. The pain was beyond the bailiwick of crushed aspirins or oil of cloves. Only one thing could help me, so I prayed earnestly that I'd be allowed to sit under the house and have the building collapse on my left jaw. Since there was no Negro dentist in Stamps, nor doctor either, for that matter, Momma had dealt with previous toothaches by pulling them out (a string tied to the tooth with the other end looped over her fist), pain killers and prayer. In this particular instance the medicine had proved ineffective; there wasn't enough enamel left to hook a string on, and the prayers were being ignored because the Balancing Angel was blocking their passage. 1

I lived a few days and nights in blinding pain, not so much toying with as seriously considering the idea of jumping in the well, and Momma decided I had to be taken to a dentist. The nearest Negro dentist was in Texarkana, twenty-five miles away, and I was certain that I'd be dead long before we reached half the distance. Momma said we'd go to Dr. Lincoln, right in Stamps, and he'd take care of me. She said he owed her a favor. 2

I knew there were a number of whitefolks in town that owed her favors. Bailey and I had seen the books which showed how she had lent money to Blacks and whites alike during the Depression, and most still owed her. But I couldn't aptly remember seeing Dr. Lincoln's name, nor had I ever heard of a Negro's going to him as a patient. However, Momma said we were going, and put water on the stove for our baths. I had never been to a doctor, so she told me that after the bath (which would make my mouth feel better) I had to put on freshly starched and ironed underclothes from inside out. The ache failed to respond to the bath, and I knew then that the pain was more serious than that which anyone had ever suffered. 3

Before we left the Store, she ordered me to brush my teeth and then wash my mouth with Listerine. The idea of even opening my clamped jaws increased the pain, but upon her explanation that when you go to a doctor you have to clean yourself all over, but most especially the part that's to be examined, I screwed up my courage and unlocked my teeth. The cool air in my mouth and the jarring of my molars dislodged what little remained of my reason. I had frozen to the pain, my family nearly had to tie me down to take the toothbrush away. It was no small effort to get me started on the road to the dentist. Momma spoke to all the passers-by, but didn't stop to chat. She explained over her shoulder that we were going to the doctor and she'd "pass the time of day" on our way home. 4

Until we reached the pond the pain was my world, an aura that haloed me for three feet around. Crossing the bridge into whitefolks' country, pieces of sanity pushed themselves forward. I had to stop moaning and start walking straight. The white towel, which was drawn under my chin and tied over my head, had to be arranged. If one was dying, it had to be done in style if the dying took place in whitefolks' part of town. 5

On the other side of the bridge the ache seemed to lessen as if a whitebreeze blew off the whitefolks and cushioned everything in their neighborhood—including my jaw. The gravel road was smoother, the stones smaller and the tree branches hung down around the path and nearly covered us. If the pain didn't diminish then, the familiar yet strange sights hypnotized me into believing that it had. 6

But my head continued to throb with the measured insistence of a bass drum, and how could a toothache pass the calaboose, hear the songs of the prisoners, their blues and laughter, and not be changed? How could one or two or even a mouthful of angry tooth roots meet a wagonload of powhitetrash children, endure their idiotic snobbery and not feel less important? 7

Behind the building which housed the dentist's office ran a small path used by servants and those tradespeople who catered to the butcher and Stamps' one restaurant. Momma and I followed that lane to the backstairs of Dentist Lincoln's office. The sun was bright and gave the day a hard reality as we climbed up the steps to the second floor. 8

Momma knocked on the back door and a young white girl opened it to show surprise at seeing us there. Momma said she 9 wanted to see Dentist Lincoln and to tell him Annie was there. The girl closed the door firmly. Now the humiliation of hearing Momma describe herself as if she had no last name to the young white girl was equal to the physical pain. It seemed terribly unfair to have a toothache and a headache and have to bear at the same time the heavy burden of Blackness.

It was always possible that the teeth would quiet down and 10
maybe drop out of their own accord. Momma said we would wait. We leaned in the harsh sunlight on the shaky railings of the dentist's back porch for over an hour.

He opened the door and looked at Momma. "Well, Annie, what 11
can I do for you?"

He didn't see the towel around my jaw or notice my swollen 12
face.

Momma said, "Dentist Lincoln. It's my grandbaby here. She 13
got two rotten teeth that's giving her a fit."

She waited for him to acknowledge the truth of her statement. 14
He made no comment, orally or facially.

"She had this toothache purt' near four days now, and today I 15
said, 'Young lady, you going to the Dentist.'"

"Annie?" 16

"Yes, sir, Dentist Lincoln." 17

He was choosing words the way people hunt for shells. "Annie, 18
you know I don't treat nigra, colored people."

"I know, Dentist Lincoln. But this here is just my little grand- 19
baby, and she ain't gone be no trouble to you . . ."

"Annie, everybody has a policy. In this world you have to have 20
a policy. Now, my policy is I don't treat colored people."

The sun had baked the oil out of Momma's skin and melted the 21
Vaseline in her hair. She shone greasily as she leaned out of the dentist's shadow.

"Seem like to me, Dentist Lincoln, you might look after her, 22
she ain't nothing but a little mite. And seems like maybe you owe me a favor or two."

He reddened slightly. "Favor or no favor. The money has all 23
been repaid to you and that's the end of it. Sorry, Annie." He had his hand on the doorknob. "Sorry." His voice was a bit kinder on the second "Sorry," as if he really was.

Momma said, "I wouldn't press on you like this for myself but 24
I can't take No. Not for my grandbaby. When you come to borrow

my money you didn't have to beg. You asked me, and I lent it. Now, it wasn't my policy. I ain't no moneylender, but you stood to lose this building and I tried to help you out."

"It's been paid, and raising your voice won't make me change my mind. My policy . . ." He let go of the door and stepped nearer Momma. The three of us were crowded on the small landing. "Annie, my policy is I'd rather stick my hand in a dog's mouth than in a nigger's." 25

He had never once looked at me. He turned his back and went through the door into the cool beyond. Momma backed up inside herself for a few minutes. I forgot everything except her face which was almost a new one to me. She leaned over and took the doorknob, and in her everyday soft voice she said, "Sister, go on downstairs. Wait for me. I'll be there directly." 26

Under the most common of circumstances I knew it did no good to argue with Momma. So I walked down the steep stairs, afraid to look back and afraid not to do so. I turned as the door slammed, and she was gone. 27

Momma walked in that room as if she owned it. She shoved that silly nurse aside with one hand and strode into the dentist's office. He was sitting in his chair, sharpening his mean instruments and putting extra sting into his medicines. Her eyes were blazing like live coals and her arms had doubled themselves in length. He looked up at her just before she caught him by the collar of his white jacket. 28

"Stand up when you see a lady, you contemptuous scoundrel." Her tongue had thinned and the words rolled off well enunciated. Enunciated and sharp like little claps of thunder. 29

The dentist had no choice but to stand at R.O.T.C. attention. His head dropped after a minute and his voice was humble. "Yes, ma'am, Mrs. Henderson." 30

"You knave, do you think you acted like a gentleman, speaking to me like that in front of my granddaughter?" She didn't shake him, although she had the power. She simply held him upright. 31

"No, ma'am, Mrs. Henderson." 32

"No, ma'am, Mrs. Henderson, what?" Then she did give him the tiniest of shakes, but because of her strength the action set his head and arms to shaking loose on the ends of his body. He stuttered much worse than Uncle Willie. "No, ma'am, Mrs. Henderson, I'm sorry." 33

With just an edge of her disgust showing, Momma slung him back in his dentist's chair. "Sorry is as sorry does, and you're about the 34 *sorriest dentist I ever laid my eyes on." (She could afford to slip into the vernacular because she had such eloquent command of English.)*

"I didn't ask you to apologize in front of Marguerite, because I don't want her to know my power, but I order you, now and herewith. Leave Stamps by sundown." 35

"Mrs. Henderson, I can't get my equipment . . ." He was shaking terribly now. 36

"Now, that brings me to my second order. You will never again practice dentistry. Never! When you get settled in your next place, you will be a vegetarian caring for dogs with the mange, cats with the cholera and cows with the epizootic. Is that clear?" 37

The saliva ran down his chin and his eyes filled with tears. "Yes, ma'am. Thank you for not killing me. Thank you, Mrs. Henderson." 38

Momma pulled herself back from being ten feet tall with eight-foot arms and said, "You're welcome for nothing, you varlet, I wouldn't waste a killing on the likes of you." 39

On her way out she waved her handkerchief at the nurse and turned her into a crocus sack of chicken feed. 40

Momma looked tired when she came down the stairs, but who wouldn't be tired if they had gone through what she had. She came close to me and adjusted the towel under my jaw (I had forgotten the toothache; I only knew that she made her hands gentle in order not to awaken the pain). She took my hand. Her voice never changed. "Come on, Sister." 41

I reckoned we were going home where she would concoct a brew to eliminate the pain and maybe give me new teeth too. New teeth that would grow overnight out of my gums. She led me toward the drugstore, which was in the opposite direction from the Store. "I'm taking you to Dentist Baker in Texarkana." 42

I was glad after all that I had bathed and put on Mum and Cashmere Bouquet talcum powder. It was a wonderful surprise. My toothache had quieted to solemn pain, Momma had obliterated the evil white man, and we were going on a trip to Texarkana, just the two of us. 43

On the Greyhound she took an inside seat in the back, and I sat beside her. I was so proud of being her granddaughter and sure that some of her magic must have come down to me. She asked if I was scared. I only shook my head and leaned over on her cool brown upper arm. There was no chance that a dentist, especially a Negro dentist, would dare hurt me then. Not with 44

Momma there. The trip was uneventful, except that she put her arm around me, which was very unusual for Momma to do.

The dentist showed me the medicine and the needle before he deadened my gums, but if he hadn't I wouldn't have worried. Momma stood right behind him. Her arms were folded and she checked on everything he did. The teeth were extracted and she bought me an ice cream cone from the side window of a drug counter. The trip back to Stamps was quiet, except that I had to spit into a very small empty snuff can which she had gotten for me and it was difficult with the bus humping and jerking on our country roads. 45

At home, I was given a warm salt solution, and when I washed out my mouth I showed Bailey the empty holes, where the clotted blood sat like filling in a pie crust. He said I was quite brave, and that was my cue to reveal our confrontation with the peckerwood dentist and Momma's incredible powers. 46

I had to admit that I didn't hear the conversation, but what else could she have said than what I said she said? What else done? He agreed with my analysis in a lukewarm way, and I happily (after all, I'd been sick) flounced into the Store. Momma was preparing our evening meal and Uncle Willie leaned on the door sill. She gave her version. 47

"Dentist Lincoln got right uppity. Said he'd rather put his hand in a dog's mouth. And when I reminded him of the favor, he brushed it off like a piece of lint. Well, I sent Sister downstairs and went inside. I hadn't never been in his office before, but I found the door to where he takes out teeth, and him and the nurse was in there thick as thieves. I just stood there till he caught sight of me." Crash bang the pots on the stove. "He jumped just like he was sitting on a pin. He said, 'Annie, I done tole you, I ain't gonna mess around in no niggah's mouth.' I said, 'Somebody's got to do it then,' and he said, 'Take her to Texarkana to the colored dentist' and that's when I said, 'If you paid me my money I could afford to take her.' He said, 'It's all been paid.' I tole him everything but the interest been paid. He said, ''Twasn't no interest.' I said, ''Tis now. I'll take ten dollars as payment in full.' You know, Willie, it wasn't no right thing to do, 'cause I lent that money without thinking about it. 48

"He tole that little snippety nurse of his'n to give me ten dollars and make me sign a 'paid in full' receipt. She gave it to me and I 49 signed the papers. Even though by rights he was paid up before, I figger, he gonna be that kind of nasty, he gonna have to pay for it."

Momma and her son laughed and laughed over the white man's 50
evilness and her retributive sin.

I preferred, much preferred, my version. 51

Questions for Study and Discussion

1. What is Angelou's purpose in narrating the story she tells? (Glossary: *Purpose*)
2. Compare and contrast the content and style of the interaction between Momma and the dentist that is given in italics with the one given at the end of the narrative. (Glossary: *Comparison and Contrast*)
3. Angelou tells her story chronologically and in the first person. What are the advantages of the first-person narrative? (Glossary: *Point of View*)
4. Identify three similes that Angelou uses in her narrative. Explain how each simile serves her purpose. (Glossary: *Figures of Speech*)
5. Why do you suppose Angelou says she prefers her own version of the episode to that of her grandmother?
6. This story is a story of pain and not just the pain of a toothache. How does Angelou describe the pain of the toothache? What other pain does Angelou tell of in this autobiographical narrative?

Vocabulary

Refer to your dictionary to define the following words as they are used in this selection. Then use each word in a sentence of your own.

bailiwick (1)	varlet (39)
calaboose (7)	concoct (42)
mite (22)	snippety (49)
vernacular (34)	retributive (50)

Classroom Activity Using Narration

One of Angelou's themes in "Momma, the Dentist, and Me" is that cruelty, whether racial, social, professional, or personal, is very difficult to endure and leaves a lasting impression on a person. As a way of practicing chronological order, consider a situation in which an unthinking or insensitive person made you feel inferior. Rather than write a draft of an essay at this point, simply list the sequence of events that occurred, in chronological order. Once you have completed this step, consider whether or not there is a more dramatic order you might use if you were actually to write an essay.

Suggested Writing Assignments

1. Every person who tells a story does so by putting his or her signature on it in some way—by the sequencing of events, the amount and type of details used, and the tone the teller of the story employs. If you and a relative or friend experienced the same interesting sequence of events, try telling the story of those events from your unique perspective. Once you have done so, try telling the story from what you imagine the other person's perspective to be. Perhaps you even heard the other person actually tell the story. What is the same in both versions? How do the renditions differ?
2. Write a narrative in which, like Angelou, you give two versions of an actual event—one the way you thought or wished it had happened and the other the way events actually took place.

THE STORY OF AN HOUR

Kate Chopin

Kate Chopin (1851–1904) was born in St. Louis, of Creole Irish descent. After her marriage she lived in Louisiana, where she acquired the intimate knowledge of Creole Cajun culture that provided the impetus for much of her work and earned her a reputation as a writer who captured the ambience of the bayou region. When her first novel, The Awakening *(1899), was published, however, it generated scorn and outrage for its explicit depiction of a southern woman's sexual awakening. Only recently has Chopin been recognized for her literary talent and originality. Besides* The Awakening, *her works include two collections of short fiction,* Bayou Folk *(1894) and* A Night in Acadie *(1897). In 1969,* The Complete Works of Kate Chopin *was published by Louisiana State University Press. As you read the selection below, try to gauge how your reactions to Mrs. Mallard are influenced by Chopin's use of third-person narration.*

FOR YOUR JOURNAL

How do you react to the idea of marriage—committing to someone for life? What are the advantages of such a union? What are the disadvantages?

Knowing that Mrs. Mallard was afflicted with a heart trouble, great care was taken to break to her as gently as possible the news of her husband's death. 1

It was her sister Josephine who told her, in broken sentences; veiled hints that revealed in half concealing. Her husband's friend Richards was there, too, near her. It was he who had been in the newspaper office when intelligence of the railroad disaster was received, with Brently Mallard's name leading the list of "killed." 2

He had only taken the time to assure himself of its truth by a second telegram, and had hastened to forestall any less careful, less tender friend in bearing the sad message.

She did not hear the story as many women have heard the 3
same, with a paralyzed inability to accept its significance. She wept at once, with sudden, wild abandonment, in her sister's arms. When the storm of grief had spent itself she went away to her room alone. She would have no one follow her.

There stood, facing the open window, a comfortable, roomy 4
armchair. Into this she sank, pressed down by a physical exhaustion that haunted her body and seemed to reach into her soul.

She could see in the open square before her house the tops of 5
trees that were all aquiver with the new spring life. The delicious breath of rain was in the air. In the street below a peddler was crying his wares. The notes of a distant song which some one was singing reached her faintly, and countless sparrows were twittering in the eaves.

There were patches of blue sky showing here and there through 6
the clouds that had met and piled one above the other in the west facing her window.

She sat with her head thrown back upon the cushion of the 7
chair, quite motionless, except when a sob came up into her throat and shook her, as a child who has cried itself to sleep continues to sob in its dreams.

She was young, with a fair, calm face, whose lines bespoke re- 8
pression and even a certain strength. But now there was a dull stare in her eyes, whose gaze was fixed away off yonder on one of those patches of blue sky. It was not a glance of reflection, but rather indicated a suspension of intelligent thought.

There was something coming to her and she was waiting for 9
it, fearfully. What was it? She did not know; it was too subtle and elusive to name. But she felt it, creeping out of the sky, reaching toward her through the sounds, the scents, the color that filled the air.

Now her bosom rose and fell tumultuously. She was begin- 10
ning to recognize this thing that was approaching to possess her, and she was striving to beat it back with her will—as powerless as her two white slender hands would have been.

When she abandoned herself a little whispered word escaped 11
her slightly parted lips. She said it over and over under her breath: "free, free, free!" The vacant stare and the look of terror that had

followed it went from her eyes. They stayed keen and bright. Her pulses beat fast, and the coursing blood warmed and relaxed every inch of her body.

She did not stop to ask if it were or were not a monstrous joy that held her. A clear and exalted perception enabled her to dismiss the suggestion as trivial. 12

She knew that she would weep again when she saw the kind, tender hands folded in death; the face that had never looked save with love upon her, fixed and gray and dead. But she saw beyond that bitter moment a long procession of years to come that would belong to her absolutely. And she opened and spread her arms out to them in welcome. 13

There would be no one to live for her during those coming years; she would live for herself. There would be no powerful will bending hers in that blind persistence with which men and women believe they have a right to impose a private will upon a fellow-creature. A kind intention or a cruel intention made the act seem no less a crime as she looked upon it in that brief moment of illumination. 14

And yet she had loved him—sometimes. Often she had not. What did it matter! What could love, the unsolved mystery, count for in face of this possession of self-assertion which she suddenly recognized as the strongest impulse of her being! 15

"Free! Body and soul free!" she kept whispering. 16

Josephine was kneeling before the closed door with her lips to the keyhole, imploring for admission. "Louise, open the door! I beg; open the door—you will make yourself ill. What are you doing, Louise? For heaven's sake open the door." 17

"Go away. I am not making myself ill." No; she was drinking in a very elixir of life through that open window. 18

Her fancy was running riot along those days ahead of her. Spring days, and summer days, and all sorts of days that would be her own. She breathed a quick prayer that life might be long. It was only yesterday she had thought with a shudder that life might be long. 19

She arose at length and opened the door to her sister's importunities. There was a feverish triumph in her eyes, and she carried herself unwittingly like a goddess of Victory. She clasped her sister's waist, and together they descended the stairs. Richards stood waiting for them at the bottom. 20

Some one was opening the front door with a latchkey. It was Brently Mallard who entered, a little travel-stained, composedly carrying his grip-sack and umbrella. He had been far from the scene of the accident, and did not even know there had been one. He stood amazed at Josephine's piercing cry; at Richards' quick motion to screen him from the view of his wife. 21

But Richards was too late. 22

When the doctors came they said she had died of heart disease— of joy that kills. 23

Questions for Study and Discussion

1. What assumptions do Mrs. Mallard's relatives and friends make about her feelings toward her husband? How would you describe her true feelings?
2. Reread paragraphs 5–9. What is Chopin's purpose in this section of the story? (Glossary: *Purpose*) Do these paragraphs add to the story's effectiveness? Why, or why not?
3. Why does Mrs. Mallard fight her feeling of freedom, however briefly?
4. All of the events of this story take place in an hour. Would the story be as poignant if it had taken place over the course of a day, or even several days? Explain. Why do you suppose the author selected the time frame as a title for her story? (Glossary: *Title*)
5. Chopin could have written an essay detailing the oppression of women in marriage, but she chose to write a fictional narrative. This allows her to show readers the type of situation that can arise in an outwardly happy marriage, rather than tell them about it. Why else do you think she chose to write a fictional narrative? What other advantages does it give her over nonfiction?

Vocabulary

Refer to your dictionary to define the following words as they are used in this selection. Then use each word in a sentence of your own.

afflicted (1)	exalted (12)
aquiver (5)	imploring (17)
bespoke (8)	elixir (18)
tumultuously (10)	importunities (20)

Classroom Activity Using Narration

Put the following sentences into chronological order.

1. The sky was gray and gloomy for as far as she could see, and sleet hissed off the glass.
2. "Oh, hi, I'm glad you called," she said happily, but her smile dimmed when she looked outside.
3. As Betty crossed the room, the phone rang, startling her.
4. "No, the weather's awful, so I don't think I'll get out to visit you today," she sighed.
5. "Hello," she said, and she wandered over to the window, dragging the phone cord behind her.

Write five sentences of your own that cover a progression of events. Try to include dialogue. Then scramble them and see if a classmate can put them back into the correct order.

Suggested Writing Assignments

1. Write a narrative essay in which you describe your reaction to a piece of news that you once received—good or bad—that provoked a strong emotional response. What were your emotions? What did you do in the couple of hours after you received the news? How did your perceptions of the world around you change? What made the experience memorable?
2. Write a short piece of narrative fiction in which your main character reacts to a specific, dramatic event. Portray the character's emotional response, as well as how the character perceives his or her surroundings—what does the character see, hear, touch? How are these senses affected by the situation?

12

DESCRIPTION

To describe is to create a verbal picture. A person, a place, a thing—even an idea or a state of mind—can be made vividly concrete through description. Here, for example, is Thomas Mann's brief description of a delicatessen:

> It was a narrow room, with a rather high ceiling, and crowded from floor to ceiling with goodies. There were rows and rows of hams and sausages of all shapes and colors—white, yellow, red, and black; fat and lean and round and long—rows of canned preserves, cocoa and tea, bright translucent glass bottles of honey, marmalade, and jam; round bottles and slender bottles, filled with liqueurs and punch—all these things crowded every inch of the shelves from top to bottom.

Writing any description requires, first of all, that the writer gather many details about a subject, relying not only on what the eyes see but on the other sense impressions—touch, taste, smell, hearing—as well. From this catalogue of details the writer selects those that will most effectively create a *dominant impression*—the single quality, mood, or atmosphere that the writer wishes to emphasize. Consider, for example, the details that Mary McCarthy uses to evoke the dominant impression in the following passage from *Memories of a Catholic Girlhood:*

> Whenever we children came to stay at my grandmother's house, we were put to sleep in the sewing room, a bleak, shabby, utilitarian rectangle, more office than bedroom, more attic than office, that played to the hierarchy of chambers the role of poor relation. It was a room without pride: the old sewing machine, some cast-off chairs, a shadeless lamp, rolls of wrapping paper, piles of cardboard boxes that might someday come in handy, papers of pins, and remnants of a material united with the iron folding cots put out for our use and the bare floor boards to give an impression of intense and ruthless temporality. Thin white spreads, of the kind

> used in hospitals and charity institutions, and naked blinds at the windows reminded us of our orphaned condition and of the ephemeral character of our visit; there was nothing here to encourage us to consider this our home.

The dominant impression that McCarthy creates is one of clutter, bleakness, and shabbiness. There is nothing in the sewing room that suggests permanence or warmth.

Writers must also carefully plan the order in which to present their descriptive details. The pattern of organization must fit the subject of the description logically and naturally, and must also be easy to follow. For example, visual details can be arranged spatially—from left to right, top to bottom, near to far, or in any other logical order. Other patterns include smallest to largest, softest to loudest, least significant to most significant, most unusual to least unusual. McCarthy suggests a jumble of junk not only by her choice of details but by the apparently random order in which she presents them.

How much detail is enough? There is no fixed answer. A good description includes enough vivid details to create a dominant impression and to bring a scene to life, but not so many that readers are distracted, confused, or bored. In an essay that is purely descriptive, there is room for much detail. Usually, however, writers use description to create the setting for a story, to illustrate ideas, to help clarify a definition or a comparison, or to make the complexities of a process more understandable. Such descriptions should be kept short, and should include just enough detail to make them clear and helpful.

SUBWAY STATION

Gilbert Highet

Gilbert Highet (1906–1978) was born in Scotland and became a naturalized United States citizen in 1951. A prolific writer and translator, Highet was for many years a professor of classics at Columbia University, as well as a popular radio essayist. The following selection is from his book Talents and Geniuses *(1957). Take note of Highet's keen eye for detail as you read. Concrete and vivid images help him to re-create the unseemly world of a subway station.*

FOR YOUR JOURNAL

Try to remember what it is like to be in a subway station, airport, or bus station. What are the sights, sounds, and smells you recall? What do you remember most about any of these crowded, transient places? What was your overall impression of the place?

Standing in a subway station, I began to appreciate the place—almost to enjoy it. First of all, I looked at the lighting: a row of meager electric bulbs, unscreened, yellow, and coated with filth, stretched toward the black mouth of the tunnel, as though it were a bolt hole in an abandoned coal mine. Then I lingered, with zest, on the walls and ceiling: lavatory tiles which had been white about fifty years ago, and were now encrusted with soot, coated with the remains of a dirty liquid which might be either atmospheric humidity mingled with smog or the result of a perfunctory attempt to clean them with cold water; and, above them, gloomy vaulting from which dingy paint was peeling off like scabs from an old wound, sick black paint leaving a leprous white undersurface. Beneath my feet, the floor was a nauseating dark brown with black stains upon it which might be stale oil or dry chewing gum or some worse defilement; it looked like the hallway of a condemned slum building. Then my eye traveled to the tracks, where two lines of glittering steel—the only positively clean objects in the whole place—ran out of darkness into darkness above an unspeakable mass of congealed oil, puddles of dubious liquid, and a mishmash of old cigarette packets, mutilated and filthy newspapers, and the débris that filtered down from the street above through a barred grating in the roof. As I looked up toward the sunlight, I could see more débris sifting slowly downward, and making an abominable pattern in the slanting beam of dirt-laden sunlight. I was going on to relish more features of this unique scene: such as the advertisement posters on the walls—here a text from the Bible, there a half-naked girl, here a woman wearing a hat consisting of a hen sitting on a nest full of eggs, and there a pair of girl's legs walking up the keys of a cash register—all scribbled over with unknown names and well-known obscenities in black crayon and red lipstick; but then my train came in at last, I boarded it, and began to read. The experience was over for the time.

Questions for Study and Discussion

1. What dominant impression does Highet create in his description? (Glossary: *Dominant Impression*) Make a list of those details that help Highet create his dominant impression.
2. Why do you think Highet observes the subway station with "zest" and "relish"? What does he find appealing about the experience?
3. What similes and metaphors can you find in Highet's description? How do they help to make the description vivid? (Glossary: *Figures of Speech*)
4. What mix of advertisements does Highet observe? Based on Highet's description of what they depict, their current appearance, and the atmosphere of their surroundings, suggest what product each poster might be advertising. Explain your suggestions.
5. Highet has an eye for detail that is usually displayed by those who are seeing something for the first time. Do you think it is his first time in a subway station, or is he a regu-

lar rider who is taking time out to "relish" his physical surroundings? What in the essay leads you to your conclusion?

Vocabulary

Refer to your dictionary to define the following words as they are used in this selection. Then use each word in a sentence of your own.

perfunctory	dubious
leprous	abominable
defilement	

Classroom Activity Using Description

Make a long list of the objects and people in your classroom as well as the physical features of the classroom—desks, windows, blackboard, students, professor, dirty walls, burned-out light bulb, a clock that is always ten minutes fast, and so on. Determine a dominant impression that you would like to create in describing the classroom. Now choose from your list those items that would best illustrate the dominant impression you have chosen. Your instructor may wish to have students compare their responses.

Suggested Writing Assignments

1. Using Highet's essay as a model, write an extended one-paragraph description of a room in your house or apartment where you do not spend much time. Spend some time observing the details in the room. Before you write, decide on the dominant impression you wish to communicate to the reader.
2. Write a short essay in which you describe one of the following places, or another place of your choice. Arrange the details of your description from top to bottom, left to right, near to far, or according to some other spatial organization.

a closet	a barbershop or beauty salon
a pizza parlor	a bookstore
a locker room	a campus dining hall

UNFORGETTABLE MISS BESSIE

Carl T. Rowan

In addition to being a popular syndicated newspaper columnist, Carl T. Rowan is a former ambassador to Finland and director of the United States Information Agency. Born in 1925 in Ravenscroft, Tennessee, he received degrees from Oberlin College and the University of Minnesota. He worked as a columnist for the Minneapolis Tribune *and the* Chicago Sun-Times *before moving to Washington, D.C., where he lives today. In 1991 Rowan published* Breaking Barriers: A Memoir. *His most recent book,* The Coming Race War in America, *appeared in 1996. In the following essay, he describes a high-school teacher whose lessons went far beyond the subjects she taught. After reading the details Rowan presents about Miss Bessie's background, behavior, and appearance, determine what kind of dominant impression of Miss Bessie he leaves you with.*

FOR YOUR JOURNAL

Perhaps you have at some time taught a friend or younger brother or sister how to do something—tie a shoe, hit a ball, read, solve a puzzle, drive a car—but you never thought of yourself as a teacher. Did you enjoy the experience of sharing what you know with someone else? Would you consider becoming a teacher someday?

She was only about five feet tall and probably never weighed more than 110 pounds, but Miss Bessie was a towering presence in the classroom. She was the only woman tough enough to make me read *Beowulf* and think for a few foolish days that I 1 liked it. From 1938 to 1942, when I attended Bernard High School in McMinnville, Tenn., she taught me English, history, civics—and a lot more than I realized.

I shall never forget the day she scolded me into reading 2
Beowulf.

"But Miss Bessie," I complained, "I ain't much interested in it." 3

Her large brown eyes became daggerish slits. "Boy," she said, 4
"how dare you say 'ain't' to me! I've taught you better than that."

"Miss Bessie," I pleaded, "I'm trying to make first-string end 5
on the football team, and if I go around saying 'it isn't' and 'they aren't,' the guys are gonna laugh me off the squad."

"Boy," she responded, "you'll play football because you have 6
guts. But do you know what *really* takes guts? Refusing to lower your standards to those of the crowd. It takes guts to say you've got to live and be somebody fifty years after all the football games are over."

I started saying "it isn't" and "they aren't," and I still made first- 7
string end—and class valedictorian—without losing my buddies' respect.

During her remarkable 44-year career, Mrs. Bessie Taylor 8
Gwynn taught hundreds of economically deprived black youngsters—including my mother, my brother, my sisters and me. I remember her now with gratitude and affection—especially in this era when Americans are so wrought-up about a "rising tide of mediocrity" in public education and the problems of finding competent, caring teachers. Miss Bessie was an example of an informed, dedicated teacher, a blessing to children and an asset to the nation.

Born in 1895, in poverty, she grew up in Athens, Ala., where 9
there was no public school for blacks. She attended Trinity School, a private institution for blacks run by the American Missionary Association, and in 1911 graduated from the Normal School (a "super" high school) at Fisk University in Nashville. Mrs. Gwynn, the essence of pride and privacy, never talked about her years in Athens; only in the months before her death did she reveal that she had never attended Fisk University itself because she could not afford the four-year course.

At Normal School she learned a lot about Shakespeare, but 10
most of all about the profound importance of education—espe-

cially, for a people trying to move up from slavery. "What you put in your head, boy," she once said, "can never be pulled out by the Ku Klux Klan, the Congress or anybody."

Miss Bessie's bearing of dignity told anyone who met her that she was "educated" in the best sense of the word. There was never a discipline problem in her classes. We didn't dare mess with a woman who knew about the Battle of Hastings, the Magna Carta and the Bill of Rights—and who could also play the piano. 11

This frail-looking woman could make sense of Shakespeare, Milton, Voltaire, and bring to life Booker T. Washington and W. E. B. DuBois. Believing that it was important to know who the officials were that spent taxpayers' money and made public policy, she made us memorize the names of everyone on the Supreme Court and in the President's Cabinet. It could be embarrassing to be unprepared when Miss Bessie said, "Get up and tell the class who Frances Perkins is and what you think about her." 12

Miss Bessie knew that my family, like so many others during the Depression, couldn't afford to subscribe to a newspaper. She knew we didn't even own a radio. Still, she prodded me to "look out for your future and find some way to keep up with what's going on in the world." So I became a delivery boy for the Chattanooga *Times*. I rarely made a dollar a week, but I got to read a newspaper every day. 13

Miss Bessie noticed things that had nothing to do with schoolwork, but were vital to a youngster's development. Once a few classmates made fun of my frayed, hand-me-down overcoat, calling me "Strings." As I was leaving school, Miss Bessie patted me on the back of that old overcoat and said, "Carl, never fret about what you *don't* have. Just make the most of what you *do* have—a brain." 14

Among the things that I did not have was electricity in the little frame house that my father had built for $400 with his World War I bonus. But because of her inspiration, I spent many hours squinting beside a kerosene lamp reading Shakespeare and Thoreau, Samuel Pepys and William Cullen Bryant. 15

No one in my family had ever graduated from high school, so there was no tradition of commitment to learning for me to lean on. Like millions of youngsters in today's ghettos and barrios, I needed the push and stimulation of a teacher who truly cared. Miss Bessie gave plenty of both, as she immersed me in a wonder- 16 ful world of similes, metaphors and even onomatopoeia. She led me to believe that I could write sonnets as well as Shakespeare, or iambic-pentameter verse to put Alexander Pope to shame.

In those days the McMinnville school system was rigidly "Jim Crow," and poor black children had to struggle to put anything in their heads. Our high school was only slightly larger than the once-typical little red schoolhouse, and its library was outrageously inadequate—so small, I like to say, that if two students were in it and one wanted to turn a page, the other one had to step outside. 17

Negroes, as we were called then, were not allowed in the town library, except to mop floors or dust tables. But through one of those secret Old South arrangements between whites of conscience and blacks of stature, Miss Bessie kept getting books smuggled out of the white library. That is how she introduced me to the Brontës, Byron, Coleridge, Keats and Tennyson. "If you don't read, you can't write, and if you can't write, you might as well stop dreaming," Miss Bessie once told me. 18

So I read whatever Miss Bessie told me to, and tried to remember the things she insisted that I store away. Forty-five years later, I can still recite her "truths to live by," such as Henry Wadsworth Longfellow's lines from "The Ladder of St. Augustine": 19

> The heights by great men reached and kept
> Were not attained by sudden flight.
> But they, while their companions slept,
> Were toiling upward in the night.

Years later, her inspiration, prodding, anger, cajoling and almost osmotic infusion of learning finally led to that lovely day when Miss Bessie dropped me a note saying, "I'm so proud to read your column in the Nashville *Tennessean*." 20

Miss Bessie was a spry 80 when I went back to McMinnville and visited her in a senior citizens' apartment building. Pointing out proudly that her building was racially integrated, she reached for two glasses and a pint of bourbon. I was momentarily shocked, because it would have been scandalous in the 1930s and '40s for word to get out that a teacher drank, and nobody had ever raised a rumor that Miss Bessie did. 21

I felt a new sense of equality as she lifted her glass to mine. Then she revealed a softness and compassion that I had never known as a student. 22

"I've never forgotten that examination day," she said, "when Buster Martin held up seven fingers, obviously asking you for help with question number seven, 'Name a common carrier.' I can still picture you looking at your exam paper and humming a few bars of 'Chattanooga Choo Choo.' I was so tickled, I couldn't punish either of you." 23

Miss Bessie was telling me, with bourbon-laced grace, that I never fooled her for a moment. 24

When Miss Bessie died in 1980, at age 85, hundreds of her former students mourned. They knew the measure of a great teacher: love and motivation. Her wisdom and influence had rippled out across generations. 25

Some of her students who might normally have been doomed to poverty went on to become doctors, dentists and college professors. Many, guided by Miss Bessie's example, became public-school teachers. 26

"The memory of Miss Bessie and how she conducted her classroom did more for me than anything I learned in college," recalls Gladys Wood of Knoxville, Tenn., a highly respected English teacher who spent 43 years in the state's school system. "So many times, when I faced a difficult classroom problem, I asked myself, *How would Miss Bessie deal with this?* And I'd remember that she would handle it with laughter and love." 27

No child can get all the necessary support at home, and millions of poor children get *no* support at all. This is what makes a wise, educated, warm-hearted teacher like Miss Bessie so vital to the minds, hearts and souls of this country's children. 28

Questions for Study and Discussion

1. Throughout the essay Rowan offers details of Miss Bessie's physical appearance. (Glossary: *Details*) What specific details does he give, and in what context does he give them? Did Miss Bessie's physical characteristics match the quality of her character? Explain.
2. How would you sum up the character of Miss Bessie? Make a list of the key words that Rowan uses that you feel best describe her.

3. At what point in the essay does Rowan give us the details of Miss Bessie's background? Why do you suppose he delays giving us this important information? (Glossary: *Beginnings and Endings*)
4. How does dialogue serve Rowan's purposes? (Glossary: *Dialogue*)
5. Does Miss Bessie's drinking influence your opinion of her? Explain. Why do you think Rowan included this part of her behavior in his essay?
6. In his opening paragraph Rowan states that Miss Bessie "taught me English, history, civics—and a lot more than I realized." What did she teach her students beyond the traditional public school curriculum?

Vocabulary

Refer to your dictionary to define the following words as they are used in this selection. Then use each word in a sentence of your own.

civics (1)	cajoling (20)
barrios (16)	osmotic (20)
conscience (18)	measure (25)

Classroom Activity Using Description

The verbs you use in writing a description can themselves convey much descriptive information. Take, for example, the verb *to think.* As it stands, it actually tells us little more than the general sense of "mental activity." Using more precise and descriptive alternatives—*ponder, conceive, imagine, picture, muse, consider, contemplate, cogitate, ruminate, meditate*—could easily enhance your descriptive powers and enliven your writing. For each of the following verbs, make a list of at least six descriptive alternatives:

go	throw	exercise
see	take	study
say	drink	

Suggested Writing Assignments

1. Think of all the teachers you have had, and write a description of the one who has had the greatest influence on you. Remember to give some consideration to the balance you want to achieve between physical attributes and personality traits.
2. In paragraph 18 Rowan writes the following: "'If you don't read, you can't write, and if you can't write, you might as well stop dreaming,' Miss Bessie once told me." Write an essay in which you explore this theme that, in essence, is also the theme of *Models for Writers*.

Grocer's Daughter

Marianne Wiggins

Marianne Wiggins was born in 1947 in Lancaster, Pennsylvania. She is the author of several novels and collections of short stories, most of which depict women who challenge traditional roles assigned to them by society. Her most recent novel, Eveless Eden, *was published in 1995. "Grocer's Daughter," which appeared in her book* Bet They'll Miss Us When We're Gone *(1991), is both a tribute to and a description of her father; it also reveals important aspects of her own childhood. You may detect an apparently haphazard organizational pattern in Wiggins's presentation of details and her arrangement of paragraphs, but consider how the essay's structure may be appropriate to her purpose.*

For Your Journal

Think about an important person, place, or object in your life. What are its manifestations or traits—what do your eyes, ears, taste, touch, and smell reveal about the subject? Consider whether such sense impressions tell the whole story of that person, place, or object. Is there more to know? If so, what might it be and how do you think you might be able to reveal it in writing?

I am shameless in the way I love my father. 1

Like little girls who ride big horses, big girls who hold their fathers in devotion are talked about in overtones of sexual pathology. Love is always judged. No one's love is like another's. What I feel is mine, alone. If my heart is in my mouth, and if I speak it, judgment comes. Surviving judgment, like admitting love, takes courage. Here is what John Wiggins taught me: 2

The moon at crescent is God's fingernail. 3

When your shelves look empty, stack your canned goods to- 4
ward the front.

Keep your feet off other people's furniture. 5

Don't lean your belly on the scale weighing out the produce, 6
or the Devil will tip it his way when your time comes.

Take anybody's check. 7

Go nowhere in a hurry. 8

Sing. 9

Take your hat off inside churches and in the rain, when the 10
spirit moves you.

Don't wax cucumbers. 11

Don't sleep late on Sundays. 12

Start each week with gratitude and six clean aprons. 13

He was born in Pennsylvania, died in the woods and never, to 14
my knowledge, saw an island. He sunburned easily. He wore a yellow pencil stub behind his ear for jotting orders. He was so accustomed to jotting grocery orders on a pad for a clerk to read, he lost his longhand. The supermarkets in the suburbs squeezed him out. We moved a lot. Each time we moved, the house got smaller, things we didn't need got sold. We didn't need his army helmet or the cardboard notebooks, black and white, in which he'd learned to write. One can't save everything. One trims the fat, one trims the lettuce: produce, when it comes in crates from Florida, needs trimming. For years I saved the only letter he'd written in his lifetime to me. He'd printed it, of course, so there'd be no misunderstanding in the way a pen can curve a word. I lost that letter in my latest move. It's said three moves are like a single fire in their power to destroy one's camp. We moved nine times before I was eighteen. I search in vain, sometimes, for anything my father might have touched.

He always liked a good laugh; his jokes weren't always funny. 15
He concocted odd pranks. He scared my mother half to death one year, when they were first married, by burglarizing their apartment. He rigged a water bucket on his sister's bedroom door the night of her first date: that was 1939, when cotton dresses took half an hour's pressing and a girl might spend an afternoon wrapping dark hair on a curling iron. To my mother, who gets dizzy looking in round mirrors, he wrote love letters that germinated

from the center of the page and spiraled out. Those days, he still wrote in script. I think I could identify his longhand, if need be. Handwriting speaks. I think I could remember his.

I remember what his footsteps sounded like: heavier on one leg 16
than the other, made the change rattle in his pocket. He always carried change, most grocers did, because the kids would come in to buy cookies from the bin with pennies and their pennies crowded up the cash drawer. Year in, year out, he wore pleated pants in dark colors. He had three good suits—one gray, one black, one brown. I see him in them in the photographs. The gray one took a lot of coaxing from my mother and wasn't often worn. Every year for Christmas he received:

six new pairs of black socks
six new undershirts
six pairs of boxer shorts
two new sweater vests
six white shirts
six aprons
one subdued pastel shirt from me
one knit tie from my sister

The year I knew there was no Santa Claus was the year he fell 17
asleep beneath the Christmas tree assembling my sister's tricycle.

His favorite pie was something only Grandma Wiggins made: 18
butterscotch custard. Even when my sister and I were kids and loved sweet things, its sweetness made our teeth hurt. I never knew his favorite color. I think he must have had a favorite song, I never knew it, he was always singing, had a song for each occasion, favored "Someone's in the Kitchen with Dinah" while he was washing dishes and "Oh Promise Me" while he was driving in the car. Sometimes, early in the mornings, he'd sing "Buckle Down, Winsocki." I used to think Winsocki was as funny-sounding a name as that of his favorite politician, Wendell Wilkie. He liked FDR, hated Truman, voted for Dwight Eisenhower. By 1960, I was old enough to reason through my parents' pig Latin and moderately schooled in spelling, so everything they had to say in front of me, they couldn't code. My father was Republican, my mother fell for Kennedy's charisma. "Who did you vote for, John?" my mother asked him that November.

"Mary," my father answered, needing to be secret. "What do 19
you think that curtain in the voting booth is for—?"

"What the hell," he told me later. "If I'd voted like I wanted to, 20
your mother and me, we would have canceled one another out. What's the point of voting like you want to when you know that you'll be canceled out?"

I wonder if he ever dreamed that he could change things. He 21
taught me how to pitch softball. We played croquet in the front yard. He taught me how to spot a plant called preacher-in-the-pulpit along the country roads. He taught me harmony to "Jingle Bells." He taught me how to drive a car. He unscrewed the training wheels and taught me how to ride a bike. He told me strange, portenting things: if I ate too much bread, I'd get dandruff. He read *Reader's Digest, Coronet* and *Pageant* and didn't believe in evolution. There were times I didn't like him. He left abruptly. He left me much unfinished business.

He visited New York City four times in his lifetime. He was in 22
Times Square, a tourist, on V-J Day. Somehow, I'm glad for him, as a believer is for a novitiate, that he was there: Celebration needs a crowd. He thought not badly of large cities, after that; but he never lived in one.

He never sailed, his life was landlocked. I think he clammed 23
once, with my uncle, at Virginia Beach. I cannot say for certain that he knew his body's way in water. Water was not an element he knew, except as rain on crops. He was a farmer's son. Without the farmer's land, his legacy was vending farmer's goods. I planted a garden last week, north of where he lived and died, on an island where all roads lead to water. "Now, when you plant a small plot," he once said, "plant what you and yours can eat, or plant what makes you happy, like a sunflower, and offer your surplus to the ones who want. Don't waste. For God's sake, don't waste."

I wish that he could see the things I've sown. Diluted in me is 24
John Wiggins, as today's rain will be in summer's harvest. I wish that I could see him once again, hear his footfalls on the gravel driveway, heavy on one foot: These dried leavings aren't complete in their remembrance, like the trimmings swept from green growth on the grocer's floor, they crumble on my fingertips and fly piecemeal to the wind. I do not do my father justice, that was his charge. I've borne his name, in and out of marriage, a name

that is my own, sometimes I wish his strain would leave me, sometimes I'd like to choke it to full bloom. I'd like to turn to him today and say, "I love you: too late: I'm sorry: you did the best you could: you were my father: I learned from you: you were an honest man."

25 I cultivate a tiny garden, "plot" reminds me of a cemetery. I plant only what my family guarantees to eat. The rest I give to those who want. Had you known him, I'd like to think you would have bought your groceries from John Wiggins. He always had a pleasant word. He could tell you how to plan a meal for twenty people, give you produce wholesale, trim your cut of meat before he weighed it, profit wasn't Daddy's motive, life was. Life defeated him. He taught me how to pack a grocery bag, I worked there weekends, canned goods on the bottom, perishables on top. Someone puts tomatoes on the bottom of my bag these days, I repack it. I was taught respect of certain order. One sees one's father's face, as one grows older, in the most peculiar places. I see Daddy in each bud. I see his stance on corners. I, myself, wear grocer's aprons, when I cook. My mother always said there was no cleaning that damned blood from those white aprons. My father left a stain: I miss him. I write longhand, and in ink.

Martha's Vineyard
May 1979

Questions for Study and Discussion

1. How does Wiggins's first sentence influence the rest of the essay? How effective do you find Wiggins's last sentence as a conclusion for her essay? Explain. (Glossary: *Beginnings and Endings*)
2. What does the list of things that John Wiggins taught his daughter tell the reader about him?
3. Discuss Wiggins's writing style in "Grocer's Daughter." (Glossary: *Style*) Is it effective for you? Why, or why not?
4. Why did the Wiggins family move so often?

5. Wiggins says of her father, "I wonder if he ever dreamed that he could change things" (21). How did he change things for his daughter?
6. Wiggins never states how or when her father died. Why do you think she explores the impact of his death, rather than describing its occurrence? How and when do you think John Wiggins died? Defend your answer with excerpts from the essay.

Vocabulary

Refer to your dictionary to define the following words as they are used in this selection. Then use each word in a sentence of your own.

pathology (2)
concocted (15)
germinated (15)
charisma (18)
portenting (21)
novitiate (22)
piecemeal (24)

Classroom Activity Using Description

Important advice for writing well is to show rather than tell. Let's assume that your task is to reveal a person's character. What activities might you show the person doing to give your readers the correct impression of his or her character? For example, to indicate that the person was concerned about current events without coming out and saying so, you might show him or her reading the morning newspaper or watching the evening news. Or you might show a character's degree of formality by including that person's typical greeting: *Hi, how are ya?* versus *I am very pleased to meet you.* In other words, the things a person says and does are often important indicators of personality. Choose one of the following traits, and make a list of at least six ways to show rather than tell how a particular person possesses that trait.

simple but good
reckless
sensitive to the arts
a sports lover
thoughtful
politically involved
irresponsible
independent
quick-witted
public spirited

Suggested Writing Assignments

1. Describe a close relative of yours, such as a parent or sibling. Be sure to establish a purpose and a dominant impression for your description. Your audience will not know your subject—what are the little things that make up his or her character and make him or her special?
2. In her essay Wiggins reveals something of herself—her tastes, her values, her intelligence. Write an essay in which you argue that every writer, to a lesser or greater degree, reveals something of himself or herself in writing about any subject. Choose whatever examples you wish to make your point. You might, however, decide to use Carl Rowan and his essay on Miss Bessie as your primary example. Finally, you might wish to emphasize the significance of the self-revealing qualities of writing.

GRAVITY'S RAINBOW

Guy Trebay

Guy Trebay, who was born in 1952, lives in New York City and has been a staff writer for the Village Voice *since 1980. His articles have consistently explored New York City, an interest that is also evident in his book* In the Place to Be: Guy Trebay's New York, *published in 1992. The following piece first appeared in the* Village Voice *in October 1996. Trebay's title alludes to the title of Thomas Pynchon's novel* Gravity's Rainbow *and the trajectory of a World War II German V-2 rocket. As you read this essay, notice how Trebay relies on the language and culture of skaters to provide descriptive details about the recently constructed half-pipe at Skate Park in Manhattan's Riverside Park.*

FOR YOUR JOURNAL

Recently psychologists have identified "T-type" people, those who go out of their way for the type of thrills provided by bungee jumping, sky diving, rock climbing, and other potentially dangerous activities. Are you a T-type? What sorts of things do you consider thrilling? Do you enjoy the rush of adrenaline you get when you are scared or think you are in danger? How do you feel afterward?

Rahmaan Mazone stands poised at the lip, contemplating his doom. Below him is a 10-foot drop into a steel-plated half-pipe. The arc looks even deeper when you factor in Rahmaan's own six-foot height and the wheels of his in-line skates. Only a handful of local skaters have mastered the knack. Rahmaan wants to be one. "I just love heights to death," he says. 1

"Go!" a skateboarder urges as Rahmaan pauses, hovers, seems to cantilever his bulk out over a volume of empty air. 2

He's ready. He is about to let go. He's almost there and then . . . "Aargh!" Rahmaan groans, collapsing in a heap on the platform. "I don't want to die!" 3

We are in Skate Park, a very recently constructed rectangle of asphalt at 108th Street in Riverside Park. For some time, this place was known as Tuberculosis Park, principally because numerous homeless people were encamped here. Many still inhabit an enclosed arcade beneath the park walkway, and also the park itself, and the Penn Central tunnels where the so-called Mole People live. 4

It all sounds mythical. Any Manhattan miraculously remains a place that lends itself to myth. Consider the renegade culture of skaters. Back in the 1970s, the first bikers and skaters and skateboarders were building quarter-pipes in vacant lots all over town. Without permissions or easements, and with money mostly cadged from parents, they threw up rickety illegal inverted arcs of plywood and two-by-fours. When the quarter-pipes got torn down, the skaters turned their attention to public plazas, then abandoned stairways, then civic parking lots left unattended on weekends (one of the best-kept secrets was hard by the NYPD headquarters). 5

The three worlds intersected and freely diverged as skaters took to riding in hair-raising street trains, hitched to the backs of buses and trucks, and skateboarders went looking for new hills, and bikers bought bulkier equipment to move off track. 6

Andy Kessler has lived through the permutations. For 23 of his 35 years, the main focus of Kessler's existence has been his skateboard. Raised on 71st Street, and still living just a block away, the wiry athlete with the prominent nose and animated expression has the kind of commitment you don't necessarily associate with legal activity. For Thug Life read Skate Life in his case. 7

Wood, with metal wheels, and trucks held together with cotter pins, Andy Kessler's first board was a discard. He found it in the basement of his building when he was 12. The board he rides today is also wood, although that's where the similarity ends. Technology changed, as everyone knows: better wheels, better bearings, performance-oriented design. But what's essential to skateboarding has never altered. "You're on *it, it's* not on you." 8

There is a difference, and not just a philosophical one. "Skates go where you go," says Kessler. "Getting the board to go where you go is a completely different story." Anyone who's ever watched skilled skateboarders do radical tricks can attest. 9

Ivory Serra, for instance—having skated down from Riverside Drive on an autumn afternoon so crisp that New Jersey resembles the image in a stereoscopic photo—straps his helmet and pads and drops into the half-pipe as nonchalantly as if he were stepping off a log. Down Serra caroms, flying up the pipe's south side, which rises nine feet in a curve and then is purely vertical for another foot, the better to rocket you into the air. He performs a back side-air and slides down the tube to reverse the maneuver for a front side-air on the north side. Then he skates above the rim and alights on the platform. 10

Skate Park opened just a month ago; already close to 80 skaters arrive each day. The concept originated with 20 local adolescents guided by the Salvadori Educational Center on the Built Environment. It was realized with a $50,000 grant from the National Parks Service's Innovations in Recreation Program, matched by an equivalent sum from the Department of Parks and other contributors. "We were eager to meet the needs of teens in Riverside Park," explains Riverside Park administrator Charles McKinney. "And we were searching for a project that would allow kids to design their own place. It was just lucky for us that this place was standing here derelict." 11

Crackheads had taken over. Consequently, "there was very little controversy" about reuse of the park. The project was designed with the help of four teachers who conducted a group visit to a skate park in Shimmersville, Pennsylvania, the creation of scale models, and also of a clay maquette depicting the riverside terrain. Construction took just under five weeks. That, too, was accomplished by students. The yield, besides a huge plywood hulk, was "an enormous jump in these kids' self-esteem," says McKinney. There was something else. "We've designated this area from 100th Street to 111th Street as a place to explore prototypes" for specifically adolescent park use, since "urban park environments frequently deny that the needs of some age groups and cultures exist." 12

The kids in the Salvadori program were considered "at risk," as Andy Kessler points out. "One of the teachers involved said that's ridiculous, because all kids are at risk. People think that they can shelter their kids and keep their kids from getting into all sorts of shit. But these kids already know everything. The best thing you can do is give them something to focus on." 13

Daniel Horowitz, for one, is rapt. The skinny Dalton junior is dressed geeky slacker style. He has his own blue helmet and his brother's oversize board. Wobbling up and down the half-pipe, Horowitz works up almost enough speed to reach the rim of the half-pipe, then falters and skids to his knees. "This is only my second time," Horowitz says, as an expert skater prepares to drop into the pipe. 14

"You know, the good thing here," Rahmaan Mazone remarks, "is, instead of getting dissed, people support you. The advanced people share equally with the newcomers." They flame out equally, too. 15

The guy doing aerials rockets above the lip and his board keeps going. Suddenly he's Wile E. Coyote hanging in midair. When he crashes and skids in a painful heap to the bottom of the tube, Mazone lets out a whistle. "That is mad worse than getting body-slammed." 16

Next up is Gil Boyd, a compact and muscular 24-year-old. Using his leg strength and unusually low center of gravity, Boyd carves a precise path through the pipe. He resembles a surfer and, as Andy Kessler explains, "in its purest form, skateboarding's very close to surfing, although there's not much surfing in these parts, since the Hudson doesn't break too well." 17

Boyd's aggressive approach brings to mind the new technical dynamics of skate, surf, and snowboard, and people who don't so much ride as carve and shred. "I've been doing this since 1978," Boyd explains when his own ride is ended. "And what people are doing a lot of now is aerials and lip tricks. It all looks treacherous, but the danger is overrated. There's an art to falling. I've never personally seen a broken neck." 18

Even before the Parks Department had hung a sign on Skate Park, the private sector began applying muscle: Nike, Blades, and others offered to "sponsor" the brand-new park. "I was pleased I was on the Parks Department's side with that one," says Kessler, whose salary as the park's full-time supervisor is provided in part, at least through November, by the $3 daily use fee. Kessler was among those who lobbied to forego big corporate subsidies in favor of one-day events. That way there are no permanent banners to disfigure the park. "Keep the parks as parks," he says. 19

And let them evolve. Except for a single half-pipe in the South Bronx, Skate Park is about the only legal place in all five boroughs where, at about three o'clock every afternoon, you'll find 20 intense bands of skaters (both sexes) caught up in the kind of back side-airs, inverts, lip tricks, and grinds that won't necessarily send their parents reaching for Prozac. "It's a great sport," says Kessler. "There is no one best part about it. It just feels great riding. There's really just nothing like it when you drop into that tube."

Questions for Study and Discussion

1. Trebay introduces slang into his article very carefully. (Glossary: *Slang*) Identify where he uses slang in the article, and discuss what he accomplishes through using slang in each case.
2. What is the difference between skateboards and in-line skates? Why is that difference important? Why might Trebay call the difference "philosophical" as well as physical? (Glossary: *Comparison and Contrast*)
3. What details does Trebay use to describe the style and attitude of several individual skaters who use Riverside Park? What do these specific profiles add to his essay? How do they help him achieve his purpose in writing it? (Glossary: *Purpose*)
4. Reread Trebay's description of Daniel Horowitz. Identify the type of person he represents. What in the description enables you to come to this conclusion? Why might he be an important person for Trebay to include in the essay?
5. Why is it important to Kessler and the Parks Department that the park not be supported by a single sponsor? What does that say about what they are trying to accomplish?
6. As mentioned in the headnote, Trebay's title alludes to Thomas Pynchon's novel *Gravity's Rainbow.* What for you is the significance of Trebay's title?

Vocabulary

Refer to your dictionary to define the following words as they are used in this selection. Then use each word in a sentence of your own.

easements (5)
cadged (5)
permutations (7)
maquette (12)
prototypes (12)

Classroom Activity Using Description

Write five sentences that describe the place you most like to go. What details about your place do you want to include? Choose your words carefully so that you create the dominant impression that you have of that place—beauty, danger, serenity, fun, relaxation, and so on.

Suggested Writing Assignments

1. Describe your favorite sport or recreational activity. Do your best to capture the emotions, physical sensations, thought processes, and sensory input that you associate with the recreation. Select details and use diction that help you create a dominant impression that allows the reader to understand, without being told explicitly, why you like to participate in this sport or activity.
2. Describe your high school. First, determine your purpose—what about your school would you like to emphasize? Make an extensive list of the physical features of your school. Then decide what details to present to the reader and how to present them so that you convey your dominant impression. Finally, write your descriptive essay.

13

PROCESS ANALYSIS

When you give directions for getting to your house, tell how to make ice cream, or explain how a president is elected, you are using *process analysis.*

Process analysis usually arranges a series of events in order and relates them to one another, as narration and cause and effect do, but it has different emphases. Whereas narration tells mainly *what* happens and cause and effect focuses on *why* it happens, process analysis tries to explain—in detail—*how* it happens.

There are two types of process analysis: directional and informational. The *directional* type provides instructions on how to do something. These instructions can be as brief as the directions for making instant coffee printed on the label or as complex as the directions in a manual for assembling a new gas grill. The purpose of directional process analysis is simple: to give the reader directions to follow that will lead to the desired results.

Consider the directions on the next page for constructing an Astro Tube—a cylindrical airfoil made out of a sheet of heavy writing paper.

The *informational* type of process analysis, on the other hand, tells how something works, how something is made, or how something occurred. You would use informational process analysis if you wanted to explain how the human heart functions, how an atomic bomb works, how hailstones are formed, how you selected the college you are attending, or how the polio vaccine was developed. Rather than giving specific directions, informational process analysis explains and informs.

Clarity is crucial for successful process analysis. The most effective way to explain a process is to divide it into steps and to present those steps in a clear (usually chronological) sequence. Transitional words and phrases such as *first, next, after,* and *before* help to connect steps to one another. Naturally, you must be sure that no step is omitted or given out of order. Also, you may sometimes have to explain *why* a certain step is necessary, especially if it is not obvious. With intricate, abstract, or particularly difficult steps, you might use analogy or comparison to clarify the steps for your reader.

Making an Astro Tube

Start with an 8.5-inch by 11-inch sheet of heavy writing paper. (Never use newspaper in making paper models because it isn't strongly bonded and can't hold a crease.) Follow these numbered steps, corresponding to the illustrations.

1. With the long side of the sheet toward you, fold up one third of the paper.

2. Fold the doubled section in half.

3. Fold the section in half once more and crease well.

4. Unfold preceding crease.

5. Curve the ends together to form a tube, as shown in the illustration.

6. Insert the right end inside the left end between the single outer layer and the doubled layers. Overlap the ends about an inch and a half. (This makes a tube for right-handers, to be used with an underhand throw. For an overhand tube, or an underhand version to be thrown by a lefty, reverse the directions, and insert the left end inside the right end at this step.)

7. Hold the tube at the seam with one hand, where shown by the dot in the illustration, and turn the rim inward along the crease made in step 3. Start turning in at the seam and roll the rim under, moving around the circumference in a circular manner. Then round out the rim.

8. Fold the fin to the left, as shown, then raise it so that it's perpendicular to the tube. Be careful not to tear the paper at the front.

9. Hold the tube from above, near the rim. Hold it between the thumb and fingers.

The rim end should be forward, with the fin on the bottom. Throw the tube underhanded, with a motion like throwing a bowling ball, letting it spin off the fingers as it is released. The tube will float through the air, spinning as it goes. Indoor flights of 30 feet or more are easy. With practice you can achieve remarkable accuracy.

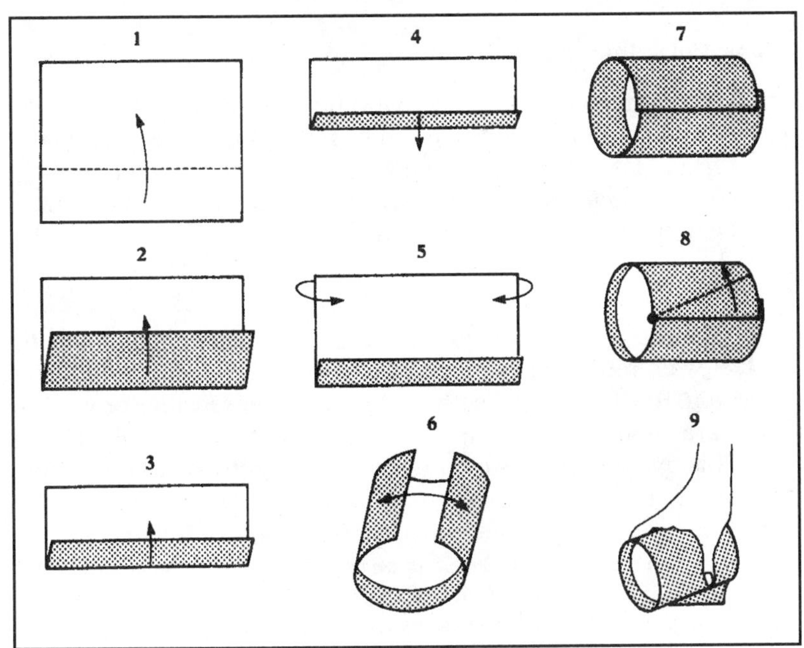

How to Organize Your Thoughts for Better Communication

Sherry Sweetnam

Sherry Sweetnam is a communications consultant for major corporations who specializes in written communication skills. She has conducted workshops on business communications all over the world and has taught at Hunter College and Queens College in New York. Her book The Executive Memo: A Guide to Persuasive Business Communications *was published in 1986. As you read the following selection, which appeared in* Personnel *in 1986, note how Sweetnam uses the writing techniques she describes to catch your attention. Her essay is a good example of a directional process analysis.*

For Your Journal

Reflect on your experiences with business communications. Have you sent and/or received business letters, memos, and reports lately? In general, how would you characterize the style of those communications? What do you think could be done to improve their clarity or directness?

Do you want to analyze the way you communicate and the way you think and organize your thoughts? Study your writing. It will tell you whether you are reader-sensitive or whether you are communicating strictly from your own point of view. 1

This example shows communication strictly from the writer's point of view: 2

The Personnel Department
is pleased to announce that
MARY R. NAKOVEY
formerly special assistant to the director
executive director of human resources

and associate executive director
Department of Manpower Planning
has joined the firm
as manager of personnel.

What's the problem with this business announcement? *It wastes time.* The big news is the new personnel manager; so why not say it up front? Instead, the writer forces you to wade through 30 words to get to the main point. Stalling the main point causes frustration, annoyance, and tension in the reader and creates negative feelings toward the writer and the information. 3

Many of us fail to get to the point when we communicate— both orally and in writing. There are logical explanations as to why we organize our thoughts like this. They are: 4

1. *We're trying to impress.* Often, we're so concerned about building our credibility and establishing our importance that we show off when we write. But showing off turns most people off. Readers don't care how great a person, department, or unit is. The readers' business concerns are: What's new? How is this going to affect me?
2. *We're trying to figure out what we think.* Writing helps us clarify thought. It is an excellent tool for moving through the thinking process itself. However, writers need to edit their work so that their key information is not buried in the maze of the process itself.
3. *We're not clear about what is important to our readers.* In writing sheerly from our own point of view, we lose sight of the reader's concerns and interests. It's fine to write this way in the initial drafts, but the final draft should be reshaped with the reader's interests in mind.
4. *We tend to organize information chronologically rather than psychologically.* Most of us are natural storytellers. ("Guess what happened on the subway today!" "Let me tell you what happened in yesterday's marketing meeting.") As storytellers, we naturally slip into a system of ordering information chronologically. There's nothing wrong with using the story format in the appropriate environment. The "right" organization to use always depends on who is reading the report and what their needs are.

5. *We were trained to write that way in school.* We learned to put the summary, conclusion, the last word, the bottom line, at the end of our school compositions and reports. We memorized and religiously followed the academic formula: (1) introduction, (2) body, (3) conclusion. And we continue to use it.

There's nothing wrong with organizing our communications that way *if* we have a captive audience, *if* we are so interesting no one can put our writing down, and *if* people have a lot of time. But that is rarely true in business. Most people are very busy with their own agendas and don't have time to wade through a lot of words to get to the point. When we bury our key points we lose credibility because we are not being sensitive to our reader's interests and time constraints. 5

Positioning Your Thoughts

Effective business communication organizes thought in the opposite way. The rule is to get to your point up front; then give the background and details. That is why executive summaries are so popular. After getting the nuggets up front, the reader can decide whether he or she wants to continue reading. 6

The most critical ideas should be in the most powerful of the three positions on the page—the beginning, middle, or end. 7

The beginning. The most powerful position is the first 50 words of a memo, letter, report, or proposal. Since the opening paragraph is key, that's where you want to load your most important ideas. 8

The middle. This is no-man's land—the weakest position on a page. It may or may not get read, depending on whether you've been able to hold your reader's interest up front. 9

The end. This is the second strongest position (assuming the reader gets to it). Why? Because it is the last thing that the reader will read. Therefore, it has greater impact than what was in no-man's land. 10

How to Do Frontload Writing

Frontloading means placing your key idea first. To do this, first go through your writing with a pencil and underline the key ideas 11 in sentences and paragraphs. Then rearrange those key phrases and ideas so that they appear at the beginning of the memo, paragraph, or sentence.

Consider, for example, the difference in impact between these titles: 12

> *Subject: Statistical Data Due Dates*
> vs.
> *Subject: Due Dates for Statistical Data*

The phrase *statistical data* is not the critical information in the title. It doesn't hook the reader because it doesn't answer such critical questions as: What do I have to do? Why is it important that I read this? The phrase *due date* is urgent; therefore, it needs to be frontloaded. 13

Frontloading Letters

Here is an example of how writers backload key information in a letter. The key information is italicized and appears at the end of the letter. 14

> Due to a processing error, your June payroll deduction, credited to your account on January 24, 1986, was inadvertently priced at $33.15145. The correct price for this transaction should have been $36.4214. *We have corrected this problem and adjusted your account accordingly.*

The last sentence should be repositioned so that it becomes the first sentence. The result could possibly read, "We have adjusted your account because we made an error in our calculations." 15

Why does this work? Because it is written from the reader's point of view. When it comes to problems and solutions, what most readers and customers want to know is: Have you solved the problem? If the news is good, then don't bury it! As a rule, give your reader the good news first instead of striking a negative note at the outset. 16

Frontloading Action Requests

The following is an example of a request for action. Notice that the request is buried in the second paragraph: 17

> Steve, I have been searching the lower Minneapolis area for over three months for qualified candidates with a strong knowledge of AVS to support the chemical data system. I have been unsuccessful. As a result, the project is in jeopardy.
>
> Therefore, *I am requesting your support to obtain the necessary approvals* required to begin reviewing candidates from outside the lower Minneapolis area.

By repositioning the request at the beginning of the piece, it would become a far more powerful communication.

Why don't we state requests up front? Because we don't want to appear too bold or too aggressive. In fact, however, stating your request up front is considered by many to be direct, forthright, and nonmanipulative. It is also good business because it gets to the point quickly. Again, there's no waste of time. 18

Frontloading to Persuade

Writing to persuade someone about an idea, service, or product is trickier than writing to inform or request action. You must decide how interested your reader is in what you're trying to persuade him of. If your reader is interested, then state your idea up front. For example, you might start out by writing: "I recommend that we buy XYZ computer." 19

However, if your reader isn't so interested, backload your recommendation and frontload the benefits of your idea or product so the reader will be sold. 20

Tough Messages: The Three Exceptions to Frontloading

There are three situations in which frontloading your key idea doesn't work: 21

1. *When you have to say "no."* When you have to tell someone "no," it makes much more sense to begin with a positive tone or a kiss. Then you can ease into the bad news or the kick in the second paragraph. In this way, the *no* isn't such a blow.
2. *When your reader is not interested in buying your new idea, service, or product.* When you have to convince someone of your ideas, then it makes sense to frontload the benefits and advantages and conclude with your recommendations.

3. *When you know your reader doesn't want to comply with your request.* The best thing to do in this instance is to ease into your request or suggestions.

Why Rethink?

One of the best ways to achieve force and interest in your writing is to frontload ideas. This means frontloading in all your writing—your titles; all types of memos, letters and reports; and at the sentence and paragraph level. Frontloading will grab your reader's interest and get your memos read. The inner voice of your reader will be saying, "Here's a writer who knows what's important and doesn't waste my time." 22

A fringe benefit of reorganizing your written communications is that you will find yourself getting to the point more often when you're speaking to people. Frontloading is a mental exercise that trains you to get to the point in all of your communications. 23

Questions for Study and Discussion

1. Analyze Sweetnam's first paragraph. (Glossary: *Beginnings and Endings*) Is it effective? What does she accomplish in these three sentences?
2. What does "frontloading" mean? Why is it important for business communications?
3. Why do people tend to avoid frontloading in their written communications? When *should* they avoid it?
4. Sweetnam's use of subheads makes it easy to see how she organizes her essay. (Glossary: *Organization*) Briefly summarize each section. Why is her organization effective?
5. Why does Sweetnam describe the middle of the page as "no-man's land"?
6. What techniques does Sweetnam use to make her article easy to read and to hold the reader's attention?
7. Who is Sweetnam's intended audience? (Glossary: *Audience*) Based on the techniques she describes in the article, do you think that the audience is receptive or skeptical of Sweetnam's advice?

Vocabulary

Refer to your dictionary to define the following words as they are used in this selection. Then use each word in a sentence of your own.

personnel (2)	chronologically (4)
credibility (4)	captive (5)
clarify (4)	inadvertently (14)
sheerly (4)	nonmanipulative (18)

Classroom Activity Using Process Analysis

One of the following sets of directions is better than the other. What specifically makes it better?

How to Get to the Thrifty Dry Cleaners

Version 1: Go down Shelburne Road for about two miles, take a right on Green Street, and you'll see the store on your right.

Version 2: You are heading south on Shelburne Road and you need to go north. Turn around in this parking lot and head back until you pass three traffic lights, about two miles. After the third light, get in your right-hand lane until you reach Green Street. Take a right on Green Street and go to the next traffic light. After the light, get to your right and you will immediately see the sign for Thrifty Dry Cleaners. Pull into the driveway and park in front of the store.

Suggested Writing Assignments

1. Write a business memo based on the techniques Sweetnam describes in her article. Include a directional process analysis in the memo. Choose an office topic, such as how to load paper into a new copier or printer, how to make good coffee in the office machine without making a mess, or how to send a fax.
2. Write a process essay in which you explain how to write a good college essay. How will it differ from the techniques Sweetnam describes for writing a good business memo?

How to Mark a Book

Mortimer Adler

Writer, editor, and educator Mortimer Adler was born in New York City in 1902. A high-school drop-out, Adler completed the undergraduate program at Columbia University in three years, but he did not graduate because he refused to take the mandatory swimming test. Adler is recognized for his editorial work on the Encyclopaedia Britannica *and for his leadership of the Great Books Program at the University of Chicago, where adults from all walks of life gathered twice a month to read and discuss the classics. In the following essay, which first appeared in the* Saturday Review of Literature *in 1940, Adler explains how to take full ownership of a book by marking it up, by making it "a part of yourself." Note how he provides verbal cues ("There are two ways," "Let me develop these three points") that indicate the organizational connections between the parts of a paragraph and, on a larger scale, between paragraphs.*

For Your Journal

When you read a book that you must understand thoroughly and remember for a class, or one that you are reading carefully for your own purposes, do you use any techniques beyond just reading it as you would for light pleasure reading? Do you take notes, mark the book with notes or a highlighter, or read certain passages more than once? What helps you to remember important parts of the book and improve your understanding of what the author is saying?

You know you have to read "between the lines" to get the most out of anything. I want to persuade you to do some- 1 thing equally important in the course of your reading. I want to persuade you to "write between the lines." Unless you do, you are not likely to do the most efficient kind of reading.

I contend, quite bluntly, that marking up a book is not an act 2
of mutilation but of love.

You shouldn't mark up a book which isn't yours. Librarians 3
(or your friends) who lend you books expect you to keep them clean, and you should. If you decide that I am right about the usefulness of marking books, you will have to buy them. Most of the world's great books are available today, in reprint editions, at less than a dollar.

There are two ways in which one can own a book. The first is 4
the property right you establish by paying for it, just as you pay for clothes and furniture. But this act of purchase is only the prelude to possession. Full ownership comes only when you have made it a part of yourself, and the best way to make yourself a part of it is by writing in it. An illustration may make the point clear. You buy a beefsteak and transfer it from the butcher's icebox to your own. But you do not own the beefsteak in the most important sense until you consume it and get it into your bloodstream. I am arguing that books, too, must be absorbed in your bloodstream to do you any good.

Confusion about what it means to *own* a book leads people to 5
a false reverence for paper, binding, and type—a respect for the physical thing—the craft of the printer rather than the genius of the author. They forget that it is possible for a man to acquire the idea, to possess the beauty, which a great book contains, without staking his claim by pasting his bookplate inside the cover. Having a fine library doesn't prove that its owner has a mind enriched by books; it proves nothing more than that he, his father, or his wife, was rich enough to buy them.

There are three kinds of book owners. The first has all the 6
standard sets and best-sellers—unread, untouched. (This deluded individual owns woodpulp and ink, not books.) The second has a great many books—a few of them read through, most of them dipped into, but all of them as clean and shiny as the day they were bought. (This person would probably like to make books his own, but is restrained by a false respect for their physical appearance.) The third has a few books or many—every one of them dog-eared and dilapidated, shaken and loosened by contin-

ual use, marked and scribbled in from front to back. (This man owns books.)

Is it false respect, you may ask, to preserve intact and unblemished a beautifully printed book, an elegantly bound edition? Of course not. I'd no more scribble all over a first edition of *Paradise Lost* than I'd give my baby a set of crayons and an original Rembrandt! I wouldn't mark up a painting or a statue. Its soul, so to speak, is inseparable from its body. And the beauty of a rare edition or of a richly manufactured volume is like that of a painting or a statue. 7

But the soul of a book *can* be separated from its body. A book is more like the score of a piece of music than it is like a painting. No great musician confuses a symphony with the printed sheets of music. Arturo Toscanini reveres Brahms, but Toscanini's score of the C-minor Symphony is so thoroughly marked up that no one but the maestro himself can read it. The reason why a great conductor makes notations on his musical scores—marks them up again and again each time he returns to study them—is the reason why you should mark your books. If your respect for magnificent binding or typography gets in the way, buy yourself a cheap edition and pay your respects to the author. 8

Why is marking up a book indispensable to reading? First, it keeps you awake. (And I don't mean merely conscious; I mean wide awake.) In the second place, reading, if it is active, is thinking, and thinking tends to express itself in words, spoken or written. The marked book is usually the thought-through book. Finally, writing helps you remember the thoughts you had, or the thoughts the author expressed. Let me develop these three points. 9

If reading is to accomplish anything more than passing time, it must be active. You can't let your eyes glide across the lines of a book and come up with an understanding of what you have read. Now an ordinary piece of light fiction, like say, *Gone with the Wind,* doesn't require the most active kind of reading. The books you read for pleasure can be read in a state of relaxation, and nothing is lost. But a great book, rich in ideas and beauty, a book that raises and tries to answer great fundamental questions, demands the most active reading of which you are capable. You don't absorb the ideas of John Dewey the way you absorb the crooning of Mr. Vallee. You have to reach for them. That you cannot do while you're asleep. 10

If, when you've finished reading a book, the pages are filled with your notes, you know that you read actively. The most famous active reader of great books I know is President Hutchins, of the University of Chicago. He also has the hardest schedule of business activities of any man I know. He invariably reads with a pencil, and sometimes, when he picks up a book and pencil in the evening, he finds himself, instead of making intelligent notes, drawing what he calls "caviar factories" on the margins. When that happens, he puts the book down. He knows he's too tired to read, and he's just wasting time. 11

But, you may ask, why is writing necessary? Well, the physical act of writing, with your own hand, brings words and sentences more sharply before your mind and preserves them better in your memory. To set down your reaction to important words and sentences you have read, and the questions they have raised in your mind, is to preserve those reactions and sharpen those questions. 12

Even if you wrote on a scratch pad, and threw the paper away when you had finished writing, your grasp of the book would be surer. But you don't have to throw the paper away. The margins (top and bottom, as well as side), the end-papers, the very space between the lines, are all available. They aren't sacred. And, best of all, your marks and notes become an integral part of the book and stay there forever. You can pick up the book the following week or year, and there are all your points of agreement, disagreement, doubt, and inquiry. It's like resuming an interrupted conversation with the advantage of being able to pick up where you left off. 13

And that is exactly what reading a book should be: a conversation between you and the author. Presumably he knows more about the subject than you do; naturally, you'll have the proper humility as you approach him. But don't let anybody tell you that a reader is supposed to be solely on the receiving end. Understanding is a two-way operation; learning doesn't consist in being an empty receptacle. The learner has to question himself and question the teacher. He even has to argue with the teacher, once he understands what the teacher is saying. And marking a book is literally an expression of your differences, or agreements of opinion, with the author. 14

There are all kinds of devices for marking a book intelligently and fruitfully. Here's the way I do it: 15

1. *Underlining:* of major points, of important or forceful statements.
2. *Vertical lines at the margin:* to emphasize a statement already underlined.
3. *Star, asterisk, or other doo-dad at the margin:* to be used sparingly, to emphasize the ten or twenty most important statements in the book. (You may want to fold the bottom corner of each page on which you use such marks. It won't hurt the sturdy paper on which most modern books are printed, and you will be able to take the book off the shelf at any time and, by opening it at the folded-corner page, refresh your recollection of the book.)
4. *Numbers in the margin:* to indicate the sequence of points the author makes in developing a single argument.
5. *Numbers of other pages in the margin:* to indicate where else in the book the author made points relevant to the point marked; to tie up the ideas in a book, which, though they may be separated by many pages, belong together.
6. *Circling of key words or phrases.*
7. *Writing in the margin, or at the top or bottom of the page, for the sake of:* recording questions (and perhaps answers) which a passage raised in your mind; reducing a complicated discussion to a simple statement; recording the sequence of major points right through the book. I use the end-papers at the back of the book to make a personal index of the author's points in the order of their appearance.

The front end-papers are, to me, the most important. Some 16
people reserve them for a fancy bookplate. I reserve them for fancy thinking. After I have finished reading the book and making my personal index on the back end-papers, I turn to the front and try to outline the book, not page by page, or point by point (I've already done that at the back), but as an integrated structure, with a basic unity and an order of parts. This outline is, to me, the measure of my understanding of the work.

If you're a die-hard anti-book-marker, you may object that the 17
margins, the space between the lines, and the end-papers don't give you room enough. All right. How about using a scratch pad slightly smaller than the page-size of the book—so that the edges

of the sheets won't protrude? Make your index, outlines, and even your notes on the pad, and then insert these sheets permanently inside the front and back covers of the book.

Or, you may say that this business of marking books is going to slow up your reading. It probably will. That's one of the reasons for doing it. Most of us have been taken in by the notion that speed of reading is a measure of our intelligence. There is no such thing as the right speed for intelligent reading. Some things should be read quickly and effortlessly, and some should be read slowly and even laboriously. The sign of intelligence in reading is the ability to read different things according to their worth. In the case of good books, the point is not to see how many of them you can get through, but rather how many can get through you—how many you can make your own. A few friends are better than a thousand acquaintances. If this be your aim, as it should be, you will not be impatient if it takes more time and effort to read a great book than it does a newspaper. 18

You may have one final objection to marking books. You can't lend them to your friends because nobody else can read them without being distracted by your notes. Furthermore, you won't want to lend them because a marked copy is a kind of intellectual diary, and lending it is almost like giving your mind away. 19

If your friend wishes to read your *Plutarch's Lives, Shakespeare,* or *The Federalist Papers,* tell him gently but firmly to buy a copy. You will lend him your car or your coat—but your books are as much a part of you as your head or your heart. 20

Questions for Study and Discussion

1. In the first paragraph, Adler writes, "I want to persuade you to do something equally important in the course of your reading. I want to persuade you to 'write between the lines.'" What assumptions does Adler make about his audience when he chooses to use the parallel structure of "I want to persuade you . . . "? (Glossary: *Audience* and *Parallelism*) Is stating his intention so blatantly an effective way of presenting his argument? Why, or why not?

2. Adler expresses himself very clearly throughout the essay, and his topic sentences are carefully crafted. (Glossary: *Topic Sentence*) Reread the topic sentences for paragraphs 3–6, and identify how each introduces the main idea for the paragraph and unifies it.
3. According to Adler, why is marking up a book indispensable to reading? Do you agree with his three arguments? Why, or why not?
4. Adler says that reading a book should be a conversation between the reader and the author. What characteristics does he say the conversation should have? How does marking a book assist in carrying on the conversation?
5. Summarize in your own words Adler's process analysis about how one should mark a book. How does Adler organize his process analysis? (Glossary: *Organization*)
6. Explain how Adler's analogy "A few friends are better than a thousand acquaintances" (18) works. (Glossary: *Analogy*) Why is it important to his overall argument?

Vocabulary

Refer to your dictionary to define the following words as they are used in this selection. Then use each word in a sentence of your own.

deluded (6)	integral (13)
dilapidated (6)	protrude (17)
typography (8)	

Classroom Activity Using Process Analysis

Number the series of steps in the following directional process analysis about how to hit a golf ball:

At contact, your head should still be over the ball.
Select the correct club, then go through any pre-shot routine you use to help you focus.

When addressing the ball, keep your body square to your target line.
Begin your backswing slowly.
When you finish the swing, your belt buckle should be facing the target, and you should be balanced over your forward leg.
Take a practice swing before you address the ball and establish your target line.
Trigger your downswing by tucking your forward elbow into your body.

Write a short (five- to seven-sentence) directional process analysis of an activity you know well. Pay close attention to your organization, and make it as easy as possible for a reader to follow your process.

Suggested Writing Assignments

1. Adler devotes a large portion of his essay to persuading his audience that marking books is a worthwhile task. Write an essay in which you instruct your audience about how to do something they do not necessarily wish to do or they do not think is necessary to do. For instance, before explaining how to buy the best renter's insurance, you may need to convince readers that they *should* buy renter's insurance. Write your directional process analysis after making a convincing argument for the validity of the process you wish to present.
2. Write a directional process analysis in which you present your technique for getting the most enjoyment out of a common activity. For example, perhaps you have a set routine you follow for spending an evening watching TV—preparing popcorn, checking the program listings, clearing off the coffee table, finding the remote control, settling into your favorite chair, and so on. Choose from the following topics:

   How to listen to music
   How to watch TV
   How to eat an ice-cream cone
   How to reduce stress

FENDER BENDERS: LEGAL DO'S AND DON'T'S

Armond D. Budish

Attorney and consumer-law journalist Armond D. Budish is the author of Avoiding the Medicaid Trap: How to Beat the Catastrophic Costs of Nursing-Home Care *(1989). In addition to practicing law in Cleveland, Budish writes regular columns for the* Cleveland Plain Dealer *and* Family Circle *magazine, concerning consumers and the law. He received the National Press Club's Consumer Journalism Award for Syndication in 1988. In the following selection, published in* Family Circle *in July 1994, Budish uses numbering and subheadings to help organize his material and emphasize key ideas, but still depends mostly on chronological order to keep his readers oriented to the steps in his process.*

FOR YOUR JOURNAL

Have you ever been in a minor automobile accident, either as a driver or passenger? How traumatic was it for you? What steps did you or the driver take immediately afterward so that you could continue on your way?

The car ahead of you stops suddenly. You hit the brakes, but you just can't stop in time. Your front bumper meets the rear end of the other car. *Ouch!* 1

There doesn't seem to be any damage, and it must be your lucky day because the driver you hit agrees that it's not worth hassling with insurance claims and risking a premium increase. So after exchanging addresses, you go your separate ways. 2

Imagine your surprise when you open the mail a few weeks later only to discover a letter from your "victim's" lawyer demand- 3 ing $10,000 to cover car repairs, pain and suffering. Apparently the agreeable gentleman decided to disagree, then went ahead and filed a police report blaming you for the incident and for his damages.

When automobiles meet by accident, do you know how to respond? Here are 10 practical tips that can help you avoid costly legal and insurance hassles. 4

1. Stop! It's the Law.

No matter how serious or minor the accident, stop immediately. If possible, don't move your car—especially if someone has been injured. Leaving the cars as they were when the accident occurred helps the police determine what happened. Of course, if your car is blocking traffic or will cause another accident where it is, then move it to the nearest safe location. 5

For every rule there are exceptions, though. If, for example, you are rear-ended at night in an unsafe area, it's wisest to keep on going and notify the police later. There have been cases in which people were robbed or assaulted when they got out of their cars. 6

2. Zip Loose Lips.

Watch what you say after an accident. Although this may sound harsh, even an innocent "I'm sorry" could later be construed as an admission of fault. Also be sure not to accuse the other driver of causing the accident. Since you don't know how a stranger will react to your remarks, you run the risk of making a bad situation worse. 7

Remember, you are not the judge or jury; it's not up to you to decide who is or is not at fault. Even if you think you caused the accident, you might be wrong. For example: Assume you were driving 15 miles over the speed limit. What you probably were not aware of is that the other driver's blood-alcohol level exceeded the legal limits, so he was at least equally at fault. 8

3. Provide Required Information.

If you are involved in an accident, you are required in most states to give your name, address and car registration number to: any person injured in the accident; the owner, driver or pas- 9 senger in any car that was damaged in the accident; a police officer on the scene. If you don't own the car (say it belongs to a friend or your parents), you should provide the name and address of the owner.

10 You must produce this information even if there are no apparent injuries or damages and even if you didn't cause the accident. Most states don't require you to provide the name of your insurance company, although it's usually a good idea to do so. However, *don't* discuss the amount of your coverage—that might inspire the other person to "realize" his injuries are more serious than he originally thought.

11 What should you do if you hit a parked car and the owner is not around? The law requires you to leave a note with your name, and the other identifying information previously mentioned, in a secure place on the car (such as under the windshield wiper).

4. Get Required Information.

12 You should obtain from the others involved in the accident the same information that you provide them with. However, if the other driver refuses to cooperate, at least get the license number and the make and model of the car to help police track down the owner.

5. Call the Police.

13 It's obvious that if it's a serious accident in which someone is injured, the police should be called immediately. That's both the law and common sense. But what if the accident seems minor? Say you're stopped, another car taps you in the rear. If it's absolutely clear to both drivers that there is no damage or injury, you each can go your merry way. But that's the exception.

14 Normally, you should call the police to substantiate what occurred. In most cities police officers will come to the scene, even for minor accidents, but if they won't, you and the other driver should go to the station (of the city where the accident occurred) to file a report. Ask to have an officer check out both cars.

15 If you are not at fault, be wary of accepting the other driver's suggestion that you leave the police out of it and arrange a private settlement. When you submit your $500 car-repair estimate several weeks later, you could discover that the other driver has

developed "amnesia" and denies being anywhere near the accident. If the police weren't present on the scene, you may not have a legal leg to stand on.

Even if you *are* at fault, it's a good idea to involve the police. Why? Because a police officer will note the extent of the other driver's damages in his or her report, limiting your liability. Without police presence the other driver can easily inflate the amount of the damages. 16

6. Identify Witnesses.

Get the names and addresses of any witnesses, in case there's a legal battle some time in the future. Ask bystanders or other motorists who stop whether they saw the accident; if they answer "yes," get their identifying information. It is also helpful to note the names and badge numbers of all police officers on the scene. 17

7. Go to the Hospital.

If there's a chance that you've been injured, go directly to a hospital emergency room or to your doctor. The longer you wait, the more you may jeopardize your health and the more difficult it may be to get reimbursed for your injuries if they turn out to be serious. 18

8. File a Report.

Every driver who is involved in an automobile incident in which injuries occur must fill out an accident report. Even if the property damage is only in the range of $200 to $1,000, most states require that an accident report be filed. You must do this fairly quickly, usually in 1 to 30 days. Forms may be obtained and filed with the local motor vehicle department or police station in the city where the accident occurred. 19

9. Consider Filing an Insurance Claim.

Talk with your insurance agent as soon as possible after an accident. He or she can help you decide if you should file an insurance claim or pay out of your own pocket. 20

For example, let's say you caused an accident and the damages totaled $800. You carry a $250 deductible, leaving you with a possible $550 insurance claim. If you do submit a claim, your insurance rates are likely to go up, an increase that will probably continue for about three years. You should compare that figure to the $550 claim to determine whether to file a claim or to pay the cost yourself. (Also keep in mind that multiple claims sometimes make it harder to renew your coverage.) 21

10. Don't Be Too Quick to Accept a Settlement.

If the other driver is at fault and there's any chance you've been injured, don't rush to accept a settlement from that person's insurance company. You may not know the extent of your injuries for some time, and once you accept a settlement, it's difficult to get an "upgrade." Before settling, consult with a lawyer who handles personal injury cases. 22

When you *haven't* been injured and you receive a fair offer to cover the damage to your car, you can go ahead and accept it. 23

Questions for Study and Discussion

1. Why does Budish use the term "fender bender" in his title? (Glossary: *Title*) Why is it important to his process analysis?
2. Write down each of Budish's ten one-sentence instructions and read them without his supplementary information. Why does Budish begin each paragraph with a short "sound bite" instruction? If you were to get into an accident, would the concise instruction list be helpful? Why, or why not?
3. How does Budish organize his essay? (Glossary: *Organization*) How does the organization help his readers to remember and possibly use his information?
4. When is it safe not to call the police to the scene of an accident? Explain your answer.
5. Budish ends his essay with his tenth and final instruction. (Glossary: *Beginnings and Endings*) Would a concluding paragraph be helpful to you as a reader? If he had added a concluding paragraph, what would you have wanted it to say?

Vocabulary

Refer to your dictionary to define the following words as they are used in this selection. Then use each word in a sentence of your own.

premium (2)	liability (16)
substantiate (14)	deductible (21)

Classroom Activity Using Process Analysis

In preparation for writing a short directional process analysis with the title "How to Make Scrambled Eggs," make a list of the steps in the process. Assume your reader has never prepared this dish. Share your paper with another member of your class to test for completeness, accuracy, and clarity.

Suggested Writing Assignments

1. In his essay, Budish presents clear, concise directions for handling a potentially upsetting situation in the best way possible. This information can be vital in such situations, especially when one might have to deal with both physical and emotional trauma. Write a directional process analysis for how to handle one of the following situations:

a mugging	a heart attack
a house fire	a water rescue

2. Write an essay in which you give directions on how to make a friend. Copy Budish's technique of offering a short instructional sentence followed by more detailed information. Decide how much information you wish to present to back up each main point—make sure the reader understands how to proceed, but keep the essay unified.

The Spider and the Wasp

Alexander Petrunkevitch

Alexander Petrunkevitch (1875–1964), a Russian-born zoologist, was a leading authority on spiders. He published his first important work, The Index Catalogue of Spiders of North, Central, and South America, *in 1911. Petrunkevitch was also widely recognized for his translations of Russian and English poetry. In this essay, first published in* Scientific American *(1952), Petrunkevitch describes the process involved in one of nature's annual occurrences, where the "intelligence" of digger wasps is pitted against the "instincts" of tarantula spiders. The essay is arranged as two distinct process analyses: the first identifying the tarantula's three tactile responses; the second describing how the wasp subdues the tarantula despite these instinctive responses. As you finish reading, notice how Petrunkevitch uses information from both processes in his final few paragraphs to help explore what "makes the tarantula behave as stupidly as it does."*

For Your Journal

Reflect on the encounters with nature you had as a child—especially the creepy crawlies, the birds that landed in the backyard feeder, your family pets, horses that you rode—and try to remember a natural process these creatures engaged in that you thought worthy of your attention. What did you learn from your observations?

In the feeding and safeguarding of their progeny insects and spiders exhibit some interesting analogies to reasoning and some crass examples of blind instinct. The case I propose to describe here is that of the tarantula spiders and their archenemy, 1 the digger wasps of the genus *Pepsis*. It is a classic example of what looks like intelligence pitted against instinct—a strange situation in which the victim, though fully able to defend itself, submits unwittingly to its destruction.

Most tarantulas live in the tropics, but several species occur in 2
the temperate zone and a few are common in the southern U.S. Some varieties are large and have powerful fangs with which they can inflict a deep wound. These formidable-looking spiders do not, however, attack man; you can hold one in your hand, if you are gentle, without being bitten. Their bite is dangerous only to insects and small mammals such as mice; for man it is no worse than a hornet's sting.

Tarantulas customarily live in deep cylindrical burrows, from 3
which they emerge at dusk and into which they retire at dawn. Mature males wander about after dark in search of females and occasionally stray into houses. After mating, the male dies in a few weeks, but a female lives much longer and can mate several years in succession. In a Paris museum is a tropical specimen which is said to have been living in captivity for 25 years.

A fertilized female tarantula lays from 200 to 400 eggs at a time; 4
thus it is possible for a single tarantula to produce several thousand young. She takes no care of them beyond weaving a cocoon of silk to enclose the eggs. After they hatch, the young walk away, find convenient places in which to dig their burrows and spend the rest of their lives in solitude. The eyesight of tarantulas is poor, being limited to a sensing of change in the intensity of light and to the perception of moving objects. They apparently have little or no sense of hearing, for a hungry tarantula will pay no attention to a loudly chirping cricket placed in its cage unless the insect happens to touch one of its legs.

But all spiders, and especially hairy ones, have an extremely 5
delicate sense of touch. Laboratory experiments prove that tarantulas can distinguish three types of touch: pressure against the body wall, stroking of the body hair, and riffling of certain very fine hairs on the legs called trichobothria. Pressure against the body, by the finger or the end of a pencil, causes the tarantula to move off slowly for a short distance. The touch excites no defensive response unless the approach is from above where the spider can see the motion, in which case it rises on its hind legs, lifts its front legs, opens its fangs and holds this threatening posture as long as the object continues to move.

The entire body of a tarantula, especially its legs, is thickly clothed with hair. Some of it is short and wooly, some long and stiff. Touching this body hair produces one of two distinct reactions. When the spider is hungry, it responds with an immediate and swift attack. At the touch of a cricket's antennae the tarantula seizes the insect so swiftly that a motion picture taken at the rate of 64 frames per second shows only the result and not the process of capture. But when the spider is not hungry, the stimulation of its hairs merely causes it to shake the touched limb. An insect can walk under its hairy belly unharmed. 6

The trichobothria, very fine hairs growing from disklike membranes on the legs, are sensitive only to air movement. A light breeze makes them vibrate slowly, without disturbing the common hair. When one blows gently on the trichobothria, the tarantula reacts with a quick jerk of its four front legs. If the front and hind legs are stimulated at the same time, the spider makes a sudden jump. This reaction is quite independent of the state of its appetite. 7

These three tactile responses—to pressure on the body wall, to moving of the common hair, and to flexing of the trichobothria—are so different from one another that there is no possibility of confusing them. They serve the tarantula adequately for most of its needs and enable it to avoid most annoyances and dangers. But they fail the spider completely when it meets its deadly enemy, the digger wasp *Pepsis*. 8

These solitary wasps are beautiful and formidable creatures. Most species are either a deep shiny blue all over, or deep blue with rusty wings. The largest have a wing span of about four inches. They live on nectar. When excited, they give off a pungent odor—a warning that they are ready to attack. The sting is much worse than that of a bee or common wasp, and the pain and swelling last longer. In the adult stage the wasp lives only a few months. The female produces but a few eggs, one at a time at intervals of two or three days. For each egg the mother must provide one adult tarantula, alive but paralyzed. The mother wasp attaches the egg to the paralyzed spider's abdomen. Upon hatching from the egg, the larva is many hundreds of times smaller than its living but helpless victim. It eats no other food and drinks no water. By the time it has finished its single gargantuan meal and become ready for wasphood, nothing remains of the tarantula but its indigestible chitinous skeleton. 9

The mother wasp goes tarantula-hunting when the egg in her ovary is almost ready to be laid. Flying low over the ground late on a sunny afternoon, the wasp looks for its victim or for the mouth of a tarantula burrow, a round hole edged by a bit of silk. The sex of the spider makes no difference, but the mother is highly discriminating as to species. Each species of *Pepsis* requires a certain species of tarantula, and the wasp will not attack the wrong species. In a cage with a tarantula which is not its normal prey, the wasp avoids the spider and is usually killed by it in the night. 10

Yet when a wasp finds the correct species, it is the other way about. To identify the species the wasp apparently must explore the spider with her antennae. The tarantula shows an amazing tolerance to this exploration. The wasp crawls under it and walks over it without evoking any hostile response. The molestation is so great and so persistent that the tarantula often rises on all eight legs, as if it were on stilts. It may stand this way for several minutes. Meanwhile the wasp, having satisfied itself that the victim is of the right species, moves off a few inches to dig the spider's grave. Working vigorously with legs and jaws, it excavates a hole 8 to 10 inches deep with a diameter slightly larger than the spider's girth. Now and again the wasp pops out of the hole to make sure that the spider is still there. 11

When the grave is finished, the wasp returns to the tarantula to complete her ghastly enterprise. First she feels it all over once more with her antennae. Then her behavior becomes more aggressive. She bends her abdomen, protruding her sting, and searches for the soft membrane at the point where the spider's legs join its body—the only spot where she can penetrate the horny skeleton. From time to time, as the exasperated spider slowly shifts ground, the wasp turns on her back and slides along with the aid of her wings, trying to get under the tarantula for a shot at the vital spot. During all this maneuvering, which can last for several minutes, the tarantula makes no move to save itself. Finally the wasp corners it against some obstruction and grasps one of its legs in her powerful jaws. Now at last the harassed spider tries a desperate but vain defense. The two contestants roll over and over on the ground. It is a terrifying sight and the outcome is always the same. The wasp finally manages to thrust her sting into the soft spot and holds it there for a few seconds while she 12 pumps in the poison. Almost immediately the tarantula falls paralyzed on its back. Its legs stop twitching; its heart stops beating. Yet it is not dead, as is shown by the fact that if taken from the wasp it can be restored to some sensitivity by being kept in a moist chamber for several months.

After paralyzing the tarantula, the wasp cleans herself by dragging her body along the ground and rubbing her feet, sucks a drop of blood oozing from the wound in the spider's abdomen, then grabs a leg of the flabby, helpless animal in her jaws and drags it down to the bottom of the grave. She stays there for many minutes, sometimes for several hours, and what she does all that time in the dark we do not know. Eventually she lays her egg and attaches it to the side of the spider's abdomen with a sticky secretion. Then she emerges, fills the grave with soil carried bit by bit in her jaws, and finally tramples the ground all around to hide any trace of the grave from prowlers. Then she flies away, leaving her descendant safely started in life. 13

In all this the behavior of the wasp evidently is qualitatively different from that of the spider. The wasp acts like an intelligent animal. This is not to say that instinct plays no part or that she reasons as man does. But her actions are to the point; they are not automatic and can be modified to fit the situation. We do not know for certain how she identifies the tarantula—probably it is by some olfactory or chemo-tactile sense—but she does it purposefully and does not blindly tackle a wrong species. 14

On the other hand, the tarantula's behavior shows only confusion. Evidently the wasp's pawing gives it no pleasure, for it tries to move away. That the wasp is not simulating sexual stimulation is certain because male and female tarantulas react in the same way to its advances. That the spider is not anesthetized by some odorless secretion is easily shown by blowing lightly at the tarantula and making it jump suddenly. What, then, makes the tarantula behave as stupidly as it does? 15

No clear, simple answer is available. Possibly the stimulation by the wasp's antennae is masked by a heavier pressure on the spider's body, so that it reacts as when prodded by a pencil. But the explanation may be much more complex. Initiative in attack is not in the nature of tarantulas; most species fight only when cornered so that escape is impossible. Their inherited patterns of behavior apparently prompt them to avoid problems rather than 16 attack them. For example, spiders always weave their webs in three dimensions, and when a spider finds that there is insufficient space to attach certain threads in the third dimension, it leaves the place and seeks another, instead of finishing the web in a single plane. This urge to escape seems to arise under all circumstances, in all phases of life, and to take the place of reasoning. For a spider to change the pattern of its web is as impossible as for an inexperienced man to build a bridge across a chasm obstructing his way.

In a way the instinctive urge to escape is not only easier but 17
often more efficient than reasoning. The tarantula does exactly what is most efficient in all cases except in an encounter with a ruthless and determined attacker dependent for the existence of her own species on killing as many tarantulas as she can lay eggs. Perhaps in this case the spider follows its usual pattern of trying to escape, instead of seizing and killing the wasp, because it is not aware of its danger. In any case, the survival of the tarantula species as a whole is protected by the fact that the spider is much more fertile than the wasp.

Questions for Study and Discussion

1. In what way is the *Pepsis* wasp's destruction of tarantulas a "classic example of what looks like intelligence pitted against instinct" (1)?
2. How has Petrunkevitch organized his essay? (Glossary: *Organization*) You may find it helpful to outline the essay in answering this question.
3. What are the three tactile responses of the tarantula? What is Petrunkevitch's purpose in discussing them? (Glossary: *Purpose*)
4. In what part of his essay does Petrunkevitch actually write a process analysis? What transitional or linking devices has he used to give coherence to his explanation of the process? (Glossary: *Transitions*)
5. What are some of the possible reasons why the tarantula does not try to escape from the wasp until it is too late? (Glossary: *Cause and Effect*)

6. How is the tarantula able to survive as a species despite its helplessness against the wasp?

Vocabulary

Refer to your dictionary to define the following words as they are used in this selection. Then use each word in a sentence of your own.

progeny (1)	molestation (11)
tactile (8)	qualitatively (14)
gargantuan (9)	olfactory (14)
chitinous (9)	initiative (16)

Classroom Activity Using Process Analysis

Read the following paragraph of informational process analysis about how leaves turn color in the fall:

> Come mid-September, people begin looking for the day when the first leaves start to "change." In fact, the leaves contain the yellows of fall throughout the summer. The leaves are green in summer because of a high concentration of chlorophyll, the pigment that plays a crucial role in photosynthesis. As the daylight hours grow shorter and shorter, the chlorophyll breaks down. Other pigments in the leaf, masked by all the chlorophyll before, can then be seen. Thus the leaf changes to yellow, the color of the "new" pigments. In some trees, such as the sugar maple, cool weather helps create yet another pigment, anthocyanin. Anthocyanin is what turns the maple leaves red and orange.

How effective do you find the explanation of how leaves turn color in the fall? What, if anything, would you suggest to the writer to make the explanation more complete, more accurate, or clearer? Compare your suggestions with those offered by other members of your class.

Suggested Writing Assignments

1. Our world is filled with a multitude of predator/prey relationships. In this piece, Petrunkevitch has written a process

analysis of an unusual relationship, but there are many more straightforward ones, such as cat and mouse, lion and antelope, wolf and moose, and so on. Write an informational process analysis of a predator/prey relationship, using Petrunkevitch's essay as a model.

2. Use a directional process analysis for a "simple" task that could prove unfortunate or even harmful if not explained correctly—for example, changing a tire, driving a standard shift, packing for a camping trip, or loading a camera.

14

DEFINITION

To communicate precisely what you want to say, you will frequently need to *define* key words. Your reader needs to know just what you mean when you use unfamiliar words, such as *accouterment,* or words that are open to various interpretations, such as *liberal,* or words that, while generally familiar, are used in a particular sense. Failure to define important terms, or to define them accurately, confuses readers and hampers communication.

There are three basic ways to define a word; each is useful in its own way. The first method is to give a *synonym,* a word that has nearly the same meaning as the word you wish to define: *face* for *countenance, nervousness* for *anxiety.* No two words ever have *exactly* the same meaning, but you can, nevertheless, pair an unfamiliar word with a familiar one and thereby clarify your meaning.

Another way to define a word quickly, often within a single sentence, is to give a *formal definition;* that is, to place the term to be defined in a general class and then to distinguish it from other members of that class by describing its particular characteristics. For example:

WORD	CLASS	CHARACTERISTICS
A *watch*	is a *mechanical device*	*for telling time* and is usually *carried* or *worn.*
Semantics	is an *area of linguistics*	*concerned with the study of the meaning of words.*

The third method is known as *extended definition.* While some extended definitions require only a single paragraph, more often than not you will need several paragraphs or even an entire essay to define a new or difficult term or to rescue a controversial word from misconceptions and associations that may obscure its meaning.

One controversial term that illustrates the need for extended definition is *obscene.* What is obscene? Books that are banned in one school system are considered perfectly acceptable in another. Movies that are shown in one town cannot be shown in a neighboring town. Clearly, the meaning of *obscene* has been clouded by contrasting personal opinions as well as by conflicting social norms. Therefore, if you use the term *obscene* (and especially if you tackle the issue of obscenity itself), you must be careful to define clearly and thoroughly what you mean by that term—that is, you have to give an extended definition. There are a number of methods you might use to develop such a definition. You could define *obscene* by explaining what it does not mean. You could also make your meaning clear by narrating an experience, by comparing and contrasting it to related terms such as *pornographic* or *exotic,* by citing specific examples, or by classifying the various types of obscenity.

A Jerk

Sydney J. Harris

For more than forty years Sydney J. Harris (1917–1986) wrote a syndicated column for the Chicago Daily News *and the* Chicago Sun-Times *entitled "Strictly Personal," in which he considered virtually every aspect of contemporary American life. In the following essay from his book* Last Things First *(1961), Harris defines the term* jerk *by differentiating it from other similar slang terms. His essay is basically an extended definition but culminates with a formal definition in the final paragraph.*

For Your Journal

Do you think that others see you as you see yourself or as someone different? How do you know? What accounts for how others see you? Are we known by anything more than the total of our actions?

I don't know whether history repeats itself, but biography certainly does. The other day, Michael came in and asked me what a "jerk" was—the same question Carolyn put to me a dozen years ago. 1

At that time, I fluffed her off with some inane answer, such as "A jerk isn't a very nice person," but both of us knew it was an unsatisfactory reply. When she went to bed, I began trying to work up a suitable definition. 2

It is a marvelously apt word, of course. Until it was coined, not more than 25 years ago, there was really no single word in English to describe the kind of person who is a jerk—"boob" and "simp" were too old hat, and besides they really didn't fit, for they could be lovable, and a jerk never is. 3

Thinking it over, I decided that a jerk is basically a person without insight. He is not necessarily a fool or a dope, because 4 some extremely clever persons can be jerks. In fact, it has little to do with intelligence as we commonly think of it; it is, rather, a kind of subtle but persuasive aroma emanating from the inner part of the personality.

I know a college president who can be described only as a jerk. 5
He is not an unintelligent man, nor unlearned, nor even unschooled in the social amenities. Yet he is a jerk *cum laude,* because of a fatal flaw in his nature—he is totally incapable of looking into the mirror of his soul and shuddering at what he sees there.

A jerk, then, is a man (or woman) who is utterly unable to see 6
himself as he appears to others. He has no grace, he is tactless without meaning to be, he is a bore even to his best friends, he is an egotist without charm. All of us are egotists to some extent, but most of us—unlike the jerk—are perfectly and horribly aware of it when we make asses of ourselves. The jerk never knows.

Questions for Study and Discussion

1. What, according to Harris, is a jerk?
2. Jerks, boobs, simps, fools, and dopes are all in the same class. How does Harris differentiate a jerk from a boob or a simp on the one hand, and a fool or a dope on the other? (Glossary: *Classification*)
3. What does Harris see as the relationship between intelligence and/or cleverness and the idea of a jerk?
4. In paragraph 5 Harris presents the example of the college president. How does this example support his definition? (Glossary: *Example*)
5. In the first two paragraphs Harris tells how both his son and daughter asked him what *jerk* means. How does this brief anecdote serve to introduce Harris's essay? (Glossary: *Beginnings and Endings*) Do you think it works well? Explain.

Vocabulary

Refer to your dictionary to define the following words as they are used in this selection. Then use each word in a sentence of your own.

inane (2)	emanating (4)
apt (3)	amenities (5)
coined (3)	tactless (6)

Classroom Activity Using Definition

Try formally defining (p. 341) one of the following terms by putting it in a class and then differentiating it from other words in that class:

potato chips	tenor saxophone
love	physical therapy
sociology	

Suggested Writing Assignments

1. Write one or two paragraphs in which you give your own definition of *jerk* or another slang term of your choice.
2. Every generation develops its own slang, which generally enlivens the speech and writing of those who use it. Ironically, however, no generation can arrive at a consensus definition of even its most popular slang terms—for example, *dweeb, rambo, nimrod, airhead, fly.* Select a slang term that you use frequently, and write an essay in which you define the term. Read your definition aloud in class. Do the other members of your class agree with your definition?

Who's a Hillbilly?

Rebecca Thomas Kirkendall

Rebecca Thomas Kirkendall was a doctoral student at the University of Missouri when this essay was first published in Newsweek *in November 1995. To some extent, Kirkendall's essay can be read as an anti-definition in the way it takes issue with the term* hillbilly. *As you read, pay particular attention to how she attacks the assumptions behind the use of this pejorative as a way of defining what it really means to be part of the rural culture of the Ozarks.*

For Your Journal

With which of the three familiar living environments—urban, suburban, rural—are you most familiar? What do you like about it? What do you dislike? If you have experience with more than one kind of environment, which do you like best? Why?

I once dated a boy who called me a hillbilly because my family has lived in the Ozarks in southern Missouri for several generations. I took offense, not realizing that as a foreigner to the United States he was unaware of the insult. He had meant it as a term of endearment. Nonetheless, it rankled. I started thinking about the implications of the term to me, my family and my community. 1

While growing up I was often surprised at the way television belittled "country" people. We weren't offended by the self-effacing humor of "The Andy Griffith Show" and "The Beverly Hillbillies" because, after all, Andy and Jed were the heroes of these shows, and through them we could comfortably laugh at ourselves. But as I learned about tolerance and discrimination in school, I wondered why stereotypes of our lifestyle went unexamined. Actors 2 playing "country" people on TV were usually comic foils or objects of ridicule. Every sitcom seemed to have an episode where country cousins, wearing high-water britches and carrying patched suitcases, visited their city friends. And movies like "Deliverance" portrayed country people as backward and violent.

As a child I laughed at the exaggerated accents and dress, never 3
imagining that viewers believed such nonsense. Li'l Abner and the folks on "Hee Haw" were amusing, but we on the farm knew that our work did not lend itself to bare feet, gingham bras and revealing cutoff jeans.

Although our nation professes a growing commitment to cul- 4
tural egalitarianism, we consistently oversimplify and misunderstand our rural culture. Since the 1960s, minority groups in America have fought for acknowledgment, appreciation and, above all, respect. But in our increasingly urban society, rural Americans have been unable to escape from the hillbilly stigma, which is frequently accompanied by labels like "white trash," "redneck" and "hayseed." These negative stereotypes are as unmerciful as they are unfounded.

When I graduated from college, I traveled to a nearby city to 5
find work. There I heard wisecracks about the uneducated rural folk who lived a few hours away. I also took some ribbing about the way I pronounced certain words, such as "tin" instead of "ten" and "agin" for "again." And my expressed desire to return to the country someday was usually met with scorn, bewilderment or genuine concern. Co-workers often asked, "But what is there to *do?*" Thoreau may have gone to Walden Pond, they argued, but he had no intention of staying there.

With the revival of country music in the early 1980s, hillbilly- 6
ness was again marketable. Country is now big business. Traditional country symbols—Minnie Pearl's hat tag and Daisy Mae—have been eclipsed by the commercially successful Nashville Network, Country Music Television and music theaters in Branson, Mo. Many "country" Americans turned the negative stereotype to their advantage and packaged the hillbilly legacy.

Yet with successful commercialization, the authentic elements 7
of America's rural culture have been juxtaposed with the stylized. Country and Western bars are now chic. While I worked in the city, I watched with amazement as my Yuppie friends hurried from their corporate desks to catch the 6:30 line-dancing

class at the edge of town. Donning Ralph Lauren jeans and ankle boots, they drove to the trendiest country bars, sat and danced together and poked fun at the local "hicks," who arrived in pickup trucks wearing Wrangler jeans and roper boots.

Every summer weekend in Missouri the freeways leading out of our cities are clogged with vacationers. Minivans and RVs edge toward a clear river with a campground and canoe rental, a quiet lake resort or craft show in a remote Ozark town. Along these popular vacation routes, the rural hosts of convenience stores, gift shops and corner cafés accept condescension along with personal checks and credit cards. On a canoeing trip not long ago, I recall sitting on the transport bus and listening, heartbroken, as a group of tourists ridiculed our bus driver. They yelled, "Hey, plowboy, ain't ya got no terbacker fer us?" They pointed at the young man's sweat-stained overalls as he, seemingly unaffected by their insults, singlehandedly carried their heavy aluminum canoes to the water's edge. That "plowboy" was one of my high-school classmates. He greeted the tourists with a smile and tolerated their derision because he knew tourism brings dollars and jobs. 8

America is ambivalent when it comes to claiming its rural heritage. We may fantasize about Thomas Jefferson's agrarian vision, but there is no mistaking that ours is an increasingly urban culture. Despite their disdain for farm life—with its manure-caked boots, long hours and inherent financial difficulties—urbanites rush to imitate a sanitized version of this lifestyle. And the individuals who sell this rendition understand that the customer wants to experience hillbillyness without the embarrassment of being mistaken for one. 9

Through it all, we Ozarkians remind ourselves how fortunate we are to live in a region admired for its blue springs, rolling hills and geological wonders. In spite of the stereotypes, most of us are not uneducated. Nor are we stupid. We are not white supremacists, and we rarely marry our cousins. Our reasons for living in the hills are as complex and diverse as our population. We have a unique sense of community, strong family ties, a beautiful environment and a quiet place for retirement. 10

We have criminals and radicals, but they are the exception. Our public-education system produces successful farmers, doctors, business professionals and educators. Country music is our favorite, but we also like rock and roll, jazz, blues and classical. We read Louis L'Amour, Maya Angelou and *The Wall Street Jour-* 11 *nal.* And in exchange for living here, many of us put up with a lower standard of living and the occasional gibe from those who persist in calling us "hillbillies."

Questions for Study and Discussion

1. In what way might the term "hillbilly" be a term of endearment? Why did being called a hillbilly bother Kirkendall so much?
2. What is Kirkendall's tone? (Glossary: *Tone*) How does she establish it?
3. What connotations do the words "hillbilly" and "hayseed" have for you? (Glossary: *Connotation/Denotation*) How do such words differ in connotation from a designation such as "someone who lives in a rural area"?
4. What are the advantages for people from rural areas of successfully merchandising the hillbilly image? What are the disadvantages? (Glossary: *Comparison and Contrast*)
5. Kirkendall states that "America is ambivalent when it comes to claiming its rural heritage" (9). What does she mean? Why is this point important to her purpose for writing the essay? (Glossary: *Purpose*)
6. According to Kirkendall, what are Ozarkians—and, by association, other rural people—really like? Why do they choose to live outside of urban areas?
7. Kirkendall does her own bit of name-calling when she identifies her friends as "Yuppies," a word that does not always carry a positive connotation. Can you think of two or three other well-known "labels" one can give urban residents? What connotations do they have? In your opinion, are they as "unmerciful" and "unfounded" as hillbilly? Why, or why not?

Vocabulary

Refer to your dictionary to define the following words as they are used in this selection. Then use each word in a sentence of your own.

rankled (1)
foils (2)
egalitarianism (4)
stigma (4)
juxtaposed (7)
derision (8)
ambivalent (9)
disdain (9)
gibe (11)

Classroom Activity Using Definition

Write a short definition of "jogger" or "tennis player." What do joggers do? What are they like? Be as inclusive as you can with your definition. Then discuss your definition with your classmates. What difficulties do you contend with when trying to quickly define such a large group of people?

Suggested Writing Assignments

1. Kirkendall comes from a rural part of the Missouri Ozarks. Where do you come from? Write a short essay in which you define what people from your area are like. In what way does that definition contrast with what people from your part of the country are "supposed" to be like? For instance, California residents might be stereotyped as mellow surfers living in La La Land, when in fact many of them are probably hard-working people who seldom see the ocean. Do you feel that stereotypes hurt residents of your area or hold them back in any way?
2. Write a short essay in which you define one of the following words. Base your definition on your working knowledge of the subject, not on a dictionary or encyclopedia entry.

   activist
   nomad
   refugee
   patriot
   terrorist
   aristocrat

   Does your essay present a well-rounded definition? Did you use any information in the essay that could be called stereotypical?

My Way!

Margo Kaufman

Freelance writer Margo Kaufman was born in York, Pennsylvania, in 1953. After spending her childhood in Baltimore, she graduated from Northwestern University and went to work as a columnist for a number of newspapers and magazines. Her essays have appeared in the New York Times, Newsweek, USA Today, Cosmopolitan, *and the* Village Voice. *She lives in Venice, California, and recently published* This Damn House! *(1996). The following selection, taken from her first book* 1-800-Am-I-Nuts *(1993), defines what it means to be a* control freak. *As you read, notice that Kaufman never really offers a formal definition, but instead relies on an accumulation of examples, descriptions, and observations, her own and those of other people, to present a clear picture of what the term means.*

For Your Journal

Do you know any "control freaks"? What do they do that earns them that designation? Do you recognize any controlling tendencies in your own behavior? What, if anything, do you have to control in order to feel comfortable?

Is it my imagination, or is this the age of the control freak? I'm standing in front of the triceps machine at my gym. I've just set the weights, and I'm about to begin my exercise when a lightly muscled bully in turquoise spandex interrupts her chest presses to bark at me. "I'm using that," she growls as she leaps up from her slant board, darts over to the triceps machine, and resets the weights. 1

I'm tempted to point out that, while she may have been planning to use the machine, she was, in fact, on the opposite side of 2 the room. And that her muscles won't atrophy if she waits for me to finish. Instead, I go work on my biceps. Life's too short to fight over a Nautilus machine. Of course, *I'm* not a control freak.

Control freaks will fight over anything: a parking space, the 3
room temperature, the last pair of marked-down Maude Frizon pumps, even whether you should barbecue with the top on or off the Weber kettle. Nothing is too insignificant. Everything has to be just so.

Just so *they* like it. "These people compulsively have to have 4
their own way," says Los Angeles psychologist Gary Emery. "Their egos are based on being right," Emery says, "on proving they're the boss." (And it isn't enough for the control freak to win. Others have to lose.)

"Control freaks are overconcerned with the means, rather than 5
the end," Emery says. "So it's more important that the string beans are the right kind than it is to just enjoy the meal."

"What do you mean just enjoy the meal?" scoffs my friend Marc. 6
"There's a right way to do things and then there's everything else." It goes without saying that he, and only he, has access to that Big Right Way in the Sky. And that Marc lives alone.

"I really hate to be in any situation where my control over what 7
I'm doing is compromised," he admits. "Like if somebody says, 'I'll handle the cooking and you can shuck the corn or slice the zucchini,' I tell them to do it without me."

A control freak's kitchen can be his or her castle. "Let me show 8
you the right way to make rice," said my husband the first time I made the mistake of fixing dinner. By the time Duke had sharpened the knives, rechopped the vegetables into two-inch squares, and chided me for using the wrong size pan, I had decided to surrender all control of the stove. (For the record, this wasn't a big sacrifice. I don't like to cook.)

"It's easier in a marriage when you both don't care about the 9
same things," says Milton Wolpin, a psychology professor at the University of Southern California. "Otherwise, everything would be a battle."

And every automobile would be a battleground. There's noth- 10
ing worse than having two control freaks in the same car. "I prefer to drive," my friend Claire says. "But no sooner do I pull out of the driveway than Fred starts telling me what to do. He thinks

that I'm an idiot behind the wheel and that I make a lot of stupid mistakes."

She doesn't think he drives any better. "I think he goes really, really fast, and I'm sure that someday he's going to kill us both," she says. "And I complain about it constantly. But it's still a little easier for me to take a back seat. I'd rather get to pick him apart than get picked on." 11

My friend Katie would withstand the abuse. "I like to control everything," she says. "From where we're going to eat to what we're going to eat to what movie we're going to see, what time we're going to see it, where we're going to see it, where we're going to park. Everything!" 12

But you can't control everything. So much of life is beyond our control. And to me, that's what makes it interesting. But not to Katie. "I don't like having my fate in someone else's hands," she says firmly. "If I take charge, I know that whatever it is will get done and it will get done well." 13

I shuffle my feet guiltily. Not too long ago I invited Katie and a bunch of friends out to dinner to celebrate my birthday. It was a control freak's nightmare. Not only did I pick the restaurant and arrange to pick up the check, but Duke also called in advance and ordered an elaborate Chinese banquet. I thought Katie was going to lose her mind. 14

"What did you order? I have to know," she cried, seizing a menu. "I'm a vegetarian. There are things I won't eat." Duke assured her that he had accounted for everybody's taste. Still, Katie didn't stop hyperventilating until the food arrived. "I was very pleasantly surprised," she confesses. "And I would trust Duke again." 15

"I'm sure there are areas where you're the control freak," says Professor Wolpin, "areas where you're more concerned about things than your husband." *Me?* The champion of laissez-faire? "You get very upset if you find something visible to the naked eye on the kitchen counter," Duke reminds me. "And you think you know much better than me what the right shirt for me to wear is." 16

But I'm just particular. I'm not a control freak. 17

"A control freak is just someone who cares about something more than you do," Wolpin says. 18

So what's wrong with being a control freak? 19

Questions for Study and Discussion

1. The title of Kaufman's essay alludes to a popular song, "My Way," recorded by Frank Sinatra. (Glossary: *Allusion*) If you are familiar with Sinatra and this song, explain how the allusion helps to make this an effective title. If not, is the title still appropriate and effective? Why, or why not?
2. What colloquial expressions does Kaufman use in paragraphs 1–3? (Glossary: *Colloquial Expressions*) Why does she use these expressions? What does their use tell the reader about her writing style? (Glossary: *Style*)
3. What is a "control freak"? How does Kaufman define this term in her essay?
4. How does Kaufman illustrate her definition? (Glossary: *Illustration*) Do you think that her mix of examples is effective? Why, or why not?
5. Why was Kaufman's friend Katie going to lose her mind over Kaufman's birthday party? How can somebody else's party cause so much distress for a control freak? (Glossary: *Cause and Effect*) What does this tell you about what life is like for a control freak?
6. Kaufman ends her essay with a question that seems to contradict most of what she has written. (Glossary: *Beginnings and Endings*) What does the question tell you about Kaufman? Is she a control freak herself? Based on the rest of the essay, what *is* wrong with being a control freak?

Vocabulary

Refer to your dictionary to define the following words as they are used in this selection. Then use each word in a sentence of your own.

atrophy (2)
compulsively (4)
scoffs (6)
compromised (7)
laissez-faire (16)

Classroom Activity Using Definition

Define one of the following terms in four sentences or less. Be sure that each sentence contributes directly to your definition.

neat freak
slob
know-it-all
party animal
smart aleck

Suggested Writing Assignments

1. Kaufman quotes a psychology professor as saying, "It's easier in a marriage when you both don't care about the same things" (9). Can the same be said of close friendships, or is caring about similar things—and agreeing about them—important to a good friendship? Write a short essay in which you define the word "friend." What trait is important for you to have in a friend that not everybody might look for? What faults might you be willing to overlook?
2. Write a short essay in which you define a word that has more than one meaning, depending on one's point of view—for example, *tourist, macho, liberal, success,* and *marriage.*

A Magic Circle of Friends

Elvira M. Franco

After returning to school in her forties and befriending a group of older students like herself, Elvira M. Franco wrote the following piece for the New York Times *in January 1990. "A Magic Circle of Friends" explores how Franco and her friends used their age and life experiences to forge a new understanding of friendship, school, and the world around them. As you read, pay particular attention to the way Franco describes and defines these individual issues as part of the larger process of defining her magic circle of friends.*

For Your Journal

What aspects of school cause you the greatest insecurity? Fear of failure? Fear of looking foolish or ignorant? What qualities do you bring to your school? Are you bright, creative, persistent, intuitive? If you are a nontraditional student, how has the time you spent away from school affected your outlook? Do you think it has affected your performance?

Older than forty and starting from scratch: I thought I was a unique item, but as soon as I peeked out of my shell I found a sea of women in similar positions. 1

The little child in us has grown mature and middle-aged, almost to our surprise. We share a fear that sits in the back of the mind like a spider ready to pounce: but we've also developed determination, almost like a religion. 2

We know we have friends; at least, I know my friends are with me, if not always, at least most of the time. And most of the time I need them, and they me. We reach over the phone lines for that word of comfort, the encouragement we need to go on when our own store of willpower has become depleted. 3

Returning to school, I found my friends were my best fans. In spite of their own insecurities, they never failed to offer me the cheering I often needed to rewrite a paper one more time or to stay up one last half-hour to re-read a difficult chapter. 4

After classes we would go to a diner, a bunch of over-forty classmates. Working together on a project that we felt strongly about ignited a part of us we did not know existed. While we were quite far from orthopedic shoes, bifocals were prominent. Underneath the artful makeup, we would measure the wrinkles on each other's cheeks across the table, almost as if these lines could form a cord to link us. 5

It was a good time. For years, in a locked-up corner of our minds, we had held the unspoken fear that we might actually be brain-dead. We were finally giving ourselves permission to celebrate our minds. 6

For some, it was a return to the carefree years of college. For others, a first-time discovery that learning can be both fun and exhilarating. Besides the intellectual surprises, we found joy in each other's company, and we delved in this new-found camaraderie with an intensity we did not know we could achieve outside of love and pregnancies. We were, and are, proud of our ages. The only woman in the group who was under thirty struck most of us as brash, angry, and, frankly, quite inappropriate. We were probably insensitive to her needs, but somehow we failed to find out how she felt in our midst and were almost relieved when she found excuses for not joining our study sessions. 7

We ended up treating her almost like a daughter, and doing for her what most of us have been doing for our own daughters: that is, picking up the slack. The hidden bonus was that now we could continue to do things our way, which, we all knew, was the best anyway. Things were smoother when she was not around: the rest of us would always agree, and even our disagreements were somehow smooth and enjoyable. 8

We had, in fact, created a sort of bubble around us, a magic circle that follows us still and says we are bright, successful, caring, ambitious, and, finally, ready to change the world. We will not do it, as we might have been ready to do at twenty, pushing and fighting and abrading. 9

We will do it instead at a slower pace, because, along the way, we have learned lessons both small and big: for example, that the 10 world is in no hurry to be changed and that we will have a better shot at it after a good night's sleep. We may not complete our plans by tomorrow, or even by the end of the week, because the details of our lives may interfere, such as a child home from college, or a neighbor's emergency.

Our goals may not even be achieved exactly as originally planned, and that is fine, too, because time has also brought us a sense of flexibility and an appreciation for the serendipitous properties of practically any action. The end product could turn out to be infinitely more complex, and in its way more perfect, more multifaceted and rich, than what we had first envisioned. The process is in itself an achievement. 11

They call us "late bloomers," they call us "returnees." We are sought by schools, thanks to the sheer numbers we represent, not to mention the life experience and the common sense that even the least bright among us brings to the classroom. We feel flattered and surprised, and our ego is bolstered by the realization that we are indeed quite capable. 12

There are fears, too ("Will it all make sense at some point?" "What if I'll never be able to get a decent job?"), but they are kept for only a few pairs of ears, where we know we will find support and understanding. 13

Graduation comes: the last papers have been handed in with trepidation, the test booklets carrying in their pages the very essence of our knowledge closed for the last time. Goodbyes, with promises and some tears, even a photograph to keep as souvenir. We've made it: watch out world, here come the mothers and the grandmothers, ready to push, cajole, smile and negotiate to achieve those goals we did not have a chance to effect the first time around. 14

We may just be beginning to feel a few arthritic pangs in our toes and fingers, but with our hair neatly streaked and some expensive dental work, we know we still look good. We know we are still strong, smart, vital, and, most especially, ready to work. This time around we will make a big difference. We know, because, for sure, we already are different. 15

Questions for Study and Discussion

1. What fear does Franco share with her friends that "sits in the back of the mind like a spider ready to pounce" (2)?

2. Why is the under-thirty woman out of place in Franco's group? How do they end up treating her?
3. What does the "bubble" or "magic circle" mean to Franco? (Glossary: *Figurative Language*) How does she define it?
4. How have the "late bloomers" changed in the way they try to get things done, to change the world? What have the added years given them that they did not have when they were younger?
5. Franco warns the world to look out—she and her friends are ready "to achieve those goals we did not have a chance to effect the first time around" (14). Why did they not have the chance before? What tools do they have now that will help them?
6. Franco's circle of friends can be considered the product of some of the recent changes in our society. For example, the group might reflect the increased presence of women in the workplace. What other changes are they both reflecting and creating? (Glossary: *Cause and Effect*)

Vocabulary

Refer to your dictionary to define the following words as they are used in this selection. Then use each word in a sentence of your own.

depleted (3)	multifaceted (11)
intellectual (7)	bolstered (12)
camaraderie (7)	cajole (14)
abrading (9)	pangs (15)

Classroom Activity Using Definition

It is said that Eastern cultures define the concept of "crisis" as encompassing both danger and opportunity. Use this model to come up with concise definitions for the following words:

stress	anxiety
challenge	invigorate

Be prepared to explain your choice of words in the definitions.

Suggested Writing Assignments

1. It is common, in times of stress, to form close bonds with those who share your experiences. In school, those who take a particularly difficult class together may bond. In sports, a successful team will often be the catalyst for close friendships. Write an essay about the "circle of friends" that has meant the most to you. What were the circumstances under which you met the others? If you have gone your separate ways, how lasting have the friendships been? Define what made them special to you.
2. Write a short essay in which you define one of the following abstract terms. You may find it useful to begin your essay with a concrete example that illustrates your point.

friendship	love	choice
freedom	hatred	charm
trust	patriotism	peace
commitment		

15

DIVISION AND CLASSIFICATION

To divide is to separate a class of things or ideas into categories, whereas to classify is to group separate things or ideas into those categories. The two processes can operate separately but often go together. Division and classification can be a useful organizational strategy in writing. Here, for example, is a passage about levers in which the writer first discusses generally how levers work and then, in the second paragraph, uses division to establish three categories of levers and then uses classification to group individual levers into those categories:

> Every lever has one fixed point called the "fulcrum" and is acted upon by two forces—the "effort" (exertion of hand muscles) and the "weight" (object's resistance). Levers work according to a simple formula: the effort (how hard you push or pull) multiplied by its distance from the fulcrum (effort arm) equals the weight multiplied by its distance from the fulcrum (weight arm). Thus two pounds of effort exerted at a distance of four feet from the fulcrum will raise eight pounds located one foot from the fulcrum.
>
> There are three types of levers, conventionally called "first kind," "second kind," and "third kind." Levers of the first kind have the fulcrum located between the effort and the weight. Examples are a pump handle, an oar, a crowbar, a weighing balance, a pair of scissors, and a pair of pliers. Levers of the second kind have the weight in the middle and magnify the effort. Examples are the handcar crank and doors. Levers of the third kind, such as a power shovel or a baseball batter's forearm, have the effort in the middle and always magnify the distance.

In writing, division and classification are affected directly by the writer's practical purpose. That purpose—what the writer wants to explain or prove—determines the class of things or ideas being divided and classified. For instance, a writer might divide television programs according to their audiences—adults, families, or children—and then classify individual programs into each of these categories in order to show how much emphasis the television stations place on reaching each audience. A different purpose would require different categories. A writer concerned about the prevalence of violence in television programming would first divide television programs into those that include fights and murders and those that do not, and would then classify a large sample of programs into those categories. Other writers with different purposes might divide television programs differently—by the day and time of broadcast, for example, or by the number of women featured in prominent roles—and then classify individual programs accordingly.

The following guidelines can help you in using division and classification in your writing:

1. *Identify a clear purpose, and be sure that your principle of division is appropriate to that purpose.* To determine the makeup of a student body, for example, you might consider the following principles of division: college or program, major, class level, sex. It would not be helpful to divide students on the basis of their favorite toothpaste unless you had a purpose and thus a reason for doing so.
2. *Divide your subject into categories that are mutually exclusive.* An item can belong to only one category. For example, it would be unsatisfactory to divide students as men, women, and athletes.
3. *Make your division and classification complete.* Your categories should account for all items in a subject class. In dividing students on the basis of geographic origin, for example, it would be inappropriate to consider only home states, for such a division would not account for foreign students. Then, for your classification to be complete, every student must be placed in one of the established categories.
4. *Be sure to state clearly the conclusion that your division and classification lead you to draw.* For example, a study of the student body might lead to the conclusion that 45 percent of the male athletes with athletic scholarships come from west of the Mississippi.

THE WAYS OF MEETING OPPRESSION

Martin Luther King, Jr.

Martin Luther King, Jr. (1929–1968) was the leading spokesman for the rights of African Americans during the 1950s and 1960s before he was assassinated in 1968. He established the Southern Christian Leadership Conference, organized many civil-rights demonstrations, and opposed the Vietnam War and the draft. In 1964 he was awarded the Nobel Prize for Peace. In the following essay, taken from his book Strive toward Freedom *(1958), King classifies the three ways oppressed people throughout history have reacted to their oppressors. As you read, pay particular attention to how King's discussions within the categories of classification lead him to the conclusion he presents in paragraph 8.*

FOR YOUR JOURNAL

Someone once said, "Violence is the last resort of the incompetent." What are your thoughts on the reasons for violent behavior on either a personal or national level? Is violence ever justified? If so, under what circumstances?

Oppressed people deal with their oppression in three characteristic ways. One way is acquiescence: the oppressed resign themselves to their doom. They tacitly adjust themselves to oppression, and thereby become conditioned to it. In every movement toward freedom some of the oppressed prefer to remain oppressed. Almost 2800 years ago Moses set out to lead the children of Israel from the slavery of Egypt to the freedom of the promised land. He soon discovered that slaves do not always welcome their deliverers. They become accustomed to being slaves. They would rather bear those ills they have, as Shakespeare pointed out, than 1 flee to others that they know not of. They prefer the "fleshpots of Egypt" to the ordeals of emancipation.

There is such a thing as the freedom of exhaustion. Some people are so worn down by the yoke of oppression that they give up. A few years ago in the slum areas of Atlanta, a Negro guitarist used to sing almost daily: "Been down so long that down don't bother me." This is the type of negative freedom and resignation that often engulfs the life of the oppressed. 2

But this is not the way out. To accept passively an unjust system is to cooperate with that system; thereby the oppressed become as evil as the oppressor. Noncooperation with evil is as much a moral obligation as is cooperation with good. The oppressed must never allow the conscience of the oppressor to slumber. Religion reminds every man that he is his brother's keeper. To accept injustice or segregation passively is to say to the oppressor that his actions are morally right. It is a way of allowing his conscience to fall asleep. At this moment the oppressed fails to be his brother's keeper. So acquiescence—while often the easier way—is not the moral way. It is the way of the coward. The Negro cannot win the respect of his oppressor by acquiescing; he merely increases the oppressor's arrogance and contempt. Acquiescence is interpreted as proof of the Negro's inferiority. The Negro cannot win the respect of the white people of the South or the peoples of the world if he is willing to sell the future of his children for his personal and immediate comfort and safety. 3

A second way that oppressed people sometimes deal with oppression is to resort to physical violence and corroding hatred. Violence often brings about momentary results. Nations have frequently won their independence in battle. But in spite of temporary victories, violence never brings permanent peace. It solves no social problem; it merely creates new and more complicated ones. 4

Violence as a way of achieving racial justice is both impractical and immoral. It is impractical because it is a descending spiral ending in destruction for all. The old law of an eye for an eye leaves everybody blind. It is immoral because it seeks to humiliate the opponent rather than win his understanding; it seeks to annihilate rather than to convert. Violence is immoral because it thrives on hatred rather than love. It destroys community and makes brotherhood impossible. It leaves society in monologue rather than dialogue. Violence ends by defeating itself. It creates 5 bitterness in the survivors and brutality in the destroyers. A voice echoes through time saying to every potential Peter, "Put up your sword."* History is cluttered with the wreckage of nations that failed to follow this command.

6 If the American Negro and other victims of oppression succumb to the temptation of using violence in the struggle for freedom, future generations will be the recipients of a desolate night of bitterness, and our chief legacy to them will be an endless reign of meaningless chaos. Violence is not the way.

7 The third way open to oppressed people in their quest for freedom is the way of nonviolent resistance. Like the synthesis in Hegelian philosophy, the principle of nonviolent resistance seeks to reconcile the truths of two opposites—acquiescence and violence—while avoiding the extremes and immoralities of both. The nonviolent resister agrees with the person who acquiesces that one should not be physically aggressive toward his opponent; but he balances the equation by agreeing with the person of violence that evil must be resisted. He avoids the nonresistance of the former and the violent resistance of the latter. With nonviolent resistance, no individual or group need submit to any wrong, nor need anyone resort to violence in order to right a wrong.

8 It seems to me that this is the method that must guide the actions of the Negro in the present crisis in race relations. Through nonviolent resistance the Negro will be able to rise to the noble height of opposing the unjust system while loving the perpetrators of the system. The Negro must work passionately and unrelentingly for full stature as a citizen, but he must not use inferior methods to gain it. He must never come to terms with falsehood, malice, hate, or destruction.

9 Nonviolent resistance makes it possible for the Negro to remain in the South and struggle for his rights. The Negro's problem will not be solved by running away. He cannot listen to the glib suggestion of those who would urge him to migrate en masse to other sections of the country. By grasping his great opportunity in the South he can make a lasting contribution to the moral strength of the nation and set a sublime example of courage for generations yet unborn.

---

*The apostle Peter had drawn his sword to defend Christ from arrest. The voice was Christ's, who surrendered himself for trial and crucifixion (John 18:11).

By nonviolent resistance, the Negro can also enlist all men of 10
good will in his struggle for equality. The problem is not a purely racial one, with Negroes set against whites. In the end, it is not a struggle between people at all, but a tension between justice and injustice. Nonviolent resistance is not aimed against oppressors but against oppression. Under its banner consciences, not racial groups, are enlisted.

Questions for Study and Discussion

1. What are the disadvantages that King sees in meeting oppression with acquiescence or with violence?
2. Why, according to King, do slaves not always welcome their deliverers?
3. What does King mean in paragraph 2 by the "freedom of exhaustion"?
4. What is King's purpose in writing this essay? How does classifying the three types of resistance to oppression serve this purpose? (Glossary: *Purpose*)
5. What principle of division does King use in this essay?
6. Why do you suppose King discusses acquiescence, violence, and nonviolent resistance in that order? (Glossary: *Organization*)
7. King states that he favors nonviolent resistance over the other two ways of meeting oppression. Look closely at the words he uses to describe nonviolent resistance and those he uses to describe acquiescence and violence. How does his choice of words contribute to his argument? Show examples. (Glossary: *Connotation/Denotation*)

Vocabulary

Refer to your dictionary to define the following words as they are used in this selection. Then use each word in a sentence of your own.

acquiescence (1)
tacitly (1)
corroding (4)
annihilate (5)
desolate (6)
synthesis (7)
sublime (9)

Classroom Activity Using Division and Classification

Examine the following lists of hobbies, books, and buildings. Determine at least six criteria that could be used to classify the items listed in each group. Finally, classify the items in each group according to three of the criteria you have established.

HOBBIES

watching sports on TV
stamp collecting
scuba diving
surfing the Web
hiking
dancing
running

BOOKS

The Adventures of Huckleberry Finn
Guinness Book of World Records
The Joy of Cooking
American Heritage Dictionary (College Edition)
To Kill a Mockingbird
Gone with the Wind

BUILDINGS

World Trade Center
White House
The Alamo
Taj Mahal
Library of Congress
Buckingham Palace

Suggested Writing Assignments

1. Write an essay about a problem of some sort in which you use division and classification to discuss various possible solutions. You might discuss something personal, such as the problems of giving up smoking, or something that concerns everyone, such as the difficulties of coping with homelessness. Whatever your topic, use an appropriate principle of division to establish categories that suit the purpose of your discussion.
2. Consider any one of the following topics for an essay of classification:

movies	country music
college courses	newspapers
sports fans	pets
teenage lifestyles	students

FRIENDS, GOOD FRIENDS—AND SUCH GOOD FRIENDS

Judith Viorst

Judith Viorst was born in Newark, New Jersey, in 1931 and attended Rutgers University. She has published several volumes of light verse and collections of prose, as well as many articles in popular magazines. Her numerous children's books include the perennial favorite Alexander and the Terrible, Horrible, No Good, Very Bad Day *(1972).* Murdering Mr. Monti, *her most recent book of prose, was published in 1994. The following selection appeared in her regular column in* Redbook. *In it she analyzes and classifies the various types of friends that a person can have. As you read, assess the validity of Viorst's analysis by trying to place your own friends into her categories. Determine also whether the categories themselves are mutually exclusive.*

FOR YOUR JOURNAL

Think about your friends. Do you regard them all in the same light? Would you group them in any way? On what basis would you group them?

Women are friends, I once would have said, when they totally love and support and trust each other, and bare to each other the secrets of their souls, and run—no questions asked—to help each other, and tell harsh truths to each other (no, you can't wear that dress unless you lose ten pounds first) when harsh truths must be told. 1

Women are friends, I once would have said, when they share the same affection for Ingmar Bergman, plus train rides, cats, 2 warm rain, charades, Camus, and hate with equal ardor Newark and brussels sprouts and Lawrence Welk and camping.

In other words, I once would have said that a friend is a friend 3
all the way, but now I believe that's a narrow point of view. For the friendships I have and the friendships I see are conducted at many levels of intensity, serve many different functions, meet different needs and range from those as all-the-way as the friendship of the soul sisters mentioned above to that of the most nonchalant and casual playmates.

Consider these varieties of friendship: 4

1. Convenience friends. These are women with whom, if our 5
paths weren't crossing all the time, we'd have no particular reason to be friends: a next-door neighbor, a woman in our car pool, the mother of one of our children's closest friends or maybe some mommy with whom we serve juice and cookies each week at the Glenwood Co-op Nursery.

Convenience friends are convenient indeed. They'll lend us 6
their cups and silverware for a party. They'll drive our kids to soccer when we're sick. They'll take us to pick up our car when we need a lift to the garage. They'll even take our cats when we go on vacation. As we will for them.

But we don't, with convenience friends, ever come too close or 7
tell too much; we maintain our public face and emotional distance. "Which means," says Elaine, "that I'll talk about being overweight but not about being depressed. Which means I'll admit being mad but not blind with rage. Which means that I might say that we're pinched this month but never that I'm worried sick over money."

But which doesn't mean that there isn't sufficient value to be 8
found in these friendships of mutual aid, in convenience friends.

2. Special-interest friends. These friendships aren't intimate, 9
and they needn't involve kids or silverware or cats. Their value lies in some interest jointly shared. And so we may have an office friend or a yoga friend or a tennis friend or a friend from the Women's Democratic Club.

"I've got one woman friend," says Joyce, "who likes, as I do, to 10
take psychology courses. Which makes it nice for me—and nice for her. It's fun to go with someone you know and it's fun to discuss what you've learned, driving back from the classes." And for the most part, she says, that's all they discuss.

"I'd say that what we're doing is *doing* together, not being together," Suzanne says of her Tuesday-doubles friends. "It's mainly a tennis relationship, but we play together well. And I guess we all need to have a couple of playmates." 11

I agree. 12

My playmate is a shopping friend, a woman of marvelous taste, a woman who knows exactly *where* to buy *what,* and furthermore is a woman who always knows beyond a doubt what one ought to be buying. I don't have the time to keep up with what's new in eyeshadow, hemlines and shoes and whether the smock look is in or finished already. But since (oh, shame!) I care a lot about eyeshadow, hemlines and shoes, and since I don't *want* to wear smocks if the smock look is finished, I'm very glad to have a shopping friend. 13

3. Historical friends. We all have a friend who knew us when . . . maybe way back in Miss Meltzer's second grade, when our family lived in that three-room flat in Brooklyn, when our dad was out of work for seven months, when our brother Allie got in that fight where they had to call the police, when our sister married the endodontist from Yonkers and when, the morning after we lost our virginity, she was the first, the only, friend we told. 14

The years have gone by and we've gone separate ways and we've little in common now, but we're still an intimate part of each other's past. And so whenever we go to Detroit we always go to visit this friend of our girlhood. Who knows how we looked before our teeth were straightened. Who knows how we talked before our voice got un-Brooklyned. Who knows what we ate before we learned about artichokes. And who, by her presence, puts us in touch with an earlier part of ourself, a part of ourself it's important never to lose. 15

"What this friend means to me and what I mean to her," says Grace, "is having a sister without sibling rivalry. We know the texture of each other's lives. She remembers my grandmother's cabbage soup. I remember the way her uncle played the piano. There's simply no other friend who remembers those things." 16

4. Crossroads friends. Like historical friends, our crossroads friends are important for *what was*—for the friendship we shared at a crucial, now past, time of life. A time, perhaps, when we roomed in college together; or worked as eager young singles in the Big City together; or went together, as my friend Elizabeth 17

and I did, through pregnancy, birth and that scary first year of new motherhood.

Crossroads friends forge powerful links, links strong enough to endure with not much more contact than once-a-year letters at Christmas. And out of respect for those crossroad years, for those dramas and dreams we once shared, we will always be friends. 18

5. Cross-generational friends. Historical friends and crossroads friends seem to maintain a special kind of intimacy—dormant but always ready to be revived—and though we may rarely meet, whenever we do connect, it's personal and intense. Another kind of intimacy exists in the friendships that form across generations in what one woman calls her daughter–mother and her mother–daughter relationships. 19

Evelyn's friend is her mother's age—"but I share so much more than I ever could with my mother"—a woman she talks to of music, of books and of life. "What I get from her is the benefit of her experience. What she gets—and enjoys—from me is a youthful perspective. It's a pleasure for both of us." 20

I have in my own life a precious friend, a woman of 65 who has lived very hard, who is wise, who listens well; who has been where I am and can help me understand it; and who represents not only an ultimate ideal mother to me but also the person I'd like to be when I grow up. 21

In our daughter role we tend to do more than our share of self-revelation; in our mother role we tend to receive what's revealed. It's another kind of pleasure—playing wise mother to a questing younger person. It's another very lovely kind of friendship. 22

6. Part-of-a-couple friends. Some of the women we call our friends we never see alone—we see them as part of a couple at couples' parties. And though we share interests in many things and respect each other's views, we aren't moved to deepen the relationship. Whatever the reason, a lack of time or—and this is more likely—a lack of chemistry, our friendship remains in the context of a group. But the fact that our feeling on seeing each other is always, "I'm *so* glad she's here" and the fact that we spend half the evening talking together says that this too, in its own way, counts as a friendship. 23

(Other part-of-a-couple friends are the friends that came with the marriage, and some of these are friends we could live without. But sometimes, alas, she married our husband's best friend; 24

and sometimes, alas, she *is* our husband's best friend. And so we find ourself dealing with her, somewhat against our will, in a spirit of what I'll call *reluctant* friendship.)

25 7. Men who are friends. I wanted to write just of women friends, but the women I've talked to won't let me—they say I must mention man–woman friendships too. For these friendships can be just as close and as dear as those that we form with women. Listen to Lucy's description of one such friendship:

26 "We've found we have things to talk about that are different from what he talks about with my husband and different from what I talk about with his wife. So sometimes we call on the phone or meet for lunch. There are similar intellectual interests—we always pass on to each other the books that we love—but there's also something tender and caring too."

27 In a couple of crises, Lucy says, "he offered himself for talking and for helping. And when someone died in his family he wanted me there. The sexual, flirty part of our friendship is very small, but *some*—just enough to make it fun and different." She thinks—and I agree—that the sexual part, though small, is always *some,* is always there when a man and a woman are friends.

28 It's only in the past few years that I've made friends with men, in the sense of a friendship that's *mine,* not just part of two couples. And achieving with them the ease and the trust I've found with women friends has value indeed. Under the dryer at home last week, putting on mascara and rouge, I comfortably sat and talked with a fellow named Peter. Peter, I finally decided, could handle the shock of me minus mascara under the dryer. Because we care for each other. Because we're friends.

29 8. There are medium friends, and pretty good friends, and very good friends indeed, and these friendships are defined by their level of intimacy. And what we'll reveal at each of these levels of intimacy is calibrated with care. We might tell a medium friend, for example, that yesterday we had a fight with our husband. And we might tell a pretty good friend that this fight with our husband made us so mad that we slept on the couch. And we might tell a very good friend that the reason we got so mad in that fight that we slept on the couch had something to do with that girl that works in his office. But it's only to our very best friends that we're willing to tell all, to tell what's going on with that girl in his office.

The best of friends, I still believe, totally love and support and 30
trust each other, and bare to each other the secrets of their souls, and run—no questions asked—to help each other, and tell harsh truths to each other when they must be told.

But we needn't agree about everything (only 12-year-old girl 31
friends agree about *everything*) to tolerate each other's point of view. To accept without judgment. To give and to take without ever keeping score. And to *be* there, as I am for them and as they are for me, to comfort our sorrows, to celebrate our joys.

Questions for Study and Discussion

1. In her opening paragraph Viorst explains how she once would have defined friendship. Why does she now think differently?
2. What is Viorst's purpose in this essay? Why is division and classification an appropriate strategy for her to use? (Glossary: *Purpose*)
3. Into what categories does Viorst divide her friends?
4. What principles of division does Viorst use to establish her categories of friends? Where does she state these principles?
5. Discuss the ways in which Viorst makes her categories distinct and memorable.
6. Viorst wrote this essay for *Redbook,* and so her audience was women between the ages of twenty-five and thirty-five. If she had been writing on the same topic for an audience of men of the same age, how might her categories have been different? How might her examples have been different? (Glossary: *Audience*)

Vocabulary

Refer to your dictionary to define the following words as they are used in this selection. Then use each word in a sentence of your own.

ardor (2)
nonchalant (3)
sibling (16)
forge (18)
dormant (19)
perspective (20)

Classroom Activity Using Division and Classification

Review the categories of friends that Viorst establishes in her essay. Make a list of no more than three of your friends that you would place in each of her categories. Write a sentence or two explaining the reasons for each placement. Does Viorst's classification work for your friends?

Suggested Writing Assignments

1. If for any reason you dislike or disagree with Viorst's classification of friends, write a classification essay of your own on the same topic. In preparation for writing, you may wish to interview your classmates and dorm members for their ideas on the various types of friends a person can have.
2. The accompanying drawing is a basic exercise in classification. By determining the features that the figures have in common, establish the general class to which they all belong. Next, establish subclasses by determining the distinctive features that distinguish one subclass from another. Finally, place each figure in an appropriate subclass within your classification system. You may wish to compare your classification system with those developed by other members of your class and to discuss any differences that exist.

a
b
c
d
e
f
g
h
i
j
k
l
m
n
o

What You Do Is What You Are

Nickie McWhirter

Nickie McWhirter was born in Peoria, Illinois, in 1929. She graduated from the University of Michigan in 1951 and began her writing career soon thereafter. She joined the staff of the Detroit Free Press *in 1963 as a features writer and in 1977 began writing her own column. She has received numerous local awards for her writing. As you read the following selection, note that the purpose McWhirter establishes in the first sentences of paragraphs 1 and 2 provides a basis for dividing and classifying in the rest of the essay. Mild sarcasm also helps to emphasize her point.*

For Your Journal

In America, we do not have a monarchy or noble class of people as some countries do. Are we a society without classes, a society in which everyone is equally regarded? If we are not, how are privilege and prestige determined in our society?

Americans, unlike people almost everywhere else in the world, tend to define and judge everybody in terms of the work they do, especially work performed for pay. Charlie is a doctor; Sam is a carpenter; Mary Ellen is a copywriter at a small ad agency. It is as if by defining how a person earns his or her rent money, we validate or reject that person's existence. Through the work and job title, we evaluate the worth of the life attached. Larry is a laid-off auto worker; Tony is a retired teacher; Sally is a former showgirl and blackjack dealer from Vegas. It is as if by learning that a person currently earns no money at a job—and maybe hasn't earned any money at a job for years—we assign that person to limbo, at least for the present. We define such non-employed persons in terms of their past job history. 1

This seems peculiar to me. People aren't cast in bronze because of the jobs they hold or once held. A retired teacher, for example, may spend a lot of volunteer time working with handicapped children or raising money for the Loyal Order of Hibernating Hibiscus. That apparently doesn't count. Who's Tony? A retired teacher. A laid-off auto worker may pump gas at his cousin's gas station or sell encyclopedias on weekends. But who's Larry? Until and unless he begins to work steadily again, he's a laid-off auto worker. This is the same as saying he's nothing now, but he used to be something: an auto worker. 2

There is a whole category of other people who are "just" something. To be "just" anything is the worst. It is not to be recognized by society as having much value at all, not now and probably not in the past either. To be "just" anything is to be totally discounted, at least for the present. There are lots of people who are "just" something. "Just" a housewife immediately and painfully comes to mind. We still hear it all the time. Sometimes women who have kept a house and reared six children refer to themselves as "'just' a housewife." "Just" a bum, "just" a kid, "just" a drunk, bag lady, old man, student, punk are some others. You can probably add to the list. The "just" category contains present non-earners, people who have no past job history highly valued by society and people whose present jobs are on the low-end of pay and prestige scales. A person can be "just" a cab driver, for example, or "just" a janitor. No one is ever "just" a vice-president, however. 3

We're supposed to be a classless society, but we are not. We don't recognize a titled nobility. We refuse to acknowledge dynastic privilege. But we certainly separate the valued from the valueless, and it has a lot to do with jobs and the importance or prestige we attach to them. 4

It is no use arguing whether any of this is correct or proper. Rationally it is silly. That's our system, however, and we should not only keep it in mind, we should teach our children how it works. It is perfectly swell to want to grow up to be a cowboy or a nurse. Kids should know, however, that quite apart from earnings potential, the cattle breeder is much more respected than the hired hand. The doctor gets a lot more respect and privilege than the nurse. 5

I think some anthropologist ought to study our uncataloged system of awarding respect and deference to each other based on jobs we hold. Where does a vice-president–product planning 6 fit in? Is that better than vice-president–sales in the public consciousness, or unconsciousness? Writers earn diddly dot, but I suspect they are held in higher esteem than wealthy rock musicians—that is, if everybody older than 40 gets to vote.

How do we decide which jobs have great value and, therefore, 7
the job-holders are wonderful people? Why is someone who builds shopping centers called an entrepreneur while someone who builds freeways is called a contractor? I have no answers to any of this, but we might think about the phenomenon the next time we are tempted to fawn over some stranger because we find out he happens to be a judge, or the next time we catch ourselves discounting the personal worth of the garbage collector.

Questions for Study and Discussion

1. What is McWhirter's thesis? (Glossary: *Thesis*) Does she state it outright or is it implied?
2. Add several more people to McWhirter's list of people who are "just" housewives, old men, and so on.
3. According to McWhirter, why should we teach our children how the system works? Do you think her recommendation is serious or tongue-in-cheek? Why?
4. What is McWhirter's tone? (Glossary: *Tone*) Support your answer with examples from the essay.
5. Does income necessarily dictate how others view each job? What are the most important factors?
6. According to McWhirter, how are unemployed people viewed in America's "job classification"?

Vocabulary

Refer to your dictionary to define the following words as they are used in this selection. Then use each word in a sentence of your own.

validate (1)	dynastic (4)
limbo (1)	deference (6)
prestige (3)	fawn (7)

Classroom Activity Using Division and Classification

Visit a local supermarket, and from the many department or product areas (frozen foods, dairy products, cereals, soft drinks, meats, produce) select one for an exercise in classification. First, establish the general class of products in the area you have selected by determining the features that the products have in common. Next, establish subclasses by determining the features that distinguish one subclass from another. Finally, place the products from your selected area in appropriate subclasses within your classification system.

Suggested Writing Assignments

1. Within each classification that we make, there are subclassifications. For instance, Michael Jordan and Dan Jansen are both great athletes, but there are obvious differences between them: summer vs. winter sport, amateur vs. professional, etc. The same holds true for Stephen King and Jamaica Kincaid—they are both writers, but their works are nonetheless very different in content and style. Choose one of the following jobs (or another of your own choosing) and write a short essay in which you establish three or four subclassifications, with examples of each:

   postal workers
   construction workers
   farmers
   retail-store workers
   entertainers

2. Do you agree with McWhirter's contention that we are classified in society by what job we do? Write an essay stating why you agree or do not agree with McWhirter. Provide some evidence to support your reasons; for instance, how has job classification influenced your current choice of careers?

What We Now Know about Memory

Lee Smith

Lee Smith has been a writer for Fortune *magazine since 1977. He was born in New York in 1937 and received his bachelor's degree from Yale University in 1959. After a stint in the army, he joined the Associated Press in Olympia, Washington, before moving on to* Newsweek, *where he worked as a writer for five years. During his years at* Fortune, *Smith has also served as bureau chief in Tokyo and Washington. The selection below first appeared in* Fortune *in April 1995. As you read it, pay particular attention to the way Smith embeds his classification of the types of memory within a larger discussion of the processes of remembering and of what we can do to maintain or improve our memories as we age.*

For Your Journal

Do you find it easy to memorize information for classes, or do you have to go over your notes and textbooks several times before it all seems to stick? How well do you remember names and faces of people you just met? Have you developed any techniques that help you remember important information?

The alarm finally goes off in your head around 3 P.M. Your face flushes and your hands plow through the papers on your desk. You have accidentally stood someone up for lunch. It gets worse. You can't remember who. And still worse: You can't recall where you left your glasses, so you can't look up the name in your appointment book. This is the afternoon you find yourself at a different place in life. Ten years ago, when you were 40, you would not have—could not have—forgotten anything. 1

2 Why do our memories betray us? Is this a precursor of Alzheimer's or some other serious mental disorder? How can some people command a loyal and prodigious memory well into old age? Are there ways to make everyone's memory clear again?

3 First, reassurance: A momentary loss of memory is most probably not a sign of Alzheimer's, or if so it's a very distant one. People between 65 and 75 face only a 4% chance of suffering from that sad, destructive disease, vs. a frightening 50% chance for those over 85. Yet almost all of us will be tripped up by forgetfulness from time to time as we age. Memory may begin to get a little shaky even in our late 30s, but the decline is so gradual that we don't start to stumble until we're 50ish.

4 The vanguard of 78 million baby-boomers will be 49 this year, so an ever larger share of the population will be turning desktops upside down. For many, their anxiety in already difficult careers could rise significantly. Moderate memory loss may be easily manageable for those who spend their entire working lives in the same company. In that steady-state universe, new people arrive and rules change slowly. The 45-year-olds who are downsized out and working as consultants, on the other hand, suddenly must master the rosters of half a dozen clients and as many ways of doing business.

5 Neuroscience, in a timely way, has begun to pay more attention to this condition. Researchers call it AAMI, age-associated memory impairment. The Charles A. Dana Foundation, named for an early manufacturer of differential joints for cars, has given $8.4 million to five major university medical centers to study AAMI. Researchers get the help of powerful instruments like PET (positron emission tomography) scanners that can detect the chemical changes taking place in the brains of subjects as they perform such tasks as memorizing vocabulary lists.

6 Some 450 middle-aged and elderly volunteers visit Johns Hopkins Hospital in Baltimore once a year to take a series of memory exams, the results of which are tracked over decades. The brains of some of these good sports will be examined after they die to see if their declining scores over the years relate to physical signs of disease and atrophy.

7 Much about memory is still baffling. "Despite all the noise we scientists make about memory, it is remarkable how little we know," says Dr. Arnold Scheibel, director of the UCLA Brain

Research Institute. He and his colleagues can be forgiven. The brain has as many as 100 billion neurons, many with 100,000 or more connections through which they can send signals to neighboring neurons. The number of potential pathways would be beyond the ability of the most advanced supercomputers to map.

Some of the predetermined roadways seem bizarre. In early February, for example, researchers discovered that men process language in one part of their brain, women in several. As for memory, the names of natural things, such as plants and animals, are apparently stored in one part of the brain; the names of chairs, machines, and other man-made stuff in another. Nouns seem to be separated from verbs. (That may explain the resistance of some brains to neologisms that turn nouns into verbs, such as "Let's dialogue on this" or "I'll liaise with Helen's team.") 8

Aspects of memory are scattered throughout the brain, but many researchers believe the hippocampus (Greek for "sea horse," the shape of the tiny organ) has an especially important role. That is where new information is turned into memory. How memories are made—and fade—is still mysterious. But this much is known. Neuron No. 28, say, fires an electrical signal, and in the synapse where one of 28's connectors touches a receiver of neuron No. 29, a chemical change takes place that triggers an electrical signal in 29. That signal gets passed on to neuron No. 30, and on and on. If the connection between 28 and 29 is made often enough, the bond between the two neurons grows stronger. This crucial marriage, the stuff that memory seems to be made of, neuroscientists have dubbed, unpoetically, long-term potentiation, or LTP. 9

Though memories may be created in the hippocampus, they are stored elsewhere. In TV soap operas the amnesiac is the ingenue who has forgotten she is already married to her fiancé's brother in another city, but is otherwise able to function more or less normally. That doesn't happen often, if ever. Real amnesiacs are people who remember the past but not the present. Their hippocampi have been severely damaged, so they are unable to form new memories, but most old memories remain intact. 10

Daniel L. Schacter, 42, a Harvard psychology professor, played a round of golf with one such victim. M.T., who was 58, remembered the rules and all the lingo from bogie to wedge. But he couldn't recall where he hit his ball. If Schacter drove first and M.T. followed, M.T. had half a chance of holding on to the image 11 of where his ball went long enough to track it down. But if M.T. drove first and had to wait for Schacter to drive, he had no chance. After M.T. walked off one green, Schacter noted in his journal, "the patient was surprised and confused when told he had not yet putted."

Amnesia can be caused by a virus, a blow to the head, a near 12
drowning or stroke that deprives the brain of oxygen for a time, or a faulty gene that programs parts of the brain to deteriorate early. Stress can play a part as well. Lab animals exposed to low levels of shock they cannot control produce glucosteroids that damage their hippocampi. Marilyn Albert, 51, a researcher at Massachusetts General Hospital, notes that among the elderly she is studying in the Boston area, those who are less educated, are less active physically, and feel less able to influence what happens to them day to day tend to experience greater memory loss than the better educated who regard themselves as more commanding. (This kind of stress is not the same as pressure to finish a job or perform well. Pressure can stir strong emotions that actually help imprint memories more deeply.)

As we age, most of us will experience at least some slowdown 13
in ability to remember. What do we have to fear and how do we avoid it? Laypeople are accustomed to distinguishing between long-term and short-term memory. That oversimplifies the phenomenon. Dr. Murray Grossman, 43, a University of Pennsylvania Medical Center neurologist, has helped develop a model that separates memory into five types. He assigns each a locale, or a possible locale, in the brain and assesses the likelihood of each type's decaying over time. In order of durability, the memory types are as follows:

> SEMANTIC: The memory of what words and symbols mean is highly resilient—even some Alzheimer's patients retain much of their semantic memory. It's unlikely you'll forget what "Tinkertoy," "prom," and "mess hall" mean even though you haven't used the words in years. Nor do you forget religious symbols and corporate trademarks or what distinguishes a cat from a dog. You can add words to your semantic memory until death.

IMPLICIT: Years ago someone taught you to ride a bike. You may not recall the specific instructions of those wobbly, knee-banging first outings, but you will not forget all that you have learned about bike riding over a lifetime—without even being conscious of learning—from turning corners at high speeds to stopping on a dime. How to swim or drive a car and many other skills that depend on automatic recall of a series of motions don't disappear either. Nor do conditioned responses. Like Pavlov's dogs, once you've learned to salivate at the sound of a bell, you'll do it forever. Nor will you neglect to reach for a handkerchief when you sense a sneeze, or for a dollar bill when you see a doorman. Loss of implicit memory is a sure sign of serious mental deterioration.

REMOTE: This is the kind of memory that wins money on *Jeopardy*. It is data collected over the years from schools, magazines, movies, conversations, wherever. Remote memory appears to diminish with age in normal people, though the decline could be simply a retrieval problem. "It could be interference," says Johns Hopkins neurologist Dr. Barry Gordon, 44. "We have to keep sorting through the constant accumulation of information as we age."

When a 60-year-old hears "war," it has many more associations than Vietnam or the Gulf. And compared with the 30-year-old, the 60-year-old may have to rummage through twice as much data before digging way back to the lessons of a high school history course and finding the names of the five Presidents after Lincoln.

WORKING: Now we enter territory that does erode, at least for most people. This is extremely short-term memory, lasting for no more than a few seconds. It is the brain's boss, telling it what to cling to. In conversation, working memory enables you to hang on to the first part of your companion's sentence while she gets to the end. It also lets you keep several things in mind simultaneously—to riffle through your mail, talk on the

> phone, and catch the attention of a colleague walking by the door to ask him if he wants to go to lunch—all without losing your place.
>
> For reasons that aren't altogether clear, working memory in many people starts to slow down noticeably between 40 and 50. "Certain environments become more difficult, like the trading floor of a stock exchange, where you have to react very fast to a lot of information," says Richard Mohs, 45, a psychiatry professor at Mount Sinai School of Medicine in New York City. Jetfighter combat is out.
>
> EPISODIC: This is the memory of recent experience—everything from the movie you saw last week and the name of the client with whom you booked lunch to where you put your glasses—and it too dwindles over time. This is the form of memory loss, the AAMI, that does, or will, trouble most people. You remember how to drive your car, but that's academic because you can't recall where you parked it.
>
> Episodic memory could begin to dwindle in the late 30s, but the downward glide is so gentle that unless you are trying to memorize the *Iliad* or pass a bar exam, you probably won't notice for a couple of decades. At 50, however, you are likely to feel a little anxiety as you watch the younger people in the office, even the non-techies, learn how to operate the new computer software much more quickly than you do.

Several years ago a Massachusetts insurance company, observing that malpractice suits are brought against old doctors more often than young ones, asked researchers to develop tests for identifying physicians at risk. Dean K. Whitla, 69, a Harvard psychologist, was on a team that examined 1,000 doctors, ages 30 to 80. In one test the subjects were seated in front of computers and asked to read stories crammed with details, such as street addresses. A few minutes later they took a multiple-choice test. 14

Ability declined steadily with age, says Whitla. Though some of the 80-year-olds were as good as the 30s, on average the 80s could remember only half as much as the 30s. But there were 15 also some 80s who on further investigation couldn't match the patients they had seen that day with their complaints. (The insurance company has not yet disclosed whether it plans to act on the results.)

What's going on up there? Unlike cells elsewhere in the body, neurons don't divide. They age, and at the rate of 100,000 a day they die, says Dr. Daniel Alkon, 52, chief of the neural science lab at the National Institutes of Health. By the time someone reaches 65 or 70, he may have lost 20% of his 100 billion. Return to the hippocampus, where episodic memory is first recorded. Neuron 28 and some of its neighbors may be dead or so feeble they no longer transmit electrical charges efficiently. 16

Still, 80 billion remaining neurons is a lot. And even though the brain cannot grow new ones, the neurons can likely sprout new synapses late into life and thereby form new connections with one another. William Greenough, 50, a researcher at the University of Illinois, supplied lab rats with new balls, dolls, and other toys to play with daily and changed the chutes and tunnels in their cages. When he cut open their brains, he counted many more synapses than in rats that got no toys and no new decor. 17

It's a good guess that the human brain, too, grows more synapses when stimulated and challenged. So the brain—even while shrinking—may be able to blaze ever more trails for laying down memory. If the neuron 28 path is no longer easily passable, the number of alternate routes may be virtually limitless. The trick is to force the brain to make them. 18

The habits of highly intelligent people offer a clue as to how to do that. By and large, says Harvard's Schacter, the higher people score on the Wechsler Adult Intelligence Scale (100 is the mean), the higher they score on the Wechsler Memory Scale. "Memory depends on processing," he says. "Very smart people process information very deeply." Perhaps they relate a magazine article on memory to a book on artificial intelligence and a play about prison camp survivors. Doing so, they could be laying networks of neuron highways that will make the recollection of the article, book, or play accessible by multiple routes. 19

With effort, people with average intellects can boost their memories substantially. For example, most people have trouble remembering numbers of more than seven digits or so, a limitation long recognized by telephone companies. But a decade ago, researchers 20 at Carnegie Mellon University trained otherwise undistinguished undergraduates to memorize hundred-digit numbers. Focusing hard on that long string of digits, the students found patterns they could relate to meaningful number series, such as birthdays.

Forgetting names bedevils most people, the more so as they age. So meet Harry Lorayne, 68, a memory coach and theatrical wonder already familiar to many insomniacs. His half-hour TV infomercials with Dick Cavett run at 4 A.M. and other off-price times. Lorayne has also appeared on *The Tonight Show* and memorized the names of as many as 500 people in the audience. His gift is that he can quickly invent a dramatic, often grotesque, image to slap on the face of everyone he encounters. "I meet Mr. Benavena, and I notice he has a big nose," rasps Lorayne in a voice that was trained on New York's Lower East Side. "So I think 'vane,' like weather vane, a nose that's a bent weather vane." Lorayne's Memory Power package of videotapes, audiotapes, and a book sells for $115. 21

Frank Felberbaum, 58, refers to himself as a corporate memory consultant. "Think of bottles of beer falling like bombs," he introduces himself unforgettably. Felberbaum's clients include GE Capital, Condé Nast, and some Marriott hotels. For about $6,000, Felberbaum trains a group of 20 or so executives in a two-day course that instructs them on how to retain such critical data as a range of interest rates and the names of hotel guests. 22

The methods of Lorayne and Felberbaum are legitimate, say the neuroscientists. The routines they teach—fastening names and other information to vivid pictures—have been around since the ancient Greeks. Lorayne likes to trace his intellectual roots to Aristotle, who taught that in order to think, we must speculate with images. Matteo Ricci, a 16th-century Jesuit missionary to China, "built" a memory palace in his mind and wandered the halls, storing the dosage for a new medicine in one room, perhaps, and retrieving a Thomistic proof for the existence of God from another. 23

There are modest ways to build, if not a palace, at least a comfortable home for memory. College students may be superior at memorizing not only because their neurons are young but also because they develop mnemonic devices to survive exams. That's an easy practice to resume. For example, memory is WIRES—working, implicit, remote, episodic, and semantic. One of the 24 clichéd pieces of advice for improving your brain, including memory, is to marry someone smarter than yourself. If that's inconvenient, at least hang out with challenging, fast-thinking company. Or study accounting, zoology, or a new language.

Coming someday, perhaps, is a memory pill. Cortex Pharma- 25
ceuticals, founded by three neuroscientists from the University of California at Irvine, claims to have developed a class of drugs called ampakines that revive tired neurons. Gary Lynch, 52, one of the founders and a prominent LTP researcher, says ampakines heighten the ability of the remaining receptors in weakened neurons to carry on after some of their synapses have died. "We know that this works in middle-aged and old rats," says Lynch. "If you give them ampakines, they will remember in the afternoon where they found food in the morning."

Cortex President Alan Steigrod, 57, says that preliminary clin- 26
ical trials on humans in Germany have been encouraging. The company hopes to test the drugs soon on about 100 Alzheimer's victims in the U.S. Ampakines, or another series of drugs, may eventually prove to be the easy, safe, and effective way to freshen old memories. Or they may not. A Salk Institute researcher questions whether they are any more useful than caffeine. And they might have dangerous side effects. So the Food and Drug Administration could approve ampakines for Alzheimer's sufferers, who don't have much to lose, but keep them off the market for a long time for those afflicted by normal memory loss. Waiting for the FDA's okay, you could probably learn Chinese.

Questions for Study and Discussion

1. Why are the causes of memory disorders still so mysterious?
2. Is Smith's purpose to inform, give practical advice, or both in his essay? (Glossary: *Purpose*) What categories of memory does Smith establish in his classification, and how does he order them? How does this order relate to his purpose?
3. Find the examples Smith uses to illustrate each memory type. (Glossary: *Illustration*) Do you find them effective in quickly communicating the required information? Why, or why not? Provide an example of your own for each memory type.

4. What is the relationship between intelligence and memory? Why is this relationship significant to the research into memory retention for average people?
5. Smith organizes his essay so that he discusses the mechanics of memory before he discusses ways to improve it. (Glossary: *Organization*) Why is the information about memory important for readers to know before they learn about the new techniques for improving it?
6. Smith suggests WIRES as an easy aid in remembering the five categories of memory. Does WIRES assist you or hinder you in memorizing the essay's information?

Vocabulary

Refer to your dictionary to define the following words as they are used in this selection. Then use each word in a sentence of your own.

precursor (2)
synapse (5)
hippocampus (6)
semantic (9)
implicit (10)
clinical (28)

Classroom Activity Using Division and Classification

Divide each of the following into at least three different categories and be prepared to discuss the reasons for your division:

checking accounts
computers
fast-food restaurants
colleges
soft drinks

Suggested Writing Assignments

1. Music can be classified into many different types, such as jazz, country, pop, rock, hard rock, alternative, classical, big band, and so on. Each of these large classifications has a lot of variety within it. Write an essay in which you identify

your favorite type of music, then identify at least three subclassifications of the music. Explain the characteristics of each of your categories, using at least two artists to illustrate each.

2. Consider the following classes of items and determine at least two principles of division that can be used for each class. Then write a paragraph or two in which you classify one of the groups of items according to a single principle of division. For example, in discussing crime, one could use the seriousness of the crime or the type of crime as principles of division. If the seriousness of the crime were used, this would yield two categories: felonies and misdemeanors. If the type of crime were used, this would yield categories such as burglary, murder, assault, larceny, and embezzlement.

professional sports	roommates
social sciences	cars
slang used by college students	movies

16

COMPARISON AND CONTRAST

A *comparison* points out the ways that two or more persons, places, or things are alike. A *contrast* points out how they differ. The subjects of a comparison or contrast should be in the same class or general category; if they have nothing in common, there is no good reason for setting them side by side.

The function of any comparison or contrast is to clarify and explain. The writer's purpose may be simply to inform, or to make readers aware of similarities or differences that are interesting and significant in themselves. Or, the writer may explain something unfamiliar by comparing it with something very familiar, perhaps explaining squash by comparing it with tennis. Finally, the writer can point out the superiority of one thing by contrasting it with another—for example, showing that one product is the best by contrasting it with all its competitors.

As a writer, you have two main options for organizing a comparison or contrast: the subject-by-subject pattern or the point-by-point pattern. For a short essay comparing and contrasting the Atlanta Braves and the Seattle Mariners, you would probably follow the *subject-by-subject* pattern of organization. By this pattern you first discuss the points you wish to make about one team, and then go on to discuss the corresponding points for the other team. An outline of your essay might look like this:

I. Atlanta Braves
  A. Pitching
  B. Fielding
  C. Hitting
II. Seattle Mariners
  A. Pitching
  B. Fielding
  C. Hitting

The subject-by-subject pattern presents a unified discussion of each team by placing the emphasis on the teams and not on the three points of comparison. Since these points are relatively few, readers should easily remember what was said about the Braves' pitching when you later discuss the Mariners' pitching and should be able to make the appropriate connections between them.

For a somewhat longer essay comparing and contrasting solar energy and wind energy, however, you should consider the *point-by-point* pattern of organization. With this pattern, your essay is organized according to the various points of comparison. Discussion alternates between solar and wind energy for each point of comparison. An outline of your essay might look like this:

I. Installation Expenses
   A. Solar
   B. Wind
II. Efficiency
   A. Solar
   B. Wind
III. Operating Costs
   A. Solar
   B. Wind
IV. Convenience
   A. Solar
   B. Wind
V. Maintenance
   A. Solar
   B. Wind
VI. Safety
   A. Solar
   B. Wind

The point-by-point pattern allows the writer to make immediate comparisons between solar and wind energy, thus enabling readers to consider each of the similarities and differences separately.

Each organizational pattern has its advantages. In general, the subject-by-subject pattern is useful in short essays where there are few points to be considered, whereas the point-by-point pattern is preferable in long essays where there are numerous points under consideration.

A good essay of comparison and contrast tells readers something significant that they do not already know. That is, it must do more than merely point out the obvious. As a rule, therefore, writers tend to draw contrasts between things that are usually perceived as being similar or comparisons between things usually perceived as different. In fact, comparison and contrast often go together. For example, an essay about Minneapolis and St. Paul might begin by showing how much they are alike, but end with a series of contrasts revealing how much they differ. Or, a consumer magazine might report the contrasting claims made by six car manufacturers, and then go on to demonstrate that the cars all actually do much the same thing in the same way.

Analogy is a special form of comparison. When a subject is unobservable, complex, or abstract—when it is so generally unfamiliar that readers may have trouble understanding it—*analogy* can be most effective. By pointing out certain similarities between a difficult subject and a more familiar or concrete subject, writers can help their readers achieve a firmer grasp of the difficult subject. Unlike a true comparison, though, which analyzes items that belong to the same class—breeds of dogs or types of engines—analogy pairs things from different classes, things that have nothing in common except through the imagination of the writer. In addition, whereas comparison seeks to illuminate specific features of both subjects, the primary purpose of analogy is to clarify the one subject that is complex or unfamiliar. For example, an exploration of the similarities (and differences) between short stories and novels—two forms of fiction—would constitute a logical comparison; short stories and novels belong to the same class (fiction), and your purpose is to reveal something about both. If, however, your purpose is to explain the craft of fiction writing, you might note its similarities to the craft of carpentry. Then, you would be drawing an analogy, because the two subjects clearly belong to different classes. Carpentry is the more concrete subject and the one more people will have direct experience with. If you use your imagination, you will easily see many ways the tangible work of the carpenter can be used to help readers understand the more abstract work of the novelist. Depending on its purpose, an analogy can be made in several paragraphs to clarify a particular aspect of the larger topic being discussed, as in the example below, or it can provide the organizational strategy for an entire essay.

> It has long struck me that the familiar metaphor of "climbing the ladder" for describing the ascent to success or fulfillment in any field is inappropriate and misleading. There are no ladders that lead to success, although there may be some escalators for those lucky enough to follow in a family's fortunes.
>
> A ladder proceeds vertically, rung by rung, with each rung evenly spaced, and with the whole apparatus leaning against

a relatively flat and even surface. A child can climb a ladder as easily as an adult, and perhaps with a surer footing.

Making the ascent in one's vocation or profession is far less like ladder climbing than mountain climbing, and here the analogy is a very real one. Going up a mountain requires a variety of skills, and includes a diversity of dangers, that are in no way involved in mounting a ladder.

Young people starting out should be told this, both to dampen their expectations and to allay their disappointments. A mountain is rough and precipitous, with uncertain footing and a predictable number of falls and scrapes, and sometimes one has to take the long way around to reach the shortest distance.

Sydney J. Harris

Grammy Rewards

Deborah Dalfonso

Deborah Dalfonso first published the following piece in Parenting *magazine. As you read it, note that she uses a point-by-point pattern of contrasts in the first six paragraphs to help clarify and emphasize the idea she explores in the final three.*

For Your Journal

Did any or all of your grandparents have a large influence in your life as you grew up? What interaction did you have with them? How did they influence you?

Our daughter, Jill, has two grandmothers who are as different as chalk and cheese. One taught her to count cards and make her face blank when she bluffed at blackjack. The other taught her where to place salad forks. When Jill was three, this grandmother taught her not to touch anything until invited to do so. The other one taught her to slide down carpeted stairs on a cookie sheet. 1

Both grandmothers are widows. One lives in a trailer park in Florida from October until May, then moves to an old lake-front camp in Maine for the summer. The camp is a leaning structure filled with furniture impervious to wet swimsuits. Raccoons sleep on the deck every night. 2

The other grandmother resides in a town house at the Best Address in the City—a regal-looking brick building boasting a security system and plants tended by florists. 3

One grandmother plays the lottery and bingo. The other plays bridge with monogrammed playing cards. One grandmother wears primary colors, favoring fluorescents when she has a tan; the other wears suits, largely taupe or black. 4

One grandmother would be delighted to learn that many people think of her as eccentric. The other hopes that people will re- 5 fer to her as "correct." This grandmother, when startled, says "Oh, my word," her strongest expletive. The other one says "hot damn," or worse.

During Hurricane Bob, one of Jill's grandmothers bought her a duckling-yellow slicker and took her to the beach to watch the surf. She believes the ocean throws off positive ions, excellent for growth and peace of mind. While they were experiencing the elements, Jill's other grandmother called to make sure we were safe in the cellar. 6

"Are there many ways to live?" my puzzled six-year-old asked me. 7

"Yes," I said gently, "and you may choose which feels right for you." And, I promised myself, I will let her make her own choice. 8

Two grandmothers, two different worlds. Both want for Jill no less than the lion's share. One will be her anchor; the other, her mainsail. 9

Questions for Study and Discussion

1. Why do you think Dalfonso chose to use a point-by-point organization?
2. Dalfonso uses an unusual turn of phrase when she introduces Jill's grandmothers as being "as different as chalk and cheese." (Glossary: *Figurative Language*) Which of Jill's grandmothers might one classify as chalk and which one as cheese? Explain your choice.
3. It is quite apparent after the first paragraph which grandmother is which in Dalfonso's essay, yet she never identifies them other than by "one" and "the other." What point does Dalfonso make by doing this? How does it add to the effectiveness of the essay?
4. What is Dalfonso's purpose for writing the essay? (Glossary: *Purpose)* How does Jill's response to the extremes her two grandmothers represent help Dalfonso present her purpose?
5. Why do you think Dalfonso uses metaphors to represent the grandmothers' projected influence in Jill's life? Is Dalfonso's use of metaphors an effective way to conclude her essay? (Glossary: *Beginnings and Endings*) Why, or why not?

Vocabulary

Refer to your dictionary to define the following words as they are used in this selection. Then use each word in a sentence of your own.

impervious (2)
regal (3)
taupe (4)
expletive (5)
ions (6)

Classroom Activity Using Comparison and Contrast

Dalfonso writes an effective essay by contrasting the responses of two very different people to the same situations. To do so in such a short essay, she needed to focus on the situations that brought out the differences between the two grandmothers and at the same time revealed as much as possible about what each was like as an individual. Think of two friends or relatives whom you know well who have different personalities. Write a sentence about how each reacted or would react to four situations. Select the situations carefully, so that you capture the personality of each person. For example, the following situations would probably provoke strong and varied reactions:

learning to snorkel
having a picnic
going out to a Halloween party
choosing a pet

Suggested Writing Assignments

1. In what ways are your grandparents similar to your parents when it comes to hobbies, conversation topics, cooking, discipline, and so on? How do they differ? In a comparison and contrast essay, discuss how you interact with your grandparents as compared with your parents.
2. Select one of the following topics for an essay of comparison and contrast:

   two cities
   two friends
   two ways to heat a home
   two fast-food restaurants
   two actors
   two teachers
   two brands of pizza
   two books by the same author

A Case of "Severe Bias"

Patricia Raybon

A resident of Denver, Colorado, Patricia Raybon is a practicing journalist as well as an associate professor of journalism at the University of Colorado School of Journalism and Mass Communication in Boulder. She was born in 1941, graduated from Ohio State University in 1971, and earned her master's degree from the University of Colorado in 1977. She has worked as a reporter and editor, and her writing has appeared in such publications as the New York Times, *the* Wall Street Journal, USA Today, *and the* Washington Post. *Her book* My First White Friend: Confessions on Race, Love, and Forgiveness *was published in 1996. The following essay, which first appeared in* Newsweek *in 1989, reflects two of Raybon's main interests—race and the media. Here, Raybon highlights the differences she sees between the portrayal of African Americans by the media and the reality of their lives as she knows it. Notice how her use of contrast demonstrates the superiority of one view over another, in this case the superiority of the more accurate and truthful representation of African Americans.*

For Your Journal

We live in a complex, complicated society, one that is so vast and diverse that it is perhaps never really possible to know who we are as Americans. Naturally, we rely on both our own experiences and media information for our sense of ourselves. How much value do you place on your own experiences and how much do you rely on the media in building a sense of who we are as a people?

This is who I am not. I am not a crack addict. I am not a wel- 1
fare mother. I am not illiterate. I am not a prostitute. I have

never been in jail. My children are not in gangs. My husband doesn't beat me. My home is not a tenement. None of these things defines who I am, nor do they describe the other black people I've known and worked with and loved and befriended over these forty years of my life.

Nor does it describe most of black America, period. 2

Yet in the eyes of the American news media, this is what black 3 America is: poor, criminal, addicted, and dysfunctional. Indeed, media coverage of black America is so one-sided, so imbalanced that the most victimized and hurting segment of the black community—a small segment, at best—is presented not as the exception but as the norm. It is an insidious practice, all the uglier for its blatancy.

In recent months, I have observed a steady offering of media 4 reports on crack babies, gang warfare, violent youth, poverty, and homelessness—and in most cases, the people featured in the photos and stories were black. At the same time, articles that discuss other aspects of American life—from home buying to medicine to technology to nutrition—rarely, if ever, show blacks playing a positive role, or for that matter, any role at all.

Day after day, week after week, this message—that black Amer- 5 ica is dysfunctional and unwhole—gets transmitted across the American landscape. Sadly, as a result, America never learns the truth about what is actually a wonderful, vibrant, creative community of people.

Most black Americans are *not* poor. Most black teenagers are 6 *not* crack addicts. Most black mothers are *not* on welfare. Indeed, in sheer numbers, more *white* Americans are poor and on welfare than are black. Yet one never would deduce that by watching television or reading American newspapers and magazines.

Why do the American media insist on playing this myopic, in- 7 accurate picture game? In this game, white America is always whole and lovely and healthy, while black America is usually sick and pathetic and deficient. Rarely, indeed, is black America ever depicted in the media as functional and self-sufficient. The free press, indeed, as the main interpreter of American culture and American experience, holds the mirror on American reality—so much so that what the media say is *is,* even if it's not that way at all. The media are guilty of a severe bias and the problem screams out for correction. It is worse than simply lazy journalism, which is bad enough; it is inaccurate journalism.

For black Americans like myself, this isn't just an issue of vanity—of wanting to be seen in a good light. Nor is it a matter of closing one's eyes to the very real problems of the urban underclass—which undeniably is disproportionately black. To be sure, problems besetting the black underclass deserve the utmost attention of the media, as well as the understanding and concern of the rest of American society. 8

But if their problems consistently are presented as the *only* reality for blacks, any other experience known in the black community ceases to have validity, or to be real. In this scenario, millions of blacks are relegated to a sort of twilight zone, where who we are and what we are isn't based on fact but on image and perception. That's what it feels like to be a black American whose lifestyle is outside of the aberrant behavior that the media present as the norm. 9

For many of us, life is a curious series of encounters with white people who want to know why we are "different" from other blacks—when, in fact, most of us are only "different" from the now common negative images of black life. So pervasive are these images that they aren't just perceived as the norm, they're *accepted* as the norm. 10

I am reminded, for example, of the controversial Spike Lee film *Do the Right Thing* and the criticism by some movie reviewers that the film's ghetto neighborhood isn't populated by addicts and drug pushers—and thus is not a true depiction. 11

In fact, millions of black Americans live in neighborhoods where the most common sights are children playing and couples walking their dogs. In my own inner-city neighborhood in Denver—an area that the local press consistently describes as "gang territory"—I have yet to see a recognizable "gang" member or any "gang" activity (drug dealing or drive-by shootings), nor have I been the victim of "gang violence." 12

Yet to students of American culture—in the case of Spike Lee's film, the movie reviewers—a black, inner-city neighborhood can only be one thing to be real: drug-infested and dysfunctioning. Is this my ego talking? In part, yes. For the millions of black people like myself—ordinary, hard-working, law-abiding, tax-paying Americans—the media's blindness to the fact that we even exist, let alone to our contributions to American society, is a bitter cup to drink. And as self-reliant as most black Americans are—because we've had to be self-reliant—even the strongest among us still crave affirmation. 13

I want that. I want it for my children. I want it for all the beautiful, healthy, funny, smart black Americans I have known and loved over the years. 14

And I want it for the rest of America, too. 15

I want America to know us—all of us—for who we really are. To see us in all of our complexity, our subtleness, our artfulness, our enterprise, our specialness, our loveliness, our Americanness. That is the real portrait of black America—that we're strong people, surviving people, capable people. That may be the best-kept secret in America. If so, it's time to let the truth be known. 16

Questions for Study and Discussion

1. What is the basic contrast that Raybon establishes in her first paragraph? What examples does she use to establish the contrast that she sees? Can you think of any other examples? (Glossary: *Examples*)
2. Why do you think Raybon feels it is necessary to define herself by contrast in her opening paragraph? Why doesn't she simply say who she is in a positive manner?
3. How are paragraphs 1 and 6 stylistically similar? Why do you think Raybon wrote them in the way she did? (Glossary: *Style*)
4. What is Raybon's thesis in this essay? (Glossary: *Thesis*) Where does she present it? Does she support her thesis accurately in your view? Why, or why not?
5. What do you think is the purpose of Raybon's comparison and contrast technique? What does she want? What do you think she wants us to think and/or do as a result of reading her essay?
6. How would you describe Raybon's tone in this essay? (Glossary: *Tone*) What in the style of the essay led you to your response?

Vocabulary

Refer to your dictionary to define the following words as they are used in this selection. Then use each word in a sentence of your own.

tenement (1)
dysfunctional (3)
insidious (3)
myopic (7)
besetting (8)
scenario (9)
aberrant (9)
pervasive (10)
subtleness (16)
enterprise (16)

Classroom Activity Using Comparison and Contrast

In preparation for writing a comparison and contrast essay on two world leaders (or popular singers, actors, or subjects of your own choosing), consider, in writing answers, to the following questions:

What possibilities do I have for people to compare and contrast?
What is my purpose?
Should I emphasize similarities or differences?
What specific points should I discuss?
What organizational pattern will best suit my purposes: subject-by-subject or point-by-point?

Suggested Writing Assignments

1. Write an essay in which you compare and/or contrast the issues and argumentative strategies used by Patricia Raybon with those of Joanmarie Kalter in "Exposing Media Myths: TV Doesn't Affect You as Much as You Think," found in the Argument section of *Models for Writers* on pp. 479–84.
2. Using one of the following "before and after" situations, write a short essay of comparison and/or contrast:

   before and after a diet
   before and after urban renewal
   before and after a visit to the dentist
   before and after a physical workout

The Locket

Gary Soto

Gary Soto taught English and Chicano studies at the University of California at Berkeley for many years before deciding to write full-time in 1993. Born in Fresno, California, in 1952, Soto received a B.A. from California State University at Fresno and an M.F.A. from the University of California at Irvine. He has published volumes of poetry, short stories, and nonfiction, in addition to the children's literature he began writing in the 1990s. The essay below is from his autobiographical collection, A Summer Life *(1990). In it, Soto relies on points of comparison between himself and his sister to portray behaviors characteristic of adolescence in general. Pay particular attention to how paragraph 2 ultimately connects with the final paragraph.*

For Your Journal

Early adolescence is a time of excitement and confusion, when everything, including one's view of the world, is likely to change. What was particularly memorable about your early adolescence? What did you consider important when you were eleven, twelve, and thirteen years old?

I never liked jewelry. My sister Debra did. Twenty Bazooka comic strips and a dollar—after a three-week binge of reading teenage romances while waiting for the mailman—brought her a gold-plated locket, studded with plastic pearls and a fake diamond. I wanted her to choose the miniature binoculars because I helped her chew at least seven pieces of pink bubble gum and gave her a clean dime in exchange for our once-a-week pudding dessert. We were always selling desserts to each other. We were always short 1 a dime or a quarter, and our only bargaining chip was dessert, especially the pudding Mother served in gold-rimmed goblets, the kind kings and queens used in Robin Hood movies.

I wanted Debra to choose the binoculars. My head was large, but my eyes were small as a cat's, maybe even smaller. I could look through both lenses with one eye, and what I wanted was a better look at our neighbor, a junior college student who swam in an aluminum-sided doughboy pool. She used a ladder to get in, and often just stood on the ladder fiddling with her top and snapping her bikini bottom back into place. I could spy on her from behind our fence, the binoculars to my right eye because that one seemed to work better. 2

But Debra chose the locket. When it arrived in a business-size envelope, I waved it at her and said, "It's here." Angrily, she snatched it from me and took it to her room. I ate an afternoon bowl of Cocoa Puffs and watched a movie about giant ants no flame thrower could stop. I looked at her bedroom door now and then, wondering what was going on. Later, just before the ants got fried with a laser, she came out stinking of perfume, the locket around her brown neck. She didn't look at me as she went out the front door and crossed the street to see her friend, Jill. 3

My sister was eleven. She still clacked the plastic faces of Barbie and Ken together, made them hug, made them cry and run back to each other, stiff arms extended, faces wet with pretend tears from the bathroom sink. But she and Jill played with them less and less. Now they were going for the real thing: boys with washed faces. 4

In spite of the plastic pearls and the chip of glass centered in the middle, the locket made her look grown-up. I didn't tease her, and she didn't tease me about wearing rummage-sale baseball cleats. 5

All summer Debra wore the locket, and Jill wore one, too, an expensive one her mother had bought at Penney's. But Debra didn't care. She loved the locket whose metal chain left her neck green. Mother admired the locket, said it made her look elegant. That summer, Debra began to complain less and less about doing the dishes. 6

When a pearl fell out, she glued it back in. Another lost its grip and rolled into the floor furnace. She vacuumed the furnace of its 7 ghostly lint, and shook out the bag and ran her fingers through the stinking hair, lint, broken potato chips, Cocoa Puffs, Cheerios, staples, bits of Kleenex, dead ants, and blue, flowery marble. She searched through the debris until, miraculously, she found the tiny pearl. She glued it back into place and gave her locket a rest.

One day, while Debra was at the playground swimming, I snuck into her bedroom to peek in the locket because I knew she kept something in the frame. She was always snapping it open and closed, always feeling pretty happy when she looked down at her breasts, twin mounds that had begun to cast small shadows. When I opened it, slowly because the clasp looked fragile, I saw a face that was mostly an eyeball looking at me. I stared back at the eyeball, and after a moment realized that it was Paul of the Beatles. It was Paul's eyeball, a bit droopy, a bit sad like his songs. Paul was favored by the girls who rode their bikes up and down the block singing "Michelle, ma belle." 8

A few days later I checked the locket again. Paul's eyeball was gone, and now I was staring at a smiling Herman and the Hermits. Herman looked happy. His hair was long and soft, and his teeth were large and charmingly crooked. I smiled wide and thought for a moment that I looked like Herman. A few days later it was back to Paul in a new picture that she had cut out of a magazine. I thumbed through the magazine, emptied of all the famous pop stars, and looked around the room. Almost everything was pink. The furry rug, the canopy bed, the bottles of perfume and nail polish, the much-hugged pillow, everything except the chest of drawers which she intended to paint by fall. I left in a hurry when I heard Debra's bike skid to a halt in the driveway. 9

All summer it was Paul's eyeball, Herman's teeth, and one time Paul Revere with his colonial hat. Debra began to polish her nails and walk more slowly, erect as a ladder. By fall, the chest of drawers was pink and Mother was no longer worried about the green around her neck where the chain rested—an allergic reaction to cheap metal. Debra no longer wore the locket. She was saving Bazooka comics for a camera that came with a free roll of film. She had her first boyfriend and wanted to take his picture on the sly, wanted more than a droopy eyeball or toothy smile. She wanted the entire face, and some of the neck. 10

Questions for Study and Discussion

1. Soto never states his age directly in the essay, but he gives readers several hints. How old do you think he is during the time he writes about in the essay? Defend your answer.
2. Debra's locket means far more to her than one would think a piece of plastic jewelry obtained with the help of Bazooka comics would. What does the locket symbolize to Debra? (Glossary: *Symbol*)
3. List the objects that Debra finds of value. What connotations does each object have? (Glossary: *Connotation/Denotation*) For example, a Barbie doll connotes that its owner is young enough to spend large amounts of time in fantasy and play. What do the objects alone tell you about Debra's age and interests? Why is it important for Soto to show how she uses each object?
4. Why does Soto avoid teasing his sister about the locket? Why does she reciprocate and not tease him about his secondhand cleats?
5. What is Soto's attitude toward the changes he is observing in his sister? (Glossary: *Attitude*) How does he express his attitude?
6. Soto says that Debra wanted "the entire face, and some of the neck" in her photos of her boyfriend. How does this compare with the previous photos found in her locket? Why is the difference significant?

Vocabulary

Refer to your dictionary to define the following words as they are used in this selection. Then use each word in a sentence of your own.

goblets (1)	clacked (4)
doughboy (2)	sly (10)

Classroom Activity Using Comparison and Contrast

If you were to write a comparison/contrast essay about men and women, there would be many topics to compare and many to contrast. Based on your own experience with friends and siblings, list three activities or possessions that men tend to find more appealing than women, three activities or possessions that women tend to find more appealing than men, and three that are relatively independent of gender. For example, watching TV sports tends to appeal more to men, buying and applying cosmetics tends to appeal more to women, and hiking is gender-independent. Discuss your choices with your classmates. What do the gender-dependent answers tell you about the social differences between men and women? What do the gender-independent answers tell you about the similarities?

Suggested Writing Assignments

1. Write a comparison and contrast essay in which you examine your relationship with a sibling or a childhood best friend during your junior-high or early high-school years. How did the changes within you compare with the changes your friend was going through? Were your new interests similar, or did you go in different directions? Was there a time when you felt that you became much farther apart in maturity than you were before?
2. Before going to college, you heard stories about what you might expect at college. Now that you have settled into the college scene, you realize that some of the stories that you heard were true while others were not. Suppose you have been invited to address a group of prospective college students about what they might expect to find in college. Organize your talk using comparison-contrast analysis as your pattern of development.

A Battle of Cultures

K. Connie Kang

K. Connie Kang was born in Korea in 1942, but grew up in Japan and the United States. After graduating from the School of Journalism at the University of Missouri, Kang went on to earn a master of science degree from the Medill School of Journalism at Northwestern University. During her more than three decades in journalism, this award-winning newspaperwoman has worked as a reporter, editor, foreign correspondent, columnist, and editorial writer for the San Francisco Examiner, *the* San Francisco Chronicle, *and United Press International. Currently, she is a reporter for the* Los Angeles Times. *Kang's career began in June 1964, when there were only a handful of Asians in the metropolitan newsrooms in the United States. Always mindful of her Asian heritage, she wrote about Asians and the issues affecting their communities long before they were considered newsworthy. In 1995 she published* Home Was the Land of Morning Calm: A Saga of a Korean American Family. *The following essay, which first appeared in* Asian Week *in May 1990, reminds us that we need both "cultural insight" and understanding if we are to "make democracy work" in a multicultural society. Notice how Kang uses comparison and contrast when presenting aspects of Korean- and African-American cultures in order to demonstrate her point.*

For Your Journal

People of different ethnic, racial, and cultural backgrounds sometimes find it difficult to achieve a common ground of understanding. What suggestion(s) do you have for what we can do, either personally or through our institutions, to increase understanding? Rather than composing an answer, make a list of several suggestions that you would like to contribute to a classroom discussion.

A volatile inner-city drama is taking place in New York where blacks have been boycotting Korean groceries for four months. 1

The recent attack on three Vietnamese men by a group of blacks who mistook them for Koreans has brought this long-simmering tension between two minority groups to the world's attention. Korean newspapers from San Francisco to Seoul have been running front-page stories. Non-Asian commentators around the country, whose knowledge of Korea may not be much more than images from the Korean war and the ridiculous television series "M.A.S.H.," are making all sorts of comments. 2

As I see it, the problem in the Flatbush area of Brooklyn started with cultural misunderstanding and was compounded by a lack of bilingual and bicultural community leaders to intervene quickly. 3

Frictions between Korean store owners in New York and blacks had been building for years. Korean merchants have been complaining about thefts. On the other hand, their black customers have been accusing immigrant store owners of making money in their neighborhoods without putting anything back into the community. They have also complained about store owners being brusque. Over the past eight years, there have been sporadic boycotts but none has lasted as long as the current one, which stemmed from an accusation by a black customer in January that she had been attacked by a store employee. In defense, the store owner has said the employee caught the woman stealing. 4

The attack on the Vietnamese on May 13 wasn't the first time one group of Asians has been mistaken for another in America. But the publicity surrounding the case has made this unfortunate situation a case study in inter-ethnic tension. 5

What's missing in this inner-city drama is cultural insight. 6

What struck me more than anything was a recent remark by a black resident: "The Koreans are a very, very rude people. They don't understand you have to smile." 7

I wondered whether her reaction would have been the same, had she known that Koreans don't smile at Koreans either with- 8 out a reason. To a Korean, a smile is not a facial expression he can turn on and off mechanically. Koreans have a word for it—mu-ttuk-ttuk-hada" (stiff). In other words, the Korean demeanor is "myu-po-jung"—lack of expression.

It would be an easy thing for blacks who are naturally friendly and gregarious to misunderstand Korean ways. 9

As a Korean American I've experienced this many times. Whenever I'm in Korea, which is often, I'm chided for smiling too much. "Why do you smile so easily? You act like a Westerner," people tell me. My inclination is to retort: "Why do you always have to look like you've got indigestion?" But I restrain myself because I know better. 10

In our culture, a smile is reserved for people we know and for a proper occasion. Herein lies a big problem when newcomers from Korea begin doing business in America's poor inner-city neighborhoods. 11

Culturally and socially, many newcomers from Korea, like other Asian immigrants, are ill-equipped to run businesses in America's inner cities. But because they are denied entry into mainstream job markets, they pool resources and open mom-and-pop operations in the only places where they can afford it. They work 14 and 15 hours a day, seven days a week, dreaming of the day when their children will graduate from prestigious schools and make their sacrifices worthwhile. 12

From the other side, inner-city African Americans must wonder how these new immigrants find the money to run their own businesses, when they themselves can't even get a small loan from a bank. Their hope of getting out of the poverty cycle is grim, yet they see newcomers living in better neighborhoods and driving new cars. 13

"They ask me, 'Where do you people get the money to buy a business?'" Bong-jae Jang, owner of one of the grocery stores being boycotted, told me. "How can I explain to my neighbors in my poor English the concept of our family system, the idea of 'kye' (uniquely Korean private money-lending system), our way of life?" 14

I think a little learning is in order on both sides. Korean immigrants, like other newcomers, need orientation before they leave their country as well as when they arrive in the United States. It's also important for Korean immigrants, like other Asians who live 15 in the United States, to realize that they are indebted to blacks for the social gains won by their civil rights struggle. They face less discrimination today because blacks have paved the way. Instead of looking down on their culture, it would be constructive to learn their history, literature, music and values and see our African American brothers and sisters in their full humanity.

I think it is also important to remind ourselves that while the 16
Confucian culture has taught us how to be good parents, sons and daughters and how to behave with people we know, it has not prepared us for living in a democracy. The Confucian ethos lacks the value of social conscience, which makes democracy work.

It isn't enough that we think of educating our children and send 17
them to the best schools. We need to think of other peoples' children, too. Most of all, we need to be more tolerant of other peoples' cultures. We need to celebrate our similarities as well as our differences.

Jang, the grocer, told me this experience has been painful but 18
he has learned an important lesson. "We Koreans must learn to participate in this society," he said. "When this is over, I'm going to reach out. I want to give part-time work to black youths."

He also told me that he has been keeping a journal. "I'm not a 19
writer but I've been keeping a journal," he said. "I want to write about this experience someday. It may help someone."

By reaching out, we can make a difference. The Korean gro- 20
cer's lesson is a reminder to us all that making democracy work in a multicultural society is difficult but we have no choice but to strive for it.

Questions for Study and Discussion

1. What is the "battle of cultures" named in the title? (Glossary: *Title*)
2. Why are the Korean grocery stores being boycotted by African American customers? (Glossary: *Cause and Effect*)
3. What is causing the conflict, according to Kang? How does she use comparison and contrast to argue her thesis? (Glossary: *Thesis*)

4. Why are most Asian immigrants ill-equipped to run businesses in the inner cities of the United States? Why are they indebted to African Americans?
5. How does Kang's point of view contribute to the effectiveness of the essay? (Glossary: *Point of View*)
6. What is it about their culture that makes it difficult for Koreans to adapt to life in a multicultural society?

Vocabulary

Refer to your dictionary to define the following words as they are used in this selection. Then use each word in a sentence of your own.

volatile (1)
boycotting (1)
bilingual (3)
intervene (3)
brusque (4)
sporadic (4)
gregarious (9)
inclination (10)
ethos (16)

Classroom Activity Using Comparison and Contrast

Review the discussion of analogy in the introduction to Comparison and Contrast (p. 394), and then create an analogy to explain your relationship with one of your parents or a relative with whom you are close.

Suggested Writing Assignments

1. Choose an ethnic group other than your own that lives in the United States. Compare and/or contrast its culture with your own. What could you do to understand the other culture better?
2. Choose a country that you have studied, visited, or at least read about. Compare who you are now with who you think you would be if you had been born in that country. How do you think you would be different? Why?

17

CAUSE AND EFFECT

Every time you try to answer a question that asks *why,* you engage in the process of *causal analysis*—you attempt to determine a *cause* or series of causes for a particular *effect.* When you try to answer a question that asks *what if,* you attempt to determine what *effect* will result from a particular *cause.* You will have frequent opportunity to use cause and effect analysis in the writing that you will do in college. For example, in history you might be asked to determine the causes for the breakup of the former Soviet Union; in political science you might be asked to determine the reasons why Bill Clinton won the 1996 presidential election; in sociology you might be asked to analyze the effects that the AIDS epidemic has had on sexual-behavior patterns among Americans; and in economics you might be asked to predict what will happen to our country if we do not address the problem of our national debt.

Determining causes and effects is usually thought-provoking and quite complex. One reason for this is that there are two types of causes: *immediate causes,* which are readily apparent because they are closest to the effect, and *ultimate causes,* which, being somewhat removed, are not so apparent and may perhaps even be hidden. Furthermore, ultimate causes may bring about effects which themselves become immediate causes, thus creating a *causal chain.* For example, consider the following causal chain: Sally, a computer salesperson, prepared extensively for a meeting with an important client (ultimate cause), impressed the client (immediate cause), and made a very large sale (effect). The chain did not stop there: the large sale caused her to be promoted by her employer (effect).

A second reason why causal analysis can be so complex is that an effect may have any number of possible or actual causes, and a cause may have any number of possible or actual effects. An upset stomach may be caused by eating spoiled food, but it may also be caused by overeating, flu, allergy, nervousness, pregnancy, or any combination of factors. Similarly, the high cost of electricity may have multiple effects: higher profits for utility companies, fewer sales of electrical appliances, higher prices for other products, and the development of alternative sources of energy.

Sound reasoning and logic, while present in all good writing, are central to any causal analysis. Writers of believable causal analysis examine their material objectively and develop their essays carefully. They examine methodically all causes and effects and evaluate them. They are convinced by their own examination of the material but are not afraid to admit other possible causes and effects. Above all, they do not let their own prejudices interfere with the logic of their analyses and presentations.

Because people are accustomed to thinking of causes with their effects, they sometimes commit an error in logic known as the "after this, therefore because of this" fallacy (in Latin, *post hoc, ergo propter hoc*). This fallacy leads people to believe that because one event occurred after another event the first event somehow caused the second; that is, they sometimes make causal connections that are not proven. For example, if students began to perform better after a free breakfast program was instituted at their school, one could not assume that the improvement was caused by the breakfast program. There could of course be any number of other causes for this effect, and a responsible writer on the subject would analyze and consider them all before suggesting the cause.

The Effects of the Telephone

John Brooks

John Brooks (1920–1993) wrote for the New Yorker *for forty years. Although he published respected novels such as* The Big Wheel *(1949) and* The Man Who Broke Things *(1958), he was best known for his nonfiction. His book on corporate culture in the 1980s,* The Takeover Game, *was a best-seller in 1987. Brooks was also a trustee of the New York Public Library for fifteen years. In the essay below, he identifies the telephone as the ultimate cause of numerous changes in society over a period of decades. After reading his analysis, see if you can identify some of the more immediate cause-and-effect relationships that would constitute causal chains leading from the telephone as ultimate cause to the end-effects he discusses.*

For Your Journal

The twentieth century has seen technology advance at a dizzying speed. Many new products or services have become integrated into our culture so thoroughly that it is now hard to envision what life was like sixty years ago, before television, or even twenty years ago, before personal computers. Yet many of these advances are dependent on services that were not around just one hundred years ago. Think about the last time your electricity or phone service went out. How did you feel? How dependent *are* we on our utilities?

What has the telephone done to us, or for us, in the hundred years of its existence? A few effects suggest themselves at once. It has saved lives by getting rapid word of illness, injury, or famine from remote places. By joining with the elevator to make possible the multistory residence or office building, it has made 1 possible—for better or worse—the modern city. By bringing about a quantum leap in the speed and ease with which information moves from place to place, it has greatly accelerated the rate of scientific and technological change and growth in industry. Beyond doubt it has crippled if not killed the ancient art of letter writing. It has made living alone possible for persons with normal social impulses; by so doing, it has played a role in one of the greatest social changes of this century, the breakup of the multigenerational household. It has made the waging of war chillingly more efficient than formerly. Perhaps (though not provably) it has prevented wars that might have arisen out of international misunderstanding caused by written communication. Or perhaps—again not provably—by magnifying and extending irrational personal conflicts based on voice contact, it has caused wars. Certainly it has extended the scope of human conflicts, since it impartially disseminates the useful knowledge of scientists and the babble of bores, the affection of the affectionate and the malice of the malicious.

But the question remains unanswered. The obvious effects just 2
cited seem inadequate, mechanistic; they only scratch the surface. Perhaps the crucial effects are evanescent and unmeasurable. Use of the telephone involves personal risk because it involves exposure; for some, to be "hung up on" is among the worst of fears; others dream of a ringing telephone and wake up with a pounding heart. The telephone's actual ring—more, perhaps, than any other sound in our daily lives—evokes hope, relief, fear, anxiety, joy, according to our expectations. The telephone is our nerve-end to society.

In some ways it is in itself a thing of paradox. In one sense a 3
metaphor for the times it helped create, in another sense the telephone is their polar opposite. It is small and gentle—relying on low voltages and miniature parts—in times of hugeness and violence. It is basically simple in times of complexity. It is so nearly human, re-creating voices so faithfully that friends or lovers need not identify themselves by name even when talking across oceans, that to ask its effects on human life may seem hardly more fruitful than to ask the effect of the hand or the foot. The Canadian philosopher Marshall McLuhan—one of the few who have addressed themselves to these questions—was perhaps not far from the mark when he spoke of the telephone as creating "a kind of extra-sensory perception."

Questions for Study and Discussion

1. Brooks opens his essay with a rhetorical question. (Glossary: *Rhetorical Question*) Why is the question difficult, if not impossible, to fully answer?
2. Brooks says that telephones and elevators made modern cities possible, but he does little to illustrate this statement. (Glossary: *Illustration*) How did these two inventions pave the way for the development of modern cities? Provide an example of how this influence might have worked.
3. Brooks characterizes the effects of personal use of the telephone as the "crucial" effects. Why do they make charting the overall effects of the telephone so difficult?
4. Brooks says that the telephone is "a metaphor for the times it helped create" (3). (Glossary: *Figurative Language*) What does he mean? What aspect of modern society does the telephone represent?
5. Brooks describes the telephone as being "nearly human" and equates its effects on human life to those of hands and feet. What do you think he means by this? Do you agree with his assessment? Why, or why not?

Vocabulary

Refer to your dictionary to define the following words as they are used in this selection. Then use each word in a sentence of your own.

quantum (1)
impartially (1)
disseminates (1)
mechanistic (2)
evanescent (2)
paradox (3)
polar (4)

Classroom Activity Using Cause and Effect

In preparing to write a cause-and-effect essay, list two effects on society and two effects on personal behavior of a common item that is important in our society. For example, a car could be said to have the following effects:

SOCIETY:

development of an asphalt-road–based infrastructure
expansion of the size and influence of the petroleum and insurance industries

PERSONAL:

convenient transportation
freedom and independence

Suggested Writing Assignments

1. Write an essay on the effects of computers on society. Computers are already having an enormous impact on society as a whole as well as on how we live our daily lives. For example, telecommuting, in which a worker works at home and communicates with coworkers via phone, modem, and fax, has the potential to eliminate the need for much of the work force to live near cities. What other effects do you see? Which do you think are the most important to society? Which are the most important to you personally? Be sure to explain your reasoning.
2. There is often more than one cause for an event. Make a list of at least six possible causes for one of the following:

   an upset victory in a game or competition
   your excellent performance on an exam
   an injury you suffered
   changing your major
   a quarrel you had with a friend

   Examine your list, and identify the causes that seem most probable. Which of these are immediate causes, and which are ultimate causes? Using this material, write a short cause-and-effect essay on one of the topics.

I Refuse to Live in Fear

Diana Bletter

Diana Bletter is an American presently living in Israel. She was born in New York in 1957 and received a degree in comparative literature from Cornell University in 1978. A freelance writer since her graduation, with the exception of a year she spent on staff with the National Lampoon, *Bletter's many articles have appeared in well-known periodicals such as the* International Herald Tribune *and* Newsday. *She is also the author of* The Invisible Thread: A Portrait of Jewish American Women, *which was nominated for a national Jewish book award in 1989. Bletter and Samia Zina, the friend she mentions in her essay, helped organized Dove of Peace, a friendship group for Arab and Jewish women. The following selection was first published in the November 1996 issue of* Mademoiselle. *As you finish reading it, consider how Bletter's final paragraph offers an ironic twist to what might be a more expected cause-and-effect relationship between terrorism and fear.*

For Your Journal

Think about how you reacted to the news that the Atlanta Olympic Park and Oklahoma City bombings were most likely acts of domestic terrorism. Have those events altered the way you look at your surroundings? If so, how? Do you feel safe from the threat of terrorism?

For most of my life, I thought a shoe box was just a shoe box. Until the afternoon I discovered that it could also be considered a lethal weapon. 1

This is what happened: I had just gone shopping for shoes—one of my favorite pastimes—in the small Mediterranean town of Nahariyya in northern Israel, where I've lived for the last five years. I sat down on a bench to change into my new purchase. I was so busy admiring my feet that I left the shoe box (with my old shoes) on the bench. Fifteen minutes later, I suddenly remembered it and turned back. When I approached the street, I saw crowds of people, barricades and at least five policemen. 2

"What happened?" I asked. 3

"Everyone's been evacuated. Someone reported a suspicious object on a bench down the street." 4

"Oh, no!" I shouted. "My shoes!" 5

Had I arrived even a few seconds later, a special bomb squad—complete with robot—would have imploded my shoe box to deactivate what could have been a bomb hidden inside. The policeman shook his finger at me. "This is the Middle East!" he said angrily. "You can't be careless like that!" 6

Reality Bites, Hard

Moving to Israel from America's tranquil suburbia has taught me about living with the threat of terrorism, something we Americans—after the bomb at Atlanta's Olympic Games and the explosion of TWA Flight 800—are finally being forced to think about on our own turf. The brutal fact of a terrorist attack is that it shatters the innocent peace of our days, the happy logic of our lives. It inalterably changes the way we live. 7

I can no longer daydream as I walk down a street—now I know that, to stay alive, I have to remain aware of who and what surrounds me. As my fiancé always tells me, "Your eyes are your best friends!" and I use them to keep track of emergency exits, the closest windows, the nearest heavy object that could be used in self-defense. 8

I used to be a reflexive litter-grabber—in my hometown, I never hesitated to pick up a coffee cup from the sidewalk and toss it in a nearby garbage can. In Israel, I've learned not to touch litter and to stay away from garbage cans—on several occasions, bombs have been placed in them. If I see a knapsack, shopping bag or—yes—a shoe box left unattended, I now do three things: One, ask 9 passersby if they forgot the package; two, get away from it as fast as I can; and three, report it to the police.

Necessary Inconveniences

Living in a country where terrorism is always a possibility means that at every entrance to a public place, guards search every bag. I forgot this the first time I walked into Nahariyya's lone department store; a guard stopped me to look through my pocketbook. "How could I have shoplifted?" I asked. "I haven't set foot in the store." Then I remembered that in America, people worry about what someone might sneak *out* of a store; in Israel, people worry what weapons or bombs someone might sneak *in* to a store. 10

The first few days after a terrorist attack seem very quiet. Since all of Israel is only the size of New Jersey, everybody usually knows someone who was hurt or killed. The nation slips into mourning: People avoid going out, attending parties, sitting in cafés. 11

Gradually, though, daily life returns to normal. Israelis (and now, Americans) have to prove again and again to potential terrorists that we're not giving in to our fears. If we voluntarily restrict our movements and our lives, terrorists have vanquished us. 12

During the latest hostilities in Lebanon (whose border is about seven miles from Nahariyya), Samia Zina, my dear friend—and a Muslim Arab—dreamed about me, one of those vivid dreams that seems prophetic when you wake. She dreamed that the fighting had forced her to flee her home, and that I'd hidden her and her children in my house (and I certainly would have, had the nightmare been a reality). The next day, Samia popped by to tell me her dream and give me the two stuffed chickens she'd been moved to cook for me. 13

"Thank you," I said, astonished by the food and the dream. "But I know you would have hidden me, too." 14

Terrorists attempt to divide people by fear, but in our community they've brought so-called enemies together: Even Arabs and Jews watch out for each other in public places, knowing that terrorists target everyone. By resisting the temptation to become paranoid and isolated, by sticking up for one another, we remain undefeated. 15

Questions for Study and Discussion

1. Bletter's shoe box story provides an effective glimpse of life in a society threatened by terrorism. What connotation does an unattended shoe box carry with it in Israel? (Glossary: *Connotation/Denotation*) How does it differ from a shoe box in the United States? (Glossary: *Comparison and Contrast*)
2. Why does Bletter quote the policeman's response to her carelessness? (Glossary: *Dialogue*) Why is it important for the reader to "hear" what he said?
3. Why is daydreaming a dangerous activity in public places in Israel? What pieces of information are vital to perceive in one's surroundings?
4. What does Samia Zina's dream symbolize to Bletter? (Glossary: *Symbol*) Why is her relationship with Zina important to the effectiveness of the essay?
5. How is terrorism defeated? What is the cause-and-effect relationship between terrorism and the way Bletter says one should live one's life?
6. What is Bletter's tone in her essay? (Glossary: *Tone*) Explain your answer.

Vocabulary

Refer to your dictionary to define the following words as they are used in this selection. Then use each word in a sentence of your own.

imploded (6)
suburbia (7)
vanquished (12)
prophetic (13)
paranoid (15)

Classroom Activity Using Cause and Effect

Develop a causal chain for each of the following cause-and-effect pairs:

terrorism/fear
giving a speech/anxiety
party/excitement
vacation/relaxation

Then mix two of the pairs. For example, develop a causal chain for vacation/anxiety. Be prepared to discuss your answers with the class.

Suggested Writing Assignments

1. According to Bletter, terrorism succeeds only if it frightens and divides the general public. It is therefore important to show terrorists that "we're not giving in to our fears" (12). Terrorism is an extreme example, but we all face events and situations in our lives that cause fear, and we must learn to control or moderate our fear in order to succeed or, at times, even to function. Write a cause-and-effect essay in which you present something that frightens you, how and why it frightens you, and how you control the involuntary effect—fear.
2. Write a cause-and-effect essay that explores some of the effects of your choice of where to live on how you live your life. Is your area urban or rural? Is crime a problem or not? How easy is it to get around? Do you like where you live?

HALFWAY TO DICK AND JANE

Jack Agueros

Jack Agueros was born in Harlem in 1934. As a Puerto Rican in New York City, he became very aware of the problems that people of other ethnic groups faced as they moved into American society. Some of those problems are examined in "Halfway to Dick and Jane," which comes from Agueros's book The Immigrant Experience: The Anguish of Becoming American *(1971). As you read the essay, note how deliberately he sets up the cause-and-effect relationship in paragraph 7 and marks his discussion of that relationship with a distinct shift in writing style and tone.*

FOR YOUR JOURNAL

Think back on the books that you read as a child. Which ones were important to you and left a lasting impression? What made them unforgettable?

I am an only child. My parents and I always talked about my becoming a doctor. The law and politics were not highly regarded in my house. Lawyers, my mother would explain, had to defend people whether they were guilty or not, while politicians, my father would say, were all crooks. A doctor helped everybody, rich and poor, white and black. If I became a doctor, I could study hay fever and find a cure for it, my godmother would say. Also, I could take care of my parents when they were old. I like the idea of helping, and for nineteen years my sole ambition was to study medicine. 1

My house had books, not many, but my parents encouraged me to read. As I became a good reader they bought books for me and never refused me money for their purchase. My father once built a bookcase for me. It was an important moment, for I had 2 always believed that my father was not too happy about my being a bookworm. The atmosphere at home was always warm. We seemed to be a popular family. We entertained frequently, with two standing parties a year—at Christmas and for my birthday. Parties were always large. My father would dismantle the beds and move all the furniture so that the full two rooms could be used for dancing. My mother would cook up a storm, particularly at Christmas. *Pasteles, lechon asado, arroz con gandules,* and a lot of *coquito* to drink (meat-stuffed plantain, roast pork, rice with pigeon peas, and coconut nog). My father always brought in a band. They played without compensation and were guests at the party. They ate and drank and danced while a Victrola covered the intermissions. One year my father brought home a whole pig and hung it in the foyer doorway. He and my mother prepared it by rubbing it down with oil, orègano, and garlic. After preparation, the pig was taken down and carried over to a local bakery where it was cooked and returned home. Parties always went on till daybreak, and in addition to the band, there were always volunteers to sing and declaim poetry.

My mother kept an immaculate household. Bedspreads (chenille seemed to be very in) and lace curtains, washed at home like everything else, were hung up on huge racks with rows of tight nails. The racks were assembled in the living room, and the moisture from the wet bedspreads would fill the apartment. In a sense, that seems to be the lasting image of that period of my life. The house was clean. The neighbors were clean. The streets, with few cars, were clean. The buildings were clean and uncluttered with people on the stoops. The park was clean. The visitors to my house were clean, and the relationships that my family had with other Puerto Rican families, and the Italian families that my father had met through baseball and my mother through the garment center, were clean. Second Avenue was clean and most of the apartment windows had awnings. There was always music, there seemed to be no rain, and snow did not become slush. School was fun, we wrote essays about how grand America was, we put up hunchbacked cats at Halloween, we believed Santa Claus visited everyone. I believed everyone was Catholic. I grew up with dogs, nightingales, my godmother's guitar, rocking chair, cat, guppies, my father's occasional roosters, kept in a cage on the fire escape. Laundry delivered and collected by horse and wagon, fruits and vegetables sold the same way, windowsill refrigeration 3 in winter, iceman and box in summer. The police my friends, likewise the teachers.

4 In short, the first seven or so years of my life were not too great a variation on Dick and Jane, the schoolbook figures who, if my memory serves me correctly, were blond Anglo-Saxons, not immigrants, not migrants like the Puerto Ricans, and not the children of either immigrants or migrants.

5 My family moved in 1941 to Lexington Avenue into a larger apartment where I could have my own room. It was a light, sunny, railroad flat on the top floor of a well-kept building. I transferred to a new school, and whereas before my classmates had been mostly black, the new school had few blacks. The classes were made up of Italians, Irish, Jews, and a sprinkling of Puerto Ricans. My block was populated by Jews, Italians, and Puerto Ricans.

6 And then a whole series of different events began. I went to junior high school. We played in the backyards, where we tore down fences to build fires to cook stolen potatoes. We tore up whole hedges, because the green tender limbs would not burn when they were peeled, and thus made perfect skewers for our stolen "mickies." We played tag in the abandoned buildings, tearing the plaster off the walls, tearing the wire lath off the wooden slats, tearing the wooden slats themselves, good for fires, for kites, for sword fighting. We ran up and down the fire escapes playing tag and over and across many rooftops. The war ended and the heavy Puerto Rican migration began. The Irish and the Jews disappeared from the neighborhood. The Italians tried to consolidate east of Third Avenue.

7 What caused the clean and open world to end? Many things. Into an ancient neighborhood came pouring four to five times more people than it had been designed to hold. Men who came running at the promise of jobs were jobless as the war ended. They were confused. They could not see the economic forces that ruled their lives as they drank beer on the corners, reassuring themselves of good times to come while they were hell-bent toward alcoholism. The sudden surge in numbers caused new resentments, and prejudice was intensified. Some were forced to live in cellars, and were then characterized as cave dwellers. Kids came who were confused by the new surroundings; their Puerto Rican-ness forced us against a mirror asking, "If they are Puerto Ricans, what are we?" and thus they confused us. In our confusion we were sometimes pathetically reaching out, sometimes

pathologically striking out. Gangs. Drugs. Wine. Smoking. Girls. Dances and slow-drag music. Mambo. Spics, Spooks, and Wops. Territories, brother gangs, and war councils establishing rules for right of way on blocks and avenues and for seating in the local theater. Pegged pants and zip guns. Slang.

Dick and Jane were dead, man. Education collapsed. Every 8
classroom had ten kids who spoke no English. Black, Italian, Puerto Rican relations in the classroom were good, but we all knew we couldn't visit one another's neighborhoods. Sometimes we could not move too freely within our own blocks. On 109th, from the lamp post west, the Latin Aces, and from the lamp post east, the Senecas, the "club" I belonged to. The kids who spoke no English became known as Marine Tigers, picked up from a popular Spanish song. (The Marine Tiger and the Marine Shark were two ships that sailed from San Juan to New York and brought over many, many migrants from the island.)

The neighborhood had its boundaries. Third Avenue and east, 9
Italian. Fifth Avenue and west, black. South, there was a hill on 103rd Street known locally as Cooney's Hill. When you got to the top of the hill, something strange happened: America began, because from the hill south was where the "Americans" lived. Dick and Jane were not dead: they were alive and well in a better neighborhood.

When, as a group of Puerto Rican kids, we decided to go swim- 10
ming to Jefferson Park Pool, we knew we risked a fight and a beating from the Italians. And when we went to La Milagrosa Church in Harlem, we knew we risked a fight and a beating from the blacks. But when we went over Cooney's Hill, we risked dirty looks, disapproving looks, and questions from the police like, "What are you doing in this neighborhood?" and "Why don't you kids go back where you belong?"

Where we belonged! Man, I had written compositions about 11
America. Didn't I belong on the Central Park tennis courts, even if I didn't know how to play? Couldn't I watch Dick play? Weren't these policemen working for me too? . . .

Questions for Study and Discussion

1. What does the title "Halfway to Dick and Jane" mean? (Glossary: *Title*) Why is it an effective title?

2. What was Agueros's early childhood like? Why does he describe it in such detail? (Glossary: *Details* and *Description*)
3. Agueros says in the third paragraph: "There was always music, there seemed to be no rain, and snow did not become slush." Why does he use exaggeration here?
4. What, besides his family's move to Lexington Avenue, caused Agueros's ideal world to change so drastically?
5. What does Agueros mean when he says "Dick and Jane were dead, man" (8)?
6. What happens to the Puerto Ricans when they leave "their" neighborhood?
7. What is the cause and effect in Agueros's essay?

Vocabulary

Refer to your dictionary to define the following words as they are used in this selection. Then use each word in a sentence of your own.

compensation (2)
declaim (2)
immaculate (3)
consolidate (6)
pathologically (7)

Classroom Activity Using Cause and Effect

William V. Haney has developed the following test to determine your ability to analyze accurately evidence that is presented to you. After completing Haney's test, discuss your answers with other members of your class.

THE UNCRITICAL INFERENCE TEST

DIRECTIONS

1. You will read a brief story. Assume that all of the information presented in the story is definitely accurate and true. Read the story carefully. You may refer back to the story whenever you wish.

2. You will then read statements about the story. Answer them in numerical order. DO NOT GO BACK to fill in answers or to change answers. This will only distort your test score.
3. After you read carefully each statement, determine whether the statement is:

   a. "T"—meaning: On the basis of the information presented in the story the statement is DEFINITELY TRUE.
   b. "F"—meaning: On the basis of the information presented in the story the statement is DEFINITELY FALSE.
   c. "?"—meaning: The statement MAY be true (or false) but on the basis of the information presented in the story you cannot be definitely certain. (If any part of the statement is doubtful, mark the statement "?".)

4. Indicate your answer by circling either "T" or "F" or "?" opposite the statement.

THE STORY

Babe Smith has been killed. Police have rounded up six suspects, all of whom are known gangsters. All of them are known to have been near the scene of the killing at the approximate time that it occurred. All had substantial motives for wanting Smith killed. However, one of these suspected gangsters, Slinky Sam, has positively been cleared of guilt.

STATEMENTS ABOUT THE STORY

1. Slinky Sam is known to have been near the scene of the killing of Babe Smith.	T	F	?
2. All six of the rounded-up gangsters were known to have been near the scene of the murder.	T	F	?
3. Only Slinky Sam has been cleared of guilt.	T	F	?
4. All six of the rounded-up suspects were near the scene of Smith's killing at the approximate time that it took place.	T	F	?
5. The police do not know who killed Smith.	T	F	?
6. All six suspects are known to have been near the scene of the foul deed.	T	F	?

7. Smith's murderer did not confess of his own free will.	T	F	?
8. Slinky Sam was not cleared of guilt.	T	F	?
9. It is known that the six suspects were in the vicinity of the cold-blooded assassination.	T	F	?

Suggested Writing Assignments

1. Write a cause-and-effect essay in which you identify how prejudice develops, using Agueros's essay as a reference. For instance, how would overcrowding and high unemployment in a neighborhood contribute to general prejudice toward its inhabitants? Also identify ways in which prejudice can be stopped.
2. Write an essay about the neighborhood of your childhood. How has the neighborhood changed? What has caused the changes?

HOW NOT TO LOSE FRIENDS OVER MONEY

Lois Duncan

Lois Duncan is a versatile writer with more than five hundred periodical articles to her credit, in addition to books of both fiction and nonfiction. Young adults know her primarily for her novels of mystery, suspense, and the supernatural. She has also written books for younger children, including some books of poetry. Adult readers, particularly women, recognize her as a columnist for Woman's Day. *In 1982 she published* Chapters: My Growth as a Writer. *Duncan was born in 1934 in Philadelphia, received her B.A. from the University of New Mexico, and currently lives in Albuquerque. In the essay below, she identifies a cause-and-effect relationship in her first few paragraphs that serves as the underlying rationale for each of the solutions she goes on to discuss. Notice, however, that each of these solutions introduces its own stated or implied cause-and-effect relationship as well.*

FOR YOUR JOURNAL

One of Shakespeare's best-known quotes is "Neither a borrower nor a lender be." How do you feel about lending friends money? Have money issues ever caused tension between you and any of your friends?

When I was in the third grade, a girl named Olivia borrowed money from me to buy a Coke. She never paid it back. I was too embarrassed to ask for it. I didn't want my friend to think I didn't trust her. 1

One day Olivia was absent from school. She had moved to Philadelphia, and my money had gone with her. I was outraged! 2

Many years later, I am still outraged. I wake in the night with the feel of Olivia's throat in my hands! Surpassing my fury, however, is contempt for my eight-year-old self because I did not stand up to that pigtailed shyster and demand what was mine. 3

I'd like to say that the experience taught me a lesson. But the sad truth is I still have problems with friends and money. Almost everyone I know has similar difficulties. The stickiest situations seem to be those in which the amounts are so small that it doesn't seem worth the risk of alienating a friend to make a fuss. At the same time, we all resent being treated unfairly, and our buried hostility often threatens the very friendship we are struggling so hard to preserve. 4

As Dr. Signey Rosenblum, professor of psychology and psychiatry at the University of New Mexico, explains, "Money is important not just for what it can buy, but for what it may symbolize—power, social status, even love. When a friend takes advantage of us financially, it is hard to be objective. Subconsciously, we get the message that we are not important enough to that person to merit fair treatment." 5

What seems fair to one person, however, often seems totally unfair to another. A candid discussion may help, but differences in values cannot always be resolved. In some cases, you simply have to decide how much a friendship is worth—and act accordingly. But most of these problems can be handled successfully—sometimes with surprising ease. 6

I consulted psychologists and counselors on this issue, but found that some of the best advice came from women who had learned to cope through trial and error. Here are their solutions to ten common money problems that come between friends: 7

1. A companion suggests splitting a restaurant tab in half when her share is much larger than yours. Randy and Sally get together for a long, gossipy lunch at least once a month. Randy, who is perennially on a diet, always orders a salad and coffee, while skinny Sally goes for broke with veal scallopini and a lavish dessert. Many times, she also has a glass or two of wine. When the bill arrives, Sally always says, "Let's just split it, OK?" Although Randy's meal usually cost about a third of Sally's, she's reluctant to appear cheap. 8

"I used to tell myself that such inequities even out in the long run," Randy says, "but they *don't.* The person who orders the 9 most expensive dish on the menu one day is usually the one who does it the next time too."

Her solution is a pocket calculator. "Before Sally can suggest going halfsies," she says, "I offer to do the accounting. I tell her I love to use this nifty gadget my husband gave me for my birthday. Then I do a quick calculation and plunk down cash to cover my share; Sally pays the rest. She's never complained so maybe she just hates to do arithmetic." 10

2. You become involved in an unequal gift exchange. Nobody expects the presents she receives to cost exactly the same as those she gives, but a wide disparity is embarrassing for both parties. Some women avoid this problem by getting friends to agree on a maximum amount in advance. This can only work, however, when the gift exchange is an established tradition. 11

"The most distressing situations occur when you're taken by surprise," says Reneé, a schoolteacher. "The day school let out for Christmas, a colleague stopped me to say she had a little gift for me in her car. I had nothing for her, so I rushed out and bought a pair of lovely earrings on my lunch hour. Her present turned out to be a dime-store joke gift. She thanked me profusely for the earrings, but it was obvious that she was embarrassed—and so was I." 12

If this were to happen again, Reneé says she'd open the package before deciding on an appropriate form of reciprocation. "I might not give a present at all," she says. "Instead, I could invite her over for eggnog during the holidays or ask her to be my guest at a Christmas program. Every gesture of friendship doesn't have to be repaid in kind." 13

Many other women agreed. Said one: "I think people should give what they want to and can afford—without worrying overmuch about equality of cost. When you're hung up on monetary value, you're not *giving,* you're *trading.* If you're going to do that, you might just as well exchange checks for equal amounts." 14

3. A passenger in your car neglects to pay her share of expenses. "When Amy and I took a long trip in my car," says Phyllis, "I just assumed we'd each pay half. Amy did her part as she saw it, paying for every other tank of gas. But when the radiator hose burst in Salt Lake City, I paid for the replacement. When the fuel pump went out in Chicago, I paid for repairs. The cost of a tune- 15 up and oil change before the trip and the car wash when we got back—I absorbed them all."

Phyllis realizes that she was partly to blame for not discussing finances in advance, but will not make the same mistake again. "When I use my own car for business," she says, "I get reimbursed twenty cents a mile. So the next time I furnish transportation for a pleasure trip, I'll make it clear from the start that I expect my companion to contribute ten cents a mile." 16

A more common problem arises when one person provides regular chauffeur service for a friend who never chips in for gas. "I don't think most nondrivers mean to take advantage," one woman said; "they just don't realize how much it costs to operate a car. One day I pulled into a self-service station and asked my friend to finish filling the tank while I dashed to the ladies' room. By the time I got back, she was staring in horror at the price gauge and fishing for her wallet." 17

4. You are given a check that bounces. When Roberta went out to dinner and the theater with a friend from out of town, she paid both bills with her credit card. Lisa then paid for her share of the evening's expenses by giving Roberta a check—one that later bounced. 18

"It was very awkward," Roberta recalls. "I considered absorbing the whole cost of the evening myself just to avoid embarrassing Lisa. I knew, though, that if I did that I'd always feel resentful. Our friendship would be bound to suffer—and Lisa wouldn't even know why." 19

Roberta handled the situation by sending Lisa the bounced check, along with a lighthearted note saying, "If your bank is like mine, they botched up your account. Shall we try again?" Lisa responded with a note of apology and another check—one that cleared—and the incident was never referred to by either woman again. 20

5. A friend invites you to participate in an activity that costs more than you can afford—or want—to spend. "When my college roommate asked me to be matron-of-honor at her wedding, I was flattered," Louise recalls. "My immediate response was, 'I'd love to!' After I hung up, however, I began to realize how much expense was involved. The dress had to be specially made, with new shoes dyed to match—and the wedding was halfway across 21 the country. My husband and I were saving to go to Europe and couldn't afford to do both."

Louise decided to be honest. "I called her back and explained the situation," she says. "My roommate was hurt, of course, and I felt bad about that. But I'd have felt even worse if I'd sacrificed the trip I'd been looking forward to for so long." 22

Not everyone I polled agreed with this approach. All thought Louise had been right to turn down the invitation, but some felt she could have done it more kindly. "She might have said that previous plans made it impossible for her to attend the wedding," one woman suggested. "She didn't have to explain that the plans were for a trip to Europe. In Louise's place, I'd have tried to spare my friend's feelings by not mentioning that this milestone in her life was not nearly as important to me as it was to her." 23

6. You are asked to contribute toward a gift for someone you don't know well or don't like. "Every week it seems," says Eileen, "I'm asked to make a contribution toward another gift or a party to celebrate somebody's new baby, birthday or retirement. I resent forking over money for people I hardly know, but how do you get out of it when everybody else is doing it?" 24

The simplest solution: just say no. "It doesn't sound that bad if you do it regretfully," one woman suggests. "'I wish I could contribute,' I'd say, 'but it just isn't possible.'" 25

Another friend handles this problem differently. "If the honored person is somebody I'd be buying for anyway," she explains, "I donate the amount I'd have spent myself. If it's someone I know only slightly, I give a few coins as a token. What I *don't* do is apologize for my contribution—or let myself be pressured into giving more than I feel is really appropriate." 26

7. A friend is able to spend far more—or far less—than you can. We don't choose friends on the basis of how much money they have, of course, but vast differences can be disturbing to both sides. Erin, for example, is single and earns a very good salary. Her friend Pat, a divorced mother of three, is struggling to make ends meet. 27

"We're both theater buffs," Erin explains. "And I'd gladly pay for two tickets just to have Pat's company at plays and concerts. But she won't go anywhere unless she can pay her own way. I hate to go alone, so we both stay home. It all seems so silly." 28

Pat sees the situation differently. "After an unhappy marriage to a domineering man," she says, "it's very important to me to carry my own weight. I'm not comfortable in any relationship where all I do is take." 29

The impasse was finally broken when Erin moved recently. Pat's children were with their father so she took a picnic lunch to her friend's new place, then spent the day helping her unpack and get settled. "I was so grateful," Erin says, "that I persuaded Pat to let me return the favor in my own way—with season tickets to our little theater group. I think she is beginning to recognize that she contributes as much to our friendship as I do." 30

8. Social pressure forces you to overspend. "When you're out with a group, weird things can happen to common sense," says Valerie. "For example, my husband and I often meet after work on Fridays at a club we belong to. We always run into people we know there, and inevitably somebody snatches the bar tab and says, 'I'll get this round; you can get the next one.' That seems fair on the surface, but a single beer is my husband's limit and I drink club soda. More often than not, we find ourselves hosting a round of double martinis for casual acquaintances." 31

After several such occasions, Valerie and her husband agreed to refuse to be shoved into "picking up a round" again. "Now when a second batch of drinks is ordered, we just insist, 'No more for us, thanks,'" Valerie says. "We don't make excuses or offer prolonged explanations. If the person who paid for the first round gets upset, that's *his* problem. *Ours* is solved!" 32

9. A friend asks personal questions about your finances. "Some people don't seem to mind being asked how much they earn or what they spend for their clothes, but I am offended by such questions," says Heather. "To my way of thinking, our finances are nobody else's business. Yet when we were first married, a nosy acquaintance asked what my husband's salary was and I was so startled I actually *told* her!" 33

In the years since, Heather has developed techniques for putting money snoops in their place. "It's a state secret," she tells them, or "I can't remember what I paid." Today, if someone is crass enough to ask about her husband's salary, she responds with questions of her own: "Why do you care about that? Are you planning to apply for his job?" 34

10. A companion borrows money and "forgets" to repay it. 35
Large loans are seldom the issue; they're usually treated as business transactions, with the terms spelled out on paper. But many women suffer in silence over problems like Carol's. "My friend Ginny is always short of cash," she says. "I hate to recall how often I've 'loaned' her a dollar or two for a drink or a movie. Each loan is so small I'd feel really cheap making a big deal out of it; still, I *do* resent the fact that she never pays me back."

Carol admits to being "too inhibited or something" to demand 36
repayment, but she has resolved to stop giving money to Ginny. "The last time she asked for five dollars to pay for her dry cleaning, I just told her I couldn't spare it."

Another woman suggests a gutsier response. "When somebody 37
cops out on repaying a loan, I turn the tables by requesting one myself," she says. "'I left home without my wallet,' I'll say. 'Can you lend me enough to cover lunch?' Then, when the money is safely in hand, I am struck by a sudden realization. 'Why, this is exactly the amount I loaned you last week! How convenient! Now you won't have to repay me!'" She says it works like a charm.

Then, there's the *really* gutsy solution in which we simply ask, 38
straight out, in no-nonsense language, for what is rightfully ours. This, I've come to realize, is what I should have done with Olivia. If I were to run into her today, I like to think I'd have the strength of character to step right up and say, "Olivia, I have an overwhelming desire for a soda. How about giving me the cash I loaned you forty years ago?"

If she did hand it over, I think I might forgive her and renew 39
our friendship—despite the fact that you can no longer buy a Coke with a dime!

Questions for Study and Discussion

1. Duncan's anecdote about Olivia and the Coke seems trivial, yet she says she is still outraged many years later. (Glossary: *Anecdote*) How do the anecdote and Duncan's response to it serve to communicate the importance of Duncan's topic?
2. Why is money such a volatile topic between friends? Why do you think Duncan's best sources were laypeople, not psy-

chologists and counselors? What does Duncan gain by using concrete examples provided by friends instead of abstract theories provided by experts in the field? (Glossary: *Concrete/ Abstract* and *Illustration*)

3. In her seventh point, Duncan presents an ultimate cause—Pat is getting over an unhappy marriage and is struggling with self-esteem and finances—leading to an immediate cause—Pat resents Erin's attempts to pay for her theater tickets—leading to the effect that both stay home from the theater. Summarize the cause-and-effect relationship of four of Duncan's other "common money problems." What are the causes of the problems? What are the effects?
4. How does Duncan organize her essay? (Glossary: *Organization*) Do you think that her organization is an effective way to present her information? Why, or why not?
5. Duncan presents more than one method for handling three of her ten situations. Which ones are they? Are such choices a help or a hindrance? Why do you think she presented the different viewpoints?
6. Duncan concludes with her solution to the annoying situation presented at the beginning of her essay. Is presenting this solution an effective technique for ending her essay? (Glossary: *Beginnings and Endings*) Why, or why not?

Vocabulary

Refer to your dictionary to define the following words as they are used in this selection. Then use each word in a sentence of your own.

inequities (9)	milestone (23)
disparity (11)	impasse (30)
reciprocation (13)	crass (34)

Classroom Activity Using Cause and Effect

Develop a causal chain in which you examine the potential ramifications of an action of yours. Identify each part of the chain. For example, you decided you wanted to do well in the course (ultimate cause), so you got started on a research project early (immediate cause), which enabled you to write several drafts of your paper (immediate cause), which earned you an A for the project (effect), which earned you an excellent grade in the class (effect), which enabled you to take the advanced seminar you wanted (effect).

Suggested Writing Assignments

1. Friendship is a complex give-and-take relationship that changes and evolves over time. Duncan focuses on money, but changes are caused by a variety of issues and situations. Write an essay about a sudden change you had in a close friendship. What do you think was the ultimate cause? What was the immediate cause? What were the effects? What is your current relationship with this person?
2. Write an essay in which you establish the cause-and-effect relationship that exists in one of the following pairs:

winter and depression	health and happiness
poverty and crime	old age and wisdom
wealth and power	good looks and popularity

18

ARGUMENT

The word *argument* probably brings to mind a verbal disagreement of the sort that everyone has at least witnessed, if not participated in directly. Such disputes are occasionally satisfying; you can take pleasure in knowing you have converted someone to your point of view. More often, though, verbal arguments are inconclusive, frustrating you when you realize that you have failed to make your position understood, or enraging you when you feel that your opponent has been stubborn and unreasonable. Such dissatisfaction is inevitable, because verbal arguments generally arise spontaneously and so cannot be thoughtfully planned or researched; it is difficult to come up with appropriate evidence on the spur of the moment or to find the language that will make a point hard to deny. Indeed, it is often not until later, in retrospect, that the convincing piece of evidence, the forcefully phrased assertion, finally comes to mind.

Written arguments share common goals with spoken ones: They attempt to convince a reader to agree with a particular point of view, to make a particular decision, to pursue a particular course of action. Written arguments, however, involve the presentation of well-chosen evidence and the artful control of language. Writers of arguments have no one around to dispute their words directly, so they must imagine their probable audience in order to predict the sorts of objections that may be raised. Written arguments, therefore, must be much more carefully planned—the writer must settle in advance on a specific, sufficiently detailed thesis or proposition. There is a greater need for organization, for choosing the most effective types of evidence from all that is available, for determining the strategies of rhetoric, language, and style that will best suit the argument's subject, its purpose, and its thesis, as well as ensure its effect on the intended audience. In the end, however, such work can be far more satisfying than spontaneous oral argument.

Most people who specialize in the study of arguments identify two essential categories: persuasion and logic. *Persuasive appeals* are directed at readers' emotions, at their subconscious, even at their biases and prejudices. These appeals involve diction, slanting, figurative language, analogy, rhythmic patterns of speech, and the establishment of a tone that will encourage a positive response. It is important to understand, as well, that persuasion very often attempts to get the audience to take action. Examples of persuasive argument are found in the exaggerated claims of advertisers and the speechmaking of political and social activists.

Logical appeals, on the other hand, are directed primarily at the audience's intellectual faculties, understanding, and knowledge. Such appeals depend on the reasoned movement from assertion to evidence to conclusion and on an almost mathematical system of proof and counterproof. Logical argument, unlike persuasion, does not normally impel its audience to action. Logical argument is commonly found in scientific or philosophical articles, in legal decisions, and in technical proposals.

Most arguments, however, are neither purely persuasive nor purely logical. A well-written newspaper editorial, for example, will present a logical arrangement of assertions and evidence, but it will also employ striking diction and other persuasive patterns of language to reinforce its effectiveness. Thus, the kinds of appeals a writer emphasizes depend on the nature of the topic, the thesis or proposition of the argument, the writer's purpose, the various kinds of support (for example, evidence, opinions, examples, facts, statistics) offered, and a thoughtful consideration of the audience. Knowing the differences between persuasive and logical appeals is, then, essential in learning both to read and to write arguments.

True arguments make assertions about which there is a legitimate and recognized difference of opinion. It is unlikely that anyone will ever need to convince a reader that falling in love is a rare and intense experience, that crime rates should be reduced, or that computers are changing the world; most everyone would agree with such assertions. But not everyone would agree that women experience love more intensely than men, that reinstating the death penalty will reduce the incidence of crime, or that computers are changing the world for the worse; these assertions are arguable and admit of differing perspectives. Similarly, a leading heart specialist might argue in a popular magazine that too many doctors are advising patients to have pacemakers implanted when the devices are not necessary; the editorial writer for a small-town newspaper could write urging that a local agency supplying food to poor families be given a larger percentage of the tax budget; in a long and complex book, a foreign-policy specialist might attempt to prove that the current administration exhibits no consistent policy in its relationship with other countries and that the Department of State needs to be overhauled. No matter what its forum or its structure, an argument has as its chief purpose the detailed setting forth of a particular point of view and the rebuttal of any opposing views.

Argumentation frequently utilizes the other rhetorical strategies. In your efforts to argue convincingly, you may find it necessary to define, to compare and contrast, to analyze causes and effects, to classify, to describe, to narrate. Nevertheless, it is the writer's attempt to convince, not explain, that is of primary importance in an argumentative essay. In this respect, it is helpful to keep in mind that there are two basic patterns of thinking and presenting our thoughts that are followed in argumentation: *induction* and *deduction.*

Inductive reasoning, the more common type of reasoning, moves from a set of specific examples to a general statement. In doing so, the writer makes what is known as an *inductive leap* from the evidence to the generalization. For example, after examining enrollment statistics, we can conclude that students do not like to take courses offered early in the morning or late in the afternoon.

Deductive reasoning, on the other hand, moves from a general statement to a specific conclusion. It works on the model of the *syllogism,* a simple three-part argument that consists of a major premise, a minor premise, and a conclusion, as in the following example:

a. All women are mortal. *(major premise)*
b. Jeanne is a woman. *(minor premise)*
c. Jeanne is mortal. *(conclusion)*

Obviously, a syllogism will fail to work if either of the premises is untrue.

a. All living creatures are mammals. *(major premise)*
b. A butterfly is a living creature. *(minor premise)*
c. A butterfly is a mammal. *(conclusion)*

The problem is immediately apparent. The major premise is obviously false: many living creatures are not mammals, and a butterfly happens to be one of the non-mammals. Consequently, the conclusion is invalid.

Writing an argument is a difficult assignment but one that can be very rewarding. By nature, an argument must be carefully reasoned and thoughtfully structured in order to have maximum effect. Allow yourself, therefore, enough time to think about your thesis, to gather the evidence you need, and to draft, revise, edit, and proofread your essay. Fuzzy thinking, confused expression, and poor organization will be immediately evident to your reader and will diminish your chances for completing the assignment successfully. The following steps will remind you of some key features of arguments and will help you sequence your activities as you research and write.

1. Determine the Thesis or Proposition

Begin by deciding on a topic that interests you and about which there is some significant difference of opinion or about which you have a number of questions. Find out what's in the news about your topic, what people are saying about it, what authors and instructors are emphasizing as important intellectual arguments. As you pursue your research, consider what assertion or assertions you can make about the topic you choose. The more specific this thesis or proposition, the more directed your research can become and the more focused your ultimate argument will be. Don't hesitate along the way to modify or even reject an initial thesis as your continued research warrants.

A thesis can be placed anywhere in an argument, but it is probably best while learning to write arguments to place the statement of your controlling idea somewhere near the beginning of your composition. Explain the importance of the thesis, and make clear to your reader that you share a common concern or interest in this issue. You may wish to state your central assertion directly in your first or second paragraph so that your reader will have no doubt or confusion about your position. You may, as well, wish to lead off with a particularly striking piece of evidence, to capture your reader's interest.

2. Take Account of Your Audience

In no other type of writing is the question of audience more important than in argumentation. The tone you establish, the type of diction you choose, the kinds of evidence you select to buttress your assertions, and indeed the organizational pattern you follow can influence your audience to trust you and believe your assertions. If you judge the nature of your audience accurately, respect its knowledge of the subject, and correctly envision whether or not it is likely to be hostile, neutral, complacent, or receptive, you will be able to tailor the various aspects of your argument appropriately.

3. Gather the Necessary Supporting Evidence

For each point of your argument, be sure to provide appropriate and sufficient evidence: verifiable facts and statistics, illustrative examples and narratives, or quotations from authorities. Don't overwhelm your reader with evidence, but don't skimp either; it is important to demonstrate your command of the topic and control of the thesis by choosing carefully among all the evidence at your disposal.

4. Settle on an Organizational Pattern

Once you think you have sufficient evidence to make your assertion convincing, consider how best to organize your argument. To some extent, your organization will depend on your method of reasoning: inductive, deductive, or a combination of the two. For example, is it necessary to establish a major premise before moving on to discuss a minor premise? Should most of your evidence precede your direct statement of an assertion, or follow it? Will induction work better with the particular audience you have targeted? As you present your primary points, you may find it effective to move from least important to most important, or from least familiar to most familiar. A scratch outline can help; but often a writer's most crucial revisions in an argument involve rearranging its components into a sharper, more coherent order. Very often it is difficult to tell what that order should be until the revision stage of the writing process.

5. Consider Refutations to Your Argument

As you proceed with your argument, you may wish to take into account well-known and significant opposing arguments. To ignore opposing views would be to suggest to your readers any one of the following: You don't know about them; you know about them and are obviously and unfairly weighting the arguments in your favor; or you know about them and have no reasonable answers for them. Grant the validity of opposing arguments or refute them, but respect your reader's intelligence by addressing the objections to your assertion. Your readers will in turn respect you for doing so.

6. Avoid Faulty Reasoning

Have someone read your argument for errors in judgment and for faulty reasoning. Sometimes others can see easily what you can't see because you are so intimately tied to your assertion. Review the following list of errors in reasoning, making sure that you have not committed any of them.

OVERSIMPLIFICATION: A foolishly simple solution to what is clearly a complex problem: *We have a balance-of-trade deficit because foreigners make better products than we do.*

HASTY GENERALIZATION: In inductive reasoning, a generalization that is based on too little evidence or on evidence that is not representative: *My grandparents eat bran flakes for breakfast, just like most older folks do.*

POST HOC, ERGO PROPTER HOC: "After this, therefore because of this." Confusing chance or coincidence with causation. The fact that one event comes after another does not necessarily mean that the first event caused the second: *I went to the hockey game last night. The next thing I knew I had a cold.*

BEGGING THE QUESTION: Assuming in a premise something that needs to be proven: *Parking fines work because they keep people from parking illegally.*

FALSE ANALOGY: Making a misleading analogy between logically unconnected ideas: *If we can clone mammals, we should be able to find a cure for cancer.*

EITHER/OR THINKING: Seeing only two alternatives when there may in fact be other possibilities: *Either you love your job or you hate it.*

NON SEQUITUR: "It does not follow." An inference or conclusion that is not clearly related to the established premises or evidence: *She is very sincere. She must know what she's talking about.*

7. Conclude Forcefully

In the conclusion of your essay, be sure to restate your position in new language, at least briefly. Besides persuading your reader to accept your point of view, you may also want to encourage some specific course of action. Above all, your conclusion should not introduce new information that may surprise your reader; it should seem to follow naturally, almost seamlessly, from the series of points that have been carefully established in the body of the essay. Don't overstate your case, but at the same time don't qualify your conclusion with the use of too many words or phrases like *I think, in my opinion, maybe, sometimes,* and *probably.* These words can often make you sound indecisive and fuzzy-headed rather than rational and sensible.

As They Say, Drugs Kill

Laura Rowley

Laura Rowley was born in Oak Lawn, Illinois, in 1965, and graduated from the University of Illinois at Champaign–Urbana in 1987 with a degree in journalism. While in college, Rowley was the city editor of the Daily Illini. *After graduation she worked at the* United Nations Chronicle *in New York City. Rowley now works as a freelance writer and hopes someday to travel and work in Africa under the auspices of either the United Nations or the Peace Corps. In the following essay, which first appeared in* Newsweek on Campus *in 1987, Rowley argues against substance abuse by recounting a particularly poignant experience. Although her narrative appeals primarily to readers' emotions, she nonetheless attempts to persuade without preaching.*

For Your Journal

What is your own best argument against the use of drugs? If you could tell a story that argues against drugs and that would persuade young people not to use them, what would that story be? It might be a personal story, or a story about friends who were unlucky in their use of drugs, or a story that you read about or saw portrayed in the movies or on television.

The fastest way to end a party is to have someone die in the middle of it. 1

At a party last fall I watched a 22-year-old die of cardiac arrest after he had used drugs. It was a painful, undignified way to die. And I would like to think that anyone who shared the experience would feel his or her ambivalence about substance abuse dissolving. 2

This victim won't be singled out like Len Bias as a bitter ex- 3
ample for "troubled youth." He was just another ordinary guy celebrating with friends at a private house party, the kind where they roll in the keg first thing in the morning and get stupefied while watching the football games on cable all afternoon. The living room was littered with beer cans from last night's party—along with dirty socks and the stuffing from the secondhand couch.

And there were drugs, as at so many other college parties. The 4
drug of choice this evening was psilocybin, hallucinogenic mushrooms. If you're cool you call them "'shrooms."

This wasn't a crowd huddled in the corner of a darkened room 5
with a single red bulb, shooting needles in their arms. People played darts, made jokes, passed around a joint and listened to the Grateful Dead on the stereo.

Suddenly, a thin, tall, brown-haired young man began to gasp. 6
His eyes rolled back in his head, and he hit the floor face first with a crash. Someone laughed, not appreciating the violence of his fall, thinking the afternoon's festivities had finally caught up with another guest. The laugh lasted only a second, as the brown-haired guest began to convulse and choke. The sound of the stereo and laughter evaporated. Bystanders shouted frantic suggestions:

"It's an epileptic fit, put something in his mouth!" 7

"Roll him over on his stomach!" 8

"Call an ambulance; God, somebody breathe into his mouth." 9

A girl kneeling next to him began to sob his name, and he 10
seemed to moan.

"Wait, he's semicoherent." Four people grabbed for the tele- 11
phone, to find no dial tone, and ran to use a neighbor's. One slammed the dead phone against the wall in frustration—and miraculously produced a dial tone.

But the body was now motionless on the kitchen floor. "He 12
has a pulse, he has a pulse."

"But he's not breathing!" 13

"Well, get away—give him some f——ing air!" The three or 14
four guests gathered around his body unbuttoned his shirt.

"Wait—is he OK? Should I call the damn ambulance?" 15

A chorus of frightened voices shouted, "Yes, yes!" 16

"Come on, come on, breathe again. Breathe!" 17

Over muffled sobs came a sudden grating, desperate breath that 18
passed through bloody lips and echoed through the kitchen and living room.

"He's had this reaction before—when he did acid at a concert last 19
spring. But he recovered in 15 seconds . . . ," one friend confided.

The rest of the guests looked uncomfortably at the floor or 20
paced purposelessly around the room. One or two whispered, "Oh, my God," over and over, like a prayer. A friend stood next to me, eyes fixed on the kitchen floor. He mumbled, just audibly, "I've seen this before. My dad died of a heart attack. He had the same look. . . ." I touched his shoulder and leaned against a wall, repeating reassurances to myself. People don't die at parties. People don't die at parties.

Eventually, no more horrible, gnashing sounds tore their way 21
from the victim's lungs. I pushed my hands deep in my jeans pockets wondering how much it costs to pump a stomach and how someone could be so careless if he had had this reaction with another drug. What would he tell his parents about the hospital bill?

Two uniformed paramedics finally arrived, lifted him onto a 22
stretcher and quickly rolled him out. His face was grayish blue, his mouth hung open, rimmed with blood, and his eyes were rolled back with a yellowish color on the rims.

The paramedics could be seen moving rhythmically forward 23
and back through the small windows of the ambulance, whose lights threw a red wash over the stunned watchers on the porch. The paramedics' hands were massaging his chest when someone said, "Did you tell them he took psilocybin? Did you tell them?"

"No, I . . ." 24

"My God, so tell them—do you want him to die?" Two people 25
ran to tell the paramedics the student had eaten mushrooms five minutes before the attack.

It seemed irreverent to talk as the ambulance pulled away. My 26
friend, who still saw his father's image, muttered, "That guy's dead." I put my arms around him half to comfort him, half to stop him from saying things I couldn't believe.

The next day, when I called someone who lived in the house, I 27
found that my friend was right.

My hands began to shake and my eyes filled with tears for some- 28
one I didn't know. Weeks later the pain has dulled, but I still can't

unravel the knot of emotion that has moved from my stomach to my head. When I told one friend what happened, she shook her head and spoke of the stupidity of filling your body with chemical substances. People who would do drugs after seeing that didn't value their lives too highly, she said.

But others refused to read any universal lessons from the incident. Many of those I spoke to about the event considered him the victim of a freak accident, randomly struck down by drugs as a pedestrian might be hit by a speeding taxi. They speculated that the student must have had special physical problems; what happened to him could not happen to them. 29

Couldn't it? Now when I hear people discussing drugs I'm haunted by the image of him lying on the floor, his body straining to rid itself of substances he chose to take. Painful, undignified, unnecessary—like a wartime casualty. But in war, at least, lessons are supposed to be learned, so that old mistakes are not repeated. If this death cannot make people think and change, that will be an even greater tragedy. 30

Questions for Study and Discussion

1. What is Rowley's purpose in this essay? What does she want us to believe? What does she want us to do? (Glossary: *Purpose*)
2. Rowley uses an extended narrative example to develop her argument. How does she use dialogue, diction choices, and appropriate details to enhance the drama of her story? (Glossary: *Narration, Dialogue, Diction,* and *Details*)
3. What does Rowley gain by sharing this powerful experience with her readers? How did Rowley's friends react when she told them her story?
4. Why do you think Rowley chose not to name the young man who died? In what ways is this young man different from Len Bias, the talented basketball player who died of a drug overdose after signing a contract with the Boston Celtics?
5. What in Rowley's tone—her attitude toward her subject and audience—particularly contributes to the persuasiveness of

the essay? Cite examples from the selection that support your conclusion. (Glossary: *Tone*)

6. How did Rowley's opening paragraph affect you? What would have been lost had she combined the first two paragraphs? (Glossary: *Beginnings and Endings*)
7. For what audience do you suppose Rowley wrote this essay? In your opinion, would most readers be convinced by what Rowley says about drugs? Are you convinced? Why, or why not? (Glossary: *Audience*)

Vocabulary

Refer to your dictionary to define the following words as they are used in this selection. Then use each word in a sentence of your own.

ambivalence (2)	gnashing (21)
stupefied (3)	irreverent (26)
convulse (6)	unravel (28)
semicoherent (11)	speculated (29)
audibly (20)	tragedy (30)

Classroom Activity Using Argument

Choose one of the following position statements for an exercise in argumentation:

1. More parking spaces should be provided on campus for students.
2. English should be declared the official language of the United States.
3. Performance standards in our schools should be raised.
4. The Food and Drug Administration takes too long to decide whether or not new drugs will be made available to consumers.
5. Job placement is not the responsibility of colleges and universities.

Make a list of the types of information and evidence you would need in order to write an argumentative essay on the topic you chose. Indicate where and how you might obtain this information.

Suggested Writing Assignments

1. Write a persuasive essay in which you support or refute the following proposition:

   > Television advertising is in large part responsible for Americans' belief that over-the-counter drugs are cure-alls.

   Does such advertising, in fact, promote drug dependence and/or abuse?
2. Write an essay in which you argue against either drinking or smoking. What would drinkers and smokers claim are the benefits of their habits? What are the key arguments against these types of substance abuse? Use examples from your personal experience or from your reading to document your essay.
3. What is the most effective way to bring about social change and to influence societal attitudes? Concentrating on the sorts of changes you have witnessed over the last ten years, write an essay in which you describe how best to influence public opinion.

In Praise of the F Word

Mary Sherry

Mary Sherry was born in Bay City, Michigan, and received her B.A. from Rosary College in River Forest, Illinois. She owns her own research and publishing company specializing in information for economic and development organizations. Sherry also teaches in adult-literacy programs and has written essays on educational problems for various newspapers, including the Wall Street Journal *and* Newsday. *In the following essay, reprinted from* Newsweek, *Sherry takes a provocative stance—that the threat of flunking is a "positive teaching tool." She believes students would all be better off if they had a "healthy fear of failure," and she marshals a series of logical appeals to both clarify and support her argument.*

For Your Journal

Comment on what you see as the relationship between learning and grades. Is too much attention paid to grades by faculty and students at the expense of learning? Or are grades not seen as important enough?

Tens of thousands of 18-year-olds will graduate this year and be handed meaningless diplomas. These diplomas won't look any different from those awarded their luckier classmates. Their validity will be questioned only when their employers discover that these graduates are semiliterate. 1

Eventually a fortunate few will find their way into educational-repair shops—adult-literacy programs, such as the one where I teach basic grammar and writing. There, high-school graduates and high-school dropouts pursuing graduate-equivalency certificates will learn the skills they should have learned in school. 2

They will also discover they have been cheated by our educational system.

As I teach, I learn a lot about our schools. Early in each session I ask my students to write about an unpleasant experience they had in school. No writers' block here! "I wish someone would have made me stop doing drugs and made me study." "I liked to party and no one seemed to care." "I was a good kid and didn't cause any trouble, so they just passed me along even though I didn't read well and couldn't write." And so on. 3

I am your basic do-gooder, and prior to teaching this class I blamed the poor academic skills our kids have today on drugs, divorce and other impediments to concentration necessary for doing well in school. But, as I rediscover each time I walk into the classroom, before a teacher can expect students to concentrate, he has to get their attention, no matter what distractions may be at hand. There are many ways to do this, and they have much to do with teaching style. However, if style alone won't do it, there is another way to show who holds the winning hand in the classroom. That is to reveal the trump card of failure. 4

I will never forget a teacher who played that card to get the attention of one of my children. Our youngest, a world-class charmer, did little to develop his intellectual talents but always got by. Until Mrs. Stifter. 5

Our son was a high-school senior when he had her for English. "He sits in the back of the room talking to his friends," she told me. "Why don't you move him to the front row?" I urged, believing the embarrassment would get him to settle down. Mrs. Stifter looked at me steely-eyed over her glasses. "I don't move seniors," she said. "I flunk them." I was flustered. Our son's academic life flashed before my eyes. No teacher had ever threatened him with that before. I regained my composure and managed to say that I thought she was right. By the time I got home I was feeling pretty good about this. It was a radical approach for these times, but, well, why not? "She's going to flunk you," I told my son. I did not discuss it any further. Suddenly English became a priority in his life. He finished out the semester with an A. 6

I know one example doesn't make a case, but at night I see a parade of students who are angry and resentful for having been passed along until they could no longer even pretend to keep up. Of average intelligence or better, they eventually quit school, 7 concluding they were too dumb to finish. "I should have been held back" is a comment I hear frequently. Even sadder are those students who are high-school graduates who say to me after a few weeks of class, "I don't know how I ever got a high-school diploma."

Passing students who have not mastered the work cheats them and the employers who expect graduates to have basic skills. We excuse this dishonest behavior by saying kids can't learn if they come from terrible environments. No one seems to stop to think that—no matter what environments they come from—most kids don't put school first on their list unless they perceive something is at stake. They'd rather be sailing. 8

Many students I see at night could give expert testimony on unemployment, chemical dependency, abusive relationships. In spite of these difficulties, they have decided to make education a priority. They are motivated by the desire for a better job or the need to hang on to the one they've got. They have a healthy fear of failure. 9

People of all ages can rise above their problems, but they need to have a reason to do so. Young people generally don't have the maturity to value education in the same way my adult students value it. But fear of failure, whether economic or academic, can motivate both. 10

Flunking as a regular policy has just as much merit today as it did two generations ago. We must review the threat of flunking and see it as it really is—a positive teaching tool. It is an expression of confidence by both teachers and parents that the students have the ability to learn the material presented to them. However, making it work again would take a dedicated, caring conspiracy between teachers and parents. It would mean facing the tough reality that passing kids who haven't learned the material—while it might save them grief for the short term—dooms them to long-term illiteracy. It would mean that teachers would have to follow through on their threats, and parents would have to stand behind them, knowing their children's best interests are indeed at stake. This means no more doing Scott's assignments for him because he might fail. No more passing Jodi because she's such a nice kid. 11

This is a policy that worked in the past and can work today. A wise teacher, with the support of his parents, gave our son the opportunity to succeed—or fail. It's time we return this choice to all students. 12

Questions for Study and Discussion

1. What is the "F" word discussed in the essay? Does referring to it as the "F" word increase the effectiveness of the essay? Why?
2. Who is Sherry's audience? (Glossary: *Audience*) Is it receptive to the "F" word? Explain your answer.
3. What is Sherry's thesis? (Glossary: *Thesis*) What evidence does she use to support it?
4. What does Sherry accomplish in paragraph 3?
5. In what way is Sherry qualified to comment on the potential benefits of flunking students? Do you think her induction is accurate?
6. Why does Sherry think flunking is a valuable tool for educators and for students?

Vocabulary

Refer to your dictionary to define the following words as they are used in this selection. Then use each word in a sentence of your own.

validity (1)
semiliterate (1)
impediments (4)
trump (4)
testimony (9)

Classroom Activity Using Argument

An essential component of a good argument is reliable evidence, but what are the various ways that a writer can test evidence? For example, if you learned that more than one source made the same claim, would that be enough to convince you of the validity of the claim? Why, or why not? Would you be convinced if you found out that the person who made the claim was an authority on the subject? What kinds of evidence are convincing for you?

Suggested Writing Assignments

1. Think of something that involves short-term pain or sacrifice, but can lead to a brighter future. For example, exercising involves pain now, but it may help to save one from health problems down the road. Studying and writing papers when you'd rather be having fun or even sleeping may seem painful, but a college degree leads to personal growth and development. Even if the benefits are obvious, imagine a skeptical audience and write an argument in favor of the short-term sacrifice over the long-term consequences of avoiding it.
2. Write an essay in which you argue against Sherry's thesis. In what ways is flunking bad for students? Are there techniques more positive than a "fear of failure" that can be used to motivate students?

The Right to Fail

William Zinsser

William Zinsser was born in New York City in 1922. After graduating from Princeton University, he worked for the New York Herald Tribune, *first as a features writer and later as its drama and film critic. He has also taught writing at Yale University and served as the general editor of the Book-of-the-Month Club. He is currently the series editor for The Writer's Craft Series—publications of talks given by writers sponsored by the Book-of-the-Month Club and the New York Public Library. Zinsser's own published works cover many aspects of contemporary American culture, but he is best known as the author of lucid and accessible books about writing, including* Writing with a Word Processor *(1983),* Writing to Learn *(1988), and* On Writing Well *(1976), a perennial favorite for college-writing courses as well as the general public. Zinsser now teaches at the New School for Social Research in New York. In the following essay, he argues the benefits of failing or dropping out and uses numerous examples to illustrate his points. As you read, consider the degree to which these examples serve as compelling evidence for the validity of Zinsser's point of view.*

For Your Journal

Think about a time when, despite your best efforts, you could be said to have failed at something. Perhaps it was a loss in sports, a poor performance on a test in school, or even a vocational or educational path that you tried but were not able to see through for whatever reason. How did it feel to fail? Were you able to learn from the experience? How long did it take you to put it behind you?

I like "dropout" as an addition to the American language because it's brief and it's clear. What I don't like is that we use it almost entirely as a dirty word. 1

We only apply it to people under twenty-one. Yet an adult who spends his days and nights watching mindless TV programs is more of a dropout than an eighteen-year-old who quits college, with its frequently mindless courses, to become, say, a VISTA volunteer. For the young, dropping out is often a way of dropping in. 2

To hold this opinion, however, is little short of treason in America. A boy or girl who leaves college is branded a failure—and the right to fail is one of the few freedoms that this country does not grant its citizens. The American dream is a dream of "getting ahead," painted in strokes of gold wherever we look. Our advertisements and TV commercials are a hymn to material success, our magazine articles a toast to people who made it to the top. Smoke the right cigarette or drive the right car—so the ads imply—and girls will be swooning into your deodorized arms or caressing your expensive lapels. Happiness goes to the man who has the sweet smell of achievement. He is our national idol, and everybody else is our national fink. 3

I want to put in a word for the fink, especially the teen-age fink, because if we give him time to get through his finkdom—if we release him from the pressure of attaining certain goals by a certain age—he has a good chance of becoming our national idol, a Jefferson or a Thoreau, a Buckminster Fuller or an Adlai Stevenson, a man with a mind of his own. We need mavericks and dissenters and dreamers far more than we need junior vice-presidents, but we paralyze them by insisting that every step be a step up to the next rung of the ladder. Yet in the fluid years of youth, the only way for boys and girls to find their proper road is often to take a hundred side trips, poking out in different directions, faltering, drawing back, and starting again. 4

"But what if we fail?" they ask, whispering the dreadful word across the Generation Gap to their parents, who are back home at the Establishment, nursing their "middle-class values" and cultivating their "goal-oriented society." The parents whisper back: "Don't!" 5

What they should say is "Don't be afraid to fail!" Failure isn't fatal. Countless people have had a bout with it and come out stronger as a result. Many have even come out famous. History is strewn with eminent dropouts, "loners" who followed their 6 own trail, not worrying about its odd twists and turns because they had faith in their own sense of direction. To read their biographies is always exhilarating, not only because they beat the system, but because their system was better than the one that they beat.

Luckily, such rebels still turn up often enough to prove that individualism, though badly threatened, is not extinct. Much has been written, for instance, about the fitful scholastic career of Thomas P. F. Hoving, New York's former Parks Commissioner and now director of the Metropolitan Museum of Art. Hoving was a dropout's dropout, entering and leaving schools as if they were motels, often at the request of the management. Still, he must have learned something during those unorthodox years, for he dropped in again at the top of his profession. 7

His case reminds me of another boyhood—that of Holden Caulfield in J. D. Salinger's *The Catcher in the Rye,* the most popular literary hero of the postwar period. There is nothing accidental about the grip that this dropout continues to hold on the affections of an entire American generation. Nobody else, real or invented, has made such an engaging shambles of our "goal-oriented society," so gratified our secret belief that the "phonies" are in power and the good guys up the creek. Whether Holden has also reached the top of his chosen field today is one of those speculations that delight fanciers of good fiction. I speculate that he has. Holden Caulfield, incidentally, is now thirty-six. 8

I'm not urging everyone to go out and fail just for the sheer therapy of it, or to quit college just to coddle some vague discontent. Obviously it's better to succeed than to flop, and in general a long education is more helpful than a short one. (Thanks to my own education, for example, I can tell George Eliot from T. S. Eliot. I can handle the pluperfect tense in French, and I know that Caesar beat the Helvetii because he had enough frumentum.) I only mean that failure isn't bad in itself, or success automatically good. 9

Fred Zinnemann, who has directed some of Hollywood's most honored movies, was asked by a reporter, when *A Man for All Seasons* won every prize, about his previous film *Behold a Pale Horse,* which was a box-office disaster. "I don't feel any obligation to be successful," Zinnemann replied. "Success can be dangerous—you feel you know it all. I've learned a great deal from my failures." A similar point was made by Richard Brooks about 10 his ambitious money loser, *Lord Jim.* Recalling the three years of his life that went into it, talking almost with elation about the troubles that befell his unit in Cambodia, Brooks told me that he learned more about his craft from this considerable failure than from his many earlier hits.

It's a point, of course, that applies throughout the arts. Writers, playwrights, painters and composers work in the expectation of periodic defeat, but they wouldn't keep going back into the arena if they thought it was the end of the world. It isn't the end of the world. For an artist—and perhaps for anybody—it is the only way to grow. 11

Today's younger generation seems to know that this is true, seems willing to take the risks in life that artists take in art. "Society," needless to say, still has the upper hand—it sets the goals and condemns as a failure everybody who won't play. But the dropouts and the hippies are not as afraid of failure as their parents and grandparents. This could mean, as their elders might say, that they are just plumb lazy, secure in the comforts of an affluent state. It could also mean, however, that they just don't buy the old standards of success and are rapidly writing new ones. 12

Recently it was announced, for instance, that more than two hundred thousand Americans have inquired about service in VISTA (the domestic Peace Corps) and that, according to a Gallup survey, "more than three million American college students would serve VISTA in some capacity if given the opportunity." This is hardly the road to riches or to an executive suite. Yet I have met many of these young volunteers, and they are not pining for traditional success. On the contrary, they appear more fulfilled than the average vice-president with a swimming pool. 13

Who is to say, then, if there is any right path to the top, or even to say what the top consists of? Obviously the colleges don't have more than a partial answer—otherwise the young would not be so disaffected with an education that they consider vapid. Obviously business does not have the answer—otherwise the young would not be so scornful of its call to be an organization man. 14

The fact is, nobody has the answer, and the dawning awareness of this fact seems to me one of the best things happening in America today. Success and failure are again becoming individual visions, as they were when the country was younger, not rigid categories. Maybe we are learning again to cherish this right 15 of every person to succeed on his own terms and to fail as often as necessary along the way.

Questions for Study and Discussion

1. Zinsser wrote "The Right to Fail" more than twenty years ago. His reasoning and his argument remain sound, but at times his diction places him in a different era. (Glossary: *Diction*) Find the words that you perceive as being dated. What would their modern equivalents be?
2. How does Zinsser characterize society's definition of success? (Glossary: *Definition*) According to Zinsser, what must one do to fulfill this definition?
3. Look up "fink" in the dictionary. Why do you think Zinsser chose this word to characterize those who do not have the "sweet smell of achievement" (3)? In what way are those who are willing to risk failure—as defined by society—"finks"?
4. What is Zinsser's thesis? (Glossary: *Thesis*) Does he state it outright? If so, where? If not, how does he present it to the reader?
5. Zinsser argues that many people who are considered very successful have "failed" at various times in their careers. Why does Zinsser use movie directors to illustrate his point? (Glossary: *Illustration*) What makes them good examples?
6. Why does Zinsser use VISTA volunteers to represent those who are not pursuing society's definition of success? In what way might one say they are "dropping in," not dropping out?

Vocabulary

Refer to your dictionary to define the following words as they are used in this selection. Then use each word in a sentence of your own.

dissenters (4)	coddle (9)
strewn (6)	affluent (12)
eminent (6)	vapid (14)

Classroom Activity Using Argument

Which of the following syllogisms work well and which do not?

1. All of my CDs have blue lettering on them.
   I saw the new Youssou N'Dour CD the other day.
   The new Youssou N'Dour CD has blue lettering on it.
2. I have never lost a tennis match.
   I played a tennis match yesterday.
   I won my tennis match yesterday.
3. Surfers all want to catch the perfect wave.
   Jenny is a surfer.
   Jenny wants to catch the perfect wave.
4. Writers enjoy reading books.
   Bill enjoys reading books.
   Bill is a writer.
5. Cotton candy is an incredibly sticky kind of candy.
   Amy ate some incredibly sticky candy.
   Amy ate cotton candy.

Write two effective syllogisms of your own.

Suggested Writing Assignments

1. Based on your own experience, argue for or against the statement "You learn more from failure than you do from success." If you agree with this statement, do you think that you need to fail in order to eventually achieve more than you would have otherwise? If you disagree, what do you think success teaches you? How do you get strong and adaptable if all you encounter for a long time is success?
2. Zinsser's article is critical of the tyranny of the American dream of "getting ahead." Write an essay in which you discuss Americans' materialistic tendencies. When did we lose our ability to tell the difference between what we need and what we want? How would our quality of life improve if we were able to be content with fewer possessions? What changes would you propose to reduce the conspicuous-consumption mentality of our society?

Less Is More: A Call for Shorter Work Hours

Barbara Brandt

In her book Whole Life Economics: Revaluing Daily Life *(1993), Barbara Brandt writes extensively on how our society places too high a value on work and productivity and not enough on quality of life. The following excerpt argues that shorter working hours would actually benefit our society economically but would be difficult to implement. As you read the essay, pay particular attention to Brandt's reliance on statistics, examples, and expert testimony to bolster her argument. Note also that she addresses potential objections, indicating an awareness that her audience may be skeptical of her point of view.*

For Your Journal

Write two paragraphs, one pro and one con, in response to the following statement:

Work is nothing more than a source of income.

In your opinion, which paragraph is more convincing? Why?

America is suffering from overwork. Too many of us are too busy, trying to squeeze more into each day while having less to show for it. Although our growing time crunch is often portrayed as a personal dilemma, it is in fact a major social problem that has reached crisis proportions over the past 20 years. 1

The simple fact is that Americans today—both women and men—are spending too much time at work, to the detriment of their homes, their families, their personal lives, and their communities. The American Dream promised that our individual hard work paired with the advances of modern technology would bring about the good life for all. Glorious visions of the leisure 2 society were touted throughout the '50s and '60s. But now most people are working more than ever before, while still struggling to meet their economic commitments. Ironically, the many advances in technology, such as computers and fax machines, rather than reducing our workload, seem to have speeded up our lives at work. At the same time, technology has equipped us with "conveniences" like microwave ovens and frozen dinners that merely enable us to adopt a similar frantic pace in our home lives so we can cope with more hours at paid work.

A recent spate of articles in the mainstream media has focused on the new problems of overwork and lack of time. Unfortunately, overwork is often portrayed as a special problem of yuppies and professionals on the fast track. In reality, the unequal distribution of work and time in America today reflects the decline in both standard of living and quality of life for most Americans. Families whose members never see each other, women who work a double shift (first on the job, then at home), workers who need more flexible work schedules, and unemployed and underemployed people who need more work are all casualties of the crisis of overwork. 3

Americans often assume that overwork is an inevitable fact of life—like death and taxes. Yet a closer look at other times and other nations offers some startling surprises. 4

Anthropologists have observed that in pre-industrial (particularly hunting and gathering) societies, people generally spend 3 to 4 hours a day, 15 to 20 hours a week, doing the work necessary to maintain life. The rest of the time is spent in socializing, partying, playing, storytelling, and artistic or religious activities. The ancient Romans celebrated 175 public festivals a year in which everyone participated, and people in the Middle Ages had at least 115. 5

In our era, almost every other industrialized nation (except Japan) has fewer annual working hours and longer vacations than the United States. This includes all of Western Europe, where many nations enjoy thriving economies and standards of living equal to or higher than ours. Jeremy Brecher and Tim Costello, writing in *Z Magazine* (Oct. 1990), note that "European unions during the 1980s made a powerful and largely successful push to cut working hours. In 1987 German metalworkers struck and won a 37.5-hour week; many are now winning a 35-hour week. In 1990, hundreds of thousands of British workers have won a 37-hour week." 6

In an article about work-time in the *Boston Globe,* Suzanne Gordon notes that workers in other industrialized countries "enjoy—as a statutory right—longer vacations [than in the U.S.] from the moment they enter the work force. In Canada, workers are legally entitled to two weeks off their first year on the job. . . . After two or three years of employment, most get three weeks of vacation. After 10 years, it's up to four, and by 20 years, Canadian workers are off for five weeks. In Germany, statutes guarantee 18 days minimum for everyone, but most workers get five or six weeks. The same is true in Scandinavian countries, and in France." 7

In contrast to the extreme American emphasis on productivity and commitment, which results in many workers, especially in professional-level jobs, not taking the vacations coming to them, Gordon notes that "In countries that are America's most successful competitors in the global marketplace, all working people, whether lawyers or teachers, CEOs or janitors, take the vacations to which they are entitled by law. 'No one in West Germany,' a West German embassy's officer explains, 'no matter how high up they are, would ever say they couldn't afford to take a vacation. Everyone takes their vacation.'" 8

And in Japan, where dedication to the job is legendary, Gordon notes that the Japanese themselves are beginning to consider their national workaholism a serious social problem leading to stress-related illnesses and even death. As a result, the Japanese government recently established a commission whose goal is to promote shorter working hours and more leisure time. 9

Most other industrialized nations also have better family-leave policies than the United States, and in a number of other countries workers benefit from innovative time-scheduling opportunities such as sabbaticals. 10

While the idea of a shorter workweek and longer vacations sounds appealing to most people, any movement to enact shorter work-time as a public policy will encounter surprising pockets of resistance, not just from business leaders but even from some workers. Perhaps the most formidable barrier to more free time for Americans is the widespread mind-set that the 40-hour workweek, 8 hours a day, 5 days a week, 50 weeks a year, is a natural rhythm of the universe. This view is reinforced by the media's complete silence regarding the shorter work-time and more favorable vacation and family-leave policies of other countries. 11

This lack of information, and our leaders' reluctance to suggest that the United States can learn from any other nation (except workaholic Japan) is one reason why more Americans don't identify overwork as a major problem or clamor for fewer hours and more vacation. Monika Bauerlein, a journalist originally from Germany now living in Minneapolis, exclaims, "I can't believe that people here aren't rioting in the streets over having only two weeks of vacation a year."

A second obstacle to launching a powerful shorter work-time movement is America's deeply ingrained work ethic, or its modern incarnation, the workaholic syndrome. The work ethic fosters the widely held belief that people's work is their most important activity and that people who do not work long and hard are lazy, unproductive, and worthless. 12

For many Americans today, paid work is not just a way to make money but is a crucial source of their self-worth. Many of us identify ourselves almost entirely by the kind of work we do. Work still has a powerful psychological and spiritual hold over our lives—and talk of shorter work-time may seem somehow morally suspicious. 13

Because we are so deeply a work-oriented society, leisure-time activities—such as play, relaxation, engaging in cultural and artistic pursuits, or just quiet contemplation and "doing nothing"—are not looked on as essential and worthwhile components of life. Of course, for the majority of working women who must work a second shift at home, much of the time spent outside of paid work is not leisure anyway. Also, much of our non-work time is spent not just in personal renewal, but in building and maintaining essential social ties—with family, friends, and the larger community. 14

Today, as mothers and fathers spend more and more time on the job, we are beginning to recognize the deleterious effects—especially on our young people—of the breakdown of social ties and community in American life. But unfortunately, our nation reacts to these problems by calling for more paid professionals—more police, more psychiatrists, more experts—without recognizing the possibility that shorter work hours and more free time could enable us to do much of the necessary rebuilding and healing, with much more gratifying and longer-lasting results. 15

Of course, the stiffest opposition to cutting work hours comes not from citizens but from business. Employers are reluctant to 16 alter the 8-hour day, 40-hour workweek, 50 weeks a year because it seems easier and more profitable for employers to hire fewer employees for longer hours rather than more employees—each of whom would also require health insurance and other benefits—with flexible schedules and work arrangements.

Harvard University economist Juliet B. Schor, who has been studying issues of work and leisure in America, reminds us that we cannot ignore the larger relationship between unemployment and overwork: While many of us work too much, others are unable to find paid work at all. Schor points out that "workers who work longer hours lose more income when they lose their jobs. The threat of job loss is an important determinant of management's power on the shop floor." A system that offers only two options—long work hours or unemployment—serves as both a carrot and a stick. Those lucky enough to get full-time jobs are bribed into docile compliance with the boss, while the spectre of unemployment always looms as the ultimate punishment for the unruly. 17

Some observers suggest that keeping people divided into "the employed" and "the unemployed" creates feelings of resentment and inferiority/superiority between the two groups, thus focusing their discontent and blame on each other rather than on the corporations and political figures who actually dictate our nation's economic policies. 18

Our role as consumers contributes to keeping the average workweek from falling. In an economic system in which addictive buying is the basis for corporate profits, working a full 40 hours or more each week for 50 weeks a year gives us just enough time to stumble home and dazedly—almost automatically—shop; but not enough time to think about deeper issues or to work effectively for social change. From the point of view of corporations and policymakers, shorter work-time may be bad for the economy, because people with enhanced free time may begin to find other things to do with it besides mindlessly buying products. It takes more free time to grow vegetables, cook meals from scratch, sew clothes, or repair broken items than it does to just buy these things at the mall. 19

Any serious proposal to give employed Americans a break by cutting into the 8-hour work day is certain to be met with anguished cries about international competitiveness. The United States seems gripped by the fear that our nation has lost its economic dominance, and pundits, policymakers, and business lead- 20 ers tell us that no sacrifice is too great if it puts America on top again.

As arguments like this are put forward (and we can expect them to increase in the years to come), we need to remember two things. First, even if America maintained its dominance (whatever that means) and the economy were booming again, this would be no guarantee that the gains—be they in wages, in employment opportunities, or in leisure—would be distributed equitably between upper management and everyone else. Second, the entire issue of competitiveness is suspect when it pits poorly treated workers in one country against poorly treated workers in another; and when the vast majority of economic power, anyway, is in the control of enormous multinational corporations that have no loyalty to the people of any land. 21

Questions for Study and Discussion

1. According to Brandt, why has technology contributed to the problem of overwork in the United States instead of improving it?
2. What are some of the reasons that it will be difficult to enact a shorter workweek in the United States?
3. What does Brandt mean by the term "workaholic syndrome" in paragraph 12? How is it related to America's work ethic?
4. What is Brandt's thesis? (Glossary: *Thesis*) Is it stated or implied?
5. What does Brandt accomplish in paragraphs 5–9? Why is the information relevant to her argument?
6. Analyze the structure of Brandt's essay, paragraph by paragraph. How does she organize her essay in order to best argue her opinion? (Glossary: *Organization*)

Vocabulary

Refer to your dictionary to define the following words as they are used in this selection. Then use each word in a sentence of your own.

detriment (2)
spate (3)
statutory (7)
workaholism (9)
clamor (11)
deleterious (15)
determinant (17)
docile (17)
pundits (20)

Classroom Activity Using Argument

You may want to try to complete this activity over several class periods.

Find an editorial in your local newspaper or in a national paper that presents a view of an issue that you disagree with. Bring the editorial to class and reread it, study it for a few minutes, and then write a brief letter to the editor of the newspaper arguing against its position. Your letter should be brief; short letters have a better chance of being published than long ones.

During a subsequent class you may want to form groups of two to three students to share your letters and comment on the effectiveness of each other's arguments. Revise your letter, if necessary, and consider sending it to the newspaper for possible publication.

Suggested Writing Assignments

1. How long a workweek and how many weeks of vacation do you think represents the best compromise between productivity and adequate leisure time? Write an essay in which you argue for your "ideal" workweek. Imagine that your audience will be the management of a large corporation that currently maintains long workweeks and short vacations.
2. Write an argument paper in favor of fewer years of education in America, either in secondary school or college. How would students and the rest of society benefit? In what ways would it be better than maintaining the number of years that young people now devote to an education? Use Brandt's essay as a model, and be sure to acknowledge and effectively counter expected objections to each point you raise.

A City's Assault on Teen Pregnancy

Joe Loconte

Joe Loconte was born in 1961 and received his B.A. in journalism from the University of Illinois at Urbana. He worked at several daily newspapers and as senior news writer for Christianity Today *magazine before moving to* Policy Review: The Journal of American Citizenship, *where he now serves as deputy editor. He is currently working on a book about the impact of public money and government regulations on the delivery of social services by private nonprofit groups. Loconte is also a regular commentator on religious issues for National Public Radio's* All Things Considered. *The following selection appeared in the November–December 1996 edition of* Policy Review. *As you read Loconte's argument supporting the initiatives Indianapolis has undertaken to curb teen pregnancy, evaluate how his repeated references to the cause-and-effect relationship between teen pregnancy and social problems contribute to the essay's ability to convince.*

For Your Journal

People usually develop a personal morality by the time they reach the age when they are ready to leave home. Some develop moralities that do not conform with that demanded by society, but most of us strive to maintain some level of honor and honesty in our dealings with others. What influences helped to shape your own sense of morality? How large a role did your parents play? Did religion influence your personal development?

Eve Jackson taught "family life" classes to students in Hamilton Southeastern High School, a typical Indianapolis-area public school, for four years. They were troubling years for her Baptist conscience. 1

At the exact time when the hormones of adolescents are at flood tide, Jackson says, the most persuasive message they get about sex comes from their peers—and the message is: "Come on in, the water's fine." Other voices remain muffled. Teachers often ignore or play down a state requirement that they stress abstinence in sex-education classes. Church–state legal doctrine bans religious ideas about premarital sex from public schools. Says Jackson, "As much as I wanted to talk about God, I really couldn't." 2

And what she could talk about—responsible decision-making, peer pressure, self-esteem—had no more effect than a flashing yellow light on a lonely country road. "So many of them were sexually active. Every year I had a couple of students who had abortions," she says. "But I couldn't talk them out of being sexually involved." Jackson eventually left public education, developed a Bible-based abstinence program taught by high-school juniors and seniors, and brought it into 34 Catholic grade schools throughout the city. 3

Now the public schools—in a city with a teen pregnancy rate that has risen 40 percent over the last decade—want Jackson back. Mayor Steve Goldsmith has asked Jackson to bring her chastity program, "A Promise to Keep," into 150 public grade schools this fall. Stripped of its religious references, the program will recruit at least 100 high-school students to serve as advocates for abstinence. It's one of more than two dozen initiatives launched by the mayor in the last year, using his bully pulpit in an effort to reduce out-of-wedlock births. Citing its impact on crime, poverty, and welfare dependence, Goldsmith calls teen pregnancy "the most serious long-term issue facing this city. We can do nothing if we don't solve this problem." 4

Energize and Stigmatize

Unlike President Clinton's $30-million proposal to reduce illegitimacy, however, the mayor of the nation's 12th-largest city seems uninterested in expanding government services. Following a meeting last year that included the city's school superintendent, a 5 juvenile-court judge, and a county health director, Goldsmith mapped out a 27-point strategy for city-wide action. His aim: energize public opinion, the courts, and church and community groups to stigmatize out-of-wedlock births while supporting teen mothers.

The mayor intends to treat casual attitudes about teen pregnancy with the same tolerance that actor Jean-Claude Van Damme brings to flabbiness: Since studies show that roughly half of all teenage moms are impregnated by males older than 18, Goldsmith wants prosecutors to crack down on statutory rape. He plans to enforce laws requiring women to establish paternity as a condition of receiving welfare. He intends to publish monthly reports of teen pregnancies in every high school in the city. 6

And while local Planned Parenthood clinics seek to build "creative self-expression" through dance, art, and painting classes, Goldsmith is pressuring schools to ban pregnant teens and boys who have fathered children from extracurricular activities. He even has floated the idea of sending pregnant girls to separate schools altogether. 7

"Philosophically we're not in agreement," says Kathleen Baldwin, Planned Parenthood's director of education in Indianapolis. "They would define the problem largely as illegitimacy, and we would define it as limited opportunities for achievement." 8

Esperanza Zendejas, the superintendent of Indianapolis's public schools, opposes some of the mayor's school-based sanctions, but applauds his broad-based approach to attacking the problem of illegitimacy. "The fact that the city, as a city, is looking at teen pregnancy is extraordinary," she says. "It should be happening in every city in the nation." 9

It wouldn't be happening in Indianapolis without the active support of the religious community, Goldsmith says. Indeed, the mayor insists that the most dynamic partner in the assault on the culture of teen pregnancy—and all of the social problems it creates—will be churches and synagogues. 10

In February, he summoned 100 spiritual leaders—Protestant, Catholic, Jewish, Muslim, and Buddhist—to a summit on teen pregnancy. He asked them to speak out on the risks of sexual activity outside of marriage. More significantly, he challenged congregations to become personally involved with families on welfare by helping women to avoid more pregnancies, reunite with the father of their children, and get off of government assistance. 11

"The whole notion is to be more of a mentor and support group, not a candy store," says Richard Wiehe, the executive director of the Faith and Families project, a new effort to link congregations with welfare families.

The mayor wants religious groups to fight this culture war al- 12
most everywhere—even in city parks. Indianapolis now has 16 congregations managing 30 contracts to maintain public parks. In exchange, churches can sponsor events in the parks with minimal bureaucratic hassle. Goldsmith's explicit hope is that people of faith will form relationships with children who live in surrounding neighborhoods. "We could put police officers on every corner of the city," he says, "but if our people did not believe in God and basic moral values, then we would still not have a safe community."

Crime statistics seem to side with the mayor: Juvenile crime 13
in Indianapolis has increased nearly tenfold in the last decade, and 75 percent of those offenses were committed by fatherless children. Judge Jim Payne of the juvenile court of Marion County says at least 600 new juveniles enter the system each month. "Out-of-wedlock birth is driving every single rotten outcome in our city," says Krista Rush, Mayor Goldsmith's social-policy advisor.

At Goldsmith's request, the Indianapolis Training Center (ITC) 14
set up shop in the city a few years ago to reach out to troubled youth and their families. Payne now refers kids headed for state detention centers to the Christian-based program, which houses about two dozen teens at a time in its residential center. To overcome objections by the Indiana Civil Liberties Union, Payne argued that the program's emphasis on character and family relationships could help reverse irresponsible or predatory attitudes toward sex that have become "incredibly common" among today's youth.

Center director Benny McWha says that many of the girls at 15
the center were sexually abused as children, and are considered at high risk of teen pregnancy. Most of the boys come with no experience of responsible fatherhood. Eight mentor families and about a hundred student volunteers work to keep the kids out of trouble.

"Our primary goal is to help teach them character," McWha 16
says, which includes "moral purity from a biblical perspective." The ITC staff also offers practical support—and a message of abstinence—to unmarried mothers in some of the city's toughest neighborhoods.

Modeling the Message

Communicating an effective abstinence message may be the most difficult task facing the mayor, and the city's public schools are becoming a prime battleground. It is here where getting involved sexually is considered a badge of honor. And it is here where more and more pregnant teens are envied, admired, and applauded—but rarely shunned. "In many of our schools," Rush says, "there's a tremendous reward for getting pregnant." 17

Jackson, who coordinates adolescent-growth programs for the Catholic Archdiocese of Indianapolis, cites three principles for overturning an ethos of sexual freedom: (1) Give kids a clear message of abstinence until marriage, (2) get the message to them early, and (3) recruit credible high-school students to deliver it. 18

"There's a real need to have some positive peer pressure for a change," Jackson says. Young people are more likely to listen when student role models get involved. And, contrary to Planned Parenthood's news releases, finding chaste high schoolers is not a problem. Last year, Jackson recruited 200 peer mentors from six Catholic schools and six public schools to lead the workshops. She expects to train at least 50 students from Indianapolis high schools to work with kids in the city's middle schools this fall. 19

Though Jackson has removed all religious references from her public-school program, the six-hour curriculum parallels its religious counterpart in stressing chastity until marriage. Jackson essentially has translated religious concepts about the benefits of marriage—and the risks of sexual permissiveness—into secular language. 20

Moreover, most of Jackson's high-school mentors come from strong religious backgrounds. "We're finding that our peer mentors are people of faith," she says. "That faith component is essential, because it gives them a moral standard to live by. Otherwise, it's anything goes." 21

Questions for Study and Discussion

1. What is a "bully pulpit" (4)? Why is this an appropriate term to use in describing Goldsmith's efforts to reduce teen pregnancy in Indianapolis?

2. Loconte's article appeared in a publication that is aimed at politically conservative readers. What issues does Loconte raise that would specifically appeal to a conservative audience? (Glossary: *Audience*) What different issues might he have stressed if he were writing for a politically neutral audience?
3. Why is the religious community so important to Goldsmith's efforts? What elements of Eve Jackson's program appeal to the religious groups?
4. Richard Wiehe is quoted as equating the current welfare system with a candy store (11). Explain what he means by this analogy. (Glossary: *Analogy*) Do you think Loconte shares Wiehe's extremely critical view of welfare? Why, or why not?
5. Summarize Loconte's argument in three or four sentences. What are the national issues he brings up in the context of the specific situation in Indianapolis?
6. What are the components of the mayor's program to communicate a message about abstinence to teenagers effectively? What obstacles must those who deliver the message overcome?

Vocabulary

Refer to your dictionary to define the following words as they are used in this selection. Then use each word in a sentence of your own.

abstinence (2)
chastity (4)
initiatives (4)
stigmatize (5)
statutory rape (6)
paternity (6)
mentor (11)
explicit (12)
shunned (17)
ethos (18)
secular (20)

Classroom Activity Using Argument

The following paragraph is written for an audience that holds opinions in common with the writer. Read the paragraph carefully, then revise it so that it would be more readily accepted by a general audience.

One would have thought that the alien autopsy films would have erased any doubt that anyone might have had about the presence of aliens and UFOs on earth. There it was, an alien, right on the television screen. Incredibly, the federal government continued its tired—and increasingly feeble—drone of denials in the face of this direct evidence. "Of course the films are not authentic," snorted General Bill "Nuke" Winter when questioned about them. Noted UFOlogist Arthur Grace can only shake his head. "It defies logic that they continue to deny the obvious," he said. "It makes me very curious about what they know and what they are trying so hard to keep the public from finding out."

Suggested Writing Assignments

1. Write an essay in which you support or criticize the efforts of Mayor Goldsmith and the other proponents of the abstinence programs in Indianapolis. Is it acceptable to introduce so many components of religion into city programs? Is the teaching and promotion of abstinence a realistic solution to the problem of teenage pregnancy? Are the programs likely to reach and influence those teenagers who are most at risk?
2. Politicians cite the breakdown of the family structure as the root of many of our current problems, but there are few who offer any kind of practical solutions. The consequences vary, but it is the children who are affected the most—many grow up with few or no positive role models on whom they can model their behavior. Write a paper in which you argue how you think the family unit should be strengthened in our society, particularly when children are involved. Should absent fathers and unmarried teenage mothers be sought out and punished, along the lines of what Mayor Goldsmith is proposing? Should divorce laws be tightened when children are involved? Should single parents be given more community support, so that the children can interact with adults in constructive ways? Is it possible to legislate changes in the family structure, or do you think change needs to come from the community, through religious groups, or from privately controlled support groups?

Exposing Media Myths: TV Doesn't Affect You As Much As You Think

Joanmarie Kalter

Joanmarie Kalter has written extensively about television news and about the press in the Third World. After graduating from Cornell University in 1972 and working as a freelance writer for a number of years, Kalter received her master's degree from the Columbia Graduate School of Journalism in 1981. She joined TV Guide *as a staff writer in 1984, but returned to freelancing in 1989. Her articles have appeared in numerous and diverse periodicals, including the* New York Times, *the* Christian Science Monitor, *the* Bulletin of Atomic Scientists, *and* Africa Report. *In the following selection, note how she uses her evidence to chip away at some "false truths" about television news. The rhetorical mode of cause and effect also plays a significant role in Kalter's argument as she reveals the serious implications of the myths she exposes.*

For Your Journal

Reflect on your sense of the importance of television news. Do you watch a news program regularly? Do you find it valuable? How much of what you see and hear do you remember, and for how long?

Once upon a time, there was a new invention—television. It became so popular, so quickly, that more American homes now have a TV set (98 percent) than an indoor toilet (97 percent). Around this new invention, then, an industry rapidly grew, and around this industry, a whole mythology. It has become a virtual 1 truism, often heard and often repeated, that TV—and TV news, in particular—has an unparalleled influence on our lives.

Over the past 20 years, however, communications scholars have been quietly examining such truisms and have discovered, sometimes to their surprise, that many are not so true at all. *TV Guide* asked more than a dozen leading researchers for their findings and found an eye-opening collection of mythbusters. Indeed, they suggest that an entire body of political strategy and debate has been built upon false premises. . . . 2

Myth No. 1: Two-thirds of the American people receive most of their news from TV. This little canard is at the heart of our story. It can be traced to the now-famous Roper polls, in which Americans are queried: "I'd like to ask you where you usually get most of your news about what's going on in the world today. . . ." In 1959, when the poll was first conducted, 51 percent answered "television," with a steady increase ever since. The latest results show that 66 percent say they get most of their news from TV; only about a third credit newspapers. 3

Trouble is, that innocent poll question is downright impossible to answer. Just consider: it asks you to sort through the issues in your mind, pinpoint what and where you learned about each, tag it, and come up with a final score. Not too many of us can do it, especially since we get our news from a variety of sources. Even pollster Burns Roper concedes, "Memories do get fuzzy." 4

Scholars have found, however, that when they ask a less general, more specific question—Did you read a newspaper yesterday? Did you watch a TV news show yesterday?—the results are quite different. Dr. John Robinson, professor of sociology at the University of Maryland, found that on a typical day 67 percent read a newspaper, while 52 percent see a local or national TV newscast. Dr. Robert Stevenson, professor of journalism at the University of North Carolina, analyzed detailed diaries of TV use, and further found that only 18 percent watch network news on an average day, and only 13 percent pay full attention to it. Says Robinson, "TV is part of our overall mix, but in no way is it our number one source of news." 5

Yet it's a myth with disturbing consequences. Indeed, it is so widespread, says Dr. Mark Levy, associate professor of journalism at the University of Maryland, that it shapes—or misshapes—our political process. In the words of Michael Deaver, White House deputy chief of staff during President Reagan's first term, "The 6 majority of the people get their news from television, so . . . we construct events and craft photos that are designed for 30 seconds to a minute so that it can fit into that 'bite' on the evening news." And thus the myth, says Levy, "distorts the very dialogue of democracy, which cannot be responsibly conducted in 30-second bites."

Myth No. 2: TV news sets the public agenda. It was first said succinctly in 1963, and has long been accepted: while the mass media may not tell us what to think, they definitely tell us what to think about. And on some issues, the impact of TV is indisputable: the Ethiopian famine, the Challenger explosion. Yet for the more routine story, new research has challenged that myth, suggesting TV's influence may be surprisingly more limited. 7

For one thing, TV news most often reacts to newspapers in framing issues of public concern. Dr. David Weaver, professor of journalism at Indiana University, found that newspapers led TV through the 1976 campaign. Given the brevity of broadcasts, of course, that's understandable. "TV has no page 36," explains Dr. Maxwell McCombs, professor of communications at the University of Texas. "So TV journalists have to wait until an issue has already achieved substantial public interest." TV, then, does not so much set the public agenda as spotlight it. 8

Even among those issues spotlighted, viewers do make independent judgments. It seems the old "hypodermic" notions no longer hold, says Dr. Doris Graber, political science professor at the University of Illinois. "We're not sponges for this stuff, and while TV may provide the raw material, people do select." 9

Indeed, even TV entertainment is less influential than once was thought. According to Robinson, studies found no difference in racial attitudes among those who saw *Roots* and those who didn't. Ditto "The Day After" on nuclear war, and *Amerika* on the Soviets. As for news, Graber notes that the public took a long time to share the media's concern about Watergate, and even now are lagging the media on Iran-Contragate. And finally, there are many issues on which the press must belatedly catch up with the public. Which brings us to . . . 10

Myth No. 3: TV news changed public opinion about the war in Vietnam. Contrary to this most common of beliefs, research shows just the opposite. Lawrence Lichty, professor of radio/television/film at Northwestern University, analyzed network war coverage and found that it did not become relatively critical until 1967. By then, however, a majority of Americans already thought U.S. in- 11 volvement in Vietnam was a mistake. And they thought so not because of TV coverage, but because of the number of young Americans dying.

Yet this fable about the "living-room war" is so accepted it has become "fact": that gory TV pictures of bloody battles undermined public support for the war; that, in a 1968 TV-news special, Walter Cronkite mistakenly presented the Tet offensive as a defeat for the U.S.; and that, because President Johnson so believed in the power of TV, he concluded then that his war effort was lost. 12

In fact, Lichty found few "gory" pictures. "TV presented a distant view," he says, with less than five percent of TV's war reports showing heavy combat. Nor, as we now know, was a rapt audience watching at home in their living rooms. As for Cronkite's report on the Tet offensive, the CBS anchor said on the evening news, "First and simplest, the Vietcong suffered a military defeat." And, in his now-famous TV special, Cronkite concluded, "we are mired in a stalemate," and should "negotiate." By that time, Lichty says, "public opinion had been on a downward trend for a year and a half. A majority of Americans agreed." And so Johnson's concern, it seems, was not that Cronkite would influence public opinion, but rather that he reflected it. 13

Indeed, Professor John Mueller of the University of Rochester has compared the curve of public opinion on the war in Vietnam, covered by TV, with that of the war in Korea, hardly covered. He found the two curves strikingly similar: in both cases, public support dropped as the number of American deaths rose. 14

Disturbingly, the misconception about TV's influence in Vietnam has had broad consequences, for it has framed an important debate ever since. Can a democratic society, with a free flow of dramatic TV footage, retain the public will to fight a war? Many argue no. And this has been the rationale more recently for censoring the Western press in the Falklands and Grenada. Yet it is, says Lichty, a policy based on a myth. 15

Myth No. 4: TV today is the most effective medium in communicating news. Most of us think of TV fare as simple, direct, easy to understand—with the combination of words and pictures making it all the more powerful. But recent research shows that TV news, as distinct from entertainment, is often very confusing. In study after study, Robinson and Levy have found that viewers understand only about a third of network news stories. 16

Why is TV news so tough to understand? Dr. Dan Drew, professor of journalism at Indiana University, suggests that the verbal and visual often conflict. Unlike TV entertainment, in which the two are composed together, TV-news footage is gathered first, and the story it illustrates often diverges. We may see fighting across the Green Line in Beirut—for a story about peace talks. We may see "file footage" of Anglican envoy Terry Waite walking down the street—for a story on his disappearance. As viewers try to make sense of the visual, they lose the gist of the verbal. "The myth," says Levy, "is that since we are a visual medium, we must always have pictures. . . . But that's a disaster, a recipe for poor communication." 17

Journalists also are much more familiar with the world of public affairs, says Levy, and rely on its technical jargon: from "leading economic indicators" to "the Druse militia." Their stories, say researchers, are overillustrated, with most pictures on the screen for less than 20 seconds. They assume, mistakenly, that viewers pay complete attention, and so they often do not repeat the main theme. Yet while understanding TV news takes concentration, watching TV is full of distractions. In one study, researchers mounted cameras on top of sets and recorded the amount of time viewers also read, talked, walked in and out of the room. They concluded that viewers actually watch only 55 percent of what's on. 18

The audience does recall the extraordinary, such as a man on the moon, and better comprehends human-interest stories. But since most news is not covered night after night, tomorrow's broadcast tends to wash away today's. "People don't remember much from TV news," says Graber. "It's like the ocean washing over traces that have been very faintly formed." 19

Today's TV news is carefully watched by politicians, who keep a sharp eye on how they're covered. But while it may provide theater for a handful, this research increasingly shows it's lost on the American public. And sadly, then, hard-working TV journalists may be missing an opportunity to inform. 20

Yet TV remains a medium with great potential. And studies show that it does extend the awareness of the poor and ill-educated, who cannot afford additional sources. What's more, research suggests that the clarity of TV news can be improved—without compromising journalistic standards. "We have been glitzed by the glamour of TV, all these gee-whiz gimmicks," says Robinson. "And we have lost sight of one of the oldest and most durable findings 21 of communications research. . . . The most important element is the writer, who sits at a typewriter and tries to tell the story in a simple and organized way. That's the crucial link."

Research also shows that viewers want a broadcast they can understand. The success of "60 Minutes" proves there's an audience still hungry for sophisticated factual information. "When someone does this for news, they'll grab the ratings," says Levy. "Nobody loses!" Ironically, no corporation would launch an ad campaign without extensive testing on how best to reach its audience. But many broadcast journalists, working under intense pressure, remain unaware of the problems. "There's a lot we have to learn about how people comprehend," says William Rubens, NBC research vice-president. "But no, it hasn't been the thrust of our research." According to Robinson and Levy, this requires the attention of those in charge, a collective corporate will. With the networks under a financial squeeze, their news audiences having recently declined some 15 percent, "This may be the time for them to rethink their broadcasts," says Levy. 22

And if they do, they may just live . . . happily ever after. 23

Questions for Study and Discussion

1. Kalter uses the term "myth" to describe assumptions about TV news. Look up the definition of myth in your dictionary. How does the use of this term help Kalter influence her audience? (Glossary: *Audience*)
2. How can general survey questions lead to inaccurate data? How have the Roper polls contributed to the myths about television news?
3. According to Kalter, why is it a myth that TV news changed public opinion about the Vietnam War? (Glossary: *Cause and Effect*) What are the broad consequences of this myth?
4. Kalter begins by discussing television—and her title implies that the article is about television in general—but the focus of her article is television news. (Glossary: *Focus*) In what ways does narrowing her focus help her argue her point?
5. How does Kalter organize her argument in paragraphs 16–20? (Glossary: *Organization*) What does each paragraph accomplish? (Glossary: *Paragraph*)

6. In what ways does TV remain a "medium with great potential" (21)? How can TV news be changed to make it more effective? Why hasn't it been changed in the past?

Vocabulary

Refer to your dictionary to define the following words as they are used in this selection. Then use each word in a sentence of your own.

truism (1)	rapt (13)
canard (3)	rationale (15)
succinctly (7)	gist (17)
brevity (8)	glitzed (21)

Classroom Activity Using Argument

The effectiveness of a writer's argument depends in large part on the writer's awareness of audience. For example, if a writer wished to argue for the use of technology to solve environmental problems, that argument would normally have to be more convincing (i.e., more factual, better reasoned) for an environmentalist than it would have to be for an industrialist because environmentalists might tend to distrust technology.

Review each of the essays you have read thus far in this section. In your opinion, for what primary audience was each essay intended? What types of evidence did you use in determining your answer?

Suggested Writing Assignments

1. How much do you think television—and television news in particular—has affected you? Write an argumentative essay in which you either agree with Kalter's position or disagree based on your personal experiences.
2. How would you change television news in order to make it more effective for you? Write a letter to the head of a network news show in which you argue for your proposed changes in the format of the show.

Robbing the Cradle

Dennis A. Williams

Dennis A. Williams is director of the Center for Minority Student Affairs at Georgetown University. Born in Syracuse, New York, in 1951, Williams received a B.A. from Cornell University in 1973 and an M.F.A. from the University of Massachusetts in 1976. He then spent ten years as a writer for Newsweek *magazine. In 1985 he returned to Cornell as director of the Learning Skills Center, a position he held until moving to Georgetown in 1997. Williams's first novel,* Somebody's Child, *was published in the fall of 1997. The essay below first appeared as a "My Turn" column in* Newsweek *in July 1995. As you read it, notice how Williams sets up a comparison and contrast in paragraph 7 that he returns to repeatedly in the paragraphs that follow in order to make his central argument more convincing.*

For Your Journal

Imagine that someone calls you one evening and offers you a job with a three-year contract and a high salary in the field of your choice. The only catches are that you have to take the job immediately—you cannot complete your college degree—and there is no guarantee of a long-term career. What do you think you would do? How important to you is getting your degree?

The first four picks in this week's NBA draft are expected to be underclassmen. Three of them have been in school for only two years. While the competitive wisdom of this baby boom may be questionable—some of the players are considered not quite ready for pro stardom—in educational terms the cradle-robbing 1 trend is a disaster. More than ever, this year's draft exposes the poisonous relationship between college and professional sports.

As an educator, I often see the destructive power of the Hoop Dream. Granted, what I see in the nonscholarship Ivy League isn't the real thing; almost no one harbors serious NBA ambitions. Yet even here it is difficult for some recruited athletes to make up their minds about why they're really in school and what they will do when the ball stops bouncing. 2

But the young men who cashed in their books in the draft are not starry-eyed wanna-bes; they are highly talented players who will surely earn millions anyway when they get to the pros. So why the rush? The main reason may be that NBA owners, staggered by the multimillion-dollar contracts they are bestowing on untested players, are threatening to impose a rookie salary cap. In response, students who've gone far enough in school to count to eight digits are opting to get theirs now. 3

There was a time when such premature gold-digging was not an option. The NBA declined to draft students whose college class had not graduated. That system demanded that collegiate stars wait their turn for pro careers. In the early 1970s, as paydays grew fatter, the NBA began allowing "hardship" exemptions to the draft rules, so that financially strapped students could turn pro early. 4

By the 1980s, so many players were routinely claiming hardship status that the league dropped the pretense and simply allowed athletes to renounce their remaining college eligibility and grab the bucks. As a result, this year's draft crop is unusual only in the number of prominent youngsters and the brevity of their college tenure. The last three No. 1 picks in the NBA draft—Shaquille O'Neal, Chris Webber and Glenn Robinson—were all underclassmen. They've all been successful as pros, as the top pick should be. And their very success has helped to shatter the expectation that an outstanding college player should take school seriously. 5

The NCAA has been complicit in the dropout phenomenon by doggedly upholding the tradition, honored by time and not much else, of amateur purity. This quaint ideal predates the modern condition of colleges' serving as unabashed minor leagues for the pros. It also ignores the fact that basketball as well as football players generate enormous revenue for their schools. But in seeking to preserve college athletics from the taint of professionalism, 6 the NCAA has devised a system guaranteed to make "student athletes" permanent nonstudents.

Unlike athletes, "real" college students frequently hold paying jobs. Many receiving financial aid are required to do so. Those who condone athletic dropouts often claim that some students are in effect majoring in basketball—that is the career they are going to school to prepare for. True enough, and college students regularly accept jobs in their industry of choice, from paid summer internships to co-op work programs, without relinquishing their student status. (I worked for *Newsweek* in college while practicing "amateur" journalism on collegiate publications.) 7

The solution is simple. Allow student prospects to be drafted by the pros—and remain eligible for college play. Let them negotiate a contract that will bind them to their future team for a standard three-year hitch. An insurance policy (paid by the pro team) could guard against income lost to injury. As with ROTC, the pro team could pick up the remainder of a player's college scholarship and pay a minimum living allowance, a minuscule investment for a multimillion-dollar asset. Even more radically, such an arrangement might stipulate that the draftee couldn't join the NBA until he actually graduated—reinforcing the idea that college is something more than a highly organized tryout camp. 8

Where is the conflict of interest if a player already committed to the New York Knicks competes against a future San Antonio Spur in an NCAA game? And how is that different from a student who has interned with IBM competing in class against a student who has a job offer from Apple? Because the primary beneficiary is the player, not the program, no school would have a recruiting advantage beyond what many now enjoy with promises of starting assignments, TV exposure and tournament appearances. Coaches would be assured that a recruited player who catches the pros' eyes would be around for four years instead of jumping ship as soon as he makes the cover of *Sports Illustrated*. 9

The "curse" of professionalism in this case is a self-serving illusion compared with the real problem of exploitation: students in school only to play ball, generating millions for their colleges and all too often leaving without their only tangible payment, a college degree. On the other hand, there may be some who don't want the degree—who don't really want to be in school in the first place. Let them try their luck landing NBA jobs directly, like Kevin 10

Garnett, the high-school star who figures to be a high draft pick this week. Or they can work on their games in Rapid City or some other lower-level professional outpost. Colleges, meanwhile, can save their scholarships for students, including student athletes, as they should have been doing all along.

In order for any of this to work, the NCAA and its member institutions would have to pull their heads out of the sand and acknowledge that what's best for the athletic establishment is not necessarily what's best for students who play ball. And the NBA would have to agree, as it did in the past, to allow colleges to educate student athletes in return for developing their talent pool. It would be a tough sell, but worth the effort. Encouraging students to stay in school, as the NBA proclaims in its public-relations campaign, would be everyone's best move. 11

Questions for Study and Discussion

1. Williams alludes to the Hoop Dream. Are you familiar with this allusion? (Glossary: *Allusion*) If so, what is it? If not, guess what it is from the context of the essay.
2. What does Williams mean by the term "premature gold-digging" (4)? Who are the gold diggers? What does Williams's choice of words indicate about his attitude toward his subject? (Glossary: *Diction*)
3. Summarize the differences between the athletes Williams is writing about and those he terms "real" college students. Why is it so tempting for the athletes to leave school?
4. When Williams presents his solution to the problems he has identified, is he making a logical argument or a persuasive argument? Explain your answer.
5. What evidence does Williams present to support his statement that the NCAA has its head in the sand? Why does he say that the way student athletes are treated is a worse problem than the possibility of professional influences in collegiate sports?
6. Do you agree with Williams's contention that athletes who are not interested in a college education when they leave

high school should go straight into professional sports, at whatever level they are ready for? Why, or why not?

Vocabulary

Refer to your dictionary to define the following words as they are used in this selection. Then use each word in a sentence of your own.

brevity (5)	minuscule (8)
quaint (6)	beneficiary (9)
condone (7)	tangible (10)

Classroom Activity Using Argument

Read the following passages. What type of logical fallacy does each represent? See pages 446–47.

1. He'll be an excellent windsurfer. He won several skateboarding competitions when he was a student.
2. Ever since 1985, the year people in the United States started to eat more fish on a regular basis, the average height of ten-year-olds has increased each year.
3. Stressful jobs with long hours are the reason the divorce rate is going up.
4. This breed of dog is very loyal, so it's a good choice for people with small apartments.
5. The Internet is growing at a phenomenal rate. Other methods of communication will soon become obsolete.

Suggested Writing Assignments

1. There has been a lot of debate in recent years about the place amateur athletics should have in modern society. At both the collegiate and Olympic levels, the notion of keeping the athletes separated from the financial gains reaped through their efforts is under attack. In fact, many Olympic sports now welcome previously banned professional ath-

letes, such as the "Dream Team" basketball team, and the distinctions between "amateur" and "professional" athletes are being erased. Critics charge that the amateur system was set up in the days when athletics was the province of the rich, who sought to keep sports "pure." Outside money was seen as a potentially corrupting influence. Today, huge television contracts, lucrative sneaker endorsements, and large crowds mean that millions of dollars change hands every day in NCAA sports. The only ones who do not profit, critics say, are the very athletes at the center of it all who are still held to the outdated amateur ideal. What do you think? Is there a place for the amateur ideal in our society, or should athletes share in the profitability of their sports? Write an essay in which you argue for upholding the amateur ideal at the university level or in which you propose a way for student athletes to share in the profits while maintaining their status at the university as students first, athletes second.

2. Write an argumentative essay in which you defend or criticize the place professional sports have in our society today. Is it acceptable for athletes to be such prominent role models? How do you feel about the multimillion-dollar salaries and labor unrest of so many team sports? Do you think televised sports are an exciting diversion or an invitation to waste time in front of the TV? If you defend professional sports, discuss the contributions that they make to society. If you criticize them, discuss the aspect of the sports "culture" that you think is most damaging.

AGAINST THE GREAT DIVIDE

Brian Jarvis

When the following essay was published as a "My Turn" column in Newsweek *in May 1993, Brian Jarvis was a high-school junior in St. Louis. He now attends Claremont College in California and is working on a novel about his high-school experiences. Jarvis organizes the first part of his essay inductively, using a series of examples that lead to a generalization at the beginning of paragraph 9. After that, he explores the potential for remedying the voluntary segregation at his high school that he describes so concretely in his first eight paragraphs.*

FOR YOUR JOURNAL

Think of the four or five people you consider to be your closest friends. Are any of them of a different ethnic background than yours? If so, do you find that the differences create any challenges, either from inside or outside the relationship? If no, why not? Do you give the matter much thought?

I always notice one thing when I walk through the commons at my high school: the whites are on one side of the room and the blacks are on the other. When I enter the room, I think I'm at an African nationalist meeting. The atmosphere is lively, the clothes are colorful, the voices are loud, the students are up and about, the language is different and there's not a white face to be seen. But the moment I cross the invisible line to the other side, I feel I've moved to another country. There are three times as many people, the voices are softer, the clothes more subdued. Everyone's sitting or lying down, and one has as much chance of seeing a black student as a Martian. 1

The commons is a gathering spot where students relax on benches and talk with friends. They also buy candy and soda, 2 watch TV and make phone calls. It's a place where all sorts of things happen. But you'll never find a white student and a black student talking to each other.

3 After three years, I still feel uncomfortable when I have to walk through the "black" side to get to class. It's not that any black students threaten or harass me. They just quietly ignore me and look in the other direction, and I do the same. But there's one who sometimes catches my eye, and I can't help feeling awkward when I see him. He was a close friend from childhood.

4 Ten years ago, we played catch in our backyards, went bike riding and slept over at one another's houses. By the fifth grade, we went to movies and amusement parks, and bunked together at the same summer camps. We met while playing on the same Little League team, though we attended different grade schools. We're both juniors now at the same high school. We usually don't say anything when we see each other, except maybe a polite "Hi" or "Hey." I can't remember the last time we talked on the phone, much less got together outside of school.

5 Since entering high school, we haven't shared a single class or sport. He plays football, a black-dominated sport, while I play tennis, which is, with rare exception, an all-white team. It's as if fate has kept us apart; though, more likely, it's peer pressure.

6 In the lunchroom, I sit with my white friends and my childhood friend sits with his black ones. It's the same when we walk through the hallways or sit in the library. If Michael Jackson thinks, "It don't matter if you're black or white," he should visit my high school.

7 I wonder if proponents of desegregation realized that even if schools were integrated, students would choose to remain apart. It wasn't until 1983 that St. Louis's voluntary city–suburban desegregation program was approved. Today, my school has 25 percent black students. While this has given many young people the chance for a better education, it hasn't brought the two races closer together.

8 In high school, I've become friends with Vietnamese-Americans, Korean-Americans, Iranian-Americans, Indian-Americans, Russian-Americans and exchange students from France and Sweden. The only group that remains at a distance is the African-Americans. I've had only a handful of black students in all my classes and only one black teacher (from Haiti).

Crucial Course

In its effort to put students through as many academic classes as possible and prepare them for college, my school seems to have overlooked one crucial course: teaching black and white students how to get along, which in my opinion, would be more valuable than all the others. It's not that there haven't been efforts to improve race relations. Last fall, a group of black and white students established a program called Students Organized Against Racism. But at a recent meeting, SOAR members decided that the separation of blacks and whites was largely voluntary and there was little they could do about it. Another youth group tried to help by moving the soda machine from the "white" side of the commons to the "black" side, so that white students would have to cross the line to get a Coke. But all that's happened is that students buy their sodas, then return to their own territory. 9

Last summer, at a youth camp called Miniwanca in Michigan, I did see black and white teens get along. I don't mean just tolerate one another. I mean play sports together, dance together, walk on the beach together and become friends. The students came from all races and backgrounds, as well as from overseas. Camp organizers purposely placed me in a cabin and activity group that included whites, blacks, Southerners, Northerners and foreigners, none of whom I'd met before. 10

For 10 days, I became great friends with a group of strangers, at least half of whom were black. One wouldn't know that racism existed at that idyllic place, where we told stories around campfires, acted in plays and shared our deepest thoughts about AIDS, parents, abortion and dating. Everyone got along so well there that it was depressing for me to return to high school. But at the same time, it made me hopeful. If black and white teenagers could be friends at leadership camp, couldn't they mix in school as well? 11

Schools need to make it a real priority to involve whites and blacks together as much as possible. This would mean more multicultural activities, mandatory classes that teach black history and discussions of today's racial controversies. Teachers should mix whites and blacks more in study groups so they *have* to work together in and out of school. (Students won't do it on their own.) And most important, all students should get a chance to attend a camp like Miniwanca. Maybe the Clinton administration could find a way to help finance other camps like it. 12

As it is now, black and white teenagers just don't know one another. I think a lot about my friend from childhood—what he does on weekends, what he thinks about college, what he wants to do with his life. I have no answers, and it saddens me. 13

Questions for Study and Discussion

1. What are the two "countries" in the commons room at Jarvis's high school? Jarvis uses the two-country analogy to emphasize the differences on either side of the "border." What is he saying about the situation in the commons room? (Glossary: *Analogy*)
2. Why do Jarvis and his childhood friend interact so little now that they are in high school? Why is this specific situation an effective way to illustrate the overall situation Jarvis presents? (Glossary: *Illustration*)
3. Why do the African Americans and whites remain at a distance from one another? Why have the efforts to bring them closer together failed at Jarvis's high school?
4. What do you think of Jarvis's suggestion to have a course that would teach whites and blacks how to get along? How much impact do you think such a course would have in his high school? Explain your answer.
5. Jarvis's camp experience gave him hope, but it was an artificial setting—he even calls it an "idyllic place" (11)—with a select group of young people. Do you think it is an effective piece of supporting evidence in his argument? Why, or why not?
6. Who is Jarvis hoping to reach in his essay? (Glossary: *Audience*) Which sentences in the essay led you to your conclusion?

Vocabulary

Refer to your dictionary to define the following words as they are used in this selection. Then use each word in a sentence of your own.

commons (1)
proponents (7)
desegregation (7)
idyllic (11)
multicultural (12)

Classroom Activity Using Argument

Write a paragraph that argues that people should compliment each other more. Use one of the following quotes as evidence to support your argument:

> "Compliments are the high point of a person's day," said self-help author Melodie Bronson. "Without compliments anyone's life is sure to be much more difficult."

> "Compliments have been proven to lower blood pressure and increase endorphin production in the brain," said Dr. Ruth West of the Holistic Medicine Committee. "A compliment a day may lengthen your life span by as much as a year."

> "Compliments are a special way people communicate with each other," said Bill Goodbody, therapist at the Good Feeling Institute. "Ninety percent of our patients report happier relationships or marriages after they begin compliment therapy."

Explain your choice. How did you integrate the quotation into your paragraph?

Suggested Writing Assignments

1. Write an essay in which you argue either for or against Jarvis's contention that interaction between black and white teenagers needs to be mandatory and that a class could bring the two groups closer together. Would such measures be enough to overcome the apparently voluntary segregation at his high school? Does your own experience with this issue give you any insights into how to break down the barrier between the black and white "countries"?
2. In the past twenty-five years, a great deal of effort has gone into the attempt to desegregate public schools so that all ethnic groups, both genders, and as diverse a collection of backgrounds as possible are represented. Whether desegre-

gation is enforced, as in court-ordered busing, or pursued voluntarily, as in the current quest for diversity on campuses around the country, it has yielded increasingly heterogeneous student bodies. Write an essay in which you argue that diversity is an ideal that should be aggressively pursued, or that schools that offer voluntary segregation and a more homogeneous student body have something to offer. How much does a diverse school population increase students' understanding and appreciation of different ethnic groups and backgrounds?

What's Marriage Got to Do with Love?

Maggie Gallagher

Maggie Gallagher is an affiliate scholar at the Institute for American Values and author of The Abolition of Marriage: How We Destroy Lasting Love *(1996). She has also written an opinion column for* Newsday *since 1993, as well as many articles for such magazines and newspapers as the* New Republic, *the* Wall Street Journal, National Review, Cosmopolitan, *and the* New York Times. *Her first book,* Enemies of Eros: How the Sexual Revolution Is Killing Family, Marriage, and Sex, *appeared in 1989. Gallagher also worked as an editor at* National Review *and at the Manhattan Institute's* City Journal, *and was a senior fellow at the Center for Social Thought. She graduated from Yale in 1982 and lives with her family in Westchester, New York. The following essay, published in* Newsday *in 1996, was adapted from* The Abolition of Marriage. *Gallagher's belief in people's skepticism about marriage is borne out in the way she organizes her ideas: She explores various dimensions of both love and marriage before presenting the main point of her argument—a defense of marriage.*

For Your Journal

Do you think that you want to get married in the future? Why, or why not? What aspect of marriage concerns you the most? What kinds of marriages have you seen? Consider your parents' relationship as well as the marriages of others close to you. How might these examples have influenced your view of marriage?

Why do lovers marry? For centuries the answer might have been self evident, but in today's world, where cohabitation is more bourgeois than bohemian, it's an open question. 1

I posed it not long ago to a group of young, college-educated women. Krista, a 23-year-old writer, tried to explain why it's so important to her that she and her live-in boyfriend get married. "I just love the words 'husband' and 'wife,'" she says, almost ruefully. "I know the words are archaic, but I just love the whole idea." 2

Krista, like the other young women in the room, lives with the omnipresent reality of divorce. They know a marriage license is no guarantee of permanence. Sex and affection they already have from their boyfriends. Yet women like Krista long, almost irrationally, for the nuptial bond. 3

The words "I love you" have been drained, through overuse, of all special meanings. And the act of love no longer signifies union. All that is left is this frail, eroding word, "marriage," packed with centuries of loving, living, growing old together, in sickness and in health, until death do us part. 4

Thirty years of the divorce culture have not yet undone the work of ages. It is the only word that still speaks. 5

Americans are a marrying people—like Krista, nine out of 10 adult women tie the knot at least once. And yet Americans also have the highest divorce rate in the western world. How do we reconcile the cultural contradiction? 6

Here is one popular theory: The epidemic of divorce does not represent a failure of love so much as a sign of its increasing importance. "People are less willing to stay in a marriage without love," as sociologist Randall Collins put it. 7

Such comforting clichés are today's conventional wisdom, as commonly heard at cocktail parties or on talk shows as in scholars' texts. Marriages today are supposedly *better* than marriages in the past because they are based on love. 8

Never mind now that up to 65 percent of new marriages fail. Almost a third of American kids are born outside of wedlock. A baby today has a roughly 50-50 chance of keeping its father. Never mind, in short, that marriage as a durable child-rearing bond, a tie firm enough for a child to rely upon, is swiftly disappearing. 9

What does love mean, how do we love, in the Brave New World we are busily creating, where enduring marriage is becoming the exception rather than the rule? The answer, it seems to me, is timidly, reluctantly and, in some cases, not at all. 10

Call It Safe Love: Signs of this modern triumph of fear over love are everywhere, though they are often disguised by the most idealistic rhetoric. One powerful myth of the divorce culture is that divorce affects only the people who do it. In reality, of course, not only the frequency of divorce and the laws of divorce, but the ideas, attitudes and anecdotes that sustain a 50-percent-plus divorce rate transform what it means to be married. 11

Here is one of the biggest changes: A spouse has become a consumption item. "The reason we fall in love is to help us accomplish our external and internal developmental tasks," as one relationship guru recently put it. To this breed, relationships exist to serve the needs of the individuals. Fancy words. They sound reassuring. But what they mean is that love is not about a commitment to care for another person; it is part of the care and feeding of one's self. 12

In theory, there is not much difference between a husband and a vibrator. Which you choose depends on what "developmental tasks" you are trying to accomplish next in your life. So if, say, you have fulfilled your need to have a baby and you want to move on, yet he hasn't gotten over wanting to be a married father, that's his problem. He will have to work it out in his next relationship. Here, indeed, is a new habit of the heart. Love means getting what you want and getting out when you've gotten it all. 13

If the goal of marriage is merely or primarily the happiness of the individual, then marriage is inherently temporary. It lasts only as long as the man and woman both perceive themselves better off together than apart. And because marriage is conceived as an affair between adults, the new therapeutic love contract subordinates the needs of children to the desires of grown-ups. 14

The truth modern couples can't quite face is this: To really love is to surrender freedom—the freedom to flee, the freedom not to care any longer. Love creates ties. Every effort to escape from that essential human dilemma, to re-imagine love in such a way as to retain our utter freedom, involves reducing love to the level of appetite—re-imagining it as a set of pleasing inner feelings, elevated feelings perhaps, that promote our personal growth, but still 15 essentially internal sensations. What disappears in love imagined this way is the other person.

The ultimate expression of this new erotic timidity is cohabitation. Cohabitation comes wrapped in the language of love, but at its core it is about anxiety; commitment with fingers crossed. Living together is what lovers do when at least one of them does not dare to marry, to love without a net. 16

This interpretation may surprise the modern young woman, who almost always sees cohabitation as a sign of commitment, as well as a practical way to test love. The Duchess of York, asked what advice she would give her two daughters about men and marriage, recently chimed in: "Get to know them, perhaps live with them a bit. Really get to know what's going on." 17

It makes perfect sense, but it has proved perfect nonsense. Cohabitation does not improve marriages. Instead, researchers have found that married couples who lived together first are twice as likely to divorce in the first 10 years of marriage as other couples. Even one failed cohabitation appeared to reduce the happiness of future cohabitations (including marriages). 18

The sexual rationalists were right: People learn from experience. What people gain from the experience of cohabitation is that love ends and lovers ultimately cannot be trusted. Having learned that love is not reliable, they put down shallow emotional roots. 19

This conception of love is not just a personal attitude: It has been enshrined in our marriage laws. Since the advent of no-fault divorce, the law actually forbids men and women to make a permanent legal commitment to each other. Instead, the legal assumption is: He (or she) who wants out wins. We all gained the right to unilateral divorce and in the process lost the right to give ourselves in marriage. Thanks to no-fault divorce and the attitudes, norms and policies that support it, getting married more closely resembles taking a concubine than taking a wife. 20

So, for far too many people these days, marriage no longer represents safety but danger. But the alternative, to try to practice Safe Love, love with all the exit lights flashing, is a sad and foolish delusion. Those who try to avoid the risks by avoiding marriage discover the dangers are not embedded in the social construction of marriage but in the vulnerable nature of love itself. Ask Mia Farrow. Ask Macaulay Culkin's mom. To trust is to risk betrayal. To refuse to trust is to refuse to love. 21

Marriage as an institution frays and falls not when it makes too many demands on people, but when it makes too few: when it is too risk-averse, too accommodating (morally and legally) of our timidity. Men and women marry because they long for dependable love, not only to have it, but to give it, and to give it and have it in a way that becomes indistinguishable. We want to trust and become trustworthy. 22

A hundred years ago, when marriage vows could be taken for granted, romantics imagined that heroic acts of love must take place outside of marriage. But they were wrong, these wistful romantics. Today, we have learned through painful social experimentation that it is not free love, but the vow that is daring, not cohabitation but marriage. To pledge our whole selves to a single love is the most remarkable thing most of us will ever do. 23

With the abolition of marriage, that last possibility for heroism is being taken from us. 24

Questions for Study and Discussion

1. Gallagher begins her essay with a question. (Glossary: *Beginnings and Endings*) Is it a rhetorical question? (Glossary: *Rhetorical Question*) How does her own response to that question serve as an effective method of introducing both her topic and her argument?
2. Gallagher describes marriage as a "frail, eroding word" in our culture, yet nine out of ten women marry at least once. How does she explain this paradox? (Glossary: *Paradox*)
3. How does Gallagher say we approach love in our Brave New World? What consequences does this so-called "Safe Love" have on our entire society?
4. Gallagher defines cohabitation as "commitment with fingers crossed" (16). (Glossary: *Definition*) Why does she think that cohabitation is harmful to building lasting marriages, not helpful as is commonly believed?
5. Gallagher presents many of her own theories and opinions, but she bases her arguments on a solid skeleton of statistical evidence. List the data she presents. Summarize in two sen-

tences what your impression of modern marriage is based on her evidence alone.

6. According to Gallagher, what is heroic and daring about a successful marriage? Why are we losing the chance for such heroism?

Vocabulary

Refer to your dictionary to define the following words as they are used in this selection. Then use each word in a sentence of your own.

bourgeois (1)
bohemian (1)
archaic (2)
omnipresent (3)
nuptial (3)
rhetoric (11)
inherently (14)
subordinates (14)
unilateral (20)
concubine (20)
abolition (24)

Classroom Activity Using Argument

An important component of any argumentative essay is how one chooses to organize and present the evidence that supports the argument. Imagine that your college asked you to write an essay to help recruit students. Remember which factors were most important to you as you made your decision to attend, then list the four pieces of evidence that best support your argument that students should attend your institution. Make the evidence as concrete and easy to understand as possible—for example, "Ninety-five percent of graduates are either employed or attending graduate school within a year after leaving the school." In which order would you present your evidence? Explain your answer.

Suggested Writing Assignments

1. Write an essay in which you argue that no-fault divorce benefits our society. Gallagher presents what she thinks we lost with the ability to easily dissolve the marriage bond, but

what did we gain? What consequences would we face if we made marriage as difficult to get out of as it was one hundred years ago?

2. Write an essay in which you defend a personal choice that might be viewed as unwise in your particular social circle. For example, you might defend a decision to become engaged, which friends might view as an even more hazardous enterprise after reading Gallagher's essay. Other possibilities include taking up smoking, quitting school, living at home, or following a difficult career path, such as that of a musician or visual artist. What kinds of evidence will you need in order to convince an audience of your peers?

19

Combining Rhetorical Strategies

Previous chapters in this section of *Models for Writers* emphasize a specific rhetorical pattern or writing strategy—Narration, Description, Illustration, Process Analysis, and so forth. The essays we have selected within each of those chapters use the given pattern or strategy as the dominant method of development. It is important to remember, however, that the dominant pattern is usually not the only one used to develop an essay. To reinforce this point, after each essay in *Models for Writers* we have often asked specific questions about the author's use of other developmental strategies. For example, in Barbara Huttmann's "A Crime of Compassion," an essay utilizing illustration, we ask a question about narration: "The story in Huttmann's example covers a period of six months. In paragraphs 4–6, she describes the first five months of Mac's illness; in paragraphs 7–10, the sixth month; and in paragraphs 12–17, the final morning. What important point about narration does her use of time in this sequence demonstrate?"

Although some essays are developed through the use of a single mode, more often good writers will take advantage of several of the strategies available to them, using whatever means of development will further their purpose and thesis to produce an essay that is informative, persuasive, and interesting.

What to Look for in Reading an Essay Using a Combination of Patterns

By reading the work of professional writers, you can learn how to use multiple strategies to your advantage in your own writing—how a paragraph of narration, a passage of description, a clarifying point of comparison and contrast, or the helpful definition of a key word or concept can vary the terrain of an essay, make it more interesting, and help a reader to comprehend your purpose and thesis.

The first step in analyzing an essay for its use of rhetorical patterns is to identify what appears to be the essay's dominant pattern. Simply, what approach is most in evidence? Is the writer clearly telling a story, describing a process, looking into the causes of a particular event or action? Next, look at what the writer does when not using the dominant strategy. If you are familiar with the various rhetorical strategies—and you should be by the time you turn to this chapter of the text—this analysis will be an easy and, in fact, enjoyable exercise.

The writers of the essays in this chapter use a wide variety of patterns to develop their subjects: Deborah Tannen, arguing for the power of apologies in "I'm Sorry, I Won't Apologize," uses illustration, comparison and contrast, and cause and effect to demonstrate how and why people use apologies. Gish Jen, in "An Ethnic Trump," illustrates the problems she and her husband are having with their son by narrating a brief story about his experiences with a couple of other boys on the playground. In "Beyond the Melting Pot," William A. Henry III uses illustration, examples, comparison and contrast, and cause and effect to explore the significance of "America's becoming a majority nonwhite society." Finally, Lars Eighner, in "On Dumpster Diving," uses definition, illustration, and process analysis to explain what he has learned from his experiences as a Dumpster diver.

Just as you have found with other essays in *Models for Writers,* reading and analyzing how writers combine patterns will lead you to a greater understanding of your own writing. You will find that you have in the patterns not only useful tools for development, but also the means to sharpen and make more effective the strategies that are already a natural part of your writing process.

Let's suppose you wanted to write an essay focusing on the controversy surrounding professional athletes' high salaries. Depending on your purpose and thesis, you might want to give examples of the athletes' salaries (illustration), highlight differences between today's salaries and those paid in other eras (comparison and contrast), and investigate the driving forces behind escalating salaries and the question of whether owners and fans are well served by such extraordinary remuneration (cause and effect).

Or, to give another example, let's say you wanted to write a paper on the injustice done to Japanese Americans who were sent to internment camps during World War II. You would naturally want to use illustration to recall several particular cases of families who were sent to the camps, and narration if you were fortunate enough to be able to interview some former camp inhabitants and gather firsthand accounts of their experiences. If your essay were to lead you into a closer examination of the reasons why this injustice happened in the first place, you would need to use cause-and-effect analysis, as well as argumentative reasoning. In short, you will need to have at your disposal the means, the strategic rhetorical devices, to fulfill your purpose and to support the thesis you establish for your essay.

If you rely on a single pattern or approach, you lose, of course, the opportunity to come at your subject from a variety of angles, any one of which might be the most insightful or engaging and, therefore, the most memorable for your reader. Perhaps nowhere is this more true than with essays that attempt to argue, or persuade your readers. So strong is the need, and so difficult the task, of changing readers' beliefs and thoughts and of calling readers to a particular action that you must use a combination of strategies to develop your subjects.

I'm Sorry, I Won't Apologize

Deborah Tannen

Deborah Tannen's book You Just Don't Understand *(1990), which explores the difficulties men and women experience in trying to communicate, remained on best-seller lists in the United States for more than four years. Tannen had previously published* That's Not What I Meant! *in 1986, and she continued her exploration of daily communication patterns in 1995 with* Talking 9 to 5, *a book about how we converse at work. In addition to writing and lecturing widely on language and communications, Tannen teaches linguistics at Georgetown University. As you read the following essay, you will detect elements of narration, illustration, comparison and contrast, definition, cause and effect, and process analysis. Despite using this combination of rhetorical patterns, Tannen maintains a sense of unity by never straying from her main point about the importance of apologizing.*

For Your Journal

Think about the last time you had a conflict that you either caused or for which you were at least partially to blame. Did you apologize to the party whom you wronged? In general, do you find it easy or difficult to apologize? Explain why.

Almost daily, news reports include accounts of public figures or heads of companies being forced to say they're sorry. In a recent case, Marge Schott, managing partner of the Cincinnati Reds, at first did not want to apologize for her remark that Hitler "was good at the beginning but he just went too far." Under pressure, she finally said that she regretted her remarks "offended 1 many people." Predictably—and especially given her history with such comments—many were not satisfied with this response and successfully lobbied for her resignation.

This particular use of "I'm sorry" has a familiar ring. The other day my husband said to me, "I'm sorry I hurt your feelings." I knew he was really trying. He has learned, through our years together, that apologies are important to me. But he was grinning, because he also knew that "I'm sorry I hurt your feelings" left open the possibility—indeed, strongly suggested—that he regretted not what he did but my emotional reaction. It sometimes seems that he thinks the earth will open up and swallow him if he admits fault. 2

It may appear that insisting someone admit fault is like wanting him to humiliate himself. But I don't see it that way, since it's no big deal for me to say I made a mistake and apologize. The problem is that it becomes a big deal when he won't. 3

I think it's something about men—not all men, of course. There are plenty of men who apologize easily and often, and plenty of women who—like Marge Schott—avoid it at all costs. But there are many women, seemingly more than men, who easily say they're sorry and can't understand why it's such a big deal for others. Indeed, many women say "I'm sorry" as a conversational ritual—an automatic tip of the verbal hat to acknowledge that something regrettable happened. And others sometimes take this too literally. 4

One woman, for example, was talking on the phone when she got an interrupting call that she had to take immediately. When she rang the first caller back, she began by acknowledging that she had inconvenienced him and possibly been rude. "This is Sharon," she said. "I'm sorry." He responded, "You're sorry you're Sharon?" He may well have intended this retort as a good-natured tease, but it irritated her because it implied there was something odd about what she had said, while she felt it was run-of-the-mill, even required. I suspect it struck him as odd because he would avoid saying "sorry" if he could. One C.E.O. found that he could avoid it entirely: his deputy told me that part of his job was to make the rounds after the boss had lost his temper and apologize for him. 5

It's as if there's a tenet that real men don't say they're sorry. Take the closing scene in *Crimson Tide*. Gene Hackman plays an 6 unyieldingly authoritarian Navy captain in charge of a submarine carrying nuclear warheads. When he gets an unconfirmed order to launch, he is determined to comply, but is thwarted by his lieutenant commander, played by Denzel Washington, who defies his commanding officer, sparks a mutiny and averts nuclear war. The order to launch turns out to have been an error. The final scene is one of those exhilarating, dramatic moments when justice is served. Standing at attention before a panel that has investigated the mutiny without hearing his side, the lieutenant commander expects to be court-martialed. Instead he is promoted—on the recommendation of his captain. As the film ends, the captain turns to his deputy and says, "You were right and I was wrong. . . ." The audience gasps: this icon of authoritarian rigidity is admitting error. Then he grins mischievously and finishes the sentence, ". . . about the horses—the Lipizzaners. They *are* from Spain, not Portugal." Never mind that they're really from Austria; the two men exchange a look of intense rapport, and the audience heaves a sigh of satisfying relief.

Not me. I felt frustrated. Why couldn't he just say it? "I made a mistake. You were right. I was wrong about starting that nuclear war." 7

And saying you're sorry isn't enough in itself. You have to seem sorry: your face should look dejected, your voice should sound apologetic. Describing how bad you feel is also a plus. Furthermore, the depth of remorse should be commensurate with the significance of the offense. An offhand "Sorry about that" might be fine for an insignificant error like dropping a piece of paper, but if you drop a glass of red wine on your host's brand new white couch, a fleeting "Sorry about that" will not suffice. 8

The same people who resist displaying contrition may be eager to see it in others. Nowhere is this more evident than in court. Judges and juries are widely believed to give milder sentences to defendants who seem contrite. Prisons used to be called "penitentiaries" because inmates were expected not only to serve their time but also to repent. Nowadays many offenders seem to regard prison sentences as contractual: I served my time, I paid my debt. No apologies. 9

Apologies seem to come most easily from those who know their error was not intentional. The Japanese government, for example, quickly apologized for the obviously accidental downing of 10 an American plane during joint military exercises. But they have been much more reluctant to apologize for offenses committed during World War II, like forcing Korean, Chinese and Filipina girls to serve as "comfort women" to Japanese soldiers.

Sometimes, though, people react negatively to an apology from a public figure. The First Lady discovered this last year when she met with a group of female columnists—off the record, she thought—and talked about how she had been portrayed in the press. "I regret very much that the efforts on health care were badly misunderstood, taken out of context and used politically against the Administration. I take responsibility for that, and I'm very sorry for that," she said. 11

The first part of this quote clearly indicates that the fault was not with her actions—"the efforts on health care"—but rather with the way they were received and distorted by others. But because she went on to say the big, bad "S" word, all hell broke loose. One newspaper article quoted a political scientist as saying, "To apologize for substantive things you've done raises the white flag. There's a school of thought in politics that you never say you're sorry. The best defense is a good offense." A Republican woman in the Florida state cabinet was quoted as saying: "I've seen women who overapologize, but I don't do that. I believe you negotiate through strength." 12

And there's the rub—apologizing is seen as a sign of weakness. This explains why more men than women might resist apologizing, since most boys learn early on that their peers will take advantage of them if they appear weak. Girls, in contrast, tend to reward other girls who talk in ways that show they don't think they're better than their peers. 13

Hillary Clinton's experience also explains why those who resist saying "I apologize" may find it more palatable to say "I'm sorry," because I'm sorry is not necessarily an apology. It can be—and in the First Lady's statement it clearly was—an expression of regret. It means "I'm sorry that happened." Her experience shows how easily this expression of regret can be mistaken for an apology. 14

Given this ambiguity, shouldn't we all strike the phrase "I'm sorry" from our vocabularies? Not necessarily. I think we'd do better as a society if more people said "I'm sorry" rather than fewer. Instead of all the railing against Hillary Clinton for apolo- 15 gizing when she expressed regret, how come no one thought that either Newt Gingrich or his mother should apologize when the latter quoted her son as uttering an irrefutable insult against the First Lady? The problem seems to be not a surfeit of apologies but a dearth of them. One business manager told me he has discovered that apologies can be a powerful tool: subordinates so appreciate his admitting fault that they not only forgive his errors but also become ever more loyal employees.

History includes many examples of apologies that were not 16
weak but highly potent. Following the calamitous Bay of Pigs invasion, John F. Kennedy demonstrated the power not only of "taking responsibility" but also of actually taking blame. For someone that high up to admit fault was shocking—and effective. People forgave the President, and his Administration, for the colossal error.

I think those brave enough to admit fault would find a similar 17
power at home: it's amazing how an apology, if it seems sincere, can dissipate another's anger, calm the roiling waters. Erich Segal got it exactly wrong. Love doesn't mean never having to say you're sorry. Love means being able to say you're sorry—and, like J.F.K., being strong enough to admit you were at fault.

Questions for Study and Discussion

1. Why was it predictable that Marge Schott's "apology" failed to satisfy many people? In what way is Schott's situation analogous to that of Tannen's husband? (Glossary: *Analogy*)
2. How is apologizing—or not apologizing—related to gender? The statement "real men don't say they're sorry" (6) alludes to the tongue-in-cheek book *Real Men Don't Eat Quiche.* (Glossary: *Allusion*) What connotations does such a phrase carry with it? (Glossary: *Connotation/Denotation*)
3. Imagine that Tannen invites you to a party at her house. As the guests settle in, you enter into an animated discussion with a group of people about fishing. In demonstrating the size of the fish you once caught, you extend your arms out wide, accidentally knocking over and breaking a crystal vase containing a bouquet of roses. Having read the article,

what would you say to Tannen? Describe the expression and tone of voice you would use. (Glossary: *Description*)

4. What does it mean to apologize in our society? How does this contrast with the way the Japanese view apologies? (Glossary: *Comparison and Contrast*)
5. Why was Hillary Clinton criticized for her statement regarding the response of the press to her health care plans? How did the press misinterpret what she was trying to say?
6. What audience do you think Tannen is trying to reach? (Glossary: *Audience*) In your opinion, does she do an effective job of communicating her points to her audience? Why, or why not?

Vocabulary

Refer to your dictionary to define the following words as they are used in this selection. Then use each word in a sentence of your own.

lobbied (1)
contrition (4)
tenet (8)
rapport (8)
commensurate (10)
ambiguity (17)
surfeit (17)
dearth (17)
calamitous (18)
roiling (19)

Classroom Activity Using a Combination of Rhetorical Strategies

Classify apologies into three different categories, based on the seriousness of the mistake one has committed against the wronged party. Provide an example for what might provoke each type of apology, then give a short directional process analysis of what should be said and how one should say it. For example, you might say the following in apologizing for a minor incident:

> Quick Apology: To be used after spilling a nonstaining material on someone's rug or forgetting to do something that was not important or can be done later without a problem. Simply say, "I'm sorry, I didn't mean to do that." This will suffice if

said in a manner that communicates regret, not impatience or insincerity.

Base your responses on what you would consider acceptable for each situation if you were the wronged party.

Suggested Writing Assignments

1. Do you agree with Tannen's assertion that, in general, men find it more difficult to apologize than women? Write an essay in which you argue in support of this assertion, or argue that, in your experience, the two genders handle apologizing in a similar manner. Compare and contrast the way your friends and relatives of each gender handle apologies, and give specific examples to illustrate your argument.
2. Read a newspaper in search of what Tannen terms the "almost daily" occurrence of a public figure's or head of a company's being forced to apologize. When you find such an article, read it carefully. If possible, find at least one more article by a different writer about the same incident. Write an essay in which you analyze how the person who is apologizing is portrayed in the media. In what way is the apology presented to the reader? Is it portrayed as an admission of weakness or guilt, or is there sympathy or admiration expressed for the subject? What rhetorical techniques do the writers of the articles use to convey their assessments of the subject?

An Ethnic Trump

Gish Jen

Gish Jen's debut novel, Typical American, *received very favorable reviews when it was published in 1991. It was followed in 1996 by* Mona in the Promised Land. *Born in 1956, Jen received a B.A. from Harvard University in 1977 and an M.F.A. from the University of Iowa in 1983, before settling in Cambridge, Massachusetts, where she lives today. "An Ethnic Trump" first appeared in the* New York Times Magazine *on July 7, 1996. In the essay, Jen explores the difficult decisions parents sometimes face when trying to raise their children to be multicultural and proud of their own heritage. Take note of how the opening paragraph combines elements of definition and process analysis to establish a context for considering the situation Jen then goes on to describe, as well as the decision she and her husband make in the end.*

For Your Journal

How much do you know about your family tree? How important is it to you to know where your family came from, what it has done, and how its heritage might affect your own personality and abilities? Explain your response.

That my son, Luke, age 4, goes to Chinese-culture school 1
seems inevitable to most people, even though his father is of Irish descent. For certain ethnicities trump others; Chinese, for example, trumps Irish. This has something to do with the relative distance of certain cultures from mainstream American culture, but it also has to do with race. For as we all know, it is not only certain ethnicities that trump others but certain colors: black

trumps white, for example, always and forever; a mulatto is not a kind of white person, but a kind of black person.

And so it is, too, that my son is considered a kind of Asian person whose manifest destiny is to embrace Asian things. The Chinese language. Chinese food. Chinese New Year. No one cares whether he speaks Gaelic or wears green on St. Patrick's Day. For though Luke's skin is fair, and his features mixed, people see his straight black hair and "know" who he is. 2

But is this how we should define ourselves, by other people's perceptions? My husband, Dave, and I had originally hoped for Luke to grow up embracing his whole complex ethnic heritage. We had hoped to pass on to him values and habits of mind that had actually survived in both of us. 3

Then one day, Luke combed his black hair and said he was turning it yellow. Another day, a fellow mother reported that her son had invited all blond-haired children like himself to his birthday party. And yet another day, Luke was happily scooting around the Cambridge Common playground when a pair of older boys, apparently brothers, blocked his way. "You're Chinese!" they shouted, leaning on the hood of Luke's scooter car. "You are! You're Chinese!" So brazen were these kids, that even when I, an adult, intervened, they continued to shout. Luke answered, "No, I'm not!"—to no avail; it was not clear if the boys even heard him. Then the boys' mother called to them from some distance away, outside the fence, and though her voice was no louder than Luke's, they left obediently. 4

Behind them opened a great, rippling quiet, like the wash of a battleship. 5

Luke and I immediately went over things he could say if anything like that ever happened again. I told him that he was 100 percent American, even though I knew from my own childhood in Yonkers that these words would be met only with derision. It was a sorry chore. Since then I have not asked him about the incident, hoping that he has forgotten about it, and wishing that I could, too. For I wish I could forget the sight of those kids' fingers on the hood of Luke's little car. I wish I could forget their loud attack, but also Luke's soft defense: *No, I'm not.* 6

Chinese-culture school. After dozens of phone calls, I was elated to discover the Greater Boston Chinese Cultural Association nearby in West Newton. The school takes children at 3, has 7 a wonderful sense of community and is housed in a center paid for, in part, by great karaoke fund-raising events. (Never mind what the Japanese meant to the Chinese in the old world. In this world, people donate at least $200 each for a chance at the mike, and the singing goes on all night.) There are even vendors who bring home-style Chinese food to sell after class—stuff you can't get in a restaurant. Dave and I couldn't wait for the second class, and a chance to buy more *bao* for our freezer.

But in the car on the way to the second class, Luke announced 8
that he didn't want to go to Chinese school anymore. He said that the teacher talked mostly about ducks and bears and that he wasn't interested in ducks and bears. And I knew this was true. I knew that Luke was interested only in whales and ships. And what's more, I knew we wouldn't push him to take swimming lessons if he didn't want to, or music. Chinese school was a wonderful thing, but there was a way in which we were accepting it as somehow non-optional. Was that right? Hadn't we always said that we didn't want our son to see himself as more essentially Chinese than Irish?

Yet we didn't want him to deny his Chinese heritage, either. 9
And if there were going to be incidents on the playground, we wanted him to at least know what Chinese meant. So when Luke said again that he didn't want to go to Chinese school, I said, "Oh, really?" Later on we could try to teach him to define himself irrespective of race. For now, though, he was going to Chinese school. I exchanged glances with Dave. And then together, in a most carefully casual manner, we squinted at the road and kept going.

Questions for Study and Discussion

1. What is a trump? How does it apply to ethnicity? Do you think that it is an effective analogy in this context? (Glossary: *Analogy*) Why, or why not?
2. Jen contrasts what she and her husband believed Luke's response to his mixed ethnicity should have been with what it really was. (Glossary: *Comparison and Contrast*) What was the ideal? What was the reality? Why was the ideal so difficult to achieve?

3. Why does Jen say that she wishes she could forget not only the bullies' attack on Luke, but also his response to them? What did his response communicate to her?
4. Why is it ironic that the Chinese Cultural Association center is paid for largely by karaoke fund-raising events? (Glossary: *Irony*)
5. Why do Luke's parents not allow him to stop going to the Chinese-culture school, even though they would not force him to take music or athletic lessons that he did not want? Why is it so important that he learn about Chinese culture?

Vocabulary

Refer to your dictionary to define the following words as they are used in this selection. Then use each word in a sentence of your own.

trump (1)
mulatto (1)
manifest destiny (2)
brazen (4)
derision (6)
karaoke (7)

Classroom Activity Using a Combination of Rhetorical Strategies

Write a short paragraph of first-person narrative in which you create an evocative image using a simile or metaphor. Then write a short descriptive paragraph of the same scene using the third person. For example:

> I ran to where Arlene had fallen. I drew in my breath when I saw the blood on her forehead, but when I offered her my hand, she waved me away.
>
> "I'm fine," she said, her eyes looking at me but seeing little. She struggled to her feet, but when she stood up I watched her totter like a foal standing for the first time.

> The girl lay dazed in the dust. A crowd began to gather, concerned by the fall and the blood on the girl's forehead. A boy offered her his hand, but she did not take it and tried to

stand up on her own. Her knees buckled and she weaved back and forth, on the edge of balance. Her first steps were hesitant and shaky at best.

Suggested Writing Assignments

1. Jen says, "Later on we could try to teach him to define himself irrespective of race" (9). Based on your own experience as an adolescent and on what you observe around you, is it possible to define oneself irrespective of race or ethnicity in our society as it stands today, or is such a definition merely a noble ideal, worth working toward but not yet achievable? Write an essay in which you argue for one conclusion or the other, using as many examples as you think are necessary to support your argument. What is the cause-and-effect relationship between societal pressures and the way one sees oneself fitting into society?
2. Write an essay in which you define yourself. Does your definition include ethnic or religious heritage? Does it include what you do, or what you want to do for a career? How much do you emphasize the way you interact with others and the way others interact with you? Use self-description, personal narrative, comparison and contrast, and/or other rhetorical techniques to enable readers to readily understand your personal definition.

Beyond the Melting Pot

William A. Henry III

William A. Henry III (1950–1994) was born in South Orange, New Jersey, and received his B.A. from Yale University. He worked as a writer and critic for the Boston Globe *and the* New York Daily News *before becoming the drama critic for* Time *magazine. In 1980 he won the Pulitzer Prize for his television commentary. His books include biographies of Jackie Gleason and Jack Benny;* Visions of America *(1985), an analysis of the 1984 presidential election; and* In Defense of Elitism, *which was published posthumously in 1994. The following piece first appeared in* Time *on April 9, 1990. As you read it, notice that Henry incorporates the testimony of people from many different cultures and ethnic backgrounds to both illustrate and support his point about the growing influence of minorities in defining an American identity.*

For Your Journal

Do you consider yourself a "typical" American? Why, or why not? If you do not believe you are typical, what do you consider the typical American to be?

Someday soon, surely much sooner than most people who filled out their Census forms last week realize, white Americans will become a minority group. Long before that day arrives, the presumption that the "typical" U.S. citizen is someone who traces his or her descent in a direct line to Europe will be part of the past. By the time these elementary students at Brentwood Science Magnet School in Brentwood, California, reach mid-life, their diverse ethnic experience in the classroom will be echoed in neighborhoods and workplaces throughout the U.S. 1

Already 1 American in 4 defines himself or herself as Hispanic 2
or nonwhite. If current trends in immigration and birth rates persist, the Hispanic population will have further increased an estimated 21%, the Asian presence about 22%, blacks almost 12% and whites a little more than 2% when the 20th century ends. By 2020, a date no further into the future than John F. Kennedy's election is in the past, the number of U.S. residents who are Hispanic or nonwhite will have more than doubled, to nearly 115 million, while the white population will not be increasing at all. By 2056, when someone born today will be 66 years old, the "average" U.S. resident, as defined by Census statistics, will trace his or her descent to Africa, Asia, the Hispanic world, the Pacific Islands, Arabia—almost anywhere but white Europe.

While there may remain towns or outposts where even a black 3
family will be something of an oddity, where English and Irish and German surnames will predominate, where a traditional (some will wistfully say "real") America will still be seen on almost every street corner, they will be only the vestiges of an earlier nation. The former majority will learn, as a normal part of everyday life, the meaning of the Latin slogan engraved on U.S. coins—E PLURIBUS UNUM, one formed from many.

Among the younger populations that go to school and provide 4
new entrants to the work force, the change will happen sooner. In some places an America beyond the melting pot has already arrived. In New York State some 40% of elementary- and secondary-school children belong to an ethnic minority. Within a decade, the proportion is expected to approach 50%. In California white pupils are already a minority. Hispanics (who, regardless of their complexion, generally distinguish themselves from both blacks and whites) account for 31.4% of public school enrollment, blacks add 8.9%, and Asians and others amount to 11%—for a nonwhite total of 51.3%. This finding is not only a reflection of white flight from desegregated public schools. Whites of all ages account for just 58% of California's population. In San Jose bearers of the Vietnamese surname Nguyen outnumber the Joneses in the telephone directory 14 columns to eight.

Nor is the change confined to the coasts. Some 12,000 Hmong 5
refugees from Laos have settled in St. Paul. At some Atlanta low-rent apartment complexes that used to be virtually all black, social workers today need to speak Spanish. At the Sesame Hut restau-

rant in Houston, a Korean immigrant owner trains Hispanic immigrant workers to prepare Chinese-style food for a largely black clientele. The Detroit area has 200,000 people of Middle Eastern descent; some 1,500 small grocery and convenience stores in the vicinity are owned by a whole subculture of Chaldean Christians with roots in Iraq. "Once America was a microcosm of European nationalities," says Molefi Asante, chairman of the department of African-American studies at Temple University in Philadelphia. "Today America is a microcosm of the world."

History suggests that sustaining a truly multiracial society is 6
difficult, or at least unusual. Only a handful of great powers of the distant past—Pharaonic Egypt and Imperial Rome, most notably—managed to maintain a distinct national identity while embracing, and being ruled by, an ethnic mélange. The most ethnically diverse contemporary power, the Soviet Union, is beset with secessionist demands and near tribal conflicts. But such comparisons are flawed, because those empires were launched by conquest and maintained through an aggressive military presence. The U.S. was created, and continues to be redefined, primarily by voluntary immigration. This process has been one of the country's great strengths, infusing it with talent and energy. The "browning of America" offers tremendous opportunity for capitalizing anew on the merits of many peoples from many lands. Yet this fundamental change in the ethnic makeup of the U.S. also poses risks. The American character is resilient and thrives on change. But past periods of rapid evolution have also, alas, brought out deeper, more fearful aspects of the national soul.

A truly multiracial society will undoubtedly prove much harder 7
to govern. Even seemingly race-free conflicts will be increasingly complicated by an overlay of ethnic tension. For example, the expected showdown in the early 21st century between the rising number of retirees and the dwindling number of workers who must be taxed to pay for the elders' Social Security benefits will probably be compounded by the fact that a large majority of recipients will be white, whereas a majority of workers paying for them will be nonwhite.

While prior generations of immigrants believed they had to 8
learn English quickly to survive, many Hispanics now maintain that the Spanish language is inseparable from their ethnic and cultural identity, and seek to remain bilingual, if not primarily

Spanish-speaking, for life. They see legislative drives to make English the sole official language, which have prevailed in some fashion in at least 16 states, as a political backlash. Says Arturo Vargas of the Mexican American Legal Defense and Educational Fund: "That's what English-only has been all about—a reaction to the growing population and influence of Hispanics. It's human nature to be uncomfortable with change. That's what the Census is all about, documenting changes and making sure the country keeps up."

Racial and ethnic conflict remains an ugly fact of American 9
life everywhere, from working-class ghettos to college campuses, and those who do not raise their fists often raise their voices over affirmative action and other power sharing. When Florida Atlantic University, a state-funded institution under pressure to increase its low black enrollment, offered last month to give free tuition to every qualified black freshman who enrolled, the school was flooded with calls of complaint, some protesting that nothing was being done for "real" Americans. As the numbers of minorities increase, their demands for a share of the national bounty are bound to intensify, while whites are certain to feel ever more embattled. Businesses often feel whipsawed between immigration laws that punish them for hiring illegal aliens and antidiscrimination laws that penalize them for demanding excessive documentation from foreign-seeming job applicants. Even companies that consistently seek to do the right thing may be overwhelmed by the problems of diversifying a primarily white managerial corps fast enough to direct a work force that will be increasingly nonwhite and, potentially, resentful.

Nor will tensions be limited to the polar simplicity of white vs. 10
nonwhite. For all Jesse Jackson's rallying cries about shared goals, minority groups often feel keenly competitive. Chicago's Hispanic leaders have leapfrogged between white and black factions, offering support wherever there seemed to be the most to gain for their own community. Says Dan Solis of the Hispanic-oriented United Neighborhood Organization: "If you're thinking power, you don't put your eggs in one basket."

Blacks, who feel they waited longest and endured most in the 11
fight for equal opportunity, are uneasy about being supplanted by Hispanics or, in some areas, by Asians as the numerically largest and most influential minority—and even more, about being

outstripped in wealth and status by these newer groups. Because Hispanics are so numerous and Asians such a fast-growing group, they have become the "hot" minorities, and blacks feel their needs are getting lower priority. As affirmative action has broadened to include other groups—and to benefit white women perhaps most of all—blacks perceive it as having waned in value for them.

Political pressure has already brought about sweeping change in public school textbooks over the past couple of decades and has begun to affect the core humanities curriculum at such elite universities as Stanford. At stake at the college level is whether the traditional "canon" of Greek, Latin and West European humanities study should be expanded to reflect the cultures of Africa, Asia and other parts of the world. Many books treasured as classics by prior generations are now seen as tools of cultural imperialism. In the extreme form, this thinking rises to a value-deprived neutralism that views all cultures, regardless of the grandeur or paucity of their attainments, as essentially equal. 12

Even more troubling is a revisionist approach to history in which groups that have gained power in the present turn to remaking the past in the image of their desires. If 18th, 19th, and earlier 20th century society should not have been so dominated by white Christian men of West European ancestry, they reason, then that past society should be reinvented as pluralist and democratic. Alternatively, the racism and sexism of the past are treated as inextricable from—and therefore irremediably tainting—traditional learning and values. 13

While debates over college curriculum get the most attention, professors generally can resist or subvert the most wrong-headed changes and students generally have mature enough judgment to sort out the arguments. Elementary- and secondary-school curriculums reach a far broader segment at a far more impressionable age, and political expediency more often wins over intellectual honesty. Exchanges have been vituperative in New York, where a state task force concluded that "African-Americans, Asian-Americans, Puerto Ricans and Native Americans have all been victims of an intellectual and educational oppression. . . . Negative characterizations, or the absence of positive references, have had a terribly damaging effect on the psyche of young people." In urging a revised syllabus, the task force argued, "Chil- 14 dren from European culture will have a less arrogant perspective of being part of a group that has 'done it all.'" Many intellectuals are outraged. Political scientist Andrew Hacker of Queens College lambastes a task-force suggestion that children be taught how "Native Americans were here to welcome new settlers from Holland, Senegal, England, Indonesia, France, the Congo, Italy, China, Iberia." Asks Hacker: "Did the Indians really welcome all those groups? Were they at Ellis Island when the Italians started to arrive? This is not history but a myth intended to bolster the self-esteem of certain children and, just possibly, a platform for advocates of various ethnic interests."

Values: Something in Common

Economic and political issues, however much emotion they 15
arouse, are fundamentally open to practical solution. The deeper significance of America's becoming a majority nonwhite society is what it means to the national psyche, to individuals' sense of themselves and their nation—their idea of what it is to be American. People of color have often felt that whites treated equality as a benevolence granted to minorities rather than as an inherent natural right. Surely that condescension will wither.

Rather than accepting U.S. history and its meaning as settled, 16
citizens will feel ever more free to debate where the nation's successes sprang from and what its unalterable beliefs are. They will clash over which myths and icons to invoke in education, in popular culture, in ceremonial speechmaking from political campaigns to the State of the Union address. Which is the more admirable heroism: the courageous holdout by a few conquest-minded whites over Hispanics at the Alamo, or the anonymous expression of hope by millions who filed through Ellis Island? Was the subduing of the West a daring feat of bravery and ingenuity, or a wretched example of white imperialism? Symbols deeply meaningful to one group can be a matter of indifference to another. Says University of Wisconsin chancellor Donna Shalala: "My grandparents came from Lebanon. I don't identify with the Pilgrims on a personal level." Christopher Jencks, professor of sociology at Northwestern, asks, "Is anything more basic about turkeys and Pilgrims than about Martin Luther King and Selma? To me, it's six of one and half a dozen of the other, if children

understand what it's like to be a dissident minority. Because the civil rights struggle is closer chronologically, it's likelier to be taught by someone who really cares."

Traditionalists increasingly distinguish between a "multiracial" society, which they say would be fine, and a "multicultural" society, which they deplore. They argue that every society needs a universally accepted set of values and that new arrivals should therefore be pressured to conform to the mentality on which U.S. prosperity and freedom were built. Says Allan Bloom, author of the best-selling *The Closing of the American Mind:* "Obviously, the future of America can't be sustained if people keep only to their own ways and remain perpetual outsiders. The society has got to turn them into Americans. There are natural fears that today's immigrants may be too much of a cultural stretch for a nation based on Western values." 17

The counterargument, made by such scholars as historian Thomas Bender of New York University, is that if the center cannot hold, then one must redefine the center. It should be, he says, "the ever changing outcome of a continuing contest among social groups and ideas for the power to define public culture." Besides, he adds, many immigrants arrive committed to U.S. values; that is part of what attracted them. Says Julian Simon, professor of business administration at the University of Maryland: "The life and institutions here shape immigrants and not vice versa. This business about immigrants changing our institutions and our basic ways of life is hogwash. It's nativist scare talk." 18

Historians note that Americans have felt before that their historical culture was being overwhelmed by immigrants, but conflicts between earlier-arriving English, Germans and Irish and later-arriving Italians and Jews did not have the obvious and enduring element of racial skin color. And there was never a time when the nonmainstream elements could claim, through sheer numbers, the potential to unite and exert political dominance. Says Bender: "The real question is whether or not our notion of diversity can successfully negotiate the color line." 19

For whites, especially those who trace their ancestry back to the early years of the Republic, the American heritage is a source of pride. For people of color, it is more likely to evoke anger and sometimes shame. The place where hope is shared is in the future. Demographer Ben Wattenberg, formerly perceived as a resister 20 to social change, says, "There's a nice chance that the American myth in the 1990s and beyond is going to ratchet another step toward this idea that we are the universal nation. That rings the bell of manifest destiny. We're a people with a mission and a sense of purpose, and we believe we have something to offer the world."

Not every erstwhile alarmist can bring himself to such optimism. Says Norman Podhoretz, editor of *Commentary:* "A lot of people are trying to undermine the foundations of the American experience and are pushing toward a more Balkanized society. I think that would be a disaster, not only because it would destroy a precious social inheritance but also because it would lead to enormous unrest, even violence." 21

While know-nothingism is generally confined to the more dismal corners of the American psyche, it seems all too predictable that during the next decades many more mainstream white Americans will begin to speak openly about the nation they feel they are losing. There are not, after all, many nonwhite faces depicted in Norman Rockwell's paintings. White Americans are accustomed to thinking of themselves as the very picture of their nation. Inspiring as it may be to the rest of the world, significant as it may be to the U.S. role in global politics, world trade and the pursuit of peace, becoming a conspicuously multiracial society is bound to be a somewhat bumpy experience for many ordinary citizens. For older Americans, raised in a world where the numbers of whites were greater and the visibility of nonwhites was carefully restrained, the new world will seem ever stranger. But as the children at Brentwood Science Magnet School, and their counterparts in classrooms across the nation, are coming to realize, the new world is here. It is now. And it is irreversibly the America to come. 22

Questions for Study and Discussion

1. Why is the slogan *E Pluribus Unum* becoming more and more appropriate in describing the United States? How do most of today's immigrants differ from those of a century ago?

2. In what way is the character of the emerging multiethnic United States different from that of successful multiethnic powers of the past? Is this a significant difference? What concerns does Henry have about the "browning of America," based on American history?
3. Henry places his numerical statistics at the beginning of his essay so that he may use them as a foundation for what he has to say. (Glossary: *Beginnings and Endings*) How does he organize the rest of his essay? (Glossary: *Organization*) Do you think the way he organizes the information and issues is effective? Why, or why not?
4. Henry uses the situation at Florida Atlantic University to illustrate the potential for ethnic conflict that he speculates will become more common. (Glossary: *Illustration*) What does his example tell you about the changing nature of such conflicts? What are other likely venues for such conflicts in the future?
5. What is the difference between a multiracial society and a multicultural one? What do traditionalists fear about a multicultural society?
6. Summarize the opinions of Wattenberg and Podhoretz. Why does Henry present two such different views of what is to come in the future?
7. Summarize Henry's vision of the future. What does he fear? What opportunities does he see? What is his purpose for writing the essay? (Glossary: *Purpose*) Explain your answer.

Vocabulary

Refer to your dictionary to define the following words as they are used in this selection. Then use each word in a sentence of your own.

vestiges (3)
microcosm (5)
mélange (6)
infusing (6)
whipsawed (9)
canon (12)
paucity (12)
vituperative (14)
lambastes (14)
inherent (15)
erstwhile (21)

Classroom Activity Using a Combination of Rhetorical Strategies

Those who try to predict the future—such as some of the people quoted by Henry—are unable to supply hard evidence to back up their predictions. In order to appear credible they should carefully assemble evidence that supports their point of view, then present it in such a way that the reader will at least accept that their predictions may possibly come true. In addition, they should use a variety of strategies to present their information, including comparing and contrasting conflicting evidence, describing scenarios so that readers may better understand them, arguing for their point of view, and so on. Bring the national section of a major newspaper to class and read the headlines to look for stories that will support either the thesis "American society is currently in a state of turmoil" or "Americans will be able to accommodate the current changes in society without any upheaval." Jot down one-sentence summaries of four or five stories that support the thesis you have chosen. How would you organize the information to back up your view? What techniques would you use to present it? Be prepared to share your information with the class and to discuss the choices you made.

Suggested Writing Assignments

1. Reread paragraphs 12–14 in Henry's essay. Write an essay in which you present your view on the current debate over the importance of the "classics" versus the importance of presenting a balanced ethnic view of history. Is it a reasonable contention that a body of work that was almost entirely the product of white men of European descent is now out of date and not valid to teach in schools? Or does the traditional canon still deserve its prominent place in American education? How do you feel about a revisionist history that promotes dignity and self-esteem among the various ethnic groups but that can also be criticized as misleading or inaccurate?
2. Henry mentions the campaign to establish English as the official language of the United States, or at least the official

language of as many states as possible. Some argue that, while each state that votes to establish English as an official language represents a victory for the pro-English lobby in the short term, such legislation is dangerous. If an official language can be legislated, they argue, there may well come a day when Hispanics will have sufficient political clout to vote Spanish in as the official language of a state, a region, or, theoretically, even the entire country. And on the other side, of course, is the argument that native languages must be preserved so that immigrants can retain their ethnic heritages. Use a combination of strategies to write an essay in which you present how you feel about this issue. Do you think that English should be enforced as the official language of the United States? Why, or why not? If you think it should, what can we do to help preserve the ethnic identities of immigrants? If you think not, how can we function as a cohesive society if large segments of the population are unable to understand one another?

On Dumpster Diving

Lars Eighner

Born in Texas in 1948, Lars Eighner attended the University of Texas at Austin. After graduation, he wrote essays and fiction, and several of his articles were published in such magazines as Threepenny Review, The Guide, *and* Inches. *His volume of short stories,* Bayou Boys and Other Stories, *was published in 1985. He became homeless in 1988 when he left his job as an attendant at a mental hospital. The following piece appeared in the* Utne Reader, *abridged from a piece that appeared in* The Threepenny Review. *It eventually became part of Eighner's startling portrayal of the three years he spent as a homeless person,* Travels with Lizbeth *(1993). In 1995 he published his first novel,* Pawn to Queen Four. *Eighner uses a number of rhetorical strategies in "On Dumpster Diving," but pay particular attention to the importance of his delineation of the "stages a person goes through in learning to scavenge" (process analysis) to the success of the essay overall.*

For Your Journal

Some people believe that acquiring material objects is what life is all about, and that the measure of their own "worth" is the inventory of their possessions. Comment on the role that material objects play in your life and on whether or not your view of the importance of material objects has changed as you have grown older.

I began Dumpster diving about a year before I became homeless. 1

I prefer the term *scavenging*. I have heard people, evidently 2
meaning to be polite, use the word *foraging,* but I prefer to re-

serve that word for gathering nuts and berries and such, which I also do, according to the season and opportunity.

I like the frankness of the word *scavenging.* I live from the refuse of others. I am a scavenger. I think it a sound and honorable niche, although if I could I would naturally prefer to live the comfortable consumer life, perhaps—and only perhaps—as a slightly less wasteful consumer owing to what I have learned as a scavenger. 3

Except for jeans, all my clothes come from Dumpsters. Boom boxes, candles, bedding, toilet paper, medicine, books, a typewriter, a virgin male love doll, coins sometimes amounting to many dollars: all came from Dumpsters. And, yes, I eat from Dumpsters, too. 4

There is a predictable series of stages that a person goes through in learning to scavenge. At first the new scavenger is filled with disgust and self-loathing. He is ashamed of being seen. 5

This stage passes with experience. The scavenger finds a pair of running shoes that fit and look and smell brand-new. He finds a pocket calculator in perfect working order. He finds pristine ice cream, still frozen, more than he can eat or keep. He begins to understand: people do throw away perfectly good stuff, a lot of perfectly good stuff. 6

At this stage he may become lost and never recover. All the Dumpster divers I have known come to the point of trying to acquire everything they touch. Why not take it, they reason, it is all free. This is, of course, hopeless, and most divers come to realize that they must restrict themselves to items of relatively immediate utility. 7

The finding of objects is becoming something of an urban art. Even respectable, employed people will sometimes find something tempting sticking out of a Dumpster or standing beside one. Quite a number of people, not all of them of the bohemian type, are willing to brag that they found this or that piece in the trash. 8

But eating from Dumpsters is the thing that separates the dilettanti from the professionals. Eating safely involves three principles: using the senses and common sense to evaluate the condition of the found materials; knowing the Dumpsters of a given area and checking them regularly; and seeking always to answer the question "Why was this discarded?" 9

Yet perfectly good food can be found in Dumpsters. Canned goods, for example, turn up fairly often in the Dumpsters I frequent. I also have few qualms about dry foods such as crackers, cookies, cereal, chips, and pasta if they are free of visible contaminants and still dry and crisp. Raw fruits and vegetables with intact skins seem perfectly safe to me, excluding, of course, the obviously rotten. Many are discarded for minor imperfections that can be pared away. 10

A typical discard is a half jar of peanut butter—though nonorganic peanut butter does not require refrigeration and is unlikely to spoil in any reasonable time. One of my favorite finds is yogurt—often discarded, still sealed, when the expiration date has passed—because it will keep for several days, even in warm weather. 11

No matter how careful I am I still get dysentery at least once a month, oftener in warm weather. I do not want to paint too romantic a picture. Dumpster diving has serious drawbacks as a way of life. 12

I find from the experience of scavenging two rather deep lessons. The first is to take what I can use and let the rest go. I have come to think that there is no value in the abstract. A thing I cannot use or make useful, perhaps by trading, has no value, however fine or rare it may be. 13

The second lesson is the transience of material being. I do not suppose that ideas are immortal, but certainly they are longer-lived than material objects. 14

The things I find in Dumpsters, the love letters and rag dolls of so many lives, remind me of this lesson. Now I hardly pick up a thing without envisioning the time I will cast it away. This, I think, is a healthy state of mind. Almost everything I have now has already been cast out at least once, proving that what I own is valueless to someone. 15

I find that my desire to grab for the gaudy bauble has been largely sated. I think this is an attitude I share with the very wealthy—we both know there is plenty more where whatever we have came from. Between us are the rat-race millions who have confounded their selves with the objects they grasp and who nightly scavenge the cable channels for they know not what. 16

I am sorry for them. 17

Questions for Study and Discussion

1. Why does Eighner prefer the word *scavenging* to *foraging* or *Dumpster diving?* What does this exploration of scavenging diction tell the reader about Eighner at the beginning of the essay? (Glossary: *Diction*)
2. How does Eighner use illustration to depict the evolution of a person from a new to an experienced scavenger? What does his illustration contribute to the essay? (Glossary: *Illustration*)
3. What words does Eighner use to describe the actual items he finds while scavenging? (Glossary: *Diction*)
4. What "separates the dilettanti from the professionals" (9) of Dumpster divers?
5. What are the two lessons Eighner learns from scavenging? Why are they important to him?
6. In paragraph 12, Eighner says "Dumpster diving has serious drawbacks as a way of life." But he concludes his essay by saying "I am sorry for [the rat-race millions]." In what way has scavenging benefited him? In what way has it harmed him? (Glossary: *Cause and Effect*)
7. Eighner refers to elements of Dumpster diving that are concrete (e.g., "He finds pristine ice cream, still frozen, more than he can eat or keep" [6]), as well as abstract (e.g., "The second lesson is the transience of material being" [14]). Discuss the difference between these elements. (Glossary: *Concrete/Abstract*) What does Eighner achieve by using both types of elements?

Vocabulary

Refer to your dictionary to define the following words as they are used in this selection. Then use each word in a sentence of your own.

refuse (3)
niche (3)
dilettanti (9)
qualms (10)
transience (14)
sated (16)
rat-race (16)

Classroom Activity Using a Combination of Rhetorical Strategies

Listed below are several subjects for essays. Consider a main rhetorical strategy, as well as two minor strategies, that you could conceivably use to explore each topic. An important first step is to ask yourself a question that narrows the topic. For example:

TOPIC: happiness (What is happiness?)

MAIN STRATEGY: extended definition of *happiness*

MINOR STRATEGY: use of illustration to give examples of various types of happiness

MINOR STRATEGY: use of cause and effect to explain what events might bring about (cause) the various types of happiness (effect)

Possible Topics:

1. population growth
2. theft in cyberspace
3. job interviews
4. standardized tests
5. college sports

Suggested Writing Assignments

1. Eighner emphasizes the transience of material objects. How important are such objects to you? Why? Which ones do you enjoy most? Can you envision disposing of them? When and why? Illustrate your essay with examples and anecdotes.
2. Write an essay about a time when you experienced a transition in your way of life. It can involve moving from one place to another, starting a job or going to school, or any situation in which you had to adjust to new circumstances. Identify the dominant rhetorical pattern in your essay. What other patterns did you use in developing your essay? If you can, sharpen your use of these other patterns to enhance both the content and the purpose of your essay.

GLOSSARY OF USEFUL TERMS

Abstract See *Concrete/Abstract.*

Allusion An allusion is a passing reference to a familiar person, place, or thing often drawn from history, the Bible, mythology, or literature. An allusion is an economical way for a writer to capture the essence of an idea, atmosphere, emotion, or historical era, as in "The scandal was his Watergate" or "He saw himself as a modern Job" or "The campaign ended not with a bang but a whimper." An allusion should be familiar to the reader; if it is not, it will add nothing to the meaning.

Analogy Analogy is a special form of comparison in which the writer explains something unfamiliar by comparing it to something familiar: "A transmission line is simply a pipeline for electricity. In the case of a water pipeline, more water will flow through the pipe as water pressure increases. The same is true of electricity in a transmission line."

Anecdote An anecdote is a short narrative about an amusing or interesting event. Writers often use anecdotes to begin essays as well as to illustrate certain points.

Argumentation Argumentation is one of the four basic types of prose. (Narration, description, and exposition are the other three.) To argue is to attempt to persuade a reader to agree with a point of view, to make a given decision, or to pursue a particular course of action. There are two basic types of argumentation: logical and persuasive. See the introduction to Chapter 18 (pp. 441–47) for a detailed discussion of argumentation.

Attitude A writer's attitude reflects his or her opinion of a subject. The writer can think very positively or very negatively about a subject, or somewhere in between. See also *Tone.*

Audience An audience is the intended readership for a piece of writing. For example, the readers of a national weekly news magazine come from all walks of life and have diverse interests, opinions, and educational backgrounds. In contrast, the readership for an organic chemistry journal is made up of people whose interests and education are quite similar. The essays in *Models for Writers* are intended for general readers, intelligent people who may lack specific information about the subject being discussed.

Beginnings and Endings A beginning is that sentence, group of sentences, or section that introduces an essay. Good beginnings usually identify the thesis or controlling idea, attempt to interest readers, and establish a tone.

An ending is that sentence or group of sentences that brings an essay to a close. Good endings are purposeful and well planned. They can be a summary, a concluding example, an anecdote, or a quotation. Endings satisfy readers when they are the natural outgrowths of the essays themselves and give the readers a sense of finality or completion. Good essays do not simply stop; they conclude. See the introduction to Chapter 4 (pp. 75–79) for a detailed discussion of beginnings and endings.

Cause and Effect Cause-and-effect analysis is a type of exposition that explains the reasons for an occurrence or the consequences of an action. See the introduction to Chapter 17 (pp. 414–15) for a detailed discussion of cause and effect. See also *Exposition.*

Classification See *Division and Classification.*

Cliché A cliché is an expression that has become ineffective through overuse. Expressions such as *quick as a flash, jump for joy,* and *slow as molasses* are clichés. Writers normally avoid such trite expressions and seek instead to express themselves in fresh and forceful language. See also *Diction.*

Coherence Coherence is a quality of good writing that results when all sentences, paragraphs, and longer divisions of an essay are naturally connected. Coherent writing is achieved through (1) a logical sequence of ideas (arranged in chronological order, spatial order, order of importance, or some other appropriate order), (2) the purposeful repetition of key words and ideas, (3) a pace suitable for your topic and your reader, and (4) the use of transitional words and expressions. Coherence should not be confused with unity. (See *Unity.*) See also *Transitions.*

Colloquial Expressions A colloquial expression is an expression that is characteristic of or appropriate to spoken language or to writing that seeks the effect of spoken language. Colloquial expressions are informal, as *chem, gym, come up with, be at loose ends, won't,* and *photo* illustrate. See also *Diction.* Thus, colloquial expressions are acceptable in formal writing only if they are used purposefully.

Combined Strategies By combining rhetorical strategies, writers are able to develop their ideas in interesting ways. For example, in writing a cause-and-effect essay about a major oil spill, the writer might want to describe the damage that the spill caused, as well as explain the cleanup process step by step. See the introduction to Chapter 19 (pp. 505–7) for a detailed discussion of combining rhetorical strategies.

Comparison and Contrast Comparison and contrast is a type of exposition in which the writer points out the similarities and differences between two or more subjects in the same class or category. The function of any comparison and contrast is to clarify—to reach some conclusion about the items being compared and contrasted. See the introduction to Chapter 16 (pp. 392–95) for a detailed discussion of comparison and contrast. See also *Exposition.*

Conclusions See *Beginnings and Endings.*

Concrete/Abstract A concrete word names a specific object, person, place, or action that can be directly perceived by the senses: *car, bread, building, book, John F. Kennedy, Chicago,* or *hiking.* An abstract word, in contrast, refers to general qualities, conditions, ideas, actions, or relationships that cannot be directly perceived by the senses: *bravery, dedication, excellence, anxiety, stress, thinking,* or *hatred.* See also the introduction to Chapter 8 (pp. 177–82).

Connotation/Denotation Both connotation and denotation refer to the meanings of words. Denotation is the dictionary meaning of a word, the literal meaning. Connotation, on the other hand, is the implied or suggested meaning of a word. For example, the denotation of *lamb* is "a young sheep." The connotations of *lamb* are numerous: *gentle, docile, weak, peaceful, blessed, sacrificial, blood, spring, frisky, pure, innocent,* and so on. See also the introduction to Chapter 8 (pp. 177–82).

Controlling Idea See *Thesis.*

Coordination Coordination is the joining of grammatical constructions of the same rank (e.g., words, phrases, clauses) to indicate that they are of equal importance. For example, *They ate hot dogs,* and *we ate hamburgers.* See the introduction to Chapter 7 (pp. 150–54). See also *Subordination.*

Deduction Deduction is the process of reasoning from stated premises to a conclusion that follows necessarily. This form of reasoning moves from the general to the specific. See the introduction to Chapter 18 (pp. 441–47) for a discussion of deductive reasoning and its relation to argumentation. See also *Syllogism.*

Definition Definition is one of the types of exposition. Definition is a statement of the meaning of a word. A definition may be either brief or extended, part of an essay or an entire essay itself. See the introduction to Chapter 14 (pp. 341–42) for a detailed discussion of definition. See also *Exposition.*

Denotation See *Connotation/Denotation.*

Description Description is one of the four basic types of prose. (Narration, exposition, and argumentation are the other three.) Description tells how a person, place, or thing is perceived by the five senses. See the introduction to Chapter 12 (pp. 285–86) for a detailed discussion of description.

Details Details are the small elements that collectively contribute to the overall impression of a person, place, thing, or idea. For example, in the sentence "The *organic, whole-grain* dog biscuits were *reddish brown, beef flavored,* and in the *shape of a bone*" the italicized words are details.

Dialogue Conversation of two or more people as represented in writing. Dialogue is what people say directly to one another.

Diction Diction refers to a writer's choice and use of words. Good diction is precise and appropriate—the words mean exactly what the writer intends, and the words are well suited to the writer's subject, intended audience, and purpose in writing. The word-conscious writer knows that there are differences among *aged, old,* and *elderly; blue, navy,* and *azure;* and *disturbed, angry,* and *irritated.* Furthermore, this writer knows in which situation to use each word. See the introduction to Chapter 8 (pp. 177–82) for a detailed discussion of diction. See also *Cliché, Colloquial Expressions, Connotation/Denotation, Jargon, Slang.*

Division and Classification Division and classification is one of the types of exposition. When dividing and classifying, the writer first establishes categories and then arranges or sorts people, places, or things into these categories according to their different characteristics, thus making them more manageable for the writer and more understandable and meaningful for the reader. See the introduction to Chapter 15 (pp. 361–62) for a detailed discussion of division and classification. See also *Exposition.*

Dominant Impression A dominant impression is the single mood, atmosphere, or quality a writer emphasizes in a piece of descriptive writing. The dominant impression is created through the careful selection of details and is, of course, influenced by the writer's subject, audience, and purpose. See also the introduction to Chapter 12 (pp. 285–86).

Emphasis Emphasis is the placement of important ideas and words within sentences and longer units of writing so that they have the greatest impact. In general, what comes at the end has the most impact, and at the beginning nearly as much; what comes in the middle gets the least emphasis.

Endings See *Beginnings and Endings.*

Evaluation An evaluation of a piece of writing is an assessment of its effectiveness or merit. In evaluating a piece of writing, one should ask the following questions: What is the writer's purpose? Is it a worthwhile purpose? Does the writer achieve the purpose? Is the writer's information sufficient and accurate? What are the strengths of the essay? What are its weaknesses? Depending on the type of writing and the purpose, more specific questions can also be asked. For example, with an argument one could ask: Does the writer follow the principles of logical thinking? Is the writer's evidence sufficient and convincing?

Evidence Evidence is the information on which a judgment or argument is based or by which proof or probability is established. Evidence usually takes the form of statistics, facts, names, examples or illustrations, and opinions of authorities.

Example An example illustrates a larger idea or represents something of which it is a part. An example is a basic means of developing or clarifying an idea. Furthermore, examples enable writers to show and not simply to tell readers what they mean. See also the introduction to Chapter 10 (pp. 231–32).

Exposition Exposition is one of the four basic types of prose. (Narration, description, and argumentation are the other three.) The purpose of exposition is to clarify, explain, and inform. The methods of exposition presented in *Models for Writers* are process analysis, definition, illustration, classification, comparison and contrast, and cause and effect. For a detailed discussion of these methods of exposition, see the appropriate chapter introductions.

Facts Facts are pieces of information presented as having objective reality, that is, having actual existence. For example, water boils at 212°F, Bill Clinton won the 1996 presidential election, and the USSR no longer exists are all facts.

Fallacy See *Logical Fallacies.*

Figures of Speech Figures of speech are brief, imaginative comparisons that highlight the similarities between things that are basically dissimilar. They make writing vivid, interesting, and memorable. The most common figures of speech are:

Simile: An explicit comparison introduced by *like* or *as.* "The fighter's hands were like stone."
Metaphor: An implied comparison that makes one thing the equivalent of another. "All the world's a stage."
Personification: A special kind of simile or metaphor in which human traits are assigned to an inanimate object. "The engine coughed and then stopped."

See the introduction to Chapter 9 (pp. 208–9) for a detailed discussion of figurative language.

Focus Focus is the limitation that a writer gives his or her subject. The writer's task is to select a manageable topic given the constraints of time, space, and purpose. For example, within the general subject of sports, a writer could focus on government support of amateur athletes or narrow the focus further to government support of Olympic athletes.

General See *Specific/General.*

Idiom An idiom is a word or phrase that is used habitually with special meaning. The meaning of an idiom is not always readily apparent to nonnative speakers of that language. For example, *catch cold, hold a job, make up your mind,* and *give them a hand* are all idioms in English.

Illustration Illustration is the use of examples to explain, elucidate, or corroborate. Writers rely heavily on illustration to make their ideas both clear and concrete. See the introduction to Chapter 10 (pp. 231–32) for a detailed discussion of illustration.

Induction Induction is the process of reasoning to a conclusion about all members of a class through an examination of only a few members of the class. This form of reasoning moves from the particular to the general. See the introduction to Chapter 18 (pp. 441–47) for a discussion of inductive reasoning and its relation to argumentation.

Inductive Leap An inductive leap is the point at which a writer of an argument, having presented sufficient evidence, moves to a generalization or conclusion. See also *Induction.*

Introductions See *Beginnings and Endings.*

Irony Irony is the use of words to suggest something different from their literal meaning. For example, when Jonathan Swift suggested in *A Modest Proposal* that Ireland's problems could be solved if the people of Ireland fattened their babies and sold them to the English landlords for food, he meant that almost any other solution would be preferable. A writer can use irony to establish a special relationship with the reader and to add an extra dimension or twist to the meaning. See also the introduction to Chapter 8 (pp. 177–82).

Jargon Jargon, or technical language, is the special vocabulary of a trade, profession, or group. Doctors, construction workers, lawyers, and teachers, for example, all have a specialized vocabulary that they use "on the job." See also *Diction.*

Logical Fallacies A logical fallacy is an error in reasoning that renders an argument invalid. See the introduction to Chapter 18 (pp. 441–47) for a discussion of the more common logical fallacies.

Metaphor See *Figures of Speech.*

Narration Narration is one of the four basic types of prose. (Description, exposition, and argumentation are the other three.) To narrate is to tell a story, to tell what happened. While narration is most often used in fiction, it is also important in expository writing, either by itself or in conjunction with other types of prose. See the introduction to Chapter 11 (pp. 257–59) for a detailed discussion of narration.

Opinion An opinion is a belief or conclusion, which may or may not be substantiated by positive knowledge or proof. (If not substantiated, an opinion is a prejudice.) Even when based on evidence and sound reasoning, an opinion is personal and can be changed, and is therefore less persuasive than facts and arguments.

Organization Organization is the pattern of order that the writer imposes on his or her material. Some often-used patterns of organization include time order, space order, and order of importance. See the introduction to Chapter 3 (pp. 55–56) for a more detailed discussion of organization.

Paradox A paradox is a seemingly contradictory statement that is nonetheless true. For example, "We little know what we have until we lose it" is a paradoxical statement.

Paragraph The paragraph, the single most important unit of thought in an essay, is a series of closely related sentences. These sentences adequately develop the central or controlling idea of the paragraph. This central or controlling idea, usually stated in a topic sentence, is necessarily related to the purpose of the whole composition. A well-written paragraph has several distinguishing characteristics: a clearly stated or implied topic sentence, adequate development, unity, coherence, and an appropriate organizational strategy. See the introduction to Chapter 5 (pp. 105–8) for a detailed discussion of paragraphs.

Parallelism Parallel structure is the repetition of word order or grammatical form either within a single sentence or in several sentences that develop the same central idea. As a rhetorical device, parallelism can aid coherence and add emphasis. Franklin Roosevelt's statement "I see one-third of a nation ill-housed, ill-clad, and ill-nourished" illustrates effective parallelism.

Personification See *Figures of Speech.*

Point of View Point of view refers to the grammatical person in an essay. For example, first-person point of view uses the pronoun *I* and is commonly found in autobiography and the personal essay; third-person point of view uses the pronouns *he, she,* or *it* and is commonly found in objective writing. See the introduction to Chapter 11 (pp. 257–59) for a discussion of point of view in narration.

Process Analysis Process analysis is a type of exposition. Process analysis answers the question *how* and explains how something works or gives step-by-step directions for doing something. See the introduction to Chapter 13 (pp. 310–11) for a detailed discussion of process analysis. See also *Exposition.*

Purpose Purpose is what the writer wants to accomplish in a particular piece of writing. Purposeful writing seeks to *tell* (narration), to *describe* (description), to *explain* (process analysis, definition, classification, comparison and contrast, and cause and effect), or to *convince* (argumentation).

Rhetorical Question A rhetorical question is asked for its rhetorical effect but requires no answer from the reader. "When will nuclear proliferation end?" is such a question. Writers use rhetorical questions to introduce topics they plan to discuss or to emphasize important points. See the general introduction (pp. 1–18) and the introduction to Chapter 4 (pp. 75–79).

Sentence A sentence is a grammatical unit that expresses a complete thought. It consists of at least a subject (a noun) and a predicate (a verb). See the introduction to Chapter 7 (pp. 150–54) for a discussion of effective sentences.

Simile See *Figures of Speech.*

Slang Slang is the unconventional, very informal language of particular subgroups in our culture. Slang terms, such as *bummed, coke, split, rap, dude,* and *stoned,* are acceptable in formal writing only if used selectively for specific purposes.

Specific/General General words name groups or classes of objects, qualities, or actions. Specific words, on the other hand, name individual objects, qualities, or actions within a class or group. To some extent the terms *general* and *specific* are relative. For example, *clothing* is a class of things. *Shirt,* however, is more specific than *clothing* but more general than *T-shirt.* See also *Diction.*

Strategy A strategy is a means by which a writer achieves his or her purpose. Strategy includes the many rhetorical decisions that the writer makes about organization, paragraph structure, sentence structure, and diction. In terms of the whole essay, strategy refers to the principal rhetorical mode that a writer uses. If, for example, a writer wishes to show how to make chocolate chip cookies, the most effective strategy would be process analysis. If it is the writer's purpose to show why sales of American cars have declined in recent years, the most effective strategy would be cause-and-effect analysis.

Style Style is the individual manner in which a writer expresses his or her ideas. Style is created by the author's particular choice of words, construction of sentences, and arrangement of ideas.

Subordination Subordination is the use of grammatical constructions to make one part of a sentence dependent on, rather than equal to, another. For example, the italicized clause in the following sentence is subordinate: They all cheered *when I finished the race.* See the introduction to Chapter 7 (pp. 150–54). See also *Coordination.*

Supporting Evidence See *Evidence.*

Syllogism A syllogism is an argument that utilizes deductive reasoning and consists of a major premise, a minor premise, and a conclusion. For example,

> All trees that lose leaves are deciduous. (major premise)
> Maple trees lose their leaves. (minor premise)
> Therefore, maple trees are deciduous. (conclusion)

See also *Deduction.*

Symbol A symbol is a person, place, or thing that represents something beyond itself. For example, the eagle is a symbol of the United States, and the maple leaf, a symbol of Canada.

Syntax Syntax refers to the way in which words are arranged to form phrases, clauses, and sentences, as well as to the grammatical relationship among the words themselves.

Technical Language See *Jargon.*

Thesis A thesis is the main idea of an essay, also known as the controlling idea. A thesis may sometimes be implied rather than stated directly in a thesis statement. See the introduction to Chapter 1 (pp. 19–20) for a detailed discussion of thesis.

Title A title is a word or phrase set off at the beginning of an essay to identify the subject, to state the main idea of the essay, or to attract the reader's attention. A title may be explicit or suggestive. A subtitle, when used, explains or restricts the meaning of the main title.

Tone Tone is the manner in which a writer relates to an audience, the "tone of voice" used to address readers. Tone may be friendly, serious, distant, angry, cheerful, bitter, cynical, enthusiastic, morbid, resentful, warm, playful, and so forth. A particular tone results from a writer's diction, sentence structure, purpose, and attitude toward the subject. See the introduction to Chapter 8 (pp. 177–82) for several examples that display different tones.

Topic Sentence The topic sentence states the central idea of a paragraph and thus limits the content of the paragraph. Although the topic sentence normally appears at the beginning of the paragraph, it may appear at any other point, particularly if the writer is trying to create a special effect. Not all paragraphs contain topic sentences. See also *Paragraph.*

Transitions Transitions are words or phrases that link sentences, paragraphs, and larger units of a composition in order to achieve coherence. These devices include parallelism, pronoun references, conjunctions, and the repetition of key ideas, as well as the many conventional transitional expressions such as *moreover, on the other hand, in addition, in contrast,* and *therefore.* See the introduction to Chapter 6 (pp. 128–30) for a detailed discussion of transitions. See also *Coherence.*

Unity Unity is that quality of oneness in an essay that results when all the words, sentences, and paragraphs contribute to the thesis. The elements of a unified essay do not distract the reader. Instead, they all harmoniously support a single idea or purpose. See the introduction to Chapter 2 (pp. 37–38) for a detailed discussion of unity.

Verb Verbs can be classified as either strong verbs *(scream, pierce, gush, ravage,* and *amble)* or weak verbs *(be, has, get,* and *do).* Writers often prefer to use strong verbs in order to make writing more specific or more descriptive.

Voice Verbs can be classified as being in either the active or the passive voice. In the active voice the doer of the action is the subject. In the passive voice the receiver of the action is the grammatical subject:

Active: Glenda questioned all of the children.
Passive: All the children were questioned by Glenda.

Acknowledgments

Page 26. "Anxiety: Challenge by Another Name" by James Lincoln Collier. From *Reader's Digest,* December 1986. Reprinted with the permission of the author and *Reader's Digest.*

Page 32. "Why 'Model Minority' Doesn't Fit," by Diane Yen-Mei Wong. From *USA WEEKEND,* January 7–9, 1994, page 24. Reprinted with the permission of the author.

Page 39. "My Name" by Sandra Cisneros. From *The House on Mango Street* (New York: Alfred A. Knopf, 1984). Copyright © 1984 by Sandra Cisneros. Reprinted with the permission of Susan Bergholz Literary Services, New York. All rights reserved.

Page 42. "A Chance to Pursue My Dreams" by Cynthia Inda. From *Policy Review* (November/December 1996): 33. Copyright © 1996 by Cynthia Inda. Reprinted by permission of *Policy Review.*

Page 48. "The Meaning of a Word" by Gloria Naylor. From *The New York Times,* February 20, 1986. Copyright © 1986 by Gloria Naylor. Reprinted with the permission of Sterling Lord Literistic, Inc.

Page 57. "Reach Out and Write Someone" by Lynn Wenzel. From "My Turn," *Newsweek on Campus,* January 9, 1984. Reprinted with the permission of the author.

Page 62. "Made to Order Babies" by Geoffrey Cowley. From *Newsweek* special issue, Winter/Spring 1990. Copyright © 1990 Newsweek, Inc. Reprinted with the permission of *Newsweek.*

Page 70. "The Corner Store" by Eudora Welty. From *The Eye of the Story: Selected Essays and Reviews.* Originally titled "The Little Store." Copyright © 1975 by Eudora Welty. Reprinted with the permission of Random House, Inc.

Page 80. "Of My Friend Hector and My Achilles Heel" by Michael T. Kaufman. From *The New York Times,* November 1, 1992. Copyright © 1992 by The New York Times Company. Reprinted with the permission of *The New York Times.*

Page 86. "Even You Can Get It" by Bruce Lambert. From *The New York Times,* March 11, 1989. Copyright © 1989 by The New York Times Company. Reprinted with the permission of *The New York Times.*

Page 94. "How to Take a Job Interview" by Kirby W. Stanat. From *Job Hunting Secrets and Tactics* by Kirby W. Stanat with Patrick Reardon. Copyright © 1977 by Kirby Stanat and Patrick Reardon. Reprinted with the permission of Westwind Press, a division of Raintree Publishers Limited.

Page 100. "It's Not Just a Phase" by Katherine E. Zondlo. From *Newsweek,* June 10, 1996. Copyright © 1996 by Newsweek, Inc. Reprinted with the permission of *Newsweek.*

Page 109. "Zen and the Art of Olympic Success" by Adam Rogers. From *Newsweek,* July 22, 1996. Copyright © 1996 by Newsweek, Inc. Reprinted with the permission of *Newsweek.*

Page 114. "Simplicity" by William Zinsser. From *On Writing Well,* Fifth Edition (New York: HarperCollins Publishers, 1994). Copyright © 1976, 1980, 1985, 1988, 1990, 1994 by William Zinsser. Reprinted with the permission of the author and Carol Brissie.

Page 122. "I Just Wanna Be Average" by Mike Rose. From *Lives on the Boundary: Struggles and Achievements of America's Underprepared.* Copyright © 1989 by Mike Rose. Reprinted with the permission of The Free Press, a division of Simon & Schuster, Inc.

Page 131. "Why I Want to Have a Family" by Lisa Brown. From "My Turn," *Newsweek on Campus,* October 1984. Reprinted with the permission of the author.

Page 137. "How I Got Smart" by Steve Brody. From *The New York Times,* September 21, 1986. Originally titled, "Love, with Knowledge Aforethought." Copyright © 1986 by The New York Times Company. Reprinted with the permission of *The New York Times.*

Page 144. "Becoming a Writer" by Russell Baker. From *Growing Up.* Copyright © 1982 by Russell Baker. Reprinted with the permission of Contemporary Books.

Page 155. "Hitting Pay Dirt" by Annie Dillard. From *An American Childhood.* Copyright © 1987 by Annie Dillard. Reprinted with the permission of HarperCollins Publishers, Inc.

Page 160. "Salvation" by Langston Hughes. From *The Big Sea.* Copyright © 1940 by Langston Hughes; renewed 1969 by Arna Bontemps and George Houston Bass. Reprinted with the permission of Hill & Wang, a division of Farrar, Straus & Giroux, Inc.

Page 165. "Playing to Win" by Margaret A. Whitney. From *The New York Times,* July 3, 1988. Copyright © 1988 by The New York Times Company. Reprinted with the permission of *The New York Times.*

Page 171. "38 Who Saw Murder Didn't Call Police" by Martin Gansberg. From *The New York Times,* March 17, 1964. Copyright © 1964 by The New York Times Company. Reprinted with the permission of *The New York Times.*

Page 183. "On Being 17, Bright, and Unable to Read" by David Raymond. From *The New York Times,* April 25, 1976. Copyright © 1976 by The New York Times Company. Reprinted with the permission of *The New York Times.*

Page 189. "*La Vida Loca* (The Crazy Life): Two Generations of Gang Members" by Luis J. Rodriguez. From the *Los Angeles Times,* June 21, 1992, Section M. Reprinted with the permission of the author.

Page 196. "The Fourth of July" by Audre Lorde. From *Zami.* Copyright © 1982 by Audre Lorde. Reprinted with the permission of The Crossing Press, Freedom, CA.

Page 202. "The Dance within My Heart" by Pat Mora. From *New Chicana/Chicano Writing,* Charles M. Tatum, ed. Copyright © 1992 by Pat Mora. Reprinted with the permission of the author.

Page 210. "The Barrio" by Robert Ramirez. Originally titled "The Woolen Sarape" from *Pain and Promise: The Chicano Today* by Edward Simmens, ed. (New York: New American Library, 1972). Reprinted with the permission of the author.

Page 216. "Polaroids" by Anne Lamott. From *Bird by Bird: Instructions on Writing and Life* by Anne Lamott. Copyright © 1994 by Anne Lamott. Reprinted with the permission of Pantheon Books, a division of Random House, Inc.

Page 223. "A Hanging" by George Orwell. From *Shooting an Elephant and Other Essays.* Copyright © by Sonia Brownell Orwell; renewed 1974 by Sonia Orwell. Reprinted with the permission of Harcourt Brace and Company and The Estate of Sonia Brownell Orwell and Martin Secker & Warburg, Ltd.

Page 233. "A Crime of Compassion" by Barbara Huttmann. From *Newsweek,* August 8, 1983. Reprinted with permission.

Page 239. "The Case for Short Words" by Richard Lederer. From *The Miracle of Language.* Copyright © 1991 by Richard Lederer. Reprinted with the permission of Pocket Books.

Page 245. "A Read-Only Man in an Interactive Age" by George Felton. From *The Wall Street Journal,* May 10, 1995. Copyright © 1995 by Dow Jones & Co., Inc. Reprinted with the permission of the author.

Page 250. "Don't Let Stereotypes Warp Your Judgments" by Robert L. Heilbroner. From *Think Magazine,* June 1961. Reprinted with the permission of the author.

Page 260. "Shame" by Dick Gregory. From *Nigger: An Autobiography.* Copyright © 1964 by Dick Gregory Enterprises, Inc. Reprinted with the permission of Dutton, an imprint of New American Library, a division of Penguin Books USA, Inc.

Page 266. "The Dare" by Roger Hoffman. From "About Men," *The New York Times Magazine,* January 1, 1986. Originally titled "There's Always the Dare." Copyright © 1986 by The New York Times Company. Reprinted with the permission of *The New York Times.*

Page 271. "Momma, the Dentist, and Me" by Maya Angelou. From *I Know Why the Caged Bird Sings* by Maya Angelou. Copyright © 1969 by Maya Angelou. Reprinted with the permission of Random House, Inc.

Page 287. "Subway Station" by Gilbert Highet. From *Talents and Geniuses* (New York: Oxford University Press, 1957). Copyright © 1957 by Gilbert Highet. Reprinted with the permission of Curtis Brown, Ltd.

Page 290. "Unforgettable Miss Bessie" by Carl T. Rowan. From *Reader's Digest,* March 1985. Copyright © 1985 by The Reader's Digest Association, Inc. Reprinted with the permission of *Reader's Digest.*

Page 297. "Grocer's Daughter" by Marianne Wiggins. From *Herself in Love and Other Stories.* Originally appeared in *Parade,* June 18, 1989. Copyright © 1989 by Marianne Wiggins. Reprinted with the permission of Martin Secker & Warburg, Ltd.

Page 304. "Gravity's Rainbow" by Guy Trebay. From *The Village Voice,* October 8, 1996. Reprinted with the permission of the author and *The Village Voice.*

Page 312. "How to Organize Your Thoughts for Better Communication" by Sherry Sweetnam. From *Personnel,* March 1986. Copyright © 1986 by the American Management Association. Reprinted with the permission of the publishers.

Page 319. "How to Mark a Book" by Mortimer Adler. From *The Saturday Review of Literature,* July 1940. Copyright © 1940 by Mortimer J. Adler. Reprinted with the permission of the author.

Page 327. "Fender Benders: Legal Do's and Don't's" by Armond D. Budish. From *Family Circle,* July 19, 1994. Copyright © 1994 by Armond D. Budish. Reprinted with the permission of the author.

Page 333. "The Spider and the Wasp" by Alexander Petrunkevitch. From *Scientific American,* August 1952. Copyright © 1952 and renewed © 1980 by Scientific American, Inc. Reprinted with the permission of *Scientific American.*

Page 343. "A Jerk" by Sydney J. Harris. From *Last Things First.* Copyright © 1957, 1958, 1959, 1960 by the *Chicago Daily News* and General Features Corporation. Copyright © 1961 by Sydney J. Harris. Reprinted with the permission of Houghton Mifflin Company. All rights reserved.

Page 346. "Who's a Hillbilly?" by Rebecca Thomas Kirkendall. From *Newsweek,* November 27, 1995. Copyright © 1995 by Newsweek, Inc. Reprinted with the permission of *Newsweek.*

Page 351. "My Way!" by Margo Kaufman. From *1-800-Am-I-Nuts.* Copyright © 1993 by Margo Kaufman. Reprinted with the permission of Random House, Inc.

Page 356. "A Magic Circle of Friends" by Elvira M. Franco. From *The New York Times,* January 28, 1990. Copyright © 1990 by The New York Times Company. Reprinted with the permission of *The New York Times.*

Page 363. "The Ways of Meeting Oppression" by Martin Luther King, Jr. From *Stride toward Freedom* (New York: Harper & Row, 1958). Copyright © 1958 by Martin Luther King, Jr., renewed 1986 by Coretta Scott King, Dexter King, Martin Luther King III, Yolanda King, and Bernice King. Reprinted with the permission of Writers House, Inc.

Page 369. "Friends, Good Friends—and Such Good Friends" by Judith Viorst. From *Redbook,* 1977. Copyright © 1977 by Judith Viorst. Reprinted with the permission of Lescher & Lescher, Ltd.

Page 381. "What We Now Know about Memory" by Lee Smith. From *Fortune,* April 17, 1995. Copyright © 1995 by Time, Inc. Reprinted with the permission of *Fortune.* All rights reserved.

Page 396. "Grammy Rewards" by Deborah Dalfonso. From *Newsweek* special issue, Winter/Spring 1990. Copyright © 1990 by Newsweek, Inc. Reprinted with the permission of *Newsweek.*

Page 399. "A Case of 'Severe Bias'" by Patricia Raybon. From *Newsweek,* October 1989. Copyright © 1989. Reprinted with the permission of the author.

Page 404. "The Locket" by Gary Soto. From *A Summer Life.* Copyright © 1990 by University Press of New England. Reprinted with the permission of the publishers.

Page 409. "A Battle of Cultures" by Connie Kang. From *Asian Week,* May 25, 1990. Reprinted with the permission of the author.

Page 416. "The Effects of the Telephone" by John Brooks. From *The Telephone: The First Hundred Years.* Copyright © 1975, 1976 by John Brooks. Reprinted with the permission of HarperCollins Publishers, Inc.

Page 420. "I Refuse to Live in Fear" by Diana Bletter. From *Mademoiselle,* November 1996. Copyright © 1996 by The Condé Nast Publications, Inc. Reprinted with the permission of *Mademoiselle.*

Page 425. "Halfway to Dick and Jane" by Jack Agueros. From *The Immigrant Experience,* edited by Thomas C. Wheeler. Copyright © 1971 by Doubleday, a division of Bantam Doubleday Dell Publishing Group, Inc. Reprinted with the permission of the publishers.

Page 432. "How Not to Lose Friends over Money" by Lois Duncan. From *Woman's Day* 49: May 25, 1989. Copyright © 1989 by Hachette Magazines. Reprinted with the permission of the author.

Page 448. "As They Say, Drugs Kill" by Laura Rowley. From *Newsweek on Campus,* February 1987. Reprinted with the permission of the author.

Page 454. "In Praise of the F Word" by Mary Sherry. From *Newsweek,* May 6, 1991. Reprinted with the permission of the author.

Page 459. "The Right to Fail" by William Zinsser. From *The Lunacy Boom* (New York: Harper & Row Publishers, 1970). Copyright © 1969, 1970 by William Zinsser. Reprinted with the permission of the author and Carol Brissie.

Page 465. "Less Is More: A Call for Shorter Work Hours" by Barbara Brandt. From *Utne Reader,* July/August 1991. Reprinted with the permission of the author.

Page 472. "A City's Assault on Teen Pregnancy" by Joe Loconte. From *Policy Review* (November/December 1996). Copyright © 1996 by The Heritage Foundation. Reprinted with the permission of *Policy Review.*

Page 479. "Exposing Media Myths: TV Doesn't Affect You As Much As You Think" by Joanmarie Kalter. From *TV Guide,* May 30, 1987. Copyright © 1987 by News America Publications, Inc. Reprinted with the permission of *TV Guide.*

Page 486. "Robbing the Cradle" by Dennis A. Williams. From *Newsweek,* July 3, 1995. Copyright © 1995 by Newsweek, Inc. Reprinted with the permission of *Newsweek.*

Page 492. "Against the Great Divide" by Brian Jarvis. From *Newsweek,* May 3, 1993. Copyright © 1993 by Newsweek, Inc. Reprinted with the permission of *Newsweek.*

Page 498. "What's Marriage Got to Do with Love?" by Maggie Gallagher. Adapted from *The Abolition of Marriage: How We Destroy Lasting Love.* Copyright ©

1996 by Maggie Gallagher. Reprinted with the permission of Regnery Publishing, Inc.

Page 508. "I'm Sorry, I Won't Apologize" by Deborah Tannen. From *The New York Times Magazine,* July 21, 1996. Copyright © 1996 by Deborah Tannen. Reprinted with the permission of the author.

Page 515. "An Ethnic Trump" by Gish Jen. From *The New York Times Magazine,* July 7, 1996. Copyright © 1996 by The New York Times Company, Inc. Reprinted with the permission of *The New York Times.*

Page 520. "Beyond the Melting Pot" by William A. Henry III. From *Time,* April 9, 1990. Copyright © 1990 by Time, Inc. Reprinted with the permission of *Time.*

Page 531. "On Dumpster Diving" by Lars Eighner. From *Travels with Lizbeth.* Copyright © 1991, 1993 by Lars Eighner. This essay first appeared in *The Threepenny Review,* Fall 1991. Reprinted with the permission of St. Martin's Press.

INDEX